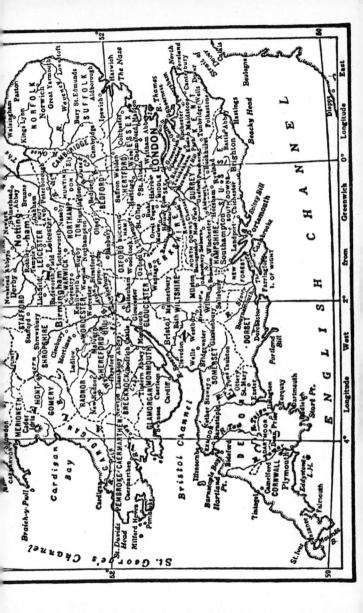

# THE VICTORIAN PERIOD

# ENGLISH LITERATURE

## THE BEGINNINGS TO 1500
James Dow McCallum

## THE RENAISSANCE
Robert Whitney Bolwell

## THE SEVENTEENTH CENTURY
Evert Mordecai Clark

## THE EIGHTEENTH CENTURY
Joseph P. Blickensderfer

## THE ROMANTIC PERIOD
Albert Granberry Reed

## THE VICTORIAN PERIOD
George Morey Miller

This series of anthologies of English literature
is under the general editorship of
James Dow McCallum

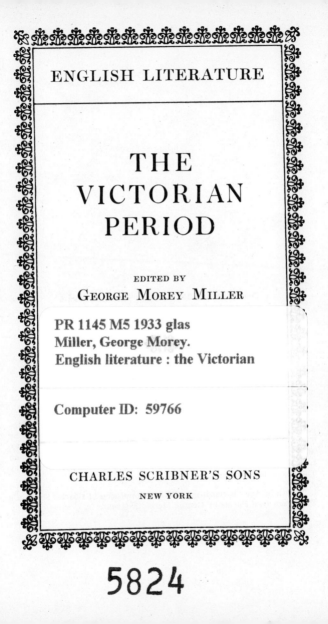

# ENGLISH LITERATURE

# THE
# VICTORIAN
# PERIOD

EDITED BY
GEORGE MOREY MILLER

CHARLES SCRIBNER'S SONS
NEW YORK

ACKNOWLEDGMENTS

"Life Laughs Onward," "Ah, Are You Digging, on my Grave?" "Misconception," and "To Sincerity" reprinted from *Collected Poems* by Thomas Hardy, by permission of The Trustees of the Hardy Estate, Macmillan and Company, Ltd., The Macmillan Company of Canada Limited, and The Macmillan Company (New York). Copyright 1925 by The Macmillan Company.

"Youth in Age" is reprinted with the permission of Charles Scribner's Sons from *Last Poems* by George Meredith (1909).

Printed in the United States of America

## PREFATORY NOTE

Any editor who attempts to compile a Victorian anthology must be as conscious as I am how impossible it is to represent that great period in English literature adequately in one small volume. My embarrassment is all the greater because I agree with the latest authoritative historian of the period, Professor Elton, when he says, "while there is a great and noble body of achievement in verse, the achievement of prose, both in range and quality, is greater still." Naturally the mass of Victorian prose far outbulks the poetry. Yet we can spare the prose drama, because drama of any quantity meeting the two-fold test of practicability for the stage and literary quality did not take its rise till after 1870. Much to my regret, the plan of the series of which this volume is a part forces me to leave out prose fiction, though to leave out Dickens and Thackeray, Eliot and Meredith is to leave out authors fully as important in their kind as Carlyle, Ruskin, and Arnold in the essay or Tennyson and Browning in poetry. Still I have had to content myself with the fact that the more important poets and essayists are well represented by characteristic selections. Pater, Hardy, and Stevenson, though not properly in the period, have been included, since these authors are the subject of study in many courses dealing with Victorian literature. The Introduction attempts to outline in brief space the environment of the Victorian Age, to connect it with the preceding periods, to give its general characteristics, and to relate the chief authors to their age and to each other.

The difficulty of providing a really adequate presentation of Victorian literature in a volume of this size has necessitated cutting down in every way possible. Consequently I have deliberately compressed the usual system of notes at the back of the volume into the smallest possible minimum to make room for more of the literature. Full notes are needed in the earlier periods of our literature. Yet ninety-five per cent of the material in the ordinary notes on Victorian literature can be found in any good dictionary, in an encyclopædia, or in a good history of the literature. Moreover, the proper interpretation, the proper appreciation, the especial significance of individual poems or essays or passages is the peculiar business, the peculiar privilege of the teacher.

My indebtedness, conscious and unconscious, for the material of the Introduction and for the choice of the illustrative selections I could not begin to enumerate—to editors, critics, literary historians, my teachers, and my own classes. I cannot refrain, however, from paying tribute to my assistant, Miss Marian Wormell, of the Lewiston State Normal School, to whose faithfulness, intelligence, and accuracy I owe much. I must add, also, that the general editor of the series has assumed the responsibility for the inclusion of certain selections and for the exclusion of others, and to him I am indebted for the correct dating of certain individual selections.

G. M. M.

*Fourth Printing.*—I have taken advantage of this reprinting to make certain corrections, and I have added a number of individual notes.

GEORGE MOREY MILLER.

# CONTENTS

vii

# CONTENTS

# INTRODUCTION

## I. THE ENVIRONMENT AND THE LIMITS OF THE PERIOD

The period illustrated in this anthology extends properly from the death of Scott to the death of Dickens, from 1832 to 1870. Some of the most important authors of the Victorian era began to write before 1832, and some of these same men continued to write after 1870; but between these dates they established their reputations and contributed their most characteristic work to English literature. Around the year 1832 cluster a mass of significant dates in literature. In the fifteen years from 1821 to 1836 the men who had made the Romantic Movement died—all the important writers except Wordsworth, and practically all his best work was completed. The necrology of the great Romantics, the bead roll of the dead between these dates, includes Keats, Shelley, Mrs. Radcliffe, Byron, Blake, Hazlitt, Scott, Coleridge, Lamb, and Godwin. At the same time in the thirteen years from 1824 to 1837 the literary work of the earlier Victorians was introduced to the world—in history and essay, Carlyle, Macaulay, and Thackeray; in poetry, Tennyson and the Brownings; in the novel, Disraeli, Lytton, Dickens, and Thackeray. Literary historians are justified, then, when they say that the close of one literary era and the beginning of another is best marked by the year 1832.

There are, however, other reasons than occurrences merely literary for using 1832 as the most significant date for the beginning of the Victorian era and 1870 essentially for its close. No literature grows in a vacuum. That is not the law of life. Plant and animal, all things in the natural world, grow in this direction or that as the total weight of their environment tends to bend them in this direction or that. All the manifestations of life, whether in the natural world, in the life of man as an individual human being, or in the life of human society, with all its institutions, develop under the interaction of two fundamental forces—their inherent tendencies and their environment. Literature is no exception to this great law of life. If we want to understand any particular piece of literature, then, we must consider it as an effect, we must trace it back to its twofold cause—first, the author's individuality, his personality, his peculiar temperament; and, second, his environment, those tremendous forces—racial, national, epochal—that great matrix of ideas and powers—economic, social, political, philosophical, moral, religious, scientific, artistic, literary—under the influence of which his personality developed. True appreciation of literature, and understanding enjoyment of literature, can come only when we can put ourselves back into the life of the time which produced that literature. If, then, we want to know what Victorian literature is, we must know those forces, historical and cultural, which made the period.

If all this is a sound theory of literary development and literary appreciation, it follows that to know Carlyle and Tennyson, Dickens and Browning, we must know their times. Now 1832 and 1870 are even more significant in the development of English civilization than in the contributions of individual authors to the development of literature. These dates mark great changes in the life of England and of all Englishmen—changes political, industrial, social, educational, scientific, philosophical, and religious.

In the year that marks the death of Scott, 1832, the

first Reform Bill became a law, and this is the first great step in England toward modern democracy. The year before, 1831, public opinion, the public opinion of the disfranchised, was invoked for the first time as a powerful weapon to secure political justice from Parliament. In 1834 William IV failed in the last attempt of royalty to control the cabinet. In 1835 reform of a still more sweeping kind was enacted on behalf of city government. In 1837-40 England proved that she had finally learned the lesson of the American Revolution by establishing self-government for Canada.

Closely connected with these great political reforms, influencing them and influenced by them, were a number of progressive measures tending toward social, religious, and educational justice. In 1828 the Dissenters and in 1829 the Catholics were emancipated politically. Through a series of struggles from 1819 to 1831 Carlile and Cobbett achieved the freedom of the press against political and religious persecution. In 1833 slavery was abolished throughout the British dominions. In the same year the Factory Act protected children against that new juggernaut of British industry, the factory. In 1834 the new Poor Law undertook to reduce pauperism. It was in 1833 that Parliament made the first national grant in behalf of elementary education, the first great step in the public education of the masses. Still earlier, in 1823-24, had begun the movement for the education of adults of the working classes in the mechanics' institutes. In 1827 secular higher education, without the religious restrictions of Oxford and Cambridge and with a new emphasis on science, was begun by the founding of University College in London; and King's College was founded in London next year under church control as a rival to University College. In 1831-32, on the general model of Oxford and Cam-

bridge in organization and method of work, Durham
University was founded under control of the chapter of
Durham Cathedral. In 1830–1833 the new world of
nineteenth century science was ushered in by the publication of Lyell's epoch-making *Principles of Geology*.
In 1833, three years after Lyell's inauguration of the
revolution in modern science, Newman and his colleagues
at Oxford began their religious retreat from the modern
world, their demand for a return to the ages of faith,
by the publication of the *Tracts for the Times*.

Back of all these movements were great industrial and
economic changes which were revolutionizing the structure of English society. The Industrial Revolution
reached a climax in the two decades from 1820 to 1840.
Its two phases, the rural revolution and the urban revolution, focussed here. Enclosures by great landlords of
lands held in common by yeomen, small farmers, and
cottagers transformed these people into miserable peas-
ants or forced them to seek the city factories; and this
transforming process in the rural world, though beginning in the eighteenth century, reached its climax and
end about 1840.

Great as the effect of this rural transformation was on
English life, it was only part of the great Industrial
Revolution proper, the transformation in manufactures,
in transportation, and in commerce, and the consequent
social results of these economic changes. The invention
of the spinning jenny, the power loom, and the steam
engine in England and of the cotton gin in America did
not give their full effect to English industry until metal
machinery, made in the machine factories, was introduced into the cotton and woolen factories, the great
mass of them now steam driven; and this took place from
1825 to 1840. Such a revolution in method would have
been impossible, however. without the bringing together

of coal and iron, and that itself was made increasingly possible only by the new transportation by means of canals and railroads. Canals, railroads, and ocean going steamships made possible not only the tremendous development of the factory system but also the development of the new commerce that grew out of it. The development of canals began in the eighteenth century; but railroad construction did not originate till 1830, and yet by 1837 seven important railroads had received the sanction of Parliament. In the meantime Morse as early as 1832 began in America the development of his telegraph, the necessary accompaniment to the great railroad development that was to follow both in England and in America. Steam transportation on the ocean first took place in 1819, when the American steamer, *Savannah,* crossed from Georgia to Liverpool; but regular voyages began when the British steamers, *Sirius* and *Great Western,* reached New York in 1838. Steam driven factories and steam driven transportation, on land and on all the oceans of the world, made the England we have known for the last hundred years, made her, until the rapid rise of American and German industry after 1870, the world's manufacturing and commercial center.

The social results of the Industrial Revolution and the new awakening of a social conscience among those who ruled England were responsible for the mass of reforms which we have already seen centered around the year 1832 and the first Reform Bill. Furthermore, the Industrial Revolution made a new type of employer in the masters and owners of the great factories, and it made a new type of laborer in the skilled workmen the masters developed. The clamor by the factory owners and upper middle class people for political and religious justice helped to remove the political disabilities of Dissenters in 1828 and to pass the Reform Bill in 1832. In the meantime their employees, skilled and unskilled, were persecuted in the courts and even ridden down by soldiers whenever they attempted to get together to devise ways and means for redressing their wrongs; but in 1824 repeal of restrictive laws against trades unions set the laborers free, at least for awhile, to combine for their own betterment. This act of justice was forced from Parliament by the new method of summoning "clouds of witnesses" from the oppressed workmen to appear before Parliament, the first notable use in English history of the legislative lobby. From now on trades unions flourished individually; but they had not yet learned how to combine their forces for common ends. Robert Owen's Grand National Trade Union (all-inclusive) failed in its immediate socialistic ends in 1833-34; yet its influence only ten years later was responsible for the founding by the Rochdale pioneers of the first cooperative store, a movement which has proved that profit, both material and spiritual, from cooperation can come not only to producers and sellers but also to buyers.

With 1832, then, there came into the world of England, a new outlook, a new spirit, a new soil from which a new literature must grow. Forty years later, centering around 1870, again a change came—a new outlook, a new spirit, a new soil, which could give complete sustenance no longer to the literature that sprang up after 1832.

Even if there were no other compelling reasons for its choice, the date chosen to mark the real end of the period, 1870, can justify itself also as marking a stage in the development of the literature alone. The literary career of Dickens, the most popular Victorian writer, spans almost exactly the whole period. He began writing only two years after the death of Scott, the most popular author of the Romantic Age, and his career was ended by death in 1870. Before 1870 death had stopped the work, also, of

Macaulay, Mrs. Browning, Clough, and Thackeray; but at the time of their deaths Clough had been publishing for thirteen years, Thackeray for nearly thirty, and Macaulay and Mrs. Browning for over thirty. In 1870 Carlyle and Tennyson had been before the public for well over forty years; Rossetti, Arnold, Meredith, George Eliot, and Huxley from some twenty to twenty-five years; Morris for about fifteen years; and even Swinburne for ten years. Not only was the characteristic work of the older men largely completed; even for the younger writers much of the work by which we know them had already been done by 1870. George Eliot had published her first big book *Adam Bede,* George Meredith his *Richard Feverel,* and Fitzgerald his *Rubaiyat* as early as 1859. Arnold had turned from poetry to prose and had already published *Essays in Criticism* (1865), *The Study of Celtic Literature* (1867), and *Culture and Anarchy* (1869). Huxley had published many scientific papers, *Man's Place in Nature* (1863), *The Classification of Animals* (1869), and *Lay Sermons* (1870). Rossetti's *Early Italian Poets* had appeared in 1861, while the first complete edition of his *Poems* came out in 1870. Morris's *The Defence of Guinevere and Other Poems* was published in 1858, his *Life and Death of Jason* in 1867, and *The Earthly Paradise* in 1868-70. Swinburne's *Atalanta in Calydon* appeared in 1865, and he had presented to the public a total of some seven other volumes by 1870.

When we consider this list, we see that we know practically all the real Victorians by 1870. Walter Pater, Thomas Hardy, Robert Louis Stevenson, Rudyard Kipling, the rise under the influence of Ibsen of the new literary drama of Jones, Pinero, and Shaw, and the change in fiction under continental influences do not properly belong in the period; for practical convenience, however, representative work of three of these men, all now dead—Pater, Hardy, and Stevenson—has been included. The last quarter of the century gave all the new people their place in English literature. But though Victoria might still be on the throne until the end of the century, the last thirty-one years of her reign are not properly "Victorian" as the first thirty-three were. These later men did their work in a changed world from that world we sometimes call Mid-Victorian.

The changed world after 1870 was ushered in by a mass of significant detailed changes in English life—changes internally in the political, industrial, social, educational, scientific, and religious life of England, and changes externally in the world environment of England. Of course important events had taken place between 1832 and 1870, things as important, for example, as the establishment of penny postage in 1839, the repeal of the Corn Laws in 1846, and the Chartist and revolutionary movements of 1848; such events do not cluster together, however, as they do with 1832 and 1870 as centers.

In politics the event that looms largest and that leads immediately to other changes was the second Reform Bill. It came in 1867, thirty-five years after the first Reform Bill. That first big step toward modern democracy in England in 1832 had declared the nation supreme, but it was a nation that consisted only of the nobility and gentry and of the upper half of the middle class—professional men and the employers of labor. In 1867 the second Reform Bill added to the nation as defined in 1832 the lower middle class and the workers of the towns. Still without the pale, still unenfranchised were some of the miners and all the workers in the country districts, and these elements of the lower classes had to wait nearly twenty years for recognition as citizens.

The new voters, however, were in a majority, and their weight told for reform in many directions. What the new basis of government would mean was indicated even the year before, in 1866, in the hitherto unheard of campaign of agitation for reform conducted by John Bright, the great radical, when the whole male population of an industrial city, perhaps 200,000 strong, would march before him and drink in his fiery eloquence. With the partnership of Gladstone the Liberal and Bright the Radical in 1868 began a program of reform that revolutionized England.

Even before the Liberals came into power on the reform wave, the Conservatives, under the guidance of Disraeli, already foreshadowing the Imperialist policy that dominated the latter part of the century, began a new treatment of the English colonies, a liberalizing and fostering treatment that would have saved America to England had their Tory predecessors realized it a hundred years before. In 1867 the British North American Act created the Dominion of Canada. In 1870 all the great central plains were ceded to Canada by the Hudson Bay Company, and in 1871 British Columbia joined the Dominion, thus making a continuous federal republic stretching from the Atlantic to the Pacific and from the United States to the Arctic Ocean. The separate colonies in New Zealand and Australia had already attained individual self-government, and in 1872 self-government was granted to Cape Colony. For the later fusing of the separate colonies in Australia and in South Africa into great self-governing republics, however, Canada had set the example, both for the mother country and for the colonies.

Internal reform began at once with the new Liberal government under Gladstone and Bright. For the first time Parliament gave real consideration to the troubles of Ireland. In 1864 it disestablished the Protestant English state church which had been imposed upon Catholic Ireland three hundred years before. In 1870, to give some relief to oppressed Irish tenants, it passed the first of a long series of Irish Land Acts. Reform in England itself began as promptly. From 1869 to 1871 the Government undertook Army Reforms, abolishing the purchase of officers' commissions and greatly ameliorating the lot of the common soldier. The Civil Service Act of 1870 killed patronage and corruption in all appointive offices and really answered Carlyle's demand for the finding of the fit by establishing competitive examinations for appointment to office. In 1871 the Government created the Local Government Board to supervise all local government throughout the nation. In 1872 came the final blow to the intimidation of the newly enfranchised citizens by the passage of the Ballot Act, thus providing for the secret ballot in all elections.

Fully as prominent as political reform at the beginning of the new age was the progress made in the industrial and social worlds. The factory system, developing under the influence of the steam engine, had long dominated English industry. The railroad, the steamship, and the telegraph had long been established. Other striking advances in communication and transportation, however, came now with the successful use of the Atlantic cable in 1866, the opening of the Suez Canal in 1869, and the Government purchase of all land telegraphs in 1870. Marking the change from the Mid-Victorian Age to the new age came the swift expansion of labor organizations in members, in power, and in privileges. In 1860-61 began the cooperative movement among trades unions known as the Permanent Trade Councils. In 1862 the first Working Men's Clubs were formed, educational and propaganda organizations that grew rapidly in power.

ln 1863 appeared the first Cooperative Wholesale Societies. From 1866 to 1876 came the successful agitation for equal justice to the laborers and their unions before the law, which so far had discriminated heavily in favor of the employers. In 1869 came the Cooperative Union, the inclusive organization of the numerous independent cooperatives. In 1871, under Gladstone, the trades unions secured from Parliament the complete protection of their funds. In the General Election of 1874 leaders of the unions were for the first time elected to Parliament. In 1876 Disraeli in the Employers' and Workmen's Act repealed all oppressive criminal law directed at the unions, employers and workmen were made equal in civil law, and strikes and peaceful picketing became possible. Trades unions had come of age.

Social betterment kept pace with the improvement in the status of labor organizations. A quickening of the social conscience demanded adequate care for the sick and the suffering. Florence Nightingale revolutionized the care for sick and wounded soldiers in the Crimean War of 1854-56, and she led in the formation of the Red Cross in 1864, in the modern type of hospital construction, and in the preparation of women for one of the greatest achievements of modern civilization, trained nursing. From 1864 to 1876 agitation for human betterment took form in many directions. In 1867 the Metropolitan (London) Common Poor Fund was established for the care of the poor unable to care for themselves— the sick, defectives, and children—adequate care away from the poorhouses. In 1869 imprisonment for debt was abolished. The betterment of the condition of the common soldier in 1871 was followed by the protection of sailors in 1876. Agitation for adequate public health measures was led by such organizations as the Commons Preservation Society, with its insistence on the necessity of public parks as breathing spaces for crowded populations. In 1875 the Public Health and the Artisans' Dwelling Acts placed under public control all such matters as city water supplies, sewage disposal, parks and public recreation, though the national agency for the enforcement of all such regulations, the Local Government Board, had already been created in 1871. The age-old protection of property had at last been balanced by protection of life and conditions of living for all the people.

The success of advancing democracy demanded increased education for the great influx of new citizens brought under the Constitution by the Second Reform Bill of 1867. The principle of state aid to elementary schools—a revolution in itself—had been put into practice at the beginning of the Victorian period. By 1860 the annual national grant was forty-two times greater than the first grant of 1833, and every grant of aid carried national inspection of schools as a condition. In 1869 Parliament abolished sectarian tests in endowed schools and made their ancient funds available for modern uses. In 1870 came the great Education Act of the Gladstone Government, making available for the first time a national system of schools under national inspection but with local support and control. The Act prohibited religious intruction in school hours, thus breaking the connection between the church and education that had existed for over twelve hundred years. From 1876 on compulsory school attendance was enforced, with its corollary prohibiting child labor until at least the "three R's" had been attained.

Higher education in the changing years around 1870 kept pace with the reforms in elementary education. One of the most significant developments in English life at this time is the growth of university education and the modernizing and liberalizing of its spirit. In 1871 all kinds of dissenters were admitted to all fellowships and appointments in Oxford and Cambridge and Durham on an equality with adherents of the Church of England. In 1873 Cambridge began to take the University to the people in the modern system of university extension lectures. This was only symptomatic of the demand for higher education throughout the country, education along modern lines in science, in modern history, and in modern languages and literatures, as against the strictly classical education that had ruled in Oxford and Cambridge for centuries. The new demand could not be satisfied merely by some slight reorganization in the old institutions. Modern higher educational institutions, therefore, began to spring up in all the great centers of the country. In 1870 Mason College was founded at Birmingham, an institution that has now developed into the great University of Birmingham. Though founded in 1831-32 along the old classical lines, the University of Durham assumed the modern character in 1871 by undertaking technical education. Higher education had begun in Manchester in 1851, but it began its modern development toward the present University of Manchester in 1872, and similar development took place at Leeds in 1875 and at Liverpool in 1881. No longer did Oxford and Cambridge have a monopoly of higher education.

Along with this extension of university education began the development of college education for women. In 1869 women were admitted as students at the University of London, but not to degrees. In 1873 Girton College and in 1875 Newnham College were founded for women at Cambridge. In 1879 Somerville College and Lady Margaret Hall were founded for them at Oxford. The year before London began conferring degrees on women. From 1870 on, as both cause and result of their better education, began that increased participation of women in the leadership of English life which has culminated in this century in granting them the right to vote and which is symbolized now by their election to Parliament.

These great changes in human relations in the changing world of 1870 were accompanied by the tremendous impact of science on modern life. The effect of science was brought about at first almost wholly outside the pale of the universities, by individuals who were university men but who did their work independently. The application of science to industry, transportation, and communication already discussed is only one part of its revolutionizing influence on English life and on the whole life of the world. Nineteenth century science affected all the thought life, all the emotional life of men; it changed economic, social, and political theory and practice; it forced a restatement of philosophy; its influence even compelled heart-searching readjustments in theology and religion; it profoundly affected literature.

To confirm the reign of law in the natural world—that was the contribution of nineteenth century science to modern life. The conception of natural law had been growing since the Renaissance. Copernicus in the sixteenth century and Newton in the seventeenth had asserted it for the astronomical world. Lyell in 1830 extended it to the development of the earth itself. Then came four great Englishmen at the end of our period, men who stand out as world figures, carrying over to all forms of life on the earth what Lyell had begun in his *Principles of Geology* at the beginning of the period. These four men were Darwin, Huxley, Wallace, and Spencer.

1859 was a notable year in English letters. The world will remember it because in that year three important figures made their first important contributions to letters with the *Adam Bede* of George Eliot, the *Rubaiyat* of

Fitzgerald, and the *Richard Feverel* of Meredith. But 1859 will be a more famous date in world annals because in that year appeared Darwin's *Origin of Species*. He and Wallace had jointly given the first statement of the development of species through natural selection before the Linnean Society in 1858; but with the publication of Darwin's full explanation of evolution in the *Origin of Species* in 1859 the storm of discussion and opposition broke forth at once. Historians of the world have rightly given great space to the revolution seventy years before, the French Revolution of 1789; yet the effect upon the world of the Revolution of 1859 may be more profound.

From 1859 the significant dates in the onslaught of science on modern life "Come not single spies but in battalions." In 1860 before the British Association for the Advancement of Science Huxley defended evolution and vindicated the right of science to investigate and to teach, whatever theology might say. In 1862 Herbert Spencer, the philosopher of the evolutionary theory, published his *First Principles*. In 1863 appeared Huxley's *Man's Place in Nature;* in 1864 Spencer's *Classification of the Sciences* and his *Principles of Biology;* in 1867 Darwin's *Variation of Plants and Animals under Domestication;* in 1869 Huxley's *Classification of Animals* and Wallace's *Malay Archipelago;* in 1870 Huxley's *Lay Sermons* and Spencer's *Principles of Psychology;* and finally in 1871 Wallace's *Contributions to the Theory of Natural Selection* and Darwin's *Descent of Man*. All four of these men—and Lyell as well—continued to write for years, amplifying what they had already done. This year 1871, however, which brought together again the work of the two great co-discoverers of biological evolution, Darwin and Wallace, thirteen years after their first joint announcement, may well stand as the center for the achievements of pure science in the times of Victoria and for its influence on the world of thought. It is these achievements which make Professor Elton declare that science is "the boldest feature of all in the intellectual map of the last century." It is these same achievements which induce Professor Louis Cazamian to assert that at the close of the Victorian Age science is of primal importance in the intellectual life even of the average man and that "it holds supreme sway during this new age."

The great influence of science on thought was very largely the work of the biological sciences—geology (so far as it is related to the history of life), botany, and zoology. To these powerful influences must be added the work of the new science dealing with primitive man—anthropology. From 1861 to 1865 appeared Sir Henry Maine's *Ancient Law, Village Communities,* and *Early History of Institutions.* Contemporary with these appeared Tylor's *Researches into the Early History of Mankind,* his *Primitive Culture,* and Max Mueller's statement of his theory of Comparative Mythology in his *Chips from a German Workshop.* The new spirit of science showed itself, moreover, in many other fields. It is found not only in the more exact physical sciences in the work of such men as Tyndall and Thompson and Tait but also in those fields of study that deal with man as man, with man and all his institutions. In governmental, social, and historical studies, for example, from 1865 to 1876 appeared Bagehot's *The English Constitution* and his *Physics and Politics,* Spencer's *The Study of Sociology* and his *Principles of Sociology,* Lecky's *History of Rationalism* and his *History of European Morals,* and Green's *Short History of the English People* —all books exerting great influence and all strongly influenced by the new spirit. The indirect influence of the new science on philosophy can hardly be measured; it shows itself directly from 1862 to 1874 in such different books as Spencer's *First Principles* and his *Classification of the Sciences,* in Maurice's *Social Morality,* in Mills's *Subjection of Women,* in Tyndall's *Imagination in Science,* and in Jevons's *The Principles of Science.* The same attitude appears in a new type of studies in language and literature—for example, in Max Mueller's *History of Ancient Sanskrit Literature* in 1859 and in his *Lectures* on the *Science of Language,* in 1861-64.

Such penetration of the spirit of science into all the fields of thought meant that the one field considered most vital by vast masses of men, the field of religion, could not escape. As was suggested above, the age-long conflict of religious dogma against secular knowledge, that is, against the science of whatever century, broke out anew with the promulgation of the theory of evolution in the fields of biology and geology. The bases of the conflict can be better understood if we take a glance backward.

The historians of Christianity tell us that the church in its earlier centuries passed through three stages, both in relation to the state and in relation to that organized attempt at the explanation of the universe which we call philosophy. In the first relationship Christianity, the church, was at first persecuted by the state; later it was established by the state; and finally it dominated the state. In the second relationship its teachings were at first alien to philosophy; then they were accepted by philosophy and given form and intellectual authority by philosophy; and finally theology, the theory of religion, became the "Queen of the Sciences" and ruled over the whole world of knowledge for centuries. But beginning with modern times and the Renaissance the state gained first unchallenged control over all secular matters and in the course of the last four centuries has gradually established its sovereignty over the church itself. One of the great missions of the nineteenth century was to bring about a similar reversal of the medieval dominance of theology over philosophy and science. Here the underlying foundation of the struggle was the deliberate assertion by the progressive thinkers in the changing world of 1870 that the subject matter and the method of science was of vital concern to the life of man, a reassertion, therefore, of an interest in this present world as against the dominant interest in medieval times in another world.

To quote from the new *Britannica* the nineteenth century proclaimed that our present world was "no longer merely the scene for the drama of the soul and God, nor is man independent of it, but man and nature constitute an organism, humanity being part of the vaster whole. Man's place is not even central, as he appears a temporary inhabitant of a minor planet in one of the lesser stellar systems. . . . The rights gained for independent research were extended over the realm of religion also; the two indeed cannot remain separate, and man must subordinate knowledge to the authority of religion—or make science supreme, submitting religion to its scrutiny and judging it like other phenomena. Under this investigation Christianity does not appear altogether exceptional. Its early logic, ontology, and cosmology, with many of its distinctive doctrines are shown to be the natural offspring of the races and ages which gave them birth. Put into their historical environment they are found to be steps in the intellectual development of man's mind. But when put forward as absolute truths to-day, they are put aside as anachronisms not worthy of dispute. The Bible is studied like other works, its origins discovered and its place in comparative religion assigned. It does not appear as altogether unique, but it is put among the other sacred books. For the great religions of the world show similar cycles of development, similar appropriations of prevalent science and philosophy, similar conservative insistence upon ancient truth, and similar claims to an exclusive authority."

It was inevitable that conservative religious leaders would at first violently oppose the introduction of such views. At the beginning of the period, in 1833, the Oxford Movement, led by Newman, was as much a revolt against the growing spirit of science as against the materialism of the new industrial revolution. At the end of the period even stronger opposition was voiced by religious conservatives, beginning immediately. After the publication of the *Origin of the Species* in 1859, it was Bishop Wilberforce's attack on evolution in 1860 that called forth Huxley's famous defense. But side by side with the cumulative evidence in a host of books of the growing strength of science, not only in the natural sciences but also in what we are learning to call the social sciences of government, sociology, and history, and even in the study of language and literature, there appeared in book after book the embodiment of the struggle between orthodox theology and dogmatic religion on the one side and a more liberal theology and the application of the scientific method and aim to the study of religion and the Bible and the church on the other side. From 1860 on for fifteen years and beyond came work after work, article after article, using the method of science in the study of the Bible, in the study of the history of the church and Christianity, and in the study of comparative religions. Liberal scholars like Colenso and Westcott and Robertson Smith and Max Mueller and liberal writers like the authors of the famous *Essays and Reviews* of 1860 and Dean Stanley and Seeley and Matthew Arnold—all these contributed to the penetration into the sphere of religion of the new spirit of fearless investigation.

Yet there can be no revolution in the world of thought

when it touches men's dearest beliefs without trouble and pain, doubt and even despair. The great conflict between the new science and orthodox religious belief was not a matter of the intellect only, something merely to be debated by scholars. It touched the faith of the millions, of those new millions who had learned to read and who did read, of those millions who had arisen in the conflict between labor and capital, in the conflict between democracy and privilege, to a stage of consciousness and articulateness which made their feelings, their opinions, their thoughts vital to every great interest of English civilization. The rise of the new science, then, as it affected industry and as it affected religion, came home, to use Bacon's great phrase, to all men's "business and bosoms."

This great mass of changes in the internal life and relationships of the English people centering around 1870—changes political, industrial, social, educational, scientific, and religious—marks only one part of the change in the environment of Victorian literature. Changes in the world environment of England were almost equally important in their effect upon English life and therefore upon English literature. The part played by England in the world movements centering around 1870 and continuing even up to the present is far from being a part to which she can always point with pride Her power, her prestige, her actual leadership in a hundred directions in mid-century world life made her a responsible trustee, whether she would or not, for the safe progress of western civilization. How she lived up to her responsibilities, her opportunities, can be shown best by a rapid enumeration of characteristic events from the middle of the century to the Great War.

With the close of the Napoleonic wars in 1815 England had forty years of peace. To a large extent peace reigned also in the rest of the world except for the wars of liberation in Greece and in Spanish America and for the easily crushed uprisings of the common people in the various European countries in 1848. Everywhere during that forty years of peace the English people on the whole were sympathetic with the attempts of oppressed subjects and peoples to secure their freedom. But with the turn into the second half of the century official England, usually supported by a majority in Parliament, was often either indifferent or even on the wrong side toward the struggles for liberty in various parts of the world. In the Crimean War of 1854-56, for example, England fought on the side of the Turks against the efforts of Russia to free the oppressed peoples of the Balkans from Turkish rule, and England justified herself on the claim that she was fighting to "maintain the balance of power." Whether England took part in them or not, the period that followed was a period of wars. From the Crimean War of 1854-56 to the Great War of 1914, a period of sixty years, war was practically continuous. In that period there were twenty-five wars and five international "incidents," each "incident" producing many of the effects of war. From the Crimean War to 1870 there were nine wars, with England taking part only in the Crimean War and the Indian Mutiny of 1857-59 against her rule; but from 1870 to 1902 England engaged in twelve wars, all waged under the new doctrine of Imperialism.

All this meant that a new theory of the state had taken possession of the English government. Disraeli secured a big majority in the General Election of 1874 with "Preservation of our Empire" as one of his chief proposals. In 1876 he obtained from Parliament the proclamation of Queen Victoria as "Empress of India," and thus the doctrine of the Empire, of Imperialism, might be considered as launched officially. It was the desire of

Disraeli and of his conservative colleagues and successors, Salisbury and Chamberlain, to change the thought of all men concerning the state and the nation from "England," from "Great Britain and Ireland," and focus it on the "British Empire." It was the doctrine of the "Map in Red," of a British Empire, to quote the vision of Daniel Webster, "whose morning drum-beat, following the sun . . . circles the earth with one continuous and unbroken strain of the martial airs of England." Imperialism was a principle of governmental action which refused to grant home rule to Ireland, which attempted to draw the greater English dominions into an imperial federation, which insisted on assuming the "white man's burden" of ruling inferior races from one end of the globe to the other, which supported the Turks in the Near East—for Imperial reasons, and which engaged in Jameson "Raids," even against a white people, if they preferred to govern themselves. Only four foreign wars of importance took place after 1870 and before 1914— Russo-Turkish, Spanish-American, Russo-Japanese, and Balkan. The very names, however, of the twelve wars of England before the close of the century are significant of her imperialistic aims, of her new spirit and her new environment—1877, forcible annexation of the Transvaal; 1877-78, the Kaffir War; 1878-80, the Afghan War; 1879, the Zulu War; 1880-81, the Transvaal War; 1882, the Egyptian War against Arabi Pasha; 1884, the first Soudan War; 1884-86, the third Burmese War; 1885, the Canadian Half-Breed Rebellion; 1895, Jameson's Raid on the Transvaal; 1898, second Soudan War; 1899-1903, the Boer War. England was using the "Big Stick."

In the meantime events of far reaching importance to the world and to England were occurring in Europe and in America. With her eyes fixed on her colonies and on the possibilities for further expansion of the Empire,

England was less interested than she should have been in the significance of three great struggles. In his *British History in the Nineteenth Century* G. M. Trevelyan asserts: "The sixties were the most formative years in history between the era of Napoleon and the revolutionary convulsions following the Great War of our own day." The brief period from 1859 to 1871 was of such vast historical importance because it saw the fusion of disparate elements into three great modern nations, a fusion symbolized by the victory of the North in the Civil War of the United States, the crowning of Victor Emanuel as King of Italy, and the crowning of William I as Emperor of Germany. England had been unjustified in the Crimean War of 1854-56; she had to wage a war of conquest in the Sepoy Rebellion in India in 1857-59; and these were but preparation for her misinterpretation of contemporary history in America and in Germany. In the American Civil War of 1861-65 official England was on the wrong side—she sided with the South. She permitted Prussia to take by force from little Denmark the provinces of Schleswig and Holstein in 1865, and she did not object to Germany's taking Alsace and Lorraine from France in 1871. In only one of these great struggles was England right. She did help in the unification of Italy by declaring, against a hostile Continent, that the Italians, under the leadership of Cavour and Garibaldi, should settle their affairs by themselves. The result was that Italy was able to achieve union, to enter the circle of modern nations under a constitutional, liberal monarchy. But England was equally wrong in being indifferent to the establishment of an imperial autocracy, a military despotism, in Germany under Bismarck and in being actively hostile to Lincoln, who achieved the salvation of modern democracy when he exterminated slavery and established the federal republic permanently. England did not have the vision to see that forty-three years later Germany, which she had permitted to become the dominant force of the Continent for that long period, would threaten her very existence and that her only salvation would be the great American republic.

The decade of the sixties, the twelve years from 1859 to 1871, settled Italian, American, and German unity; but it left unsolved for nearly half a century, till the Great War, the problems of liberation—the Irish question, Polish liberty, Russian liberty, and German liberty. A new spirit entered the world after the annexation of Alsace and Lorraine by Germany—a spirit of race and class hatred, of power as the ideal of government rather than justice, of high protective tariffs, of the grabbing of colonial "empires" and "spheres of influence," of tremendous efforts in the building of competitive armaments. The liberal hopes for social and political evolution, encouraged by the great internal reforms in England clustering around 1870, began to give way in international relations to the doctrines of survival of the strongest through class war and race war. It was an atmosphere alien to the true Victorians. Men as different as Disraeli, Chamberlain, and Kipling among Englishmen, Emperor William II for the Germans, and Roosevelt for the Americans voiced the English doctrine of "Dominion over palm and pine," the German doctrine of the "Will to Power," and the Rooseveltian doctrine of the "Big Stick."

In such an air the great Victorians—Gladstone and Bright, Dickens and Ruskin and Arnold, Tennyson and Browning—could not breathe and maintain the vigorous, pulsating life of the mid-century. The environment of the literature had changed, and the literature itself had to change. The century had arrived at 1870, with all that

that date symbolized. The Victorian Age had reached its
limits.

## II. WHAT PRECEDED

Probably a number of those who will use this volume
have already come in contact with the three preceding
volumes in this series, Professor Clark's *The Seventeenth
Century*, Professor's Blickensderfer's *The Eighteenth
Century*, and Professor Reed's *The Romantic Period*.
For a more detailed account and illustration of what preceded Victorian literature, then, the readers of this volume must be referred to the three previous volumes in
the series; but we also must at least glance at the literature and the life out of which Victorian literature pro-
ceeded.

Dates are not absolute marks in the development of
literature and civilization; but they are highly significant
as symbols around which to group facts that mark tran-
sitions and developments. It is worthwhile to keep in
mind, then, that what is called Late Modern English
Literature may be said to begin with the Restoration and
Dryden. From 1660 on to the end of the Victorian
period it is a curious fact that the development of English literature proceeds in five distinctly marked stages,
each approximately forty years in length. The Restoration Age, the Age of Dryden, extends from 1660 to the
death of Dryden in 1700 or to the accession of Queen
Anne in 1702. The Queen Anne Age, the Age of Addison and Pope, may be said to run to 1744-45, to the
deaths of Pope and Swift. The Transition Age, the Age
of Johnson, finds its terminus in 1784, the death of
Johnson, or in 1789, the outbreak of the French Revolution. Then comes the Romantic Age, or the age of
Wordsworth and Scott, extending to the death of Scott
and the First Reform Bill in 1832. The Victorian Age,

the age of Carlyle, Tennyson, and Dickens, as has been pointed out at length above, extends properly to 1870, a date which marks the death of Dickens and the center of a mass of changes in the life of England, changes internal and external.

In these two centuries the attitudes of Englishmen toward life and the results of this attitude in the spirit of their literature varies from age to age. The two periods from 1660 to 1744-45 are essentially one age in intellectual and literary ideals. They thought of themselves as "classical," called themselves "Augustans"; but with more exactness we designate the two ages combined as Pseudo-Classical. Restoration and Queen Anne literature was classical, or what it supposed was classical, in its dislike of zeal, of emotion, of mysticism, of aspiration, of originality. It was opposed to the concrete, to the individual, to color. It preferred to generalize, to build types. All this is a part of the exaltation of reason above imagination. A literature with such principles found little interest in the life of remote times or remote places. It cared nothing for nature, unless it was a "nature to advantage dress'd," like Pope's fantastically trimmed garden. Not only the pointed architecture of the Middle Ages but also mountains and medieval literature and even Elizabethan literature were all equally "Gothic," that is to say, barbarous, to the Augustans. The literature of such an age was interested in man, man of the present, man of society, of fashion, of the city, of politics. The "Town" (London) was the center of all life. Such an attitude was essentially provincial, narrow, insular, and the literature which grew out of such a society must be characterized in the same terms.

The Augustan Age in both life and literature was a partisan age. Partisan warfare permeated all life. Every literary man must be a partisan or not survive, and he received his reward in some form or other of "pudding from the public table," in offices in the government or in the church, in patronage of literary work, or in direct pay for partisan pamphleteering in pounds, shillings, and pence. Political partisanship, religious partisanship, literary partisanship—this explains the larger part of the career and the work of Dryden and Pope, of Addison and Steele, of Swift and Defoe. Even the poetry of such men was "composed in their wits, not in their souls"; it was reasoning in verse.

In manners and conduct it was an age of external polish but of fundamental coarseness and even corruptness in life; an age of powdered wigs, patches, embroidered brocades, colors, dress swords, canes, and fans; an age of elaborate artificial politeness, with cock-fighting, bull-baiting, drunkenness, and lechery. In religion and philosophy the tendency was toward either a cold conventional formality or a materialistic deistic skepticism. Men were pre-eminently gregarious. Social life, not solitariness, was their ideal, and the coffee-house was the symbol of such a life. Gossip was a most fruitful occupation, and conversation, discussion, harangue were cultivated, not meditation.

Nevertheless, the Augustan Age had distinguished merits. Pseudo-Classicism was a necessary reaction in style against the extravagance of Elizabethan literature as well as against the long, involved, Latinized style of early seventeenth century prose. The insistence of the Augustans on form, on regularity, on restraint, on condensed force, on ease was the one discipline above all others needed for the development of English style. What clearness, what simplicity and good sense we now have in style we owe largely to the Restoration and Queen Anne periods. It was to these ages, also, that we owe the origin of periodical literature, the per fecting of the essay, and the creation of an audience for the modern novel.

The Transition Age was what its name signifies—the transition from Pseudo-Classicism to Romanticism. Though Dr. Johnson, the dominant figure of the age, was a Keeper of the Faith as handed down from the Augustans, a "classical" schoolmaster who delighted to rap the knuckles of the bad boys of an incipient romanticism, yet his strong good sense and his instinctive liking for English literature made him a sound appreciator of the best among the English authors from the time of Elizabeth on. Moreover, the new movements toward Romanticism began as early as the beginning of the period. Methodism, democracy, the new patriotism of Pitt working for the expansion, the honor, and the glory of England, the new philanthropy of Howard and Wilberforce and Clarkson, the new love of nature and of solitude—all these gradually wrought on the literature of the age a change that developed later into the literary revolution of the Romantic Age. Broadly speaking each of these different movements means increased sensitiveness, increased feeling, increased sympathy.

Though they retained many traces of the Augustan manner and much of the Augustan attitude, the Transition poets responded to the new spirit with pictures of nature, with melancholy solitary musings, with "the short and simple annals of the poor." The novelists responded with presentations of the ordinary man in the realistic novels, with pictures of the past in the historical novel and the Gothic romance, with the exaltation of feeling in the sentimental novel. The critics responded with the dethronement of the Augustan idol, Pope, and with a rehabilitation of Milton, Shakespeare, Spenser, and the Middle Ages. The antiquarians and dilettante collectors responded by unearthing and publishing masses of folk material—Scandinavian, Gaelic, Welsh, Scottish, and English—all culminating in that mighty agent of Romanticism, Percy's *Reliques of Ancient English Poetry.* Even in the middle of the century, then, prophetic voices were preparing the way for the coming of the new age.

Still more important for the understanding of the Victorian Age is the period that immediately preceded it. We cannot fully know the times of Victoria until we know the Revolutionary Period, the Romantic Age, out of which the times of Victoria developed. But we cannot characterize the Romantic Age, cannot understand the wide swing of the pendulum in the times of Wordsworth and Scott, unless we know what was on the other side of the clock when the pendulum started to swing. As was indicated above, the prevailing tendency in the late seventeenth and in the early eighteenth century, the Augustan ages, was centripetal; it was center-seeking. Its ideals were wholly conventional. Organized society and its conventional rules governed all life. The Augustans boasted that they lived in the best of all possible worlds, and they knew that their conventional rules gave them such a world. But in the latter part of the eighteenth century and in the beginning of the nineteenth, in the Revolutionary Age, the general tendency was centrifugal, center-fleeing. Man in society and society in the narrower sense—these were the governing forces in the earlier period; but in the later period man became a human being, an individual. The tendency in the earlier period was to subordinate the individual to society; in the latter period it was to subordinate society to the individual. While pleading the rights of the individual, then, the revolutionists, the romanticists, were fundamentally anti-social. Their doctrine, their practice, would develop the individual richly; but, carried out completely, it would dissolve society.

In the literary development of England there was no romantic "school." The greater Romantics differed notably from each other through their insistence on their one common quality, on individuality. The conventional world around them looked upon all of them as freaks. They looked forward to a millennium still to come or backward to a past beautiful because distant. All were dissatisfied with the present, with the commonplace, with the conventional. With the exception of Scott they all were anti-conventional and more or less anti-social. Though Scott looked backward to an ideal age, and though he was a great original in literature, yet in his views on society, on politics, on religion he was conventional. Not so the others. Revolution in political and social theories, transcendentalism in philosophy, Unitarianism in religion, an insistence on personal freedom, a refusal to live in the world of the actual—some combination of these tendencies characterized all the other greater Romantics. It was a period of revolt, of emotion, of fervor, of enthusiasm, of imagination, of beauty-seeking, of dreams, of ideals, of faith in a new order—but unfortunately, with no practical plans for achieving a new world.

The characteristics of the romantic writers in relation to the real world in which they and other men were living can be summed up in one word—impracticality. They were convinced that the world was "out of joint," but they did not know how to "set it right." All their dreamy visions of a re-made world could be symbolized by the ideal community which the young Southey, the young Coleridge, and the young Wordsworth—they all changed later—would found, a "Pantisocracy on the banks of the Susquehanna." They had invented the word "Pantisocracy," but they probably could not define it, and they probably did not know where the Susquehanna was or whether anybody might already be in possession over there. But both words were orotund and mouth-filling, and that was enough! As an experiment in ideal living it would no doubt have been fully as successful as our own Brook Farm experiment, where, according to Hawthorne, Margaret Fuller's "transcendental heifer hooked all the other cows." Consider the typical hero of the later romantic poets—the Childe Harold of Byron, the Endymion of Keats, the Wanderer in Shelley's *Alastor,* and add even Wordsworth's Pedler. They are all lonely wanderers, all dreamers, all fancy-spinners. Childe Harold wanders over Europe having attacks of rhetoric. Endymion says, "I can see nought earthly worth my compassing." His search is for ideal beauty, for impossible beauty, and in this search he is joined by Shelley's Wanderer. Of course they are all scorners of the real world and all its conventions. We cannot imagine them in a dress coat, but only in wide, loose Byronic collars or flowing robes. Such heroes could never bring the ideal into the actual, could never transform the real world with their visions.

And yet the Romantics brought great gifts to the Victorians. As Professor Gates has phrased it, the Romantics were "the rediscoverers of the soul," the "reasserters of the primacy of the spirit." Even Scott quickened men to a new sympathy with the past; he added new color, new feeling, new glamour, new imaginative realization to life. Wordsworth made men alive to the beauty of the commonplace; he transformed nature for all men by making them feel intensely their spiritual kinship with the soul in nature. And so also

all the poets and all the prose writers of the Romantic
Age—Coleridge, Byron, Shelley, Keats, Lamb, Hazlitt,
DeQuincey—all of them, though in different ways,
quickened men, made them more sensitive to a thousand
sources of joy and delight, of pain and fear and terror,
of beauty and holiness, of intimate kinship with nature
and with other men. Naturally such an age—an age
of richly cultivated individuality, of love of the concrete, love of color, of imaginative interpretation not
only of the distant in time and place, the visionary, even
the supernatural, but also of the commonplace—such an
age could express itself adequately in only two great
literary forms, the lyric and the personal essay. It was
a great age in our literature.

## III. GENERAL CHARACTERISTICS OF THE AGE

The supreme task of the Victorian Age was the synthesis of the ideal and the real. Narrow as the world
was in which the Augustans lived, it was a very real
world. Their feet were always planted on the ground.
The Romantics, on the contrary, were in the clouds,
up among the stars. If an earthy realism characterized
the Augustans, the complementary quality of the Romantics was a misty idealism. It was the problem of
the Victorians to fuse these contradictory tendencies
into a progressively realized unity, to help "reason and
the will of God prevail" in a world of ugly fact, to
bring the Vision on the Mount down to the valley where
real men dwell.

That there was need for the transforming power of
ideals in the actual life of the Victorian period has already been seen. Struggle characterized the age—struggle between capital and labor, between aristocracy and

democracy, between science and religion. All the great problems of the period were inter-related. Industrial problems became social problems when the conditions of labor—wages, hours, housing, recreation, education—became the conditions of the laborer and his life. Science on the practical side was linked up to the development of industry and commerce, but on the other it became the new ferment in philosophy and religion, the agent of doubt, of revolution in thought, in education. The growth of industry made the owners and directors of industry, the middle classes, clamor for political rights, for participation in government. For a like self-protection the working man also demanded representation in the state. The advance of education became a necessity as the basis of the state broadened with the extension of the franchise; yet it was first conferred upon those who had it not because of the quickening social conscience of those who had. The Utilitarian philosophy of Bentham and his followers was right when it phrased the ideal for the growing democracy as the greatest good to the greatest number. But it was wrong when it helped to set up as the right method for the realization of its ideal the doctrine of Laissez Faire, the doctrine which applied the biological principle of the struggle for existence to economic and social life. What would happen to men's motives in their relation to their fellow-men if religion was to be broken down by the onslaughts of doubt? Would the humanitarian impulse, the sense of brotherhood and of social responsibility, continue to function without the sanctions of traditional Christianity? Could the new science and religion be reconciled? One effect of industrialism, of machinery, was to destroy the artistry of craftsmanship, to make the world uglier in every way. Could the beauty of the earlier ages be brought back into life?

These and a host of other questions called for answer. The British world was in a state of unstable equilibrium. Which way would it go when it began to move?

The Victorians had no illusions about the world in which they lived. The smug self-complacency of the Augustans in their slogan of the best of all possible worlds was re-echoed by Macaulay and a few other Victorian Philistines; but the great mass of thinking Victorians knew that their world in many ways was wrong, that it was getting worse, and that, unless something was done about it, it would eventually go to smash. What should they do about it? They were completely disillusioned as to any answers the Romantics, the Revolutionaries, had offered. They saw the failure of romantic dreaming. They realized that they had to live with actual men in a real world with institutions fitted to a world of fact. They saw the need of a return to cooperation with their fellows. They recognized the necessity of continuity in life, that men could get help not only from their fellows but also from their predecessors. Consequently among thinking men there was a return of respect for the routine of ordinary life, for the customs, even for the conventions by which men had lived and were living. Yet the Victorians knew that they must do something about the evils of their civilization. They could not destroy the whole of life to right wrongs in a part of life. They could not accept the solution of complete destruction of the old—the revolutionist's answer. Neither could they accept withdrawal from the actual world into the world of dreams —the romanticist's answer. Their answer, therefore, was—not destruction but preservation, not dreamy withdrawal but amelioration.

It is the glory of the Victorian era that more than in any other age in our literature the great Victorian writers participated in thought and feeling and action in the life of their times. Moreover, this participation was conscious and deliberate, not the unconscious reflection of environment which characterizes the literature of every age. The great Victorian authors shared in the disillusion after the Revolutionary era. They suffered in the early days of the period with the submerged eight-tenths of the laboring classes. They themselves went through the doubt, the turmoil evoked by the new science. They saw the paganism of the upper classes, the materialism of the middle classes, and the brutalizing of the lower classes. Everyone of them, directly or indirectly, gave for his own age some answer, positive or negative, to the greatest of all questions for any age—how to live life. They were concerned directly with the conduct of life.

Matthew Arnold said that true poetry was a criticism of life, that is, an interpretation of life, an evaluation of life. Such a formula may well be applied to the great mass of Victorian literature of whatever kind and type—essay and novel as well as poetry—and whoever the author. They do not talk about life in the abstract; they talk about life in their own times. In the face of a disagreeable, ugly, evil, dangerous world, "weary, stale, flat, and unprofitable," as it seemed to many of them, courageously they gird up their loins to fight the good fight. They are searchers for the truth. They are prophets crying out: "Prepare ye the way of the Lord." They are preachers of new crusades. Yet they are not merely didactic, dry moralists. Victorian literature was profoundly ethical; but it was also dynamically ethical. It had power; it produced effects. The characteristic movements in the progress of civilization in the Victorian era were: (1) the tremendous expansion of industry and commerce; (2) the growth of democracy, both political and industrial; (3) the fostering and the spread of education;

(4) the advancement of science; and (5) the direct relation of literature to life. In all these movements the Victorian Age sought for a sane balance in life, not for a
revolutionary realization of ideals but for the sane progress toward ideals. It wished to combine the best in the
common sense of the Augustans with the spiritual insight
of the Romantics. That Victorian life was more worthy in
1870 than in 1832, that England was a better country to
live in at the end of the period than at its beginning, was
due in no small measure to Victorian literature. It stimu-
lated the practical reformers in industry, in politics, in social life. It quickened Englishmen of every station to
the demands of humanity. Constantly it used the ideal to
measure the actual. Victorian literature, therefore, did
more than its full share to accomplish the great task of
its age, the synthesis of the ideal and the real.

## IV. THE WRITERS AND THEIR RELATIONS

Four distinct attitudes toward the perplexing confusion of their age can be discerned among the writers
of the Victorian era. In the first place, a very limited
number of them, of whom Macaulay was chief, accepted
the age and its tendencies with much the same smug
self-satisfaction as the Augustans expressed toward their
age. In the second place, a somewhat larger number
fled from the age, but fled in two different directions:
first, with Newman and his associates they fled from
the incurable evils of their time back to the Ages of
Faith, to the Middle Ages; and second, relatively untroubled by the great moral problems of the time but as
beauty-loving souls bothered by the disagreeableness,
the ugliness of their environment, they fled to a self-
created world of beauty with Rossetti and the Pre-
Raphaelites and Pater. In the third place, they remained

among their fellows, but they were overwhelmed by the troubles of their age, they lost faith, lost confidence in any satisfactory solution of its problems. They were the pessimists of the age, and among them we find such different men as Clough, Arnold the Poet—not Arnold of the prose, Fitzgerald of the *Rubaiyat,* James Thomson of *The City of Dreadful Night,* and Hardy the novelist, Hardy of *Tess of the D'Urbervilles* and *Jude the Obscure.* In the fourth place, we find the great group who struggled to re-make the age: Carlyle, Ruskin, Arnold, Huxley, and, to a degree, Stevenson, the essayists; Dickens, Thackeray, Disraeli, Mrs. Gaskell, Kingsley, Reade, George Eliot, and Meredith, the novelists; Tennyson, Browning, Mrs. Browning, Morris, Swinburne, and Meredith, the poets.

Of course such a grouping of Victorian writers must allow for overlapping; it can never be hard and fast. No human being with any individuality is ever merely of a class, merely a type figure. Even differences in mood at different times in the same writer often means differences in attitude toward life. Yet after making allowances for the large part played by Macaulay in welding into law the First Reform Bill, allowances for an earnestness in Newman equal to the earnestness in Carlyle and Ruskin, allowances for the appearance of Morris and Swinburn both among the Pre-Raphaelites and among the reformers and for Arnold with the pessimists and with the re-shapers of the age—after all this the classification in the preceding paragraph, on the whole, represents the attitude of the chief Victorians toward their times. Such a classification will afford, then, the easiest approach to a discussion of their likenesses and their differences.

Macaulay would be classed by Arnold among the Philistines, a "comfortable worldling," a "faithful Benthamite." Macaulay is the middle-class Whig, who believes that with the Whigs in Power in Parliament, the English world is headed straight for Paradise. He glories in industrial expansion and the "modern progress" of 1850. In his *History of England* he speaks of Manchester as "That wonderful emporium, which in population and wealth far surpasses capitals so much renowned as Berlin, Madrid, and Lisbon, was then a mean and ill-built market-town, containing under six thousand inhabitants," and he speaks of the other great manufacturing cities as having "within the memory of persons still living grown to a greatness which this generation contemplates with wonder and pride." Apparently he was untroubled by the tragic problem of the cities, even then the festering sores on the civilization of England. His faith in material progress would make him a most acceptable speaker in this year of grace, 1930, at a meeting of the United States Chamber of Commerce, and he could out-Babbitt Babbitt at a Rotarian Convention.

Nevertheless, Macaulay was the most useful member of the popularizers of knowledge and opinion for that great mass of new readers England was beginning to acquire. Many thousands of Englishmen learned what they knew about literature and about history from his *Essays* and from his *History of England*. He was never the judge but always the advocate, always a partisan. He loved contrasts and was inclined to turn gray into black and pink into a dazzling scarlet. His brilliant, balanced antithetical style is the appropriate expression for his love of contrast. He had an astounding command over concrete detail and an absolute clarity in sentence and paragraph structure that make him a master of prose style, a marvel of easy reading. But his love of contrast and of the telling phrase sometimes make his views and even what he states as alleged facts untrustworthy. To heighten the contrast, he makes Boswell the greatest biographer that ever lived because he was the meanest man that ever lived, a paradox which Carlyle explodes completely. But Macaulay never saw far beneath the surface, never got to the soul of things, as Carlyle and Ruskin and Arnold did. A great stylist, master of an astounding mass of information, a satisfied Philistine purveyor of information for the great public—that was Macaulay.

Newman has been classified as one who fled from his age. Yet that is only partially true. He also wished to remake the age; but he wished to change the whole of nineteenth century life by turning back the clock, by a return to the Middle Ages. Essentially, then, in temperament and in attitude he is as much a romanticist as Scott. Both found their ideal of the good life in medieval times. Scott made no effort to refashion the whole world to the picturesque arrangement of the feudal life; he was content with some attempt to reproduce them in his own home at Abbotsford, in his family, and among his dependents. But Newman tried with all the power of a deep sincerity, of a beautifully cultivated and sympathetic nature, of a marvelously flexible and eloquent style, to turn Victorian England back to faith in the divine mission of the church as the one true guide and Alma Mater of men. Newman's imagination was fascinated in true romantic fashion by the appeal of the pageantry of ritual, by the mystical and symbolical significance of religious art, architecture, and ceremony. He was Romantic, also, in his feeling for the mysterious significance of nature as the visible symbolical language of God to the soul of man.

In his *Idea of a University* Newman, of course, included theology as one of the necessary parts of a rounded education; but he goes on to formulate in detail the aim of a liberal education, its materials, and its processes, pointing out the great advantage of that type of education afforded by Oxford as contrasted with the newer type offered by the mere examining and certificating body called the University of London. Newman's idea of a liberal education and Arnold's idea of culture were really aiming at the same thing—to fit men to live in the world, not in the cloister, not in the study or the laboratory; Newman wished to educate a gentleman, not a specialist. But Newman could no more secure the approval of his Catholic associates for his ideas of a liberal education than he could carry the new industrial, scientific, materialistic England back with him to the medieval religion and its church. His university in Dublin failed, and he retired to England reckoning himself to have failed in another great objective. Yet he did not really fail, for he was as much the leader of a religious revival still of force in the world as John Wesley was a hundred years before.

Rossetti and the Pre-Raphaelite movement represent a much more real withdrawal from the Victorian world than Newman made. It was not through Newman's prepossession for the Middle Ages, though the colorful pageantry of the medieval church greatly attracted them, but through the inspiring praise of Ruskin for medieval art that Rossetti and his companions first caught their enthusiasm for the Middle Ages. Ruskin himself sympathized with them and to a degree became their spokesman. Their fundamental motive was the old romantic motive of escape from the sordid reality of the Victorian world, from a world of machinery and turmoil and ugliness. They, too, wished to escape from conventions, from the conventions in the art of painting that had grown up since Raphael. They wanted to get away from the artificial art of their own times by following the methods and even by using the subjects of the more primitive Italian artists. They claimed a "rigid adherence to the simplicity of nature; they desired truth in art, fidelity to the subject, fidelity in detail of both drawing and color; they loved the gorgeous coloring of medieval art; they hated convention." In other words, they were romanticists, though they lived in the Victorian era. Unlike the Romantics, they really constituted a "school" in both thought and practice, and it will be no mean "school" that can give the world another group of artists equal to Holman Hunt, George Frederick Watts, Sir John Millais, Sir Edward Burne-Jones, and Rossetti himself.

Rossetti believed, as his "school" did, that the principles of the Pre-Raphaelites were equally as valid for poetry as for painting and his own practice shows a unity of conception uniting his painting and his poetry. The gorgeous pictorial quality of his painting repeats itself in his poetry, and the same perfection of finish in weaving details into a unified whole governs both. Next to Tennyson Rossetti is unquestionably the most finished artist in poetic form in the Victorian poetry; whether in the mystical treatment of a commingled religious-love theme, like *The Blessed Damozel,* in lyrical imitation of folk ballads like *Sister Helen,* or in the sequence of love sonnets, *The House of Life,* always he is the perfect artist, with form indissolubly wedded to theme and subject. But neither he nor his associates cared whether Manchester quadrupled its population or starved its workmen. Their art was personal, without social implications; it was the art of escape, romantic art, the art of beauty and beauty alone.

William Morris was the disciple of Ruskin in his love of beauty and art. He too loved the Middle Ages, and, with some additions from classical themes, the large mass of his poetry is medieval, early Teutonic, early

Scandinavian, in subject matter and spirit. It too is romantic, the literature of escape from an unpleasant real world. He phrased it himself as the work of "the idle singer of an empty day." But whether ballad or lay or saga of "old forgotten far off things," it is beautiful, and Morris is the only rival of Chaucer and Scott in telling a tale in verse. But Morris could not rest content in his dream world. He hated ugliness, and, again under the influence of Ruskin, he tried to change the conditions of society so that the conditions of art could be improved. Consequently he became an enthusiastic socialist, working with speech and with pen in what seemed to him the cause of humanity. Not content with this alone, he became the leader in the new art of decoration, a designer, painter, and manufacturer in stained glass, tapestry, cloth, furniture—in all the arts to make the home beautiful. This is not an "idle singer of an empty day." This Morris saw the world bad through social injustice, and he worked for equal opportunity for all, for the application of the principle of human brotherhood in all the relations of men. He saw the world ugly, and if the stodgy, stuffy, depressing homes of Victorian Philistines have in our day taken on any attractiveness, any beauty, it is largely due to Morris the artist.

Swinburne was not properly a Pre-Raphaelite, though he was closely associated with them and has many points of contact with them. Swinburne was really many men in one; he was a man of "isms," though no one of them continued dominant throughout his career. He too, like the Pre-Raphaelites, found the Mid-Victorian world "weary, stale, flat, and unprofitable," and he tried many avenues of escape. Even in his earliest period we see half a dozen tendencies. Neo-paganism was perhaps the "ism," the line of escape from his Victorian environment, for which we should be most thankful. It gave us

*Atalanta in Calydon* as early as 1865 and thereby gave us in many ways the best embodiment of pagan thought, pagan reaction to life, pagan interpretation of life, in modern literature. Swinburne could write Greek, he could think in Greek, and he could feel like a Greek. Marvelous as is his command over rhythms and verse forms throughout his career, he never bettered the choric and dithyrambic songs of *Atalanta*. Swinburne was the most absorbent poet of the Victorian era. Rossetti influenced him as early as 1857. Landor, the Englishman who was a Greek in feeling, was one of his heroes, and so was the French Hugo and the Italian Mazzini. His youthful republicanism flowered magnificently in his second period under the influence of Mazzini in *Songs Before Sunrise*. But he was swept by winds from every quarter—a passing nihilism, medievalism, anti-clericalism, morbidity, sensuousness, æstheticism, decadence, pessimism—he suffered them all, and he expressed them all. Swinburne felt and imagined rather than thought. His poetic art is in general an art of detail, of images, of rhythms, of tone color, of alliteration, of music, but not of clear outline. His purple patches are spread on too thick; we can't see the drawing for the color. Yet music is there, and we are grateful for it.

The æsthetic motive, art for art's sake, is in general supreme for the Pre-Raphaelites, and it is supreme with Pater. The passion for social service, the development of a social conscience, was largely inspired by Carlyle; but Ruskin disseminated the same influence, and it was from Ruskin that the Pre-Raphaelite Morris caught the inspiration to attempt the remaking of the world. It was also from Ruskin, as was pointed out above, that the Pre-Raphaelites took their departure toward the creation of a world of beauty out of the material of the Middle Ages and with the methods of medieval artists. Though he himself could never accept its full tenets, it was Ruskin among Englishmen who gave the impulse to the æsthetic movement of which Pater was a leader. Of course in Ruskin's case art, morals, and social ideals are fused, and that is the essential Victorian attitude. It is significant that it was Swinburne the poet, born only six years before the first volume of Ruskin's *Modern Painters,* and Pater the prose writer, born only four years before *Modern Painters,* who expressed most openly the æsthetic, hedonistic, Epicurean attitude, which resolutely divorces morals from art. Without question it was largely the French doctrine of art for art's sake grafted on Ruskin's worship of art that provided for the independent development of literary æstheticism with Pater as its prophet. Pater's whole gospel of beauty, of enjoying the passing moment, of savoring the unique taste of each bit of art—all this is fully expressed in the *Preface* to the *Renaissance* on pages 457-460 of this volume. To the æsthetic critic, Pater says, "the picture, the landscape, the engaging personality in life or in a book . . . are valuable . . . for the special unique impression of pleasure." For Pater and for the art-for-art's sake æsthetic critic the highest human quality is not some moral quality —they are all ignored in the æsthetic creed—but a delicate sensitiveness to every passing shade of beauty, a sensitiveness that discriminates each momentary impression from every other moment and every other impression. Pater himself had a style exactly adapted in its perfection of finish to the portrayal of each individual moment of pleasure and to the analysis of the unique source of each impression. His exquisite style and his penetrative intuition make him one of the greatest English critics.

The group of pessimists, of the doubters who saw little hope in Victorian England or in life, though individually in some cases more important, can, as a whole, be treated more briefly than those who fled from the age. These men are all poets. Arnold as an essayist is not a pessimist, and Hardy, who chronologically does not belong to the real Victorians, is more markedly pessimistic in his novels than in his poetry. But Arnold the poet and his friend Clough are pessimists as young men because they have lost faith, faith in the possibility of realizing the romantic dreams of the age that preceded them, faith in orthodox Christianity, gone down for them under the onslaughts of science. Clough died while yet relatively a young man, only forty-two, and Arnold had practically deserted poetry and turned to prose by the time he was forty. Their tragedy of doubt, then, is the tragedy of young men. Clough did not survive to regain his grasp on life, but it was Arnold's good fortune to spend the last half of his adult life fighting to remake England in that wonderful army of three, the army of Carlyle, Ruskin, and himself.

But in poetry Arnold and Clough, most intimate of friends from early boyhood, through Oxford, and on to the end of Clough's life—these two, twins in spirit and experience, yet wore their rue with a difference. Arnold's graceful despair was not so much that he had lost faith in orthodox religion and in romantic dreaming but that in losing faith he had lost tranquility and peace and assurance of safety. Clough's sorrow is directly because of his lost faith in God and Christ and the solution of the problems of life by religion. Both men develop a certain stoicism of endurance; yet both continue to search for something they have lost. There is somewhat of humor in Clough, a humor Arnold's poetry always lacked. Clough has a frankness, an outspokenness in the expression of his doubts and of the remnants of his faith that has attracted readers when Arnold's more subtle expression of the same thing has left them cold. But Clough's poetic form is not so good as Arnold's, and his range is not so wide. Arnold's deliberate restraint, his sobriety, his classicism, his studied simplicity, his philosophical reflective approach, his academic air, his elegiac note, his sad twilight world, his lonely grievance in musical minors —all this forever estops Arnold from being a popular poet. His poetry has too little of the milk of common humanity in it ever to have more than a few readers; but it will always have some readers, because his prevailing mood represents so well the experience of a good many cultivated men, disillusioned, disenchanted, in Arnold's own words:

> "Wandering between two worlds, one dead,
>  The other powerless to be born,
>  With nowhere to rest my head,
>  Like these, on earth I wait forlorn."

The pessimism of Fitzgerald's *Rubáiyát,* of Hardy's novels, and of Thomson's *City of Dreadful Night* differs from the pessimism of Arnold and Clough, and no one of the three is like the others. Arnold and Clough despaired because of a loss in a cosmic faith. James Thomson's visions of "dreadful night" came out of personal experience, personal suffering. A man born of the people, experiencing the deprivations of Dickens's early life and of surrender to an awful physical appetite like DeQuincey —in Thomson's case drink not opium—Thomson's pessimism in this one great poem is both personal and unrelieved. It is regretable that other material has crowded out of this volume representation of one of the greatest poems of the century.

Fitzgerald's life afforded the happiest possible contrast to poor Thomson's. Wealthy, a gentleman in upbringing and in associations, happy in his friendships at

Cambridge and after with some of the choicest spirits of the time—Thackeray, the Tennysons, Carlyle, Cowell, the oriental scholar who gave him Omar, and many others, including Lowell and Charles Eliot Norton in America—living the life of a shy, diffident, but happy recluse, a country gentleman and amateur sailor—his life must be counted happy and successful, and the *Rubáiyát* is not the least personal to him, to Edward Fitzgerald. The absolutely unnoticed way in which Fitzgerald's Omar Khayyam crept into the world in 1859 is remarkable when we remember that it saw four editions in twenty years and that it became probably the best known single poem of the nineteenth century. Of the two hundred and fifty copies of the little pamphlet first printed Fitzgerald gave two hundred to Quaritch the bookseller, who sold them when he could at a penny each. But Rossetti and Swinburne paid their pennies in 1860, and the Pre-Raphaelites, charmed by its exotic flavor and color, began to proclaim it to the world. Its success was due partly, of course, to the fact that it harmonized with the spirit of disillusion, of skepticism, of cynicism, of Epicureanism which marked many of the more sensitive Victorian spirits; but it was due also to the fact that Fitzgerald's genius was exactly fitted to the creative rendering—not "translation"—in organization, in verse form, in style, of the spirit of Omar. Men felt that it said in unforgetable phrase what they wanted to say, that the Persian poet seven centuries before spoke their nineteenth century reaction to life. This modernity of the *Rubáiyát* was due to Fitzgerald's unique genius in giving to the world what is essentially an original poem. Fitzgerald was no pessimist, no hedonist; but his creative power enabled him to dramatize Omar in English with an effect fully as great as Browning's dramatizations of Saul and the Rabbi and the Bishop and Caliban.

Hardy comes later. The prevailing point of view of the greater Victorians in contact with the utilitarian theory of the greatest good to the greatest number and with the evolutionary theory of struggle was that the complex process of evolution was making for social progress. They were optimists, hesitant like Tennyson or confident like Browning or fighting like Carlyle and Ruskin and Arnold. But later men, like Hardy and George Gissing, interpret evolution in relation to human beings as the power of a mechanical universe run by mechanical laws with humanity for its victims, crushed as by some blind and pitiless Juggernaut. That is essentially Hardy's view as expressed in the best known of his novels, *Tess of the D'Urbervilles*. Hardy's novels are all close to the soil, all deal with "homely" folk, and many of these suffer from the pitiless pressure of natural law. With Hardy evolutionary science, the reign of law, is wholly hostile to men; he cannot see back of nature a force not ourselves that makes for righteousness. His poetry, often jerky and crude in form but practically always powerful and suggestive, frequently voices the same pessimistic view of humanity and its fate. But in fiction he is a great artist, and everywhere he thinks and thinks with power.

The Victorian authors who accepted their age, who found much wrong with it, but who were willing to work to set the wrongs right were more numerous and to most people much more important than those who tried to escape from the age or who despaired of it. As individuals and as a group they are much more widely known than most of the men already considered; for the average reader a dozen of this last group *are* Victorian literature. If we name Carlyle, Ruskin, and Arnold, the essayists—Dickens, Thackeray, Eliot, and **Meredith**, the novelists—Tennyson, the Brownings, **Morris, and Swin-**

burne, the poets—we have named four times the number
the average man of general education will know in a
personal way from the other groups, where those that are
likely to be known are Macaulay the essayist, Fitzgerald
the poet, and Hardy the novelist.

What is it that has given the bigger group its power
over men? It is not that they are so greatly superior as
stylists, superior in literary power and expression. Isn't
it primarily because of their attitude toward life? They
were clear-sighted. They could see evils, glaring evils,
in Victorian civilization, where Macaulay could not. Yet,
unlike Newman, they could also see great virtues in their
age. Unlike the Pre-Raphaelites, they did not propose
to leave their world if they did not like everything in it,
to shut themselves up in an ivory tower so the crude
noises of the real world could not offend their ears. They
were optimists, not pessimists. They did not say like the
third group: "The world is bad and ugly. It hurts me
horribly, and I don't know what I am going to do about
it!" Nor did they say: "The world is not God's world; it
belongs to a devil of mechanical law. There is no free
will, no choice for men; and all I can do about it is to
clamp my jaws and endure, or look around and pity the
poor fools who are the sport of what is really scientific
determinism, but what seems to humanity an all-powerful
blind chance." The big group is brave. They too were
hurt, like Newman and Clough and Arnold. Their fas-
tidious nerves were jarred, like those of the Pre-
Raphaelites. But they did not run away. If they were
to receive blows, they proposed to return blows. If the
world was sick, they would diagnose its disease and seek
a cure. People like a clear-sighted, manly man, a good
fighter, one able to estimate the enemy's strength and yet
lead the attack, even against odds. It is this quality of
character, this attitude toward life, this power to bring

the ideal into the real world that has conferred upon the great Victorians their dominion over their own and later times.

The great Victorians worked together; they supplemented each other. This is far from saying that they were alike. They would not be interesting to us if each did not have his pronounced individuality. We need only to mention them in pairs to see how they differed— Dickens and Thackeray, Tennyson and Browning, Carlyle and Arnold. But they realized that in addition to the portrayal of their individual moods, reactions, and picture of life, they had a common task. Their common question was what Carlyle called the "Condition-of-England-Question." Men sensitive to the world around them could not escape feeling the force of the tremendous changes brought into English life by the new industrialism, by the age of machinery and mass production. Such men must consider all the implications of the new science. If the rights of men of whatever class to life, liberty, and the pursuit of happiness were to be secured, then the social conscience of all England must be aroused. If men were to attain a satisfying faith, a faith they could live by, after what seemed to be the washing away of all the old faiths under the flood of science, then the natural leaders of England must be seekers after the truth. These were just the tasks the Victorians of the big group set themselves; in different degrees, in different material, and with different methods, they became awakeners of the social conscience, seekers after the truth.

It is not poetry but prose that utters first and most clearly its challenge to a self-satisfied world. The year 1833, it is true, witnessed the young Tennyson's condemnation in "The Palace of Art" of art-for-art's-sake withdrawal from the actual world to a self-created world of beauty. But 1833 is much more significant as the date of the last volume of Lyell's *Principles of Geology,* with conceptions that were to shake to their foundations the world of thought and religion. It was in 1833 that Newman and his associates first protested against the new age. In 1833 the biggest single figure in Victorian literature made his appearance with a book destined to become one of the great ferments of the age—Carlyle began the publication of *Sartor Resartus.* When we see how large they bulk in Victorian literature now, it is strange how long it took Carlyle and Browning and Fitzgerald and Meredith to secure a public. *Sartor* did not disturb the world at all in 1833, except to cause a storm of protest from readers of *Fraser's Magazine* for publishing such "clotted nonsense."

Yet practically everything the great Carlyle, the prophet of his age, wrote throughout a long life was to be found, explicit or implicit, in *Sartor Resartus.* Here we find his transcendentalism, his "world in clothes," clothes that needed patching, as the very center of the book. Here is his preaching of the brotherhood of man, his doctrine of work, of reverence and obedience for the "hero" as the divinely appointed leader and savior of men. Even the year before *Sartor* he declared Boswell was a great biographer because of his hero-worship for Johnson. In his *French Revolution* he asserts that the outworn conventions, the "old clothes," of society, politics, and religion had to be swept away by the "sans culottes," the ragged brothers of lords and princes. *Heroes and Hero Worship* shows these messengers of God at their work in saving men. *Past and Present* analyzes the way in which the leaders of contemporary England were casting "laborers" into the "Bastile," were ignoring the claims of human brotherhood. His *Cromwell* and his *Frederick the Great* are merely examples of "heroes" at work. All Carlyle's work, then, is one integrated message to the world, the thunderous cries of a John the Baptist from the wilderness of the Scottish moors calling upon the world of cities, of rank and wealth and power, to repent before it is too late.

Gradually Carlyle created his audience. His attitude toward the problems of his time has become so much the attitude of generous minded thinking men everywhere now that we fail to recognize how revolutionary his preaching was in 1833. We can almost say that he created the modern social conscience. Yet he had great help from younger men, his friends and disciples. "All visible things are emblems," said Carlyle. What a "decrepit death-sick Era" proclaimed—"that Life was a *Lie*, and the Earth Beelzebub's"—is opposed by the Everlasting, Yea—"The Universe is not dead and demoniacal, a charnel-house with specters; but godlike, and my Father's!" Carlyle, then, makes the great assertion for the Victorian age, the assertion of all transcendentalists, all idealists, the assertion of the primacy of the spirit, "of the Godlike that is in man." But Ruskin asserted it, too; Arnold asserted it; Tennyson, even through doubts, believed it and proclaimed it; it was the secret of Browning's magnificent optimism; Dickens and Thackeray, Eliot and Meredith, illustrated it, either positively or negatively. Materialism is death. "Love not pleasure," said Carlyle; "love God." The universe is spiritual, and woe be to them who deny it.

Carlyle's analysis of English society and its weaknesses was paraphrased by Arnold and expressed in different terms by all the others. Arnold speaks of an upper class materialized, a middle class vulgarized, and a lower class brutalized, and he names them Barbarians, Philistines, and Populace. But these are only other names for Carlyle's Disciples of Dilettantism, Devotees of Mammonism, and Laborers in the Bastile. Carlyle, Ruskin, and Arnold have all lost faith in a parasitical upper class that no longer "works," that fiddles while Rome burns, mere pleasure seekers, "young barbarians at play." The only men of power in Victorian England are those Carlyle calls "Captains of Industry," the Victorian owners and managers of what we now call "Big Business." To them Carlyle appeals as possible founders of a new aristocracy of service. But they are the besotted Philistines of Arnold, the Devotees of Mammonism, impervious to ideas, whose evangelical religion rules beauty out of life but permits otherwise the grossest of materialism. Their real worship is addressed only to the Goddess of Getting On. Their laborers are not their brothers, sons of a common Father, but a mere commodity to be bought at the cheapest price and, like any other broken machine, flung on the dump heap at last. The accumulation of wealth through unrestricted competition, "freedom of contract" —in labor, the tenets of Utilitarian political economy, the "Dismal Science," the "Profit and Loss Philosophy," as Carlyle called it—this was the real faith of the English Philistine, the real religion by which he lived. It was to this class, the real rulers of England, that the practical idealists of the Victorian era had to address themselves if they wanted vital reform.

Carlyle was fourteen years older than Tennyson, seventeen years older than Dickens and Browning, twenty-four years older than Ruskin, and twenty-seven years older than Arnold. He had made his diagnosis of England and had prescribed his cures before Ruskin and Arnold began any serious analysis of the condition of England. His *Sartor* appeared in 1833, *The French Revolution* in 1837, *Chartism* in 1839, *Heroes and Hero Worship* in 1841, and *Past and Present* in 1843. Ruskin and Arnold began their work as social reformers after 1860. Carlyle's own prescriptions are much vaguer than his analysis of social disease. A sentence can give them all—(1) universal brotherhood in place of the old caste prejudices; (2) universal labor—"Produce, produce"—and all honor to the workers; (3) reverence—men are brothers but not equal; (4) therefore hero-worship—society can be restored to health only by the reverent discipleship on the part of the great mass of men for the best men, for the hero, the one delegated by the Divine Spirit of the universe to lead. Be sincere, work in silence, find your superior and obey him—that is the gospel according to Carlyle. He was contemptuous of all other solutions, especially if they involved definite machinery like universal suffrage, for he did not believe in democracy—only another "Morrison's pill" prescribed by quacks. Carlyle was more destructive than constructive. Yet his terrific earnestness, his thunderous style, his lightning flashes of imagery shocked men into a belief that the universe is spiritual, not merely material, that beneath the "clothes," the conventions of society, lie the real men bound together into an indissoluble brotherhood under the common fatherhood of God. Carlyle aroused a new social conscience, but he did not invent a new social ethics.

Carlyle, unlike his successors, originated among the Populace, the Laborers in the Bastile. He was a Scotch peasant who had suffered all the hardships and deprivations of the poor. Ruskin was the son of a Captain of Industry, of the wealthy middle class. Arnold was a Barbarian, born a gentleman with generations of culture back of him. Though the three united in a common aim, their methods were necessarily different. Carlyle came to his work out of personal suffering, personal experience; but not so Ruskin and Arnold. Their own pleasant lives did not drive them into social reform; all the more credit must be given them, then, for their consecration to the common task.

More than any man in the nineteenth century Ruskin served his generation as the revealer of beauty, beauty in nature, beauty in art. Though the Pharisees of art hooted at him, the public heard him gladly. Brought up in a narrow evangelical atmosphere, surrounded with a stuffy Philistine luxury, he was the man who did most, either directly or through his influence on men like Morris, to set Englishmen free from such restraints, to open their minds and hearts and souls to the love of beauty and the hatred of ugliness. To Ruskin beauty in art and beauty in nature are sacred things, a "consecrated revelation of God . . . to be received with reverent delight."

But however great his power as the appreciator of art and the revealer of nature, he could not rest in that as his only function in the life of England. Few writers had ever attained such popularity as Ruskin at the age of twenty-four with the publication of the first volume of *Modern Painters,* and he kept that popularity for twenty years, rivaling Tennyson and Dickens. But when his insight and his conscience bade him change his work in 1860, when the art critic and nature painter became the social reformer, he lost his public, he became the reviled and the despised, not only among the Manchester "Profit-and-Loss" economists but also in the whole world of British Philistia. But like Luther, he could do no other. He was led to reform because only through reform could England achieve the necessary conditions for pure art; yet it was his awakened sympathies that made him say, "I simply cannot paint nor read nor look at minerals nor do anything else that I like . . . because of the misery I know of." He too believed in work for all. "Life without industry is guilt," he said; but "industry without art is brutality." He believed that true art could flourish only in a world filled with beauty and contentment, with honor and justice, and he began to preach a new social, a new spiritual crusade.

Unlike Carlyle and Ruskin, Arnold did not work in the spirit of a crusader. The methods, the styles of the three men revealed their temperaments—Carlyle's style filled with turgid thunder crashes and scorching lightning flashes, Ruskin's a style of marvelous rhythms and gorgeous magical colors alternating with a Biblical simplicity, Arnold's restrained, suave, insinuating, ironical. If Carlyle dealt berserker hammer blows, Arnold pierced the Philistine carcase with a pointed rapier. Carlyle and Ruskin made their appeals through the imagination and the emotions; Arnold made his appeals through the intellect and to the intellect. He believed that right thinking would result in right doing and right living. Carlyle says that life should be work and obedience. Ruskin accepted these for the result he wanted, the enjoyment, the inspiration of beauty in nature, in art, in life. Arnold's ideal for the good life, individual or collective, is that it shall have sweetness and light, and his all-embracing method to attain this is a process. In his own words, "it is *a study of perfection*"; and its objectives are twofold—"To render an intelligent being yet more intelligent!" and "To make reason and the will of God prevail!" It is a compound, then, in its motive forces of the scientific passion for knowing with the moral and social passion for doing good. Its result is "a harmonious expansion of *all* the powers which make the beauty and worth of human nature." Arnold finds modern civilization "mechanical and external," and its besetting sin is faith in what he calls "machinery"—Arnold's name for Carlyle's "clothes." Freedom, population, wealth, even religious organizations are made ends in themselves, while culture pronounces them to be mere machinery, means to an end, the end of a perfectly balanced spiritual condition. To attain a harmonious perfection of all the powers of man the narrow Hebraism of the English race, valuable as it is, must be balanced by the classic Hellenism, which gives beauty and sweetness to life. Arnold, then, would join the Hebraism of Carlyle—do good—to the Hellenism of Ruskin—see beauty, and this can be brought about only by "light," by the free play of ideas, by right education.

The quarrel of Huxley and Arnold as to what knowledge is more worth, science or literature, is after all a matter for compromise. Both are valuable. In fact these redoubtable opponents fully respect each other and each other's cause. Arnold wants to see to it that the new power of science does not crowd out of education the invaluable contribution of literature and art to the sweetness of life. Huxley insists that the entrenched position in education of literature and the classics shall not prohibit the full recognition of the importance of science to the welfare and happiness of mankind. They both won the debate. Modern science was fortunate to have for its popular interpreter a man of Huxley's personal gifts, his intelligence, his tact, his imagination, his clear, supple, engaging style.

Thackeray and Stevenson as essayists may well be omitted from this discussion. Both are illustrated here by a type of literary criticism rather than by the serious comment on life of the ethical essay. Thackeray's essay is of the personal whimsical kind, with the enjoyment of books as its theme, while Stevenson shows what makes books enjoyable. Yet both men could think seriously about life, as Thackeray's novels of Mid-Victorian life show and as Stevenson's more serious essays and his psychological novels make clear.

What is the function of the greater novelists in the age of Victoria? It was the function of the Victorian novelists to picture the society the essayists discussed. Dickens and Thackeray divided between them the classes of society as Arnold and Carlyle had named them. Thackeray took for his field what Arnold called the Barbarians and Carlyle the Disciples of Dilettantism. People "in Society," the gentry, furnish the *dramatis personæ* of Thackeray. It was the business and the delight of Dickens to give the world unforgetable pictures of the middle classes and the lower classes of London, of the Philistines, the Devotees of Mammonism on the one side, and the Populace, the Laborers in the Bastile, on the other. The world of Dickens exists to make the things, to buy and sell the things, the world of Thackeray needs. Both worlds are permeated, are shot through and through, with money or the lack of it. Thackeray's Barbarians exist to spend money, Dickens's Philistines to make money, and his Populace to earn it by cringing service to those above, to steal it, or to starve for want of it. The Victorians of Dickens and Thackeray, then, are wholly mercenary, wholly materialistic. Both novelists furnish us inexhaustible galleries of portraits; a novel by either is likely to carry a list of from sixty to seventy-five distinct people. Yet always in Thackeray we see a society corrupted by hypocrisy and immorality, without ideals, a nobility with nothing left of the old *noblesse oblige.* More soul-searching pictures of this group appeared later in the psychological novels of Meredith. Though Dickens's people may have any or all of the elementary human virtues, yet they are all essentially coarse and vulgar, with no knowledge of the finer things of life. Dickens and Thackeray, however, did not give the whole of English life. For a picture of the poor in the country we must go to Kingsley and especially to the earlier novels of George Eliot; for country and town "society," a society dominated by the clergy, Trollope is the artist; but for the great mass of the Laborers in the Bastile and for the Captains of Industry we must turn to Mrs. Gaskell's *Mary Barton* and Reade's *Put Yourself in His Place*. Of all the Victorian novelists those who worked directly to induce a new sympathy with the sufferers from evil social conditions were Kingsley, Mrs. Gaskell, George Eliot, and Dickens. Dickens's social novels, for example, were deliberate propaganda for social betterment; inspired by Carlyle and by his own early struggles, he would picture the life and death of the downtrodden and then passionately fling the picture directly at majesties, lords and gentlemen, right reverends and wrong reverends, with a "Dead . . . And dying thus around us every day!"

The Victorian poets who did not flee and who did not despair were faithful reflectors of their age. Like the age, they had their beginnings in romanticism, and a large element in their work continued to be an interest in the past. They treated the past, however, in a spirit and with a method new in literature. For the first time in the development of our literature the modern historical scientific point of view prevails and the poets strive to reproduce the actual truth of the past. The Elizabethans might be satisfied when Hamlet and Mark Antony strutted the stage of the Globe in Sir Walter Raleigh's cast off clothes; but not the Victorians. Their Neo-Paganism, the classic revival of the nineteenth century, was almost wholly Greek, not Latin as in the earlier Renaissance, as witness Tennyson's "Œnone," "Ulysses," and the "Lotos-Eaters," Swinburne's "Atalanta," Arnold's "Empedocles," and Morris's *Earthly Paradise*. The medieval revival showed itself most fully in Tennyson, as illustrated in the "Idylls of the King" and in a number of poems in this volume; but it bulked large also with the Pre-Raphaelites and especially with

**Morris.** The interpretation of the Renaissance is preeminently the work of Browning, magnificently illustrated here in "The Bishop Orders His Tomb" and a halfdozen other poems. But the Victorians, with the exception of the Pre-Raphaelites, could not remain in any past, however beautiful. Tennyson, the chief portrayer of the Middle Ages, and Browning, the revealer of the Renaissance, were the most distinctive critics of medieval and Renaissance ideals. The Victorians were children of their own time, and, troubled though it might be, they preferred to live in it.

Yes, the Victorian poets, like the essayists and the novelists, lived in their own time, and their chief responses, whether of attraction or repulsion, were to the two fundamental motivating forces of the century—science and social redress. They felt all the implications of the new science, and practically all of them accepted science and accepted the tasks of revision in thought and life which science compelled. The two greatest poets of the era reflect the two general attitudes. Browning accepted science, accepted evolution, and was never troubled; but in his superb optimism, his confident and glad welcome to science, he stands almost alone among the poets. The only parallel to him is Meredith, who is just as confident, just as superb in his faith in a universe controlled by law, but rightly controlled, controlled for the benefit of all its creatures, of whom man is not the least. As far back as 1835 Browning wrote in Act V of *Paracelsus*:

> "The centre-fire heaves underneath the earth,
> And the earth changes like a human face.
> . . . Thus God dwells in all,
> From life's minute beginnings, up at last
> To man. . . ."

From that faith Browning never departed. "All's right with the world," if "God's in his heaven" and "dwells in all." The idea of Progress received with the Victorians its first solid foundations because founded solidly on science. The idea of a fundamental Unity, a fundamental Force, at the center of things, tying all things together into one complex but coherent progressive whole, the genetic conception of man and nature—that too, confirmed by the evidence of science, Browning accepted absolutely. The sense and value of fact so prominent in all Browning's work, his realism, is again recognition of his acceptance of the universe as he found it.

But Tennyson is more nearly the representative of the average thinking Victorian in contact with the world of science. He represents more the quest for truth as against Browning's never-failing certainty. Science shook the world of Tennyson, as it shook the whole world of Victoria. He represents his age when he confronts doubt, doubt which may become, as in Arnold and Clough, despair. The poets have a way of anticipating movements of thought that come later; they are seers and prophets. Tennyson was working from 1833 for seventeen years on "In Memoriam," and he published it in 1850. It made him Laureate, gained him recognition as the leading poet of his age. It was nine years before the publication of the *Origin of Species,* and yet "In Memoriam" is the supreme recognition in the Victorian Age of the problems, the doubts raised by science for all thinking Victorians. When the poet's soul is confronted with the shock of pain, how can he believe that an indifferent universe, "Nature red in tooth and claw," can offer him any hope? That is the supreme intellectual problem of "In Memoriam," of Tennyson, and of the Victorian Age. Tennyson fought through the positions of the two minor schools of poetry. He was

All the group are as sensitive to the Condition-of-England-Question as the essayists and the novelists. In their different ways, the ways of poetry, they do their full share in arousing the social conscience of Philistines and Barbarians to the woes of their brothers, the Populace. Mrs. Browning's "Cry of the Children" was an evangel as powerful as any Dickens ever preached on behalf of childhood. Morris and Swinburne visioned the coming of social righteousness. In spite of his fundamental aristocracy of temperament, the Tennyson of 1842 sings of "men, my brothers, men the workers," and in "Locksley Hall Sixty Years After" asks

"Is it well that while we range with Science, glorying
     in the Time,
City children soak and blacken soul and sense in city
     slime?

There among the glooming alleys Progress halts on pal-
     sied feet,
Crime and hunger cast our maidens by the thousand on
     the street.

There the master scrimps his haggard semptress of her
     daily bread,
There a single sordid attic holds the living and the
     dead.

There the smouldering fire of fever creeps across the
     rotted floor,
And the crowded couch of incest in the warrens of the
     poor."

Browning, perhaps, is too much the individualist to feel the social demands of his time as much as the others do, or at least to discuss them as much. He really believes "All's right with the world," or is going to be right, because it is God's world. But no one in poetry gives us the conception of the worth and value of the individual so fully as Browning in his dramatic monologues and dramas, and it is upon a fundamental faith in the value and significance of the individual human being that the demands for social justice are based, that democracy has grown, democracy in the state, and democracy in social and industrial life.

## V. WHAT THE AGE HAS BEQUEATHED US

This is not the place to summarize the history of the nineteenth century or even of that forty years in the middle of the century which constitutes the Victorian Age proper. The historical environment of Victorian literature has been glanced at in the first sections of this introduction. The chief purpose of this introduction as a whole is to show Victorian literature in relation to Victorian life. It was said above that more than in any other age in our literature it was the peculiar glory of Victorian literature that it participated consciously and deliberately in the crucial thought and feeling and action of its age. How important that participation was, how much their own age owes to the Victorian writers, and how much we owe to them cannot be analyzed and summarized in a paragraph.

In the first place it should be remembered that Victorian literature, in its beginnings at least, is now a century in the past. It pictures an age and a spirit that ought to be as far removed from us in time as the age of Queen Anne, of Pope and Addison and Defoe, was from the early Victorians. We ought to feel that *Sartor Resartus* and *Oliver Twist* are far distant from us, that for us they are "historical"; but they do not so seem. On the contrary, the things Carlyle and Dickens, Ruskin and Tennyson talked about are the things we still talk about, or else we enjoy a world so changed for the better that we fail to realize how much these Victorians did to bring our new world into existence. Today as this is written five of the greatest powers in the world are gathered around the council table in London to devise means to still the throbbing of the war drums. The man who presides at that council table is the representative of what a century ago was that discrowned humanity, Arnold's Populace, Carlyle's Laborers in the Bastile. Today there is a Parliament of Man, a Federation of the World, which sits at Geneva, a World Court which sits at The Hague. A Labor premier in charge of a world conference, a League of Nations—either would have been inconceivable to the great mass of Englishmen a century ago. That such progress has become possible in a century is in no mean degree due to those great practical idealists, the Victorian essayists and novelists and poets. The poets kept the faith and kept the vision before the eyes of the people; forty-three years after the first "Locksley Hall" Tennyson again saw

"All the millions one at length with all the visions of
        my youth—

.        .        .        .        .

Earth at last a warless world, a single race, a single
        tongue—

.        .        .        .        .

Robed in universal harvest up to either pole she smiles,
Universal ocean softly washing all her warless Isles."

Internal reform that has affected us here in America

directly by precept and by example, social betterment in all its aspects—this also we of 1930 owe largely to the awakening of the social conscience by the Victorian writers. They were prophets whose cry of "Repent" has been heeded; it is they who taught us that we are our brothers' keepers.

One element of the revolt of the "Naughty Nineties" and of the Twentieth Century against the Mid-Victorians seems now to be losing its force. The revolters resented the covering over of the uglier details in life, they sneered at the "prunes and prisms" attitude of the Victorians, at a decency that was too decent. But aren't we of the Twentieth Century beginning to get a bit tired of reveling in the naturalistic orgies of sex novels and the poetry that goes along with them? Many of us now sympathize with Tennyson's sarcasm when he advised authors to

"Rip your brothers' vices open, strip your own foul passions bare;
Down with Reticence, down with Reverence—forward —naked—let them stare."

One final word and this introduction has completed its task. Whatever they have done for the general progress of mankind, the Victorians have contributed fully as much to the artistic enjoyment of the English speaking race. No man since Tennyson can compare with him as a master of that harp of many strings, his poetic art. No one since has given us the equal of the unforgetable portraits painted by Carlyle and Browning, by Dickens and Thackeray. No one has plumbed deeper into the souls of men than George Eliot and Meredith and Hardy. No one now can make us feel the qualities of great art and great literature as Ruskin and Arnold and Pater did, can make us see beauty so intensely. The Victorian writers were good men, men of vision, men of power; but they were also great artists.

GEORGE MOREY MILLER.

# ALFRED TENNYSON (1809-1892)

## CLARIBEL

### A MELODY

### I

Where Claribel low-lieth
  The breezes pause and die,
    Letting the rose-leaves fall:
But the solemn oak-tree sigheth,
    Thick-leaved, ambrosial,
  With an ancient melody
  Of an inward agony,
Where Claribel low-lieth.

### II

At eve the beetle boometh
  Athwart the thicket lone:
At noon the wild bee hummeth
  About the moss'd headstone;
At midnight the moon cometh,
  And looketh down alone.
Her song the lintwhite swelleth,
The clear-voiced mavis dwelleth,
  The callow throstle lispeth,
The slumbrous wave outwelleth,
  The babbling runnel crispeth,

The hollow grot replieth
Where Claribel low-lieth.

**1830**

## THE POET

THE poet in a golden clime was born,
  With golden stars above;
Dower'd with the hate of hate, the scorn of **scorn,**
  The love of love.

He saw thro' life and death, thro' good and ill,
  He saw thro' his own soul.
The marvel of the everlasting will,
  An open scroll,

Before him lay: with echoing feet he threaded
  The secretest walks of fame:
The viewless arrows of his thoughts were headed
  And wing'd with flame,

Like Indian reeds blown from his silver tongue,
  And of so fierce a flight,
From Calpe unto Caucasus they sung,
  Filling with light

And vagrant melodies the winds which bore
  Them earthward till they lit;
Then, like the arrow-seeds of the field flower,
  The fruitful wit

Cleaving, took root, and springing forth anew
  Where'er they fell, behold,
Like to the mother plant in semblance, grew
  A flower all gold,

And bravely furnish'd all abroad to fling
  Thy winged shafts of truth,
To throng with stately blooms the breathing spring
  Of Hope and Youth.

So many minds did gird their orbs with beams,
  Tho' one did fling the fire.
Heaven flow'd upon the soul in many dreams
  Of high desire.

Thus truth was multiplied on truth, the world
  Like one great garden show'd,
And thro' the wreaths of floating dark upcurl'd,
  Rare sunrise flow'd.

And Freedom rear'd in that august sunrise
  Her beautiful bold brow,
When rites and forms before his burning eyes
  Melted like snow.

There was no blood upon her maiden robes
  Sunn'd by those orient skies;
But round about the circles of the globes
  Of her keen eyes

And in her raiment's hem was traced in flame
  WISDOM, a name to shake
All evil dreams of power—a sacred name.
  And when she spake,

Her words did gather thunder as they ran,
  And as the lightning to the thunder
Which follows it, riving the spirit of man,
  Making earth wonder,

So was their meaning to her words.  No sword
  Of wrath her right arm whirl'd,
But one **poor** poet's scroll, and with *his* word
  She shook the world.

1830

## ŒNONE

THERE lies a vale in Ida, lovelier
Than all the valleys of Ionian hills.
The swimming vapour slopes athwart the glen,
Puts forth an arm, and creeps from pine to pine,
And loiters, slowly drawn.  On either hand
The lawns and meadow-ledges midway down
Hang rich in flowers, and far below them roars
The long brook falling thro' the clov'n ravine
In cataract after cataract to the sea.
Behind the valley topmost Gargarus
Stands up and takes the morning: but in front
The gorges, opening wide apart, reveal
Troas and Ilion's column'd citadel,
The crown of Troas.

            Hither came at noon
Mournful Œnone, wandering forlorn
Of Paris, once her playmate on the hills.
Her cheek had lost the rose, and round her neck
Floated her hair or seem'd to float in rest.
She, leaning on a fragment twined with vine,
Sang to the stillness, till the mountain-shade
Sloped downward to her seat from the upper cliff.

"O mother Ida, many-fountain'd Ida,
Dear mother Ida, hearken ere I die.
For now the noonday quiet holds the hill:

The grasshopper is silent in the grass:
The lizard, with his shadow on the stone,
Rests like a shadow, and the winds are dead.
The purple flower droops: the golden bee
Is lily-cradled: I alone awake.
My eyes are full of tears, my heart of love,
My heart is breaking, and my eyes are dim,
And I am all aweary of my life.

"O mother Ida, many-fountain'd Ida,
Dear mother Ida, hearken ere I die.
Hear me, O Earth, hear me, O Hills, O Caves
That house the cold crown'd snake! O mountain brooks,
I am the daughter of a River-God,
Hear me, for I will speak, and build up all
My sorrow with my song, as yonder walls
Rose slowly to a music slowly breathed,
A cloud that gather'd shape: for it may be
That, while I speak of it, a little while
My heart may wander from its deeper woe.

"O mother Ida, many-fountain'd Ida,
Dear mother Ida, hearken ere I die.
I waited underneath the dawning hills,
Aloft the mountain lawn was dewy-dark,
And dewy-dark aloft the mountain pine:
Beautiful Paris, evil-hearted Paris,
Leading a jet-black goat white-horn'd, white-hooved,
Came up from reedy Simois all alone.

"O mother Ida, hearken ere I die.
Far-off the torrent call'd me from the cleft:
Far up the solitary morning smote
The streaks of virgin snow. With down-dropt eyes
I sat alone: white-breasted like a star

Fronting the dawn he moved; a leopard skin
Droop'd from his shoulder, but his sunny hair
Cluster'd about his temples like a God's:
And his cheek brighten'd as the foam-bow brightens
When the wind blows the foam, and all my heart
Went forth to embrace him coming ere he came.

"Dear mother Ida, hearken ere I die.
He smiled, and opening out his milk-white palm
Disclosed a fruit of pure Hesperian gold,
That smelt ambrosially, and while I look'd
And listen'd, the full-flowing river of speech
Came down upon my heart.
                         "'My own Œnone,
Beautiful-brow'd Œnone, my own soul,
Behold this fruit, whose gleaming rind ingrav'n
"For the most fair," would seem to award it thine,
As lovelier than whatever Oread haunt
The knolls of Ida, loveliest in all grace
Of movement, and the charm of married brows.'

"Dear mother Ida, hearken ere I die.
He prest the blossom of his lips to mine,
And added 'This was cast upon the board,
When all the full-faced presence of the Gods
Ranged in the halls of Peleus; whereupon
Rose feud, with question unto whom 'twere due:
But light-foot Iris brought it yester-eve,
Delivering, that to me, by common voice
Elected umpire, Herè comes to-day,
Pallas and Aphroditè, claiming each
This meed of fairest. Thou, within the cave
Behind yon whispering tuft of oldest pine,
Mayst well behold them unbeheld, unheard
Hear all, and see thy Paris judge of Gods.'

"Dear mother Ida, hearken ere I die.
It was the deep midnoon: one silvery cloud
Had lost his way between the piney sides
Of this long glen.  Then to the bower they came,
Naked they came to that smooth-swarded bower,
And at their feet the crocus brake like fire,
Violet, amaracus, and asphodel,
Lotos and lilies: and a wind arose,
And overhead the wandering ivy and vine,
This way and that, in many a wild festoon
Ran riot, garlanding the gnarled boughs
With bunch and berry and flower thro' and thro'.

"O mother Ida, hearken ere I die.
On the tree-tops a crested peacock lit,
And o'er him flow'd a golden cloud, and lean'd
Upon him, slowly dropping fragrant dew.
Then first I heard the voice of her, to whom
Coming thro' Heaven, like a light that grows
Larger and clearer, with one mind the Gods
Rise up for reverence. She to Paris made
Proffer of royal power, ample rule
Unquestion'd, overflowing revenue
Wherewith to embellish state, 'from many a vale
And river-sunder'd champaign clothed with corn,
Or labour'd mine undrainable of ore.
Honour,' she said, 'and homage, tax and toll,
From many an inland town and haven large,
Mast-throng'd beneath her shadowing citadel
In glassy bays among her tallest towers.'

"O mother Ida, hearken ere I die.
Still she spake on and still she spake of power,
Which in all action is the end of all;
Power fitted to the season: wisdom-bred

And throned of wisdom—from all neighbour crowns
Alliance and Allegiance, till thy hand
Fail from the sceptre-staff. Such boon from me,
From me, Heaven's Queen, Paris, to thee king-born,
A shepherd all thy life but yet king-born,
Should come most welcome, seeing men in power
Only, are likest gods, who have attain'd
Rest in a happy place and quiet seats
Above the thunder, with undying bliss
In knowledge of their own supremacy.'

"Dear mother Ida, hearken ere I die.
She ceased, and Paris held the costly fruit
Out at arm's-length, so much the thought of power
Flatter'd his spirit; but Pallas where she stood
Somewhat apart, her clear and bared limbs
O'erthwarted with the brazen-headed spear
Upon her pearly shoulder leaning cold,
The while, above, her full and earnest eye
Over her snow-cold breast and angry cheek
Kept watch, waiting decision, made reply.

" 'Self-reverence, self-knowledge, self-control,
These three alone lead life to sovereign power.
Yet not for power (power of herself
Would come uncall'd for) but to live by law,
Acting the law we live by without fear;
And, because right is right, to follow right
Were wisdom in the scorn of consequence.'

"Dear mother Ida, hearken ere I die.
Again she said: 'I woo thee not with gifts.
Sequel of guerdon could not alter me
To fairer. Judge thou me by what I am,

So shalt thou find me fairest.
                    Yet, indeed,
If gazing on divinity disrobed
Thy mortal eyes are frail to judge of fair,
Unbiass'd by self-profit, oh! rest thee sure
That I shall love thee well and cleave to thee,
So that my vigour, wedded to thy blood,
Shall strike within thy pulses, like a God's,
To push thee forward thro' a life of shocks,
Dangers, and deeds, until endurance grow
Sinew'd with action, and the full-grown will,
Circled thro' all experiences, pure law,
Commeasure perfect freedom.'
                    "Here she ceas'd,
And Paris ponder'd, and I cried, 'O Paris,
Give it to Pallas!' but he heard me not,
Or hearing would not hear me, woe is me!

"O mother Ida, many-fountain'd Ida,
Dear mother Ida, hearken ere I die.
Idalian Aphroditè beautiful,
Fresh as the foam, new-bathed in Paphian wells,
With rosy slender fingers backward drew
From her warm brows and bosom her deep hair
Ambrosial, golden round her lucid throat
And shoulder from the violets her light foot
Shone rosy-white, and o'er her rounded form
Between the shadows of the vine-bunches
Floated the glowing sunlights, as she moved.

"Dear mother Ida, hearken ere I die.
She with a subtle smile in her mild eyes,
The herald of her triumph, drawing nigh
Half-whisper'd in his ear, 'I promise thee
The fairest and most loving wife in Greece,'

She spoke and laugh'd: I shut my sight for fear:
But when I look'd, Paris had raised his arm,
And I beheld great Herè's angry eyes,
As she withdrew into the golden cloud,
And I was left alone within the bower;
And from that time to this I am alone,
And I shall be alone until I die.

"Yet, mother Ida, hearken ere I die.
Fairest—why fairest wife? am I not fair?
My love hath told me so a thousand times.
Methinks I must be fair, for yesterday,
When I past by, a wild and wanton pard,
Eyed like the evening star, with playful tail
Crouch'd fawning in the weed. Most loving is she?
Ah me, my mountain shepherd, that my arms
Were wound about thee, and my hot lips prest
Close, close to thine in that quick-falling dew
Of fruitful kisses, thick as Autumn rains
Flash in the pools of whirling Simois.

"O mother, hear me yet before I die.
They came, they cut away my tallest pines,
My tall dark pines, that plumed the craggy ledge
High over the blue gorge, and all between
The snowy peak and snow-white cataract
Foster'd the callow eaglet—from beneath
Whose thick mysterious boughs in the dark morn
The panther's roar came muffled, while I sat
Low in the valley. Never, never more
Shall lone Œnone see the morning mist
Sweep thro' them; never see them overlaid
With narrow moon-lit slips of silver cloud,
Between the loud stream and the trembling stars.

"O mother, hear me yet before I die.
I wish that somewhere in the ruin'd folds,
Among the fragments tumbled from the glens,
Or the dry thickets, I could meet with her
The Abominable, that uninvited came
Into the fair Peleïan banquet-hall,
And cast the golden fruit upon the board,
And bred this change; that I might speak my mind,
And tell her to her face how much I hate
Her presence, hated both of Gods and men.

"O mother, hear me yet before I die.
Hath he not sworn his love a thousand times,
In this green valley, under this green hill,
Ev'n on this hand, and sitting on this stone?
Seal'd it with kisses? water'd it with tears?
O happy tears, and how unlike to these!
O happy Heaven, how canst thou see my face?
O happy earth, how canst thou bear my weight?
O death, death, death, thou ever-floating cloud,
There are enough unhappy on this earth,
Pass by the happy souls, that love to live:
I pray thee, pass before my light of life,
And shadow all my soul that I may die.
Thou weighest heavy on the heart within,
Weigh heavy on my eyelids: let me die.

"O mother, hear me yet before I die.
I will not die alone, for fiery thoughts
Do shape themselves within me, more and more,
Whereof I catch the issue, as I hear
Dead sounds at night come from the inmost hills,
Like footsteps upon wool. I dimly see
My far-off doubtful purpose, as a mother
Conjectures of the features of her child

Ere it is born: her child!—a shudder comes
Across me: never child be born of me,
Unblest, to vex me with his father's eyes!

"O mother, hear me yet before I die.
Hear me, O earth. I will not die alone,
Lest their shrill happy laughter come to me
Walking the cold and starless road of Death
Uncomforted, leaving my ancient love
With the Greek woman. I will rise and go
Down into Troy, and ere the stars come forth
Talk with the wild Cassandra, for she says
A fire dances before her, and a sound
Rings ever in her ears of armed men.
What this may be I know not, but I know
That, whereso'er I am by night and day,
All earth and air seem only burning fire."

1832

# THE LADY OF SHALOTT

### PART I

On either side the river lie
Long fields of barley and of rye,
That clothe the wold and meet the sky;
And thro' the field the road runs by
        To many-tower'd Camelot;
And up and down the people go,
Gazing where the lilies blow
Round an island there below,
        The island of Shalott.

Willows whiten, aspens quiver,
Little breezes dusk and shiver

Thro' the wave that runs forever
By the island in the river
    Flowing down to Camelot.
Four gray walls, and four gray **towers,**
Overlook a space of flowers,
And the silent isle imbowers
    The Lady of Shalott.

By the margin, willow-veil'd,
Slide the heavy barges trail'd
By slow horses; and unhail'd
The shallop flitteth silken-sail'd
    Skimming down to Camelot:
But who hath seen her wave her hand?
Or at the casement seen her stand?
Or is she known in all the land,
    The Lady of Shalott?

Only reapers, reaping early
In among the bearded barley,
Hear a song that echoes cheerly
From the river winding clearly,
    Down to tower'd Camelot:
And by the moon the reaper weary,
Piling sheaves in uplands airy,
Listening, whispers, " 'Tis the fairy
    Lady of Shalott."

### PART II

THERE she weaves by night and day
A magic web with colours gay.
She has heard a whisper say,
A curse is on her if she stay
    To look down to Camelot.

She knows not what the curse may be,
And so she weaveth steadily,
And little other care hath she,
    The Lady of Shalott.

And moving thro' a mirror clear
That hangs before her all the year,
Shadows of the world appear.
There she sees the highway near
    Winding down to Camelot:
There the river eddy whirls,
And there the surly village-churls,
And the red cloaks of market girls,
    Pass onward from Shalott.

Sometimes a troop of damsels glad,
An abbot on an ambling pad,
Sometimes a curly shepherd-lad,
Or long-hair'd page in crimson clad,
    Goes by to tower'd Camelot;
And sometimes thro' the mirror blue
The knights come riding two and two:
She hath no loyal knight and true,
    The Lady of Shalott.

But in her web she still delights
To weave the mirror's magic sights,
For often thro' the silent nights
A funeral, with plumes and lights
    And music, went to Camelot:
Or when the moon was overhead,
Came two young lovers lately wed;
"I am half sick of shadows," said
    The Lady of Shalott.

## PART III

A BOW-SHOT from her bower-eaves,
He rode between the barley-sheaves,
The sun came dazzling thro' the leaves,
And flamed upon the brazen greaves
   Of bold Sir Lancelot.
A red-cross knight forever kneel'd
To a lady in his shield,
That sparkled on the yellow field,
   Beside remote Shalott.

The gemmy bridle glitter'd free,
Like to some branch of stars we see
Hung in the golden Galaxy.
The bridle bells rang merrily
   As he rode down to Camelot:
And from his blazon'd baldric slung
A mighty silver bugle hung,
And as he rode his armour rung,
   Beside remote Shalott.

All in the blue unclouded weather
Thick-jewell'd shone the saddle-leather,
The helmet and the helmet-feather
Burn'd like one burning flame together,
   As he rode down to Camelot.
As often thro' the purple night,
Below the starry clusters bright,
Some bearded meteor, trailing light,
   Moves over still Shalott.

His broad clear brow in sunlight glow'd;
On burnish'd hooves his war-horse trode;

From underneath his helmet flow'd
His coal-black curls as on he rode,
     As he rode down to Camelot.
From the bank and from the river
He flash'd into the crystal mirror,
"Tirra lirra," by the river
     Sang Sir Lancelot.

She left the web, she left the loom,
She made three paces thro' the room,
She saw the water-lily bloom,
She saw the helmet and the plume,
     She look'd down to Camelot.
Out flew the web and floated wide;
The mirror crack'd from side to side;
"The curse is come upon me," cried
     The Lady of Shalott.

### PART IV

IN THE stormy east-wind straining,
The pale yellow woods were waning,
The broad stream in his banks complaining,
Heavily the low sky raining
     Over tower'd Camelot;
Down she came and found a boat
Beneath a willow left afloat,
And round about the prow she wrote
     *The Lady of Shalott.*

And down the river's dim expanse
Like some bold seër in a trance,
Seeing all his own mischance—
With a glassy countenance
     Did she look to Camelot.

And at the closing of the day
She loosed the chain, and down she lay;
The broad stream bore her far away,
    The Lady of Shalott.

Lying, robed in snowy white,
That loosely flew to left and right—
The leaves upon her falling light—
Thro' the noises of the night
    She floated down to Camelot:
And as the boat-head wound along
The willowy hills and fields among,
They heard her singing her last song,
    The Lady of Shalott.

Heard a carol, mournful, holy,
Chanted loudly, chanted lowly,
Till her blood was frozen slowly,
And her eyes were darken'd wholly,
    Turn'd to tower'd Camelot.
For ere she reach'd upon the tide
The first house by the water-side,
Singing in her song she died,
    The Lady of Shalott.

Under tower and balcony,
By garden-wall and gallery,
A gleaming shape she floated by,
Dead-pale between the houses high,
    Silent into Camelot.
Out upon the wharfs they came,
Knight and burgher, lord and dame,
And round the prow they read her name,
    *The Lady of Shalott.*

Who is this? and what is here?
And in the lighted palace near
Died the sound of royal cheer;
And they cross'd themselves for fear,
    All the knights at Camelot:
But Lancelot mused a little space;
He said, "She has a lovely face;
God in his mercy lend her grace,
    The Lady of Shalott."

                         1832

## THE LOTOS-EATERS

"Courage!" he said, and pointed toward the land,
"This mounting wave will roll us shoreward soon."
In the afternoon they came unto a land
In which it seemed always afternoon.
All round the coast the languid air did swoon,
Breathing like one that hath a weary dream.
Full-faced above the valley stood the moon;
And like a downward smoke, the slender stream
Along the cliff to fall and pause and fall did seem.

A land of streams! some, like a downward smoke,
Slow-dropping veils of thinnest lawn, did go;
And some thro' wavering lights and shadows broke,
Rolling a slumbrous sheet of foam below.
They saw the gleaming river seaward flow
From the inner land: far off, three mountain-tops,
Three silent pinnacles of aged snow,
Stood sunset-flush'd; and, dew'd with showery drops,
Up-clomb the shadowy pine above the woven copse.

The charmed sunset linger'd low adown
In the red West: thro' mountain clefts the dale

Was seen far inland, and the yellow down
Border'd with palm, and many a winding vale
And meadow, set with slender galingale;
A land where all things always seem'd the same!
And round about the keel with faces pale,
Dark faces pale against that rosy flame,
The mild-eyed melancholy Lotos-eaters came.

Branches they bore of that enchanted stem,
Laden with flower and fruit, whereof they gave
To each, but whoso did receive of them,
And taste, to him the gushing of the wave
Far far away did seem to mourn and rave
On alien shores; and if his fellow spake,
His voice was thin, as voices from the grave;
And deep-asleep he seem'd, yet all awake,
And music in his ears his beating heart did make.

They sat them down upon the yellow sand,
Between the sun and moon upon the shore;
And sweet it was to dream of Fatherland,
Of child and wife, and slave; but evermore
Most weary seem'd the sea, weary the oar,
Weary the wandering fields of barren foam.
Then some one said, "We will return no more;"
Then all at once they sang, "Our island home
Is far beyond the wave; we will no longer roam."

1832

## YOU ASK ME, WHY

You ask me, why, tho' ill at ease,
    Within this region I subsist,
    Whose spirits falter in the mist,
And languish for the purple seas.

It is the land that freemen till,
    That sober-suited Freedom chose,
    The land, where girt with friends or foes
A man may speak the thing he will;

A land of settled government,
    A land of just and old renown,
    Where Freedom slowly broadens down
From precedent to precedent:

Where faction seldom gathers head,
    But by degrees to fullness wrought,
    The strength of some diffusive thought
Hath time and space to work and spread.

Should banded unions persecute
    Opinion, and induce a time
    When single thought is civil crime,
And individual freedom mute;

Tho' Power should make from land to land
    The name of Britain trebly great—
    Tho' every channel of the State
Should fill and choke with golden sand—

Yet waft me from the harbour-mouth,
    Wild wind! I seek a warmer sky,
    And I will see before I die
The palms and temples of the South.

                                        1842


## OF OLD SAT FREEDOM

OF OLD sat Freedom on the heights,
    The thunders breaking at her feet:

Above her shook the starry lights:
  She heard the torrents meet.

There in her place she did rejoice,
  Self-gather'd in her prophet-mind,
But fragments of her mighty voice
  Came rolling on the wind.

Then stept she down thro' town and field
  To mingle with the human race,
And part by part to men reveal'd
  The fullness of her face—

Grave mother of majestic works,
  From her isle-altar gazing down:
Who, God-like, grasps the triple forks,
  And, King-like, wears the crown:

Her open eyes desire the truth.
  The wisdom of a thousand years
Is in them. May perpetual youth
  Keep dry their light from tears;

That her fair form may stand and shine,
  Make bright our days and light our dreams,
Turning to scorn with lips divine
  The falsehood of extremes!

                                         1842

## MORTE D'ARTHUR

So ALL day long the noise of battle roll'd
Among the mountains by the winter sea;
Until King Arthur's table, man by man,
Had fallen in Lyonness about their Lord,

King Arthur: then, because his wound was deep,
The bold Sir Bedivere uplifted him,
Sir Bedivere, the last of all his knights,
And bore him to a chapel nigh the field,
A broken chancel with a broken cross,
That stood on a dark strait of barren land.
On one side lay the Ocean, and on one
Lay a great water, and the moon was full.
　　Then spake King Arthur to Sir Bedivere:
"The sequel of to-day unsolders all
The goodliest fellowship of famous knights
Whereof this world holds record. Such a sleep
They sleep—the men I loved. I think that we
Shall nevermore, at any future time,
Delight our souls with talk of knightly deeds,
Walking about the gardens and the halls
Of Camelot, as in the days that were.
I perish by this people which I made,—
Tho' Merlin sware that I should come again
To rule once more—but let what will be, be,
I am so deeply smitten thro' the helm
That without help I cannot last till morn.
Thou therefore take my brand Excalibur,
Which was my pride: for thou rememberest how
In those old days, one summer noon, an arm
Rose up from out the bosom of the lake,
Clothed in white samite, mystic, wonderful,
Holding the sword—and how I row'd across
And took it, and have worn it, like a king:
And, wheresoever I am sung or told
In after time, this also shall be known:
But now delay not: take Excalibur,
And fling him far into the middle mere:
Watch what thou seëst, and lightly bring me word."
　　To him replied the bold Sir Bedivere:

"It is not meet, Sir King, to leave thee thus,
Aidless, alone, and smitten thro' the helm.
A little thing may harm a wounded man.
Yet I thy hest will all perform at full,
Watch what I see, and lightly bring thee word."

So saying, from the ruin'd shrine he stept
And in the moon athwart the place of tombs,
Where lay the mighty bones of ancient men,
Old knights, and over them the sea-wind sang
Shrill, chill, with flakes of foam. He, stepping down
By zig-zag paths, and juts of pointed rock,
Came on the shining levels of the lake.

There drew he forth the brand Excalibur,
And o'er him, drawing it, the winter moon,
Brightening the skirts of a long cloud, ran forth
And sparkled keen with frost against the hilt:
For all the haft twinkled with diamond sparks,
Myriads of topaz-lights, and jacinth-work
Of subtlest jewellery. He gazed so long
That both his eyes were dazzled, as he stood,
This way and that dividing the swift mind,
In act to throw: but at the last it seem'd
Better to leave Excalibur conceal'd
There in the many-knotted waterflags,
That whistled stiff and dry about the marge.
So strode he back slow to the wounded King.

Then spake King Arthur to Sir Bedivere:
"Hast thou perform'd my mission which I gave?
What is it thou hast seen? or what hast heard?"

And answer made the bold Sir Bedivere:
"I heard the ripple washing in the reeds,
And the wild water lapping on the crag."

To whom replied King Arthur, faint and pale:
"Thou hast betray'd thy nature and thy name,
Not rendering true answer, as beseem'd

Thy fealty, nor like a noble knight:
For surer sign had follow'd, either hand,
Or voice, or else a motion of the mere.
This is a shameful thing for men to lie.
Yet now, I charge thee, quickly go again
As thou art lief and dear, and do the thing
I bade thee, watch, and lightly bring me word."

Then went Sir Bedivere the second time
Across the ridge, and paced beside the mere,
Counting the dewy pebbles, fix'd in thought;
But when he saw the wonder of the hilt,
How curiously and strangely chased, he smote
His palms together, and he cried aloud,

"And if indeed I cast the brand away,
Surely a precious thing, one worthy note,
Should thus be lost for ever from the earth,
Which might have pleased the eyes of many men.
What good should follow this, if this were done?
What harm, undone? deep harm to disobey,
Seeing obedience is the bond of rule.
Were it well to obey them, if a king demand
An act unprofitable, against himself?
The King is sick, and knows not what he does.
What record, or what relic of my lord
Should be to aftertime, but empty breath
And rumours of a doubt? but were this kept,
Stored in some treasure-house of mighty kings,
Some one might show it at a joust of arms,
Saying, 'King Arthur's sword, Excalibur,
Wrought by the lonely maiden of the Lake.
Nine years she wrought it, sitting in the deeps
Upon the hidden bases of the hills.'
So might some old man speak in the aftertime
To all the people, winning reverence.
But now much honour and much fame were lost."

So spake he, clouded with his own conceit,
And hid Excalibur the second time,
And so strode back slow to the wounded King.

Then spoke King Arthur, breathing heavily:
"What is it thou hast seen? or what hast heard?"

And answer made the bold Sir Bedivere:
"I heard the water lapping on the crag,
And the long ripple washing in the reeds."

To whom replied King Arthur, much in wrath:
"Ah, miserable and unkind, untrue,
Unknightly, traitor-hearted! Woe is me!
Authority forgets a dying king,
Laid widow'd of the power in his eye
That bow'd the will. I see thee what thou art,
For thou, the latest-left of all my knights,
In whom should meet the offices of all,
Thou wouldst betray me for the precious hilt;
Either from lust of gold, or like a girl
Valuing the giddy pleasure of the eyes.
Yet, for a man may fail in duty twice,
And the third time may prosper, get thee hence:
But, if thou spare to fling Excalibur,
I will arise and slay thee with my hands."

Then quickly rose Sir Bedivere, and ran,
And, leaping down the ridges lightly, plunged
Among the bulrush-beds, and clutch'd the sword,
And strongly wheel'd and threw it. The great brand
Made lightnings in the splendour of the moon,
And flashing round and round, and whirl'd in an arch,
Shot like a streamer of the northern morn,
Seen where the moving isles of winter shock
By night, with noises of the northern sea.
So flash'd and fell the brand Excalibur:
But ere he dipt the surface, rose an arm
Clothed in white samite, mystic, wonderful,

And caught him by the hilt, and brandish'd him
Three times, and drew him under in the mere.
And lightly went the other to the King.

    Then spoke King Arthur, drawing thicker breath:
"Now see I by thine eyes that this is done.
Speak out: what is it thou hast heard, or seen?"

    And answer made the bold Sir Bedivere:
"Sir King, I closed mine eyelids, lest the gems
Should blind my purpose, for I never saw,
Nor shall see, here or elsewhere, till I die,
Not tho' I live three lives of mortal men,
So great a miracle as yonder hilt.
Then with both hands I flung him, wheeling him;
But when I look'd again, behold an arm,
Clothed in white samite, mystic, wonderful,
That caught him by the hilt, and brandish'd him
Three times, and drew him under in the mere."

    And answer made King Arthur, breathing hard:
"My end draws nigh; 'tis time that I were gone.
Make broad thy shoulders to receive my weight,
And bear me to the margin; yet I fear
My wound hath taken cold, and I shall die."

    So saying, from the pavement he half rose,
Slowly, with pain, reclining on his arm,
And looking wistfully with wide blue eyes
As in a picture. Him Sir Bedivere
Remorsefully regarded thro' his tears,
And would have spoken, but he found not words,
Then took with care, and kneeling on one knee,
O'er both his shoulders drew the languid hands,
And rising bore him thro' the place of tombs.

    But, as he walk'd, King Arthur panted hard,
Like one that feels a nightmare on his bed
When all the house is mute. So sigh'd the King,
Muttering and murmuring at his ear, "Quick, quick!

I fear it is too late, and I shall die."
But the other swiftly strode from ridge to ridge,
Clothed with his breath, and looking, as he walk'd,
Larger than human on the frozen hills.
He heard the deep behind him, and a cry
Before. His own thought drove him, like a goad.
Dry clash'd his harness in the icy caves
And barren chasms, and all to left and right
The bare black cliff clang'd round him, as he based
His feet on juts of slippery crag that rang
Sharp-smitten with the dint of armed heels—
And on a sudden, lo! the level lake,
And the long glories of the winter moon.

   Then saw they how there hove a dusky barge,
Dark as a funeral scarf from stem to stern,
Beneath them; and descending they were ware
That all the decks were dense with stately forms
Black-stoled, black-hooded, like a dream—by these
Three Queens with crowns of gold—and from them rose
A cry that shiver'd to the tingling stars,
And, as it were one voice an agony
Of lamentation, like a wind, that shrills
All night in a waste land, where no one comes,
Or hath come, since the making of the world.

   Then murmur'd Arthur, "Place me in the barge,"
And to the barge they came. There those three Queens
Put forth their hands, and took the King, and wept.
But she, that rose the tallest of them all
And fairest, laid his head upon her lap,
And loosed the shatter'd casque, and chafed his hands,
And call'd him by his name, complaining loud,
And dropping bitter tears against his brow
Striped with dark blood: for all his face was white
And colourless, and like the wither'd moon
Smote by the fresh beam of the springing east:

And all his greaves and cuisses dash'd with drops
Of onset; and the light and lustrous curls—
That made his forehead like a rising sun
High from the daïs-throne—were parch'd with dust;
Or, clotted into points and hanging loose,
Mix'd with the knightly growth that fringed his lips.
So like a shatter'd column lay the King;
Not like that Arthur who, with lance in rest,
From spur to plume a star of tournament,
Shot thro' the lists at Camelot, and charged
Before the eyes of ladies and of kings.

  Then loudly cried the bold Sir Bedivere,
"Ah! my Lord Arthur, whither shall I go?
Where shall I hide my forehead and my eyes?
For now I see the true old times are dead,
When every morning brought a noble chance,
And every chance brought out a noble knight.
Such times have been not since the light that led
The holy Elders with the gift of myrrh.
But now the whole ROUND TABLE is dissolved
Which was an image of the mighty world;
And I, the last, go forth companionless
And the days darken round me, and the years,
Among new men, strange faces, other minds."

  And slowly answered Arthur from the barge:
"The old order changeth, yielding place to new,
And God fulfils Himself in many ways,
Lest one good custom should corrupt the world.
Comfort thyself: what comfort is in me?
I have lived my life, and that which I have done
May He within Himself make pure! but thou,
If thou shouldst never see my face again,
Pray for my soul. More things are wrought by prayer
Than this world dreams of. Wherefore, let thy voice
Rise like a fountain for me night and day.

For what are men better than sheep or goats
That nourish a blind life within the brain,
If, knowing God, they lift not hands of prayer
Both for themselves and those who call. them friend?
For so the whole round earth is every way
Bound by gold chains about the feet of God.
But now farewell. I am going a long way
With these thou seëst—if indeed I go—
(For all my mind is clouded with a doubt)
To the island-valley of Avilion;
Where falls not hail, or rain, or any snow,
Nor ever wind blows loudly; but it lies
Deep-meadow'd, happy, fair with orchard-lawns
And bowery hollows crown'd with summer sea,
Where I will heal me of my grievous wound."
So said he, and the barge with oar and sail
Moved from the brink, like some full-breasted swan
That, fluting a wild carol ere her death,
Ruffles her pure cold plume, and takes the flood
With swarthy webs. Long stood Sir Bedivere
Revolving many memories, till the hull
Look'd one black dot against the verge of dawn,
And on the mere the wailing died away.

1842

# ULYSSES

It LITTLE profits that an idle king,
By this still hearth, among these barren crags,
Match'd with an aged wife, I mete and dole
Unequal laws unto a savage race,
That hoard, and sleep, and feed, and know not me.
I cannot rest from travel: I will drink
Life to the lees: all times I have enjoy'd
Greatly, have suffer'd greatly, both with those

That loved me, and alone; on shore, and when
Thro' scudding drifts the rainy Hyades
Vext the dim sea: I am become a name;
For always roaming with a hungry heart
Much have I seen and known; cities of men
And manners, climates, councils, governments,
Myself not least, but honour'd of them all;
And drunk delight of battle with my peers,
Far on the ringing plains of windy Troy.
I am a part of all that I have met;
Yet all experience is an arch wherethro'
Gleams that untravell'd world, whose margin fades
For ever and for ever when I move.
How dull it is to pause, to make an end,
To rust unburnish'd, not to shine in use!
As tho' to breathe were life. Life piled on life
Were all too little, and of one to me
Little remains: but every hour is saved
From that eternal silence, something more,
A bringer of new things; and vile it were
For some three suns to store and hoard myself,
And this gray spirit yearning in desire
To follow knowledge like a sinking star,
Beyond the utmost bound of human thought.
  This is my son, mine own Telemachus,
To whom I leave the sceptre and the isle—
Well-loved of me, discerning to fulfil
This labour, by slow prudence to make mild
A rugged people, and thro' soft degrees
Subdue them to the useful and the good.
Most blameless is he, centred in the sphere
Of common duties, decent not to fail
In offices of tenderness, and pay
Meet adoration to my household gods,
When I am gone. He works his work, I mine.

There lies the port; the vessel puffs her sail:
There gloom the dark broad seas. My mariners,
Souls that have toil'd, and wrought, and thought with
      me—
That ever with a frolic welcome took
The thunder and the sunshine, and opposed
Free hearts, free foreheads—you and I are old;
Old age hath yet his honour and his toil;
Death closes all: but something ere the end,
Some work of noble note, may yet be done,
Not unbecoming men that strove with Gods.
The lights begin to twinkle from the rocks:
The long day wanes: the slow moon climbs: the deep
Moans round with many voices. Come, my friends,
'Tis not too late to seek a newer world.
Push off, and sitting well in order smite
The sounding furrows; for my purpose holds
To sail beyond the sunset, and the baths
Of all the western stars, until I die.
It may be that the gulfs will wash us down:
It may be we shall touch the Happy Isles,
And see the great Achilles, whom we knew.
Tho' much is taken, much abides; and tho'
We are not now that strength which in old days
Moved earth and heaven; that which we are, we are;
One equal temper of heroic hearts,
Made weak by time and fate, but strong in will
To strive, to seek, to find, and not to yield.

                     1842

## LOCKSLEY HALL

COMRADES, leave me here a little, while as yet 'tis early
      morn:

Leave me here, and when you want me, sound upon the
    bugle-horn.

'Tis the place, and all around it, as of old, the curlews
    call,
Dreary gleams about the moorland flying over Locksley
    Hall;

Locksley Hall, that in the distance overlooks the sandy
    tracts,
And the hollow ocean-ridges roaring into cataracts.

Many a night from yonder ivied casement, ere I went
    to rest,
Did I look on great Orion sloping slowly to the West.

Many a night I saw the Pleiads, rising thro' the mellow
    shade,
Glitter like a swarm of fire-flies tangled in a silver braid.

Here about the beach I wander'd, nourishing a youth
    sublime
With the fairy tales of science, and the long result of
    Time;

When the centuries behind me like a fruitful land
    reposed;
When I clung to all the present for the promise that it
    closed:

When I dipt into the future far as human eye could see;
Saw the Vision of the world, and all the wonder that
    would be.—

In the Spring a fuller crimson comes upon the robin's
      breast;
In the Spring the wanton lapwing gets himself another
      crest;

In the Spring a livelier iris changes on the burnish'd
      dove;
In the Spring a young man's fancy lightly turns to
      thoughts of love.

Then her cheek was pale and thinner than should be
      for one so young,
And her eyes on all my motions with a mute observance
      hung.

And I said, "My cousin Amy, speak, and speak the
      truth to me,
Trust me, cousin, all the current of my being sets to
      thee."

On her pallid cheek and forehead came a colour and a
      light,
As I have seen the rosy red flushing in the northern
      night.

And she turn'd—her bosom shaken with a sudden
      storm of sighs—
All the spirit deeply dawning in the dark of hazel eyes—

Saying, "I have hid my feelings, fearing they should
      do me wrong;"
Saying, "Dost thou love me, cousin?" weeping, "I
      have loved thee long."

Love took up the glass of Time, and turn'd it in his
    glowing hands;
Every moment, lightly shaken, ran itself in golden
    sands.

Love took up the harp of Life, and smote on all the
    chords with might;
Smote the chord of Self that, trembling, pass'd in music
    out of sight.

Many a morning on the moorland did we hear the
    copses ring,
And her whisper throng'd my pulses with the fulness
    of the Spring.

Many an evening by the waters did we watch the stately
    ships,
And our spirits rush'd together at the touching of the
    lips.

O my cousin, shallow-hearted! O my Amy, mine no
    more!
O the dreary, dreary moorland! O the barren, barren
    shore!

Falser than all fancy fathoms, falser than all songs
    have sung,
Puppet to a father's threat, and servile to a shrewish
    tongue!

Is it well to wish thee happy?—having known me—to
    decline
On a range of lower feelings and a narrower heart than
    mine!

Yet it shall be: thou shalt lower to his level day by
    day,
What is fine within thee growing coarse to sympathize
    with clay.

As the husband is, the wife *is*: thou art mated with a
    clown,
And the grossness of his nature will have weight to
    drag thee down.

He will hold thee, when his passion shall have spent
    its novel force,
Something better than his dog, a little dearer than his
    horse.

What is this? his eyes are heavy: think not they are
    glazed with wine.
Go to him: it is thy duty: kiss him: take his hand in
    thine.

It may be my lord is weary, that his brain is over-
    wrought:
Soothe him with thy finer fancies, touch him with thy
    lighter thought.

He will answer to the purpose, easy things to under-
    stand—
Better thou wert dead before me, tho' I slew thee with
    my hand!

Better thou and I were lying, hidden from the heart's
    disgrace,
Roll'd in one another's arms, and silent in a last embrace.

Cursed be the social wants that sin against the strength
   of youth!
Cursed be the social lies that warp us from the living
   truth!

Cursed be the sickly forms that err from honest Nature's
   rule!
Cursed be the gold that gilds the straiten'd forehead of
   the fool!

Well—'tis well that I should bluster!—Hadst thou less
   unworthy proved—
Would to God—for I had loved thee more than ever
   wife was loved.

Am I mad, that I should cherish that which bears but
   bitter fruit?
I will pluck it from my bosom, tho' my heart be at the
   root.

Never, tho' my mortal summers to such length of years
   should come
As the many-winter'd crow that leads the clanging
   rookery home.

Where is comfort? in division of the records of the
   mind?
Can I part her from herself, and love her, as I knew
   her, kind?

I remember one that perish'd: sweetly did she speak
   and move:
Such a one do I remember, whom to look at was to
   love.

Can I think of her as dead, and love her for the love
  she bore?
No—she never loved me truly: love is love for evermore.

Comfort? comfort scorn'd of devils! this is truth the
  poet sings,
That a sorrow's crown of sorrow is remembering happier
  things.

Drug thy memories, lest thou learn it, lest thy heart
  be put to proof,
In the dead unhappy night, and when the rain is on
  the roof.

Like a dog, he hunts in dreams, and thou art staring at
  the wall,
Where the dying night-lamp flickers, and the shadows
  rise and fall.

Then a hand shall pass before thee, pointing to his
  drunken sleep,
To thy widow'd marriage-pillows, to the tears that thou
  wilt weep.

Thou shalt hear the "Never, never," whisper'd by the
  phantom years,
And a song from out the distance in the ringing of
  thine ears;

And an eye shall vex thee, looking ancient kindness on
  thy pain.
Turn thee, turn thee on thy pillow: get thee to thy
  rest again.

Nay, but Nature brings thee solace; for a tender
    voice will cry.
'Tis a purer life than thine; a lip to drain thy trouble
    dry.

Baby lips will laugh me down: my latest rival brings
    thee rest.
Baby fingers, waxen touches, press me from the mother's
    breast.

O, the child too clothes the father with a dearness not
    his due.
Half is thine and half is his: it will be worthy of the
    two.

O, I see thee old and formal, fitted to thy petty part,
With a little hoard of maxims preaching down a daugh-
    ter's heart.

"They were dangerous guides the feelings—she herself
    was not exempt—
Truly, she herself had suffer'd"—Perish in thy self-
    contempt!

Overlive it—lower yet—be happy! wherefore should I
    care?
I myself must mix with action, lest I wither by despair.

What is that which I should turn to, lighting upon days
    like these?
Every door is barr'd with gold, and opens but to golden
    keys.

Every gate is throng'd with suitors, all the markets over-
    flow.

I have but an angry fancy: what is that which I should
do?

I had been content to perish, falling on the foeman's
ground,
When the ranks are roll'd in vapour, and the winds are
laid with sound.

But the jingling of the guinea helps the hurt that Honour feels.
And the nations do but murmur, snarling at each other's
heels.

Can I but relive in sadness? I will turn that earlier
page.
Hide me from thy deep emotion, O thou wondrous
Mother-Age!

Make me feel the wild pulsation that I felt before the
strife,
When I heard my days before me, and the tumult of
my life;

Yearning for the large excitement that the coming
years would yield,
Eager-hearted as a boy when first he leaves his father's
field,

And at night along the dusky highway near and nearer
drawn,
Sees in heaven the light of London flaring like a dreary
dawn;

And his spirit leaps within him to be gone before him
then,

Underneath the light he looks at, in among the throngs
  of men:

Men, my brothers, men the workers, ever reaping some-
    thing new:
That which they have done but earnest of the things
    that they shall do:

For I dipt into the future, far as human eye could see,
Saw the Vision of the world, and all the wonder that
    would be;

Saw the heavens fill with commerce, argosies of magic
    sails,
Pilots of the purple twilight, dropping down with costly
    bales;

Heard the heavens fill with shouting, and there rain'd a
    ghastly dew
From the nations' airy navies grappling in the central
    blue;

Far along the world-wide whisper of the south-wind
    rushing warm,
With the standards of the peoples plunging thro' the
    thunder-storm;

Till the war-drum throbb'd no longer, and the battle-
    flags were furl'd
In the Parliament of man, the Federation of the world.

There the common sense of most shall hold a fretful
    realm in awe,
And the kindly earth shall slumber, lapt in universal
    law.

So I triumph'd ere my passion sweeping thro' me left
me dry,
Left me with the palsied heart, and left me with the
jaundiced eye;

Eye, to which all order festers, all things here are out
of joint:
Science moves, but slowly, slowly, creeping on from
point to point:

Slowly comes a hungry people, as a lion creeping nigher,
Glares at one that nods and winks behind a slowly-
dying fire.

Yet I doubt not thro' the ages one increasing purpose
runs,
And the thoughts of men are widen'd with the process
of the suns.

What is that to him that reaps not harvest of his
youthful joys,
Tho' the deep heart of existence beat for ever like a
boy's?

Knowledge comes, but wisdom lingers, and I linger on
the shore,
And the individual withers, and the world is more and
more.

Knowledge comes, but wisdom lingers, and he bears
a laden breast,
Full of sad experience, moving toward the stillness of
his rest.

Hark, my merry comrades call me, sounding on the
    bugle horn,
They to whom my foolish passion were a target for
    their scorn:

Shall it not be scorn to me to harp on such a moulder'd
    string?
I am shamed thro' all my nature to have loved so slight
    a thing.

Weakness to be wroth with weakness! woman's pleasure,
    woman's pain—
Nature made them blinder motions bounded in a shal-
    lower brain:

Woman is the lesser man, and all thy passions, match'd
    with mine,
Are as moonlight unto sunlight, and as water unto
    wine—

Here at least, where nature sickens, nothing. Ah, for
    some retreat
Deep in yonder shining Orient, where my life began to
    beat;

Where in wild Mahratta-battle fell my father evil-
    starr'd;—
I was left a trampled orphan, and a selfish uncle's ward.

Or to burst all links of habit—there to wander far
    away,
On from island unto island at the gateways of the day.

Larger constellations burning, mellow moons and happy
    skies,

Breadths of tropic shade and palms in cluster, knots of
      Paradise.

Never comes the trader, never floats an European flag,
Slides the bird o'er lustrous woodland, swings the trailer
      from the crag;

Droops the heavy-blossom'd bower, hangs the heavy-
      fruited tree—
Summer isles of Eden lying in dark-purple spheres of
      sea.

There methinks would be enjoyment more than in this
      march of mind,
In the steamship, in the railway, in the thoughts that
      shake mankind.

There the passions cramp'd no longer shall have scope
      and breathing space;
I will take some savage woman, she shall rear my dusky
      race.

Iron-jointed, supple-sinew'd, they shall dive, and they
      shall run,
Catch the wild goat by the hair, and hurl their lances
      in the sun;

Whistle back the parrot's call, and leap the rainbows of
      the brooks.
Not with blinded eyesight poring over miserable books—

Fool, again the dream, the **fancy**! but I *know* my words
      are wild,
But I count the gray barbarian lower than the Christian
      child.

I, to herd with narrow foreheads, vacant of our glorious
      gains,
Like a beast with lower pleasures, like a beast with lower
      pains!

Mated with a squalid savage—what to me were sun or
      clime?
I the heir of all the ages, in the foremost files of time—

I that rather held it better men should perish one by one,
Than that earth should stand at gaze like Joshua's moon
      in Ajalon!

Not in vain the distance beacons. Forward, forward
      let us range,
Let the great world spin for ever down the ringing
      grooves of change.

Thro' the shadow of the globe we sweep into the younger
      day:
Better fifty years of Europe than a cycle of Cathay.

Mother-Age (for mine I knew not) help me as when life
      begun:
Rift the hills, and roll the waters, flash the lightnings,
      weigh the Sun.

O, I see the crescent promise of my spirit hath not set.
Ancient founts of inspiration well thro' all my fancy yet.

Howsoever these things be, a long farewell to Locksley
      Hall!
Now for me the woods may wither, now for me the roof-
      tree fall.

Comes a vapour from the margin, blackening over heath
    and holt,
Cramming all the blast before it, in its breast a thunder-
    bolt.

Let it fall on Locksley Hall, with rain or hail, or fire or
    snow;
For the mighty wind arises, roaring seaward, and I go.
                                    1842

## SIR GALAHAD

My GOOD blade carves the casques of men,
    My tough lance thrusteth sure,
My strength is as the strength of ten,
    Because my heart is pure.
The shattering trumpet shrilleth high,
    The hard brands shiver on the steel,
The splinter'd spear-shafts crack and fly,
    The horse and rider reel:
They reel, they roll in clanging lists,
    And when the tide of combat stands,
Perfume and flowers fall in showers,
    That lightly rain from ladies' hands.

How sweet are looks that ladies bend
    On whom their favours fall!
For them I battle till the end,
    To save from shame and thrall:
But all my heart is drawn above,
    My knees are bow'd in crypt and shrine:
I never felt the kiss of love,
    Nor maiden's hand in mine.

More bounteous aspects on me beam,
　Me mightier transports move and thrill;
So keep I fair thro' faith and prayer
　A virgin heart in work and will.


When down the stormy crescent goes,
　A light before me swims,
Between dark stems the forest glows,
　I hear a noise of hymns:
Then by some secret shrine I ride;
　I hear a voice but none are there;
The stalls are void, the doors are wide,
　The tapers burning fair.
Fair gleams the snowy altar-cloth,
　The silver vessels sparkle clean,
The shrill bell rings, the censer swings,
　And solemn chaunts resound between.


Sometimes on lonely mountain-meres
　I find a magic bark;
I leap on board: no helmsman steers:
　I float till all is dark.
A gentle sound, an awful light!
　Three angels bear the holy Grail:
With folded feet, in stoles of white,
　On sleeping wings they sail.
Ah, blessed vision! blood of God!
　My spirit beats her mortal bars,
As down dark tides the glory slides,
　And star-like mingles with the stars.


When on my goodly charger borne
　Thro' dreaming towns I go,
The cock crows ere the Christmas morn
　The streets are dumb with snow.

The tempest crackles on the leads,
  And, ringing, springs from brand and mail;
But o'er the dark a glory spreads,
  And gilds the driving hail.
I leave the plain, I climb the height;
  No branchy thicket shelter yields;
But blessed forms in whistling storms
  Fly o'er waste fens and windy fields.

A maiden knight—to me is given
  Such hope, I know not fear;
I yearn to breathe the airs of heaven
  That often meet me here.
I muse on joy that will not cease,
  Pure spaces clothed in living beams,
Pure lilies of eternal peace,
  Whose odours haunt my dreams;
And, stricken by an angel's hand,
  This mortal armour that I wear,
This weight and size, this heart and eyes,
  Are touch'd, are turn'd to finest air.

The clouds are broken in the sky,
  And thro' the mountain-walls
A rolling organ-harmony
  Swells up, and shakes and falls.
Then move the trees, the copses nod,
  Wings flutter, voices hover clear:
"O just and faithful knight of God!
  Ride on! the prize is near."
So pass I hostel, hall, and grange;
  By bridge and ford, by park and pale,
All-arm'd I ride, whate'er betide,
  Until I find the holy Grail.

1842

## MOVE EASTWARD, HAPPY EARTH

Move eastward, happy earth, and leave
   Yon orange sunset waning slow:
From fringes of the faded eve,
   O, happy planet, eastward go;
Till over thy dark shoulder glow
   Thy silver sister-world, and rise
   To glass herself in dewy eyes
That watch me from the glen below.

Ah, bear me with thee, smoothly borne,
   Dip forward under starry light,
And move me to my marriage-morn,
   And round again to happy night.

1842

## BREAK, BREAK, BREAK

Break, break, break,
   On thy cold gray stones, O Sea!
And I would that my tongue could utter
   The thoughts that arise in me.

O well for the fisherman's boy,
   That he shouts with his sister at play!
O well for the sailor lad,
   That he sings in his boat on the bay!

And the stately ships go on
   To their haven under the hill;
But O for the touch of a vanish'd hand,
   And the sound of a voice that is still!

Break, break, break,
  At the foot of thy crags, O Sea!
But the tender grace of a day that is dead
  Will never come back to me.

1842

## TEARS, IDLE TEARS

(From *The Princess*)

TEARS, idle tears, I know not what they mean,
Tears from the depth of some divine despair
Rise in the heart, and gather to the eyes,
In looking on the happy Autumn-fields,
And thinking of the days that are no more.

Fresh as the first beam glittering on a sail,
That brings our friends up from the underworld,
Sad as the last which reddens over one
That sinks with all we love below the verge;
So sad, so fresh, the days that are no more.

Ah, sad and strange as in dark summer dawns
The earliest pipe of half-awaken'd birds
To dying ears, when unto dying eyes
The casement slowly grows a glimmering square;
So sad, so strange, the days that are no more.

Dear as remember'd kisses after death,
And sweet as those by hopeless fancy feign'd
On lips that are for others; deep as love,
Deep as first love, and wild with all regret;
O Death in Life, the days that are no more.

1850

## THE BUGLE SONG

(From *The Princess*)

THE splendour falls on castle walls
    And snowy summits old in story:
  The long light shakes across the lakes,
    And the wild cataract leaps in glory.
Blow, bugle, blow, set the wild echoes flying,
Blow, bugle; answer, echoes, dying, dying, dying.

    O hark, O hear! how thin and clear,
    And thinner, clearer, farther going!
  O sweet and far from cliff and scar
    The horns of Elfland faintly blowing!
Blow, let us hear the purple glens replying:
Blow, bugle; answer, echoes, dying, dying, dying.

    O love, they die in yon rich sky,
    They faint on hill or field or river:
  Our echoes roll from soul to soul,
    And grow for ever and for ever.
Blow, bugle, blow, set the wild echoes flying,
And answer, echoes, answer, dying, dying, dying.
                      1850

## SWEET AND LOW

(From *The Princess*)

SWEET and low, sweet and low,
  Wind of the western sea,
Low, low, breathe and blow,
  Wind of the western sea!

Over the rolling waters go,
Come from the dying moon, and blow,
   Blow him again to me;
While my little one, while my pretty one, sleeps.

Sleep and rest, sleep and rest,
   Father will come to thee soon;
Rest, rest, on mother's breast,
   Father will come to thee soon;
Father will come to his babe in the nest,
Silver sails all out of the west
   Under the silver moon:
Sleep, my little one, sleep, my pretty one, sleep.

1850

## IN MEMORIAM

### (Selections)

I

I HELD it truth, with him who sings
   To one clear harp in divers tones,
   That men may rise on stepping-stones
Of their dead selves to higher things.

But who shall so forecast the years
   And find in loss a gain to match?
   Or reach a hand thro' time to catch
The far-off interest of tears?

Let Love clasp Grief lest both be drown'd,
   Let darkness keep her raven gloss:
   Ah, sweeter to be drunk with loss,
To dance with death, to beat the ground,

Than that the victor Hours should scorn
    The long result of love, and boast,
    "Behold the man that loved and lost,
But all he was is overworn."


### XXVII


I envy not in any moods
    The captive void of noble rage,
    The linnet born within the cage,
That never knew the summer woods:

I envy not the beast that takes
    His license in the field of time,
    Unfetter'd by the sense of crime,
To whom a conscience never wakes;

Nor, what may count itself as blest,
    The heart that never plighted troth
    But stagnates in the weeds of sloth;
Nor any want-begotten rest.

I hold it true, what'er befall;
    I feel it, when I sorrow most;
    'Tis better to have loved and lost
Than never to have loved at all.


### LIV


Oh yet we trust that somehow good
    Will be the final goal of ill,
    To pangs of nature, sins of will,
Defects of doubt, and taints of blood;

That nothing walks with aimless feet;
   That not one life shall be destroy'd,
   Or cast as rubbish to the void,
When God hath made the pile complete;

That not a worm is cloven in vain;
   That not a moth with vain desire
   Is shrivell'd in a fruitless fire,
Or but subserves another's gain.

Behold, we know not anything;
   I can but trust that good shall fall
   At last—far off—at last, to all,
And every winter change to spring.

So runs my dream: but what am I?
   An infant crying in the night:
   An infant crying for the light:
And with no language but a cry.

LV

The wish, that of the living whole
   No life may fail beyond the grave,
   Derives it not from what we have
The likest God within the soul?

Are God and Nature then at strife,
   That nature lends such evil dreams?
   So careful of the type she seems,
So careless of the single life;

That I, considering everywhere
   Her secret meaning in her deeds,
   And finding that of fifty seeds
She often brings but one to bear,

I falter where I firmly trod,
　And falling with my weight of cares
　Upon the great world's altar-stairs
That slope thro' darkness up to God,

I stretch lame hands of faith, and grope,
　And gather dust and chaff, and call
　To what I feel is Lord of all,
And faintly trust the larger hope.

### LVII

Peace; come away: the song of woe
　Is after all an earthly song:
　Peace; come away: we do him **wrong**
To sing so wildly: let us go.

Come; let us go: your cheeks are pale;
　But half my life I leave behind:
　Methinks my friend is richly shrined;
But I shall pass; my work will fail.

Yet in these ears, till hearing dies,
　One set slow bell will seem to toll
　The passing of the sweetest soul
That ever look'd with human eyes.

I hear it now, and o'er and o'er,
　Eternal greetings to the dead;
　And "Ave, Ave, Ave," said,
"Adieu, adieu" for evermore.

### XCVI

You say, but with no touch of **scorn**,
　Sweet-hearted. you, whose light-blue eyes

Are tender over drowning flies,
You tell me, doubt is Devil-born.

I know not: one indeed I knew
    In many a subtle question versed,
    Who touch'd a jarring lyre at first,
But ever strove to make it true:

Perplext in faith, but pure in deeds,
    At last he beat his music out.
    There lives more faith in honest doubt,
Believe me, than in half the creeds.

He fought his doubts and gather'd strength,
    He would not make his judgment blind,
    He faced the spectres of the mind
And laid them: thus he came at length

To find a stronger faith his own;
    And Power was with him in the night,
    Which makes the darkness and the light,
And dwells not in the light alone,

But in the darkness and the cloud,
    As over Sinaï's peaks of old,
    While Israel made their gods of gold,
Altho' the trumpet blew so loud.

### CVI

Ring out, wild bells, to the wild sky,
    The flying cloud, the frosty light:
    The year is dying in the night;
Ring out, wild bells, and let him die.

Ring out the old, ring in the new,
　　Ring, happy bells, across the snow:
　　The year is going, let him go;
Ring out the false, ring in the true.

Ring out the grief that saps the mind,
　　For those that here we see no more;
　　Ring out the feud of rich and poor,
Ring in redress to all mankind.

Ring out a slowly dying cause,
　　And ancient forms of party strife;
　　Ring in the nobler modes of life,
With sweeter manners, purer laws.

Ring out the want, the care, the sin,
　　The faithless coldness of the times;
　　Ring out, ring out my mournful rhymes,
But ring the fuller minstrel in.

Ring out false pride in place and blood,
　　The civic slander and the spite;
　　Ring in the love of truth and right,
Ring in the common love of good.

Ring out old shapes of foul disease;
　　Ring out the narrowing lust of gold;
　　Ring out the thousand wars of old,
Ring in the thousand years of peace.

Ring in the valiant man and free,
　　The larger heart, the kindlier hand;
　　Ring out the darkness of the land.
Ring in the Christ that is to be.

## EPILOGUE

O true and tried, so well and long,
   Demand not thou a marriage lay;
   In that it is thy marriage day
Is music more than any song.

Nor have I felt so much of bliss
   Since first he told me that he loved
   A daughter of our house; nor proved
Since that dark day a day like this

Tho' I since then have number'd o'er
   Some thrice three years: they went and came,
   Remade the blood and changed the fame,
And yet is love not less, but more;

No longer caring to embalm
   In dying songs a dead regret,
   But like a statue solid-set,
And moulded in colossal calm.

Regret is dead, but love is more
   Than in the summers that are flown,
   For I myself with these have grown
To something greater than before;

Which makes appear the songs I made
   As echoes out of weaker times,
   As half but idle brawling rhymes,
The sport of random sun and shade.

But where is she, the bridal flower,
   That must be made a wife ere noon?

She enters, glowing like the moon
Of Eden on its bridal bower:

On me she bends her blissful eyes
    And then on thee; they meet thy look
    And brighten like the star that shook
Betwixt the palms of paradise.

O when her life was yet in bud,
    He too foretold the perfect rose.
    For thee she grew, for thee she grows
For ever, and as fair as good.

And thou art worthy; full of power;
    As gentle; liberal-minded, great,
    Consistent; wearing all that weight
Of learning lightly like a flower.

But now set out: the noon is near,
    And I must give away the bride;
    She fears not, or with thee beside
And me behind her, will not fear.

For I that danced her on my knee,
    That watch'd her on her nurse's arm,
    That shielded all her life from harm
At last must part with her to thee;

Now waiting to be made a wife,
    Her feet, my darling, on the dead;
    Their pensive tablets round her head,
And the most living words of life

Breathed in her ear. The ring is on,
    The "wilt thou" answer'd, and again

The "wilt thou" ask'd, till out of twain
Her sweet "I will" has made you one.

Now sign your names, which shall be read,
    Mute symbols of a joyful morn,
    By village eyes as yet unborn;
The names are sign'd, and overhead

Begins the clash and clang that tells
    The joy to every wandering breeze;
    The blind wall rocks, and on the trees
The dead leaf trembles to the bells.

O happy hour, and happier hours
    Await them. Many a merry face
    Salutes them—maidens of the place,
That pelt us in the porch with flowers.

O happy hour, behold the bride
    With him to whom her hand I gave.
    They leave the porch, they pass the grave
That has to-day its sunny side.

To-day the grave is bright for me,
    For them the light of life increased,
    Who stay to share the morning feast,
Who rest to-night beside the sea.

Let all my genial spirits advance
    To meet and greet a whiter sun;
    My drooping memory will not shun
The foaming grape of eastern France.

It circles round, and fancy plays,
    And hearts are warm'd and faces bloom,

As drinking health to bride and **groom**
We wish them store of happy days.

Nor count me all to blame if I
  Conjecture of a stiller guest,
  Perchance, perchance, among the **rest**,
And, tho' in silence, wishing joy.

But they must go, the time draws **on**,
  And those white-favour'd horses **wait**;
  They rise, but linger; it is late;
Farewell, we kiss, and they are **gone**.

A shade falls on us like the dark
  From little cloudlets on the **grass**,
  But sweeps away as out we pass
To range the woods, to roam the **park**,

Discussing how their courtship grew,
  And talk of others that are wed,
  And how she look'd, and what he said,
And back we come at fall of dew.

Again the feast, the speech, the glee,
  The shade of passing thought, the **wealth**
  Of words and wit, the double health,
The crowning cup, the three-times-three,

And last the dance;—till I retire:
  Dumb is that tower which spake so loud,
  And high in heaven the streaming cloud,
And on the downs a rising fire:

And rise, O moon, from yonder down,
  Till over down and over dale

All night the shining vapour sail
And pass the silent-lighted town,

The white-faced halls, the glancing rills,
   And catch at every mountain head,
   And o'er the friths that branch and spread
Their sleeping silver thro' the hills;

And touch with shade the bridal doors,
   With tender gloom the roof, the wall;
   And breaking let the splendour fall
To spangle all the happy shores

By which they rest, and ocean sounds,
   And, star and system rolling past,
   A soul shall draw from out the vast
And strike his being into bounds,

And, moved thro' life of lower phase,
   Result in man, be born and think,
   And act and love, a closer link
Betwixt us and the crowning race

Of those that, eye to eye, shall look
   On knowledge; under whose command
   Is Earth and Earth's, and in their hand
Is Nature like an open book;

No longer half-akin to brute,
   For all we thought and loved and did,
   And hoped, and suffer'd, is but seed
Of what in them is flower and fruit;

Whereof the man, that with me trod
   This planet, was a noble type

Appearing ere the times were ripe,
That friend of mine who lives in God,

That God, which ever lives and loves,
One God, one law, one element,
And one far-off divine event,
To which the whole creation moves.

1850

## THE CHARGE OF THE LIGHT BRIGADE

### I

HALF a league, half a league,
Half a league onward,
All in the valley of Death
Rode the six hundred.
"Forward, the Light Brigade!
Charge for the guns," he said:
Into the valley of Death
Rode the six hundred.

### II

"Forward, the Light Brigade!"
Was there a man dismay'd?
Not tho' the soldier knew
Some one had blunder'd:
Theirs not to make reply,
Theirs not to reason why,
Theirs but to do and die:
Into the valley of Death
Rode the six hundred.

### III

Cannon to right of them,
Cannon to left of them,
Cannon in front of them
    Volley'd and thunder'd;
Storm'd at with shot and shell,
Boldly they rode and well,
Into the jaws of Death,
Into the mouth of Hell
    Rode the six hundred.

### IV

Flash'd all their sabres bare,
Flash'd as they turn'd in air
Sabring the gunners there,
Charging an army, while
    All the world wonder'd:
Plunged in the battery-smoke
Right thro' the line they broke;
Cossack and Russian
Reel'd from the sabre-stroke
    Shatter'd and sunder'd.
Then they rode back, but not,
    Not the six hundred.

### V

Cannon to right of them,
Cannon to left of them,
Cannon behind them
    Volley'd and thunder'd;

Storm'd at with shot and shell,
While horse and hero fell,
They that had fought so well
Came thro' the jaws of Death,
Back from the mouth of Hell,
All that was left of them,
   Left of six hundred.

### VI

When can their glory fade?
O the wild charge they made!
   All the world wonder'd.
Honour the charge they made!
Honour the Light Brigade,
   Noble six hundred!

1854

## LYRICS FROM "MAUD"

### BIRDS IN THE HIGH HALL-GARDEN

#### I

BIRDS in the high Hall-garden
   When twilight was falling,
Maud, Maud, Maud, Maud,
   They were crying and calling.

#### II

Where was Maud? in our wood;
   And I, who else, was with her,

Gathering woodland lilies,
  Myriads blow together.


### GO NOT, HAPPY DAY

Go NOT, happy day,
  From the shining fields,
Go not, happy day,
  Till the maiden yields.
Rosy is the West,
  Rosy is the South,
Roses are her cheeks,
  And a rose her mouth.
When the happy Yes
  Falters from her lips,
Pass and blush the news
  Over glowing ships;
Over blowing seas,
  Over seas at rest,
Pass the happy news,
  Blush it thro' the West;
Till the red man dance
  By his red cedar-tree,
And the red man's babe
  Leap, beyond the sea.
Blush from West to East,
  Blush from East to West,
Till the West is East,
  Blush it thro' the West.
Rosy is the West,
  Rosy is the South,
Roses are her cheeks,
  And a rose her mouth.

### I HAVE LED HER HOME

#### I

I HAVE led her home, my love, my only friend.
There is none like her, none.
And never yet so warmly ran my blood
And sweetly, on and on
Calming itself to the long-wish'd-for end,
Full to the banks, close on the promised good.

#### II

None like her, none.
Just now the dry-tongued laurels' pattering talk
Seem'd her light foot along the garden walk,
And shook my heart to think she comes once more;
But even then I heard her close the door,
The gates of Heaven are closed, and she is gone.

#### III

There is none like her, none.
Nor will be when our summers have deceased.
O, art thou sighing for Lebanon
In the long breeze that streams to thy delicious East,
Sighing for Lebanon,
Dark cedar, tho' thy limbs have here increased,
Upon a pastoral slope as fair,
And looking to the South, and fed
With honey'd rain and delicate air,
And haunted by the starry head
Of her whose gentle will has changed my fate,
And made my life a perfumed altar-flame;
And over whom thy darkness must have spread

With such delight as theirs of old, thy great
Forefathers of the thornless garden, there
Shadowing the snow-limb'd Eve from whom she came.

### IV

Here will I lie, while these long branches sway,
And you fair stars that crown a happy day
Go in and out as if at merry play,
Who am no more so all forlorn,
As when it seem'd far better to be born
To labour and the mattock-harden'd hand,
Than nursed at ease and brought to understand
A sad astrology, the boundless plan
That makes you tyrants in your iron skies,
Innumerable, pitiless, passionless eyes,
Cold fires, yet with power to burn and brand
His nothingness into man.

### V

But now shine on, and what care I,
Who in this stormy gulf have found a pearl
The countercharm of space and hollow sky,
And do accept my madness, and would die
To save from some slight shame one simple girl.

### VI

Would die; for sullen-seeming Death may give
More life to Love than is or ever was
In our low world, where yet 'tis sweet to live.
Let no one ask me how it came to pass;
It seems that I am happy, that to me

A livelier emerald twinkles in the grass,
A purer sapphire melts into the sea.


VII


Not die; but live a life of truest breath,
And teach true life to fight with mortal wrongs.
O, why should Love, like men in drinking-songs,
Spice his fair banquet with the dust of death?
Make answer, Maud my bliss,
Maud made my Maud by that long loving kiss,
Life of my life, wilt thou not answer this?
"The dusky strand of Death inwoven here
With dear Love's tie, makes Love himself more dear."


VIII


Is that enchanted moan only the swell
Of the long waves that roll in yonder bay?
And hark the clock within, the silver knell
Of twelve sweet hours that past in bridal white,
And died to live, long as my pulses play;
But now by this my love has closed her sight
And given false death her hand, and stol'n away
To dreamful wastes where footless fancies dwell
Among the fragments of the golden day.
May nothing there her maiden grace affright!
Dear heart, I feel with thee the drowsy spell.
My bride to be, my evermore delight,
My own heart's heart, my ownest own, farewell;
It is but for a little space I go:
And ye meanwhile far over moor and fell
Beat to the noiseless music of the night!
Has our whole earth gone nearer to the glow
Of your soft splendours that you look so bright?

*I* have climb'd nearer out of lonely Hell.
Beat, happy stars, timing with things below,
Beat with my heart more blest than heart can tell,
Blest, but for some dark undercurrent woe
That seems to draw—but it shall not be so:
Let all be well, be well.

## COME INTO THE GARDEN, MAUD

### I

COME into the garden, Maud,
  For the black bat, night, has flown,
Come into the garden, Maud,
  I am here at the gate alone;
And the woodbine spices are wafted abroad,
  And the musk of the rose is blown.

### II

For a breeze of morning moves,
  And the planet of Love is on high,
Beginning to faint in the light that she loves
  On a bed of daffodil sky,
To faint in the light of the sun she loves,
  To faint in his light, and to die.

### III

All night have the roses heard
  The flute, violin, bassoon;
All night has the casement jessamine stirr'd
  To the dancers dancing in tune;
Till a silence fell with the waking bird,
  And a hush with the setting moon.

### IV

I said to the lily, "There is but one
   With whom she has heart to be gay.
When will the dancers leave her alone?
   She is weary of dance and play."
Now half to the setting moon are gone,
   And half to the rising day;
Low on the sand and loud on the stone
   The last wheel echoes away.

### V

I said to the rose, "The brief night goes
   In babble and revel and wine.
O young lord-lover, what sighs are those,
   For one that will never be thine?
But mine, but mine," so I sware to the rose,
   "For ever and ever, mine."

### VI

And the soul of the rose went into my blood,
   As the music clash'd in the hall;
And long by the garden lake I stood,
   For I heard your rivulet fall
From the lake to the meadow and on to the wood,
   Our wood, that is dearer than all;

### VII

From the meadow your walks have left so sweet
   That whenever a March-wind sighs

He sets the jewel-print of your feet
  In violets blue as your eyes,
To the woody hollows in which we meet
  And the valleys of Paradise.

### VIII

The slender acacia would not shake
  One long milk-bloom on the tree;
The white lake-blossom fell into the lake
  As the pimpernel dozed on the lea;
But the rose was awake all night for your sake,
  Knowing your promise to me;
The lilies and roses were all awake,
  They sigh'd for the dawn and thee.

### IX

Queen rose of the rosebud garden of girls,
  Come hither, the dances are done,
In gloss of satin and glimmer of pearls,
  Queen lily and rose in one;
Shine out, little head, sunning over with curls,
  To the flowers, and be their sun.

### X

There has fallen a splendid tear
  From the passion-flower at the gate.
She is coming, my dove, my dear;
  She is coming, my life, my fate;
The red rose cries, "She is near, she is near;"
  And the white rose weeps, "She is late;"
The larkspur listens, "I hear, I hear;"
  And the lily whispers, "I wait."

### XI

She is coming, my own, my sweet;
　Were it ever so airy a tread,
My heart would hear her and beat,
　Were it earth in an earthy bed;
My dust would hear her and beat,
　Had I lain for a century dead;
Would start and tremble under her feet,
　And blossom in purple and red.

#### SEE WHAT A LOVELY SHELL

### I

See what a lovely shell,
Small and pure as a pearl,
Lying close to my foot,
Frail, but a work divine,
Made so fairily well
With delicate spire and whorl,
How exquisitely minute,
A miracle of design!

### II

What is it? a learned man
Could give it a clumsy name.
Let him name it who can,
The beauty would be the same.

### III

The tiny cell is forlorn,
Void of the little living will

That made it stir on the shore.
Did he stand at the diamond door
Of his house in a rainbow frill?
Did he push, when he was uncurl'd,
A golden foot or a fairy horn
Thro' his dim water-world?

IV

Slight, to be crush'd with a tap
Of my finger-nail on the sand,
Small, but a work divine,
Frail, but of force to withstand,
Year upon year, the shock
Of cataract seas that snap
The three-decker's oaken spine
Athwart the ledges of rock,
Here on the Breton strand.

### DEAD, LONG DEAD

I

DEAD, long dead,
Long dead!
And my heart is a handful of dust,
And the wheels go over my head,
And my bones are shaken with pain,
For into a shallow grave they are thrust,
Only a yard beneath the street,
And the hoofs of the horses beat, beat,
The hoofs of the horses beat,
Beat into my scalp and my brain,
With never an end to the stream of passing feet,
Driving, hurrying, marrying, burying,

Clamour and rumble, and ringing and clatter,
And here beneath it is all as bad,
For I thought the dead had peace, but it is not so;
To have no peace in the grave, is that not sad?
But up and down and to and fro,
Ever about me the dead men go;
And then to hear a dead man chatter
Is enough to drive one mad.

1855

## TITHONUS

THE woods decay, the woods decay and fall,
The vapours weep their burthen to the ground.
Man comes and tills the field and lies beneath,
And after many a summer dies the swan.
Me only cruel immortality
Consumes: I wither slowly in thine arms,
Here at the quiet limit of the world,
A white-hair'd shadow roaming like a dream
The ever-silent spaces of the East,
Far-folded mists, and gleaming halls of morn.

Alas! for this gray shadow, once a man—
So glorious in his beauty and thy choice,
Who madest him thy chosen, that he seem'd
To his great heart none other than a God!
I ask'd thee, "Give me immortality."
Then didst thou grant mine asking with a smile,
Like wealthy men who care not how they give.
But thy strong Hours indignant work'd their wills,
And beat me down and marr'd and wasted me,
And tho' they could not end me, left me maim'd
To dwell in presence of immortal youth,

Immortal age beside immortal youth,
And all I was, in ashes. Can thy love,
Thy beauty, make amends, tho' even now,
Close over us, the silver star, thy guide,
Shines in those tremulous eyes that fill with tears
To hear me? Let me go: take back thy gift:
Why should a man desire in any way
To vary from the kindly race of men,
Or pass beyond the goal of ordinance
Where all should pause, as is most meet for all?

A soft air fans the cloud apart; there comes
A glimpse of that dark world where I was born.
Once more the old mysterious glimmer steals
From thy pure brows, and from thy shoulders pure,
And bosom beating with a heart renew'd.
Thy cheek begins to redden thro' the gloom,
Thy sweet eyes brighten slowly close to mine,
Ere yet they blind the stars, and the wild team
Which love thee, yearning for thy yoke, arise,
And shake the darkness from their loosen'd manes,
And beat the twilight into flakes of fire.

Lo! ever thus thou growest beautiful
In silence, then before thine answer given
Departest, and thy tears are on my cheek.

Why wilt thou ever scare me with thy tears,
And make me tremble lest a saying learnt,
In days far-off, on that dark earth, be true?
"The Gods themselves cannot recall their gifts."

Ay me! ay me! with what another heart
In days far-off, and with what other eyes

I used to watch—if I be he that watch'd—
The lucid outline forming round thee; saw
The dim curls kindle into sunny rings;
Changed with thy mystic change, and felt my blood
Glow with the glow that slowly crimson'd all
Thy presence and thy portals, while I lay,
Mouth, forehead, eyelids, growing dewy-warm
With kisses balmier than half-opening buds
Of April, and could hear the lips that kiss'd
Whispering I knew not what of wild and sweet,
Like that strange song I heard Apollo sing,
While Ilion like a mist rose into towers.

Yet hold me not for ever in thine East:
How can my nature longer mix with thine?
Coldly thy rosy shadows bathe me, cold
Are all thy lights, and cold my wrinkled feet
Upon thy glimmering thresholds, when the steam
Floats up from those dim fields about the homes
Of happy men that have the power to die,
And grassy barrows of the happier dead.
Release me, and restore me to the ground;
Thou seëst all things, thou wilt see my grave:
Thou wilt renew thy beauty morn by morn;
I earth in earth forget these empty courts,
And thee returning on thy silver wheels.

1860


## THE HIGHER PANTHEISM

The sun, the moon, the stars, the seas, the hills, and the
        plains—
Are not these, O Soul, the Vision of Him who reigns?

Is not the Vision He? tho' He be not that which He
    seems?
Dreams are true while they last, and do we not live in
    dreams?

Earth, these solid stars, this weight of body and limb,
Are they not sign and symbol of thy division from Him?

Dark is the world to thee: thyself art the reason why;
For is He not all but thou, that hast power to feel "I
    am I"?

Glory about thee, without thee; and thou fulfillest thy
    doom
Making Him broken gleams, and a stifled splendour and
    gloom.

Speak to Him thou for He hears, and Spirit with Spirit
    can meet—
Closer is He than breathing, and nearer than hands and
    feet.

God is law, say the wise; O Soul, and let us rejoice,
For if He thunder by law the thunder is yet His voice.

Law is God, say some: no God at all, says the fool;
For all we have power to see is a straight staff bent in a
    pool;

And the ear of man cannot hear, and the eye of man
    cannot see;
But if we could see and hear, this Vision—were it not
    He?

1869

## FLOWER IN THE CRANNIED WALL

FLOWER in the crannied wall,
I pluck you out of the crannies,
I hold you here, root and all, in my hand,
Little flower—but *if* I could understand
What you are, root and all, and all in all,
I should know what God and man is.

                                1869

## THE REVENGE

### A BALLAD OF THE FLEET

I

AT FLORES in the Azores Sir Richard Grenville lay,
And a pinnace, like a flutter'd bird, came flying from far
        away:
"Spanish ships of war at sea! we have sighted fifty-
        three!"
Then sware Lord Thomas Howard: "'Fore God I am
        no coward;
But I cannot meet them here, for my ships are out of
        gear,
And the half my men are sick. I must fly, but follow
        quick.
We are six ships of the line; can we fight with fifty-
        three?"

II

Then spake Sir Richard Grenville: "I know you are no
        coward;

You fly them for a moment to fight with them again.
But I've ninety men and more that are lying sick ashore.
I should count myself the coward if I left them, my Lord
      Howard,
To these Inquisition dogs and the devildoms of Spain."

### III

So Lord Howard past away with five ships of war that
      day,
Till he melted like a cloud in the silent summer heaven;
But Sir Richard bore in hand all his sick men from the
      land
Very carefully and slow,
Men of Bideford in Devon,
And we laid them on the ballast down below;
For we brought them all aboard,
And they blest him in their pain, that they were not left
      to Spain,
To the thumbscrew and the stake, for the glory of the
      Lord.

### IV

He had only a hundred seamen to work the ship and to
      fight,
And he sailed away from Flores till the Spaniard came
      in sight,
With his huge sea-castles heaving upon the weather bow.
"Shall we fight or shall we fly?
Good Sir Richard, tell us now,
For to fight is but to die!
There'll be little of us left by the time this sun be set."
And Sir Richard said again: "We be all good English
      men.

Let us bang these dogs of Seville, the children of the
　　　devil,
For I never turn'd my back upon Don or devil yet."

### V

Sir Richard spoke and he laugh'd, and we roar'd a
　　　hurrah, and so
The little Revenge ran on sheer into the heart of the foe,
With her hundred fighters on deck, and her ninety sick
　　　below;
For half of their fleet to the right and half to the left
　　　were seen,
And the little Revenge ran on thro' the long sea-lane
　　　between.

### VI

Thousands of their soldiers look'd down from their decks
　　　and laugh'd,
Thousands of their seamen made mock at the mad little
　　　craft
Running on and on, till delay'd
By their mountain-like San Philip that, of fifteen hun-
　　　dred tons,
And up-shadowing high above us with her yawning tiers
　　　of guns,
Took the breath from our sails, and we stay'd.

### VII

And while now the great San Philip hung above us like
　　　a cloud
Whence the thunderbolt will fall

Long and loud,
Four galleons drew away
From the Spanish fleet that day,
And two upon the larboard and two upon the starboard
    lay,
And the battle-thunder broke from them all.

### VIII

But anon the great San Philip, she bethought herself and
    went
Having that within her womb that had left her ill
    content;
And the rest they came aboard us, and they fought us
    hand to hand,
For a dozen times they came with their pikes and
    musqueteers,
And a dozen times we shook 'em off as a dog that shakes
    his ears
When he leaps from the water to the land.

### IX

And the sun went down, and the stars came out far over
    the summer sea,
But never a moment ceased the fight of the one and the
    fifty-three.
Ship after ship, the whole night long, their high-built
    galleons came,
Ship after ship, the whole night long, with her battle-
    thunder and flame;
Ship after ship, the whole night long, drew back with
    her dead and her shame.

For some were sunk and many were shatter'd, and so
    could fight us no more—
God of battles, was ever a battle like this in the world
    before?

### X

For he said "Fight on! fight on!"
Tho' his vessel was all but a wreck;
And it chanced that, when half of the short summer night
    was gone,
With a grisly wound to be drest he had left the deck,
But a bullet struck him that was dressing it suddenly
    dead,
And himself he was wounded again in the side and the
    head,
And he said "Fight on! fight on!"

### XI

And the night went down, and the sun smiled out far
    over the summer sea,
And the Spanish fleet with broken sides lay round us all
    in a ring;
But they dared not touch us again, for they fear'd that
    we still could sting,
So they watch'd what the end would be.
And we had not fought them in vain,
But in perilous plight were we,
Seeing forty of our poor hundred were slain,
And half of the rest of us maim'd for life
In the crash of the cannonades and the desperate strife;
And the sick men down in the hold were most of them
    stark and cold,

And the pikes were all broken or bent, and the powder
       was all of it spent;
And the masts and the rigging were lying over the side;
But Sir Richard cried in his English pride,
"We have fought such a fight for a day and a night
As may never be fought again!
We have won great glory, my men!
And a day less or more
At sea or ashore,
We die—does it matter when?
Sink me the ship, Master Gunner—sink her, split her in
       twain!
Fall into the hands of God, not into the hands of Spain!"

XII

And the gunner said "Ay, ay," but the seamen made
       reply:
"We have children, we have wives,
And the Lord hath spared our lives.
We will make the Spaniard promise, if we yield, to let
       us go;
We shall live to fight again and to strike another blow."
And the lion there lay dying, and they yielded to the
       foe.

XIII

And the stately Spanish men to their flagship bore him
       then,
Where they laid him by the mast, old Sir Richard caught
       at last,

And they praised him to his face with their courtly for-
eign grace;
But he rose upon their decks, and he cried:
"I have fought for Queen and Faith like a valiant man
and true;
I have only done my duty as a man is bound to do:
With a joyful spirit I Sir Richard Grenville die!"
And he fell upon their decks, and he died.


### XIV


And they stared at the dead that had been so valiant
and true,
And had holden the power and glory of Spain so cheap
That he dared her with one little ship and his English
few;
Was he devil or man? He was devil for aught they
knew,
But they sank his body with honour down into the deep,
And they mann'd the Revenge with a swarthier alien
crew,
And away she sail'd with her loss and long'd for her
own;
When a wind from the lands they had ruin'd awoke from
sleep,
And the water began to heave and the weather to moan,
And or ever that evening ended a great gale blew,
And a wave like the wave that is raised by an earthquake
grew,
Till it smote on their hulls and their sails and their masts
and their flags,
And the whole sea plunged and fell on the shot-shatter'd
navy of Spain,

And the little Revenge herself went down by the island
      crags
To be lost evermore in the main.

                           1878

## DE PROFUNDIS:

### THE TWO GREETINGS

### I

Out of the deep, my child, out of the deep,
Where all that was to be, in all that was,
Whirl'd for a million æons thro' the vast
Waste dawn of multitudinous-eddying light—
Out of the deep, my child, out of the deep,
Thro' all this changing world of changeless law,
And every phase of ever-heightening life,
And nine long months of antenatal gloom,
With this last moon, this crescent—her dark orb
Touch'd with earth's light—thou comest, darling boy;
Our own; a babe in lineament and limb
Perfect, and prophet of the perfect man;
Whose face and form are hers and mine in one,
Indissolubly married like our love;
Live, and be happy in thyself, and serve
This mortal race thy kin so well, that men
May bless thee as we bless thee, O young life
Breaking with laughter from the dark; and may
The fated channel where thy motion lives
Be prosperously shaped, and sway thy course
Along the years of haste and random youth
Unshatter'd; then full-current thro' full man;
And last in kindly curves, with gentlest fall,

By quiet fields, a slowly-dying power,
To that last deep where we and thou are still.

## II

### I

Out of the deep, my child, out of the deep,
From that great deep, before our world begins,
Whereon the Spirit of God moves as he will—
Out of the deep, my child, out of the deep,
From that true world within the world we see,
Whereof our world is but the bounding shore—
Out of the deep, Spirit, out of the deep,
With this ninth moon, that sends the hidden sun
Down yon dark sea, thou comest, darling boy.

### II

For in the world, which is not ours, They said
"Let us make man" and that which should be man,
From that one light no man can look upon,
Drew to this shore lit by the suns and moons
And all the shadows. O dear Spirit half-lost
In thine own shadow and this fleshly sign
That thou art thou—who wailest being born
And banish'd into mystery, and the pain
Of this divisible-indivisible world
Among the numerable-innumerable
Sun, sun, and sun, thro' finite-infinite space
In finite-infinite Time—our mortal veil
And shatter'd phantom of that infinite One,

Who made thee unconceivably Thyself
Out of His whole World-self and all in all—

Live thou! and of the grain and husk, the grape
And ivyberry, choose; and still depart
From death to death thro' life and life, and find
Nearer and ever nearer Him, who wrought
Not Matter, nor the finite-infinite,
But this main-miracle, that thou art thou,
With power on thine own act and on the world.

                                        1880


### THE HUMAN CRY

#### I

HALLOWED be Thy name—Halleluiah!—
    Infinite Ideality!
    Immeasurable Reality!
    Infinite Personality!
Hallowed be Thy name—Halleluiah!


#### II

We feel we are nothing—for all is Thou and in Thee;
We feel we are something—that also has come from
        Thee;
We know we are nothing—but Thou wilt help us to be.
Hallowed be Thy name—Halleluiah!

                                        1880


## MERLIN AND THE GLEAM

#### I

    O YOUNG Mariner,
    You from the haven
    Under the sea-cliff,

You that are watching
The gray Magician
With eyes of wonder,
*I* am Merlin,
And *I* am dying,
*I* am Merlin
Who follow The Gleam.

## II

Mighty the Wizard
Who found me at sunrise
Sleeping, and woke me
And learn'd me Magic!
Great the Master,
And sweet the Magic,
When over the valley,
In early summers,
Over the mountain,
On human faces,
And all around me,
Moving to melody,
Floated The Gleam.

## III

Once at the croak of a Raven
      who crost it,
A barbarous people,
Blind to the magic,
And deaf to the melody,
Snarl'd at and cursed me.
A demon vext me,
The light retreated,
The landskip darken'd,

The melody deaden'd,
The Master whisper'd,
"Follow The Gleam."

IV

Then to the melody,
Over a wilderness
Gliding, and glancing at
Elf of the woodland,
Gnome of the cavern,
Griffin and Giant,
And dancing of Fairies
In desolate hollows,
And wraiths of the mountain,
And rolling of dragons
By warble of water,
Or cataract music
Of falling torrents,
Flitted The Gleam.

V

Down from the mountain
And over the level,
And streaming and shining on
Silent river,
Silvery willow,
Pasture and plowland,
Horses and oxen,
Innocent maidens,
Garrulous children,
Homestead and harvest,
Reaper and gleaner,
And rough-ruddy faces

Of lowly labour,
Slided The Gleam.—

VI

Then, with a melody
Stronger and statelier,
Led me at length
To the city and palace
Of Arthur the king;
Touch'd at the golden
Cross of the churches,
Flash'd on the Tournament,
Flicker'd and bicker'd
From helmet to helmet,
And last on the forehead
Of Arthur the blameless
Rested The Gleam.

VII

Clouds and darkness
Closed upon Camelot;
Arthur had vanish'd
I knew not whither,
The king who loved me,
And cannot die;
For out of the darkness
Silent and slowly
The Gleam, that had waned to a
          wintery glimmer
On icy fallow
And faded forest,
Drew to the valley
Named of the shadow,

And slowly brightening
Out of the glimmer,
And slowly moving again to a
     melody
Yearningly tender,
Fell on the shadow,
No longer a shadow,
But clothed with The Gleam.

### VIII

And broader and brighter
The Gleam flying onward,
Wed to the melody,
Sang thro' the world;
And slower and fainter,
Old and weary,
But eager to follow,
I saw, whenever
In passing it glanced upon
Hamlet or city,
That under the Crosses
The dead man's garden,
The mortal hillock,
Would break into blossom;
And so to the land's
Last limit I came ——
And can no longer.
But die rejoicing,
For thro' the Magic
Of Him the Mighty,
Who taught me in childhood,
There on the border
Of boundless Ocean,

And all but in Heaven
Hovers The Gleam.

### IX

Not of the sunlight,
Not of the moonlight,
Not of the starlight!
O young Mariner,
Down to the haven,
Call your companions,
Launch your vessel,
And crowd your canvas,
And, ere it vanishes
Over the margin,
After it, follow it,
Follow The Gleam.

1889

## BY AN EVOLUTIONIST

THE Lord let the house of a brute to the soul of a man,
  And the man said "Am I your debtor?"
And the Lord—"Not yet: but make it as clean as you
      can,
  And then I will let you a better."

### I

If my body come from brutes, my soul uncertain, or a
      fable,
  Why not bask amid the senses while the sun of morn-
      ing shines,
I, the finer brute rejoicing in my hounds, and in my
      stable,

Youth and Health, and birth and wealth, and choice
of women and of wines?

II

What hast thou done for me, grim Old Age, save breaking my bones on the rack?
Would I had past in the morning that looks so bright
from afar!

OLD AGE

Done for thee? starved the wild beast that was linkt
with thee eighty years back.
Less weight now for the ladder-of-heaven that hangs
on a star.

I

If my body come from brutes, tho' somewhat finer than
their own,
I am heir, and this my kingdom. Shall the royal
voice be mute?
No, but if the rebel subject seek to drag me from the
throne,
Hold the sceptre, Human Soul, and rule thy Province
of the brute.

II

I have climb'd to the snows of Age, and I gaze at a field
in the Past,
Where I sank with the body at times in the sloughs
of a low desire,

But I hear no yelp of the beast, and the Man is quiet
    at last
 As he stands on the heights of his life with a glimpse
    of a height that is higher.

1889

## CROSSING THE BAR

SUNSET and evening star,
    And one clear call for me!
And may there be no moaning of the bar,
    When I put out to sea,

But such a tide as moving seems asleep,
    Too full for sound and foam,
When that which drew from out the boundless deep
    Turns again home.

Twilight and evening bell,
    And after that the dark!
And may there be no sadness of farewell,
    When I embark;

For tho' from out our bourne of Time and Place
    The flood may bear me far,
I hope to see my Pilot face to face
    When I have crost the bar.

1889

## ROBERT BROWNING (1812-1889)

### PORPHYRIA'S LOVER

THE rain set early in to-night,
    The sullen wind was soon awake,

It tore the elm-tops down for spite,
    And did its worst to vex the lake:
I listened with heart fit to break.
When glided in Porphyria; straight
    She shut the cold out and the storm,
And kneeled and made the cheerless grate
    Blaze up, and all the cottage warm;
Which done, she rose, and from her form
Withdrew the dripping cloak and shawl,
    And laid her soiled gloves by, untied
Her hat and let the damp hair fall,
    And, last, she sat down by my side
And called me. When no voice replied,
She put my arm about her waist,
    And made her smooth white shoulder bare,
And all her yellow hair displaced,
    And, stooping, made my cheek lie there,
And spread, o'er all, her yellow hair,
Murmuring how she loved me—she
    Too weak, for all her heart's endeavor,
To set its struggling passion free
    From pride, and vainer ties dissever,
And give herself to me forever.
But passion sometimes would prevail,
    Nor could to-night's gay feast restrain
A sudden thought of one so pale
    For love of her, and all in vain:
So, she was come through wind and rain.
Be sure I looked up at her eyes
    Happy and proud; at last I knew
Porphyria worshipped me; surprise
    Made my heart swell, and still it grew
While I debated what to do.
That moment she was mine, mine, fair,
    Perfectly pure and good: I found

A thing to do, and all her hair
　In one long yellow string I wound
Three times her little throat around,
And strangled her. No pain felt she;
　I am quite sure she felt no pain.
As a shut bud that holds a bee,
　I warily oped her lids: again
Laughed the blue eyes without a stain.
And I untightened next the tress
　About her neck; her cheek once more
Blushed bright beneath my burning kiss:
　I propped her head up as before,
Only, this time my shoulder bore
Her head, which droops upon it still:
　The smiling rosy little head,
So glad it has its utmost will,
　That all it scorned at once is fled,
And I, its love, am gained instead!
Porphyria's love: she guessed not how
　Her darling one wish would be heard.
And thus we sit together now,
　And all night long we have not stirred,
And yet God has not said a word!

1836

## PIPPA'S SONG

The year's at the spring
And day's at the morn;
Morning's at seven;
The hill-side's dew-pearled;
The lark's on the wing;
The snail's on the thorn:

> God's in his heaven—
> All's right with the world!

**1841**

## MARCHING ALONG

KENTISH Sir Byng stood for his king,
Bidding the crop-headed Parliament swing:
And, pressing a troop unable to stoop
And see the rogues flourish and honest folk droop,
Marched them along, fifty-score strong,
Great-hearted gentlemen, singing this song.

God for King Charles! Pym and such carles
To the Devil that prompts 'em their treasonous parles!
Cavaliers, up! Lips from the cup,
Hands from the pasty, nor bite take nor sup
Till you're—
   Chorus.—Marching along, fifty-score strong,
      Great-hearted gentlemen, singing this song.

Hampden to hell, and his obsequies' knell
Serve Hazelrig, Fiennes, and young Harry as well!
England, good cheer! Rupert is near!
Kentish and loyalists, keep we not here
   Chorus.—Marching along, fifty-score strong,
      Great-hearted gentlemen, singing this song!

Then, God for King Charles! Pym and his snarls
To the Devil that pricks on such pestilent carles!
Hold by the right, you double your might;
So, onward to Nottingham, fresh for the fight,
   Chorus.—March we along, fifty-score strong,
      Great-hearted gentlemen, singing this song!

**1842**

## INCIDENT OF THE FRENCH CAMP

You know, we French stormed Ratisbon:
  A mile or so away,
On a little mound, Napoleon
  Stood on our storming-day;
With neck out-thrust, you fancy how,
  Legs wide, arms locked behind,
As if to balance the prone brow
  Oppressive with its mind.

Just as perhaps he mused "My plans
  That soar, to earth may fall,
Let once my army-leader Lannes
  Waver at yonder wall,"—
Out 'twixt the battery-smokes there flew
  A rider, bound on bound
Full-galloping; nor bridle drew
  Until he reached the mound.

Then off there flung in smiling joy,
  And held himself erect
By just his horse's mane, a boy:
  You hardly could suspect—
(So tight he kept his lips compressed,
  Scarce any blood came through)
You looked twice ere you saw his breast
  Was all but shot in two.

"Well," cried he, "Emperor, by God's grace
  We've got you Ratisbon!
The Marshal's in the market-place,
  And you'll be there anon

To see your flag-bird flap his vans
  Where I, to heart's desire,
Perched him!" The chief's eye flashed; his plans
  Soared up again like fire.
The chief's eye flashed; but presently
  Softened itself, as sheathes
A film the mother-eagle's eye
  When her bruised eaglet breathes;
"You're wounded!" "Nay," the soldier's pride
  Touched to the quick, he said:
"I'm killed, Sire!" And his chief beside,
  Smiling the boy fell dead.

1842

## SOLILOQUY OF THE SPANISH CLOISTER

Gr-r-r—there go, my heart's abhorrence!
  Water your damned flower-pots, do!
If hate killed men, Brother Lawrence,
  God's blood, would not mine kill you!
What? your myrtle-bush wants trimming?
  Oh, that rose has prior claims—
Needs its leaden vase filled brimming?
  Hell dry you up with its flames!

At the meal we sit together:
  *Salve tibi!* I must hear
Wise talk of the kind of weather,
  Sort of season, time of year:
*Not a plenteous cork-crop: scarcely*
  *Dare we hope oak-galls, I doubt:*
*What's the Latin name for "parsley"?*
  What's the Greek name for Swine's Snout?

Whew! We'll have our platter burnished,
   Laid with care on our own shelf!
With a fire-new spoon we're furnished,
   And a goblet for ourself,
Rinsed like something sacrificial
   Ere 'tis fit to touch our chaps—
Marked with L for our initial!
   (He-he! There his lily snaps!)

*Saint,* forsooth! While brown Dolores
   Squats outside the Convent bank
With Sanchicha, telling stories,
   Steeping tresses in the tank,
Blue-black, lustrous, thick like horse-hairs,
   —Can't I see his dead eye glow,
Bright as 'twere a Barbary corsair's?
   (That is, if he'd let it show!)

When he finishes refection,
   Knife and fork he never lays
Cross-wise, to my recollection,
   As do I, in Jesu's praise.
I the Trinity illustrate,
   Drinking watered orange-pulp—
In three sips the Arian frustrate;
   While he drains his at one gulp.

Oh, those melons! If he's able
   We're to have a feast! so nice!
One goes to the Abbot's table,
   All of us get each a slice.
How go on your flowers? None double?
   Not one fruit-sort can you spy?
Strange!—And I, too, at such trouble
   Keep them close-nipped on the sly!

There's a great text in Galatians,
    Once you trip on it, entails
Twenty-nine distinct damnations,
    One sure, if another fails:
If I trip him just a-dying,
    Sure of heaven as sure can be,
Spin him round and send him flying
    Off to hell, a Manichee?

Or, my scrofulous French novel
    On gray paper with blunt type!
Simply glance at it, you grovel
    Hand and foot in Belial's gripe:
If I double down its pages
    At the woeful sixteenth print,
When he gathers his greengages,
    Ope a sieve and slip it in't?

Or, there's Satan!—one might venture
    Pledge one's soul to him, yet leave
Such a flaw in the indenture
    As he'd miss till, past retrieve,
Blasted lay that rose-acacia
    We're so proud of! *Hy, Zy, Hine* . . .
'St, there's Vespers! *Plena gratiâ,*
    *Ave, Virgo!* Gr-r-r—you swine!

                                    **1842**

## MY LAST DUCHESS

THAT's my last Duchess painted on the wall,
Looking as if she were alive. I call
That piece a wonder, now; Frà Pandolf's hands
Worked busily a day, and there she stands.
Will't please you sit and look at her? I said

"Frà Pandolf" by design, for never read
Strangers like you that pictured countenance,
The depth and passion of its earnest glance,
But to myself they turned (since none puts by
The curtain I have drawn for you, but I)
And seemed as they would ask me, if they durst,
How such a glance came there; so, not the first
Are you to turn and ask thus. Sir, 't was not
Her husband's presence only, called that spot
Of joy into the Duchess' cheek: perhaps
Frà Pandolf chanced to say, "Her mantel laps
Over my lady's wrist too much," or "Paint
Must never hope to reproduce the faint
Half-flush that dies along her throat:" such stuff
Was courtesy, she thought, and cause enough
For calling up that spot of joy. She had
A heart—how shall I say?—too soon made glad,
Too easily impressed; she liked whate'er
She looked on, and her looks went everywhere.
Sir, 't was all one! My favour at her breast,
The dropping of the daylight in the West,
The bough of cherries some officious fool
Broke in the orchard for her, the white mule
She rode with round the terrace—all and each
Would draw from her alike the approving speech,
Or blush, at least. She thanked men,—good! but
        thanked
Somehow—I know not how—as if she ranked
My gift of a nine-hundred-years-old name
With anybody's gift. Who'd stoop to blame
This sort of trifling? Even had you skill
In speech—(which I have not)—to make your will
Quite clear to such an one, and say, "Just this
Or that in you disgusts me; here you miss,
Or there exceed the mark"—and if she let

Herself be lessoned so, nor plainly set
Her wits to yours, forsooth, and made excuse,
—E'en then would be some stooping; and I choose
Never to stoop. Oh sir, she smiled, no doubt,
Whene'er I passed her; but who passed without
Much the same smile? This grew; I gave commands:
Then all smiles stopped together. There she stands
As if alive. Will 't please you rise? We'll meet
The company below, then. I repeat,
The Count your master's known munificence
Is ample warrant that no just pretence
Of mine for dowry will be disallowed;
Though his fair daughter's self, as I avowed
At starting, is my object. Nay, we'll go
Together down, sir. Notice Neptune, though,
Taming a sea-horse, thought a rarity,
Which Claus of Innsbruck cast in bronze for me!

1842

## THE LOST LEADER

### I

Just for a handful of silver he left us,
    Just for a riband to stick in his coat—
Found the one gift of which fortune bereft us,
    Lost all the others she lets us devote;
They, with the gold to give, doled him out silver,
    So much was theirs who so little allowed:
How all our copper had gone for his service!
    Rags—were they purple, his heart had been proud!
We that had loved him so, followed him, honoured him,
    Lived in his mild and magnificent eye,
Learned his great language, caught his clear accents,
    Made him our pattern to live and to die!

Shakespeare was of us, Milton was for us,
  Burns, Shelley, were with us,—they watch from their
      graves!
He alone breaks from the van and the freemen,
  —He alone sinks to the rear and the slaves!

## II

We shall march prospering,—not thro' his presence;
  Songs may inspirit us,—not from his lyre;
Deeds will be done,—while he boasts his quiescence,
  Still bidding crouch whom the rest bade aspire:
Blot out his name, then, record one lost soul more,
  One task more declined, one more footpath untrod,
One more devils'-triumph and sorrow for angels,
  One wrong more to man, one more insult to God!
Life's night begins: let him never come back to us!
  There would be doubt, hesitation and pain,
Forced praise on our part—the glimmer of twilight,
  Never glad confident morning again!
Best fight on well, for we taught him—strike gallantly,
  Menace our heart ere we master his own;
Then let him receive the new knowledge and wait us,
  Pardoned in Heaven, the first by the throne!

                                                1845

## HOME-THOUGHTS, FROM ABROAD

OH, TO be in England
Now that April's there,
And whoever wakes in England
Sees, some morning, unaware,
That the lowest boughs and the brush-wood sheaf
Round the elm-tree bole are in tiny leaf,

While the chaffinch sings on the orchard bough
In England—now!

And after April, when May follows,
And the whitethroat builds, and all the swallows!
Hark, where my blossomed pear-tree in the hedge
Leans to the field and scatters on the clover
Blossoms and dewdrops—at the bent spray's edge—
That's the wise thrush; he sings each song twice over,
Lest you should think he never could recapture
The first fine careless rapture!
And though the fields look rough with hoary dew,
All will be gay when noontide wakes anew
The buttercups, the little children's dower
—Far brighter than this gaudy melon-flower!

1845

## THE BISHOP ORDERS HIS TOMB AT SAINT PRAXED'S CHURCH

### ROME, 15—

VANITY, saith the preacher, vanity!
Draw round my bed: is Anselm keeping back?
Nephews—sons mine . . . ah God, I know not! Well——
She, men would have to be your mother once,
Old Gandolf envied me, so fair she was!
What's done is done, and she is dead beside,
Dead long ago, and I am Bishop since,
And as she died so must we die ourselves,
And thence ye may perceive the world's a dream.
Life, how and what is it? As here I lie
In this state-chamber, dying by degrees,
Hours and long hours in the dead night, I ask
"Do I live, am I dead?" Peace, peace seems all.

Saint Praxed's ever was the church for peace;
And so, about this tomb of mine.  I fought
With tooth and nail to save my niche, ye know:
—Old Gandolf cozened me, despite my care;
Shrewd was that snatch from out the corner South
He graced his carrion with, God curse the same!
Yet still my niche is not so cramped but thence
One sees the pulpit o' the epistle-side,
And somewhat of the choir, those silent seats,
And up into the aery dome where live
The angels, and a sunbeam's sure to lurk:
And I shall fill my slab of basalt there,
And 'neath my tabernacle take my rest,
With those nine columns round me, two and two,
The odd one at my feet where Anselm stands:
Peach-blossom marble all, the rare, the ripe
As fresh-poured red wine of a mighty pulse.
—Old Gandolf with his paltry onion-stone,
Put me where I may look at him! True peach,
Rosy and flawless: how I earned the prize!
Draw close: that conflagration of my church
—What then? So much was saved if aught were missed!
My sons, ye would not be my death? Go dig
The white-grape vineyard where the oil-press stood,
Drop water gently till the surface sink,
And if ye find . . . Ah God, I know not, I! . . .
Bedded in store of rotten fig-leaves soft,
And corded up in a tight olive-frail,
Some lump, ah God, of *lapis lazuli,*
Big as a Jew's head cut off at the nape,
Blue as a vein o'er the Madonna's breast . . .
Sons, all have I bequeathed you, villas, all,
That brave Frascati villa with its bath,
So, let the blue lump poise between my knees,
Like God the Father's globe on both his hands

Ye worship in the Jesu Church so gay,
For Gandolf shall not choose but see and burst!
Swift as a weaver's shuttle fleet our years:
Man goeth to the grave, and where is he?
Did I say basalt for my slab, sons? Black—
'Twas ever antique-black I meant! How else
Shall ye contrast my frieze to come beneath?
The bas-relief in bronze ye promised me,
Those Pans and Nymphs ye wot of, and perchance
Some tripod, thyrsus, with a vase or so,
The Saviour at his sermon on the mount,
Saint Praxed in a glory, and one Pan
Ready to twitch the Nymph's last garment off,
And Moses with the tables . . . but I know
Ye mark me not! What do they whisper thee,
Child of my bowels, Anselm? Ah, ye hope
To revel down my villas while I gasp
Bricked o'er with beggar's mouldy travertine
Which Gandolf from his tomb-top chuckles at!
Nay, boys, ye love me—all of jasper, then!
'Tis jasper ye stand pledged to, lest I grieve
My bath must needs be left behind, alas!
One block, pure green as a pistachio-nut,
There's plenty jasper somewhere in the world—
And have I not Saint Praxed's ear to pray
Horses for ye, and brown Greek manuscripts,
And mistresses with great smooth marbly limbs?
—That's if ye carve my epitaph aright,
Choice Latin, picked phrase, Tully's every word,
No gaudy ware like Gandolf's second line—
Tully, my masters? Ulpian serves his need!
And then how I shall lie through centuries,
And hear the blessed mutter of the mass,
And see God made and eaten all day long,
And feel the steady candle-flame, and taste

Good strong thick stupefying incense-smoke!
For as I lie here, hours of the dead night,
Dying in state and by such slow degrees,
I fold my arms as if they clasped a crook,
And stretch my feet forth straight as stone can point,
And let the bedclothes, for a mortcloth, drop
Into great laps and folds of sculptor's-work:
And as yon tapers dwindle, and strange thoughts
Grow, with a certain humming in my ears,
About the life before I lived this life,
And this life too, popes, cardinals and priests,
Saint Praxed at his sermon on the mount,
Your tall pale mother with her talking eyes,
And new-found agate urns as fresh as day,
And marble's language, Latin pure, discreet,
—Aha, ELUCESCEBAT quoth our friend?
No Tully, said I, Ulpian at the best!
Evil and brief hath been my pilgrimage.
All *lapis,* all, sons! Else I give the Pope
My villas! Will ye ever eat my heart?
Ever your eyes were as a lizard's quick,
They glitter like your mother's for my soul,
Or ye would heighten my impoverished frieze,
Piece out its starved design, and fill my vase
With grapes, and add a vizor and a Term,
And to the tripod ye would tie a lynx
That in his struggle throws the thyrsus down,
To comfort me on my entablature
Whereon I am to lie till I must ask
"Do I live, am I dead?" There, leave me, there!
For ye have stabbed me with ingratitude
To death—ye wish it—God, ye wish it! Stone—
Gritstone, a-crumble! Clammy squares which sweat
As if the corpse they keep were oozing through—
And no more *lapis* to delight the world!

Well, go! I bless ye. Fewer tapers there,
But in a row: and, going, turn your backs
—Ay, like departing altar-ministrants,
And leave me in my church, the church for peace,
That I may watch at leisure if he leers—
Old Gandolf—at me, from his onion-stone,
As still he envied me, so fair she was!

1845

## MEETING AT NIGHT

THE gray sea and the long black land;
And the yellow half-moon large and low;
And the startled little waves that leap
In fiery ringlets from their sleep,
As I gain the cove with pushing prow,
And quench its speed i' the slushy sand.

Then a mile of warm sea-scented beach;
Three fields to cross till a farm appears;
A tap at the pane, the quick sharp scratch
And blue spurt of a lighted match,
And a voice less loud, through its joys and fears.
Than the two hearts beating each to each!

1845

## PARTING AT MORNING

ROUND the cape of a sudden came the sea,
And the sun looked over the mountain's rim:
And straight was a path of gold for him,
And the need of a world of men for me.

1845

## MEMORABILIA

AH, DID you once see Shelley plain,
  And did he stop and speak to you
And did you speak to him again?
  How strange it seems and new!

But you were living before that,
  And also you are living after;
And the memory I started at—
  My starting moves your laughter!

I crossed a moor, with a name of its own
  And a certain use in the world no doubt,
Yet a hand's-breadth of it shines alone
  'Mid the blank miles round about:

For there I picked up on the heather
  And there I put inside my breast
A moulted feather, an eagle-feather!
  Well, I forget the rest.

1855

## ONE WORD MORE

### TO E. B. B.

### I

THERE they are, my fifty men and women
Naming me the fifty poems finished!
Take them, Love, the book and me together:
Where the heart lies, let the brain lie also.

## II

Rafael made a century of sonnets,
Made and wrote them in a certain volume
Dinted with the silver-pointed pencil
Else he only used to draw Madonnas:
These, the world might view—but one, the volume.
Who that one, you ask? Your heart instructs you.
Did she live and love it all her lifetime?
Did she drop, his lady of the sonnets,
Die, and let it drop beside her pillow
Where it lay in place of Rafael's glory,
Rafael's cheek so duteous and so loving—
Cheek, the world was wont to hail a painter's,
Rafael's cheek, her love had turned a poet's?

## III

You and I would rather read that volume,
(Taken to his beating bosom by it)
Lean and list the bosom-beats of Rafael,
Would we not? than wonder at Madonnas—
Her, San Sisto names, and Her, Foligno,
Her, that visits Florence in a vision,
Her, that's left with lilies in the Louvre—
Seen by us and all the world in circle.

## IV

You and I will never read that volume.
Guido Reni, like his own eye's apple
Guarded long the treasure-book and loved it.
Guido Reni dying, all Bologna

Cried, and the world cried too, "Ours, the treasure!"
Suddenly, as rare things will, it vanished.

### v

Dante once prepared to paint an angel:
Whom to please? You whisper "Beatrice."
While he mused and traced it and retraced it,
(Peradventure with a pen corroded
Still by drops of that hot ink he dipped for,
When, his left hand i' the hair o' the wicked,
Back he held the brow and pricked its stigma,
Bit into the live man's flesh for parchment,
Loosed him, laughed to see the writing rankle,
Let the wretch go festering through Florence)—
Dante, who loved well because he hated,
Hated wickedness that hinders loving,
Dante standing, studying his angel,—
In there broke the folk of his Inferno.
Says he—"Certain people of importance"
(Such he gave his daily dreadful line to)
"Entered and would seize, forsooth, the poet."
Says the poet—"Then I stopped my painting."

### vi

You and I would rather see that angel,
Painted by the tenderness of Dante,
Would we not?—than read a fresh Inferno.

### vii

You and I will never see that picture.
While he mused on love and Beatrice,
While he softened o'er his outlined angel,

In they broke, those "people of importance":
We and Bice bear the loss forever.

VIII

What of Rafael's sonnets, Dante's picture?
This: no artist lives and loves, that longs not
Once, and only once, and for one only,
(Ah, the prize!) to find his love a language
Fit and fair and simple and sufficient—
Using nature that's an art to others,
Not, this one time, art that's turned his nature.
Ay, of all the artists living, loving,
None but would forego his proper dowry,—
Does he paint? he fain would write a poem,—
Does he write? he fain would paint a picture,
Put to proof art alien to the artist's,
Once, and only once, and for one only,
So to be the man and leave the artist,
Gain the man's joy, miss the artist's sorrow.

IX

Wherefore? Heaven's gift takes earth's abatement!
He who smites the rock and spreads the water,
Bidding drink and live a crowd beneath him,
Even he, the minute makes immortal,
Proves, perchance, but mortal in the minute,
Desecrates, belike, the deed in doing.
While he smites, how can he but remember,
So he smote before, in such a peril,
When they stood and mocked—"Shall smiting help us?"
When they drank and sneered—"A stroke is easy!"
When they wiped their mouths and went their journey,
Throwing him for thanks—"But drought was pleasant."

Thus old memories mar the actual triumph;
Thus the doing savors of disrelish;
Thus achievement lacks a gracious somewhat;
O'er-importuned brows becloud the mandate,
Carelessness or consciousness—the gesture.
For he bears an ancient wrong about him,
Sees and knows again those phalanxed faces,
Hears, yet one time more, the 'customed prelude—
"How shouldst thou, of all men, smite, and save us?"
Guesses what is like to prove the sequel—
"Egypt's flesh-pots—nay, the drought was better."

x

Oh, the crowd must have emphatic warrant!
Theirs, the Sinai-forehead's cloven brilliance,
Right-arm's rod-sweep, tongue's imperial fiat.
Never dares the man put off the prophet.

xi

Did he love one face from out the thousands,
(Were she Jethro's daughter, white and wifely,
Were she but the Æthiopian bondslave,)
He would envy yon dumb patient camel,
Keeping a reserve of scanty water
Meant to save his own life in the desert;
Ready in the desert to deliver
(Kneeling down to let his breast be opened)
Hoard and life together for his mistress.

xii

I shall never, in the years remaining,
Paint you pictures, no, nor carve you statues,

Make you music that should all-express me;
So it seems: I stand on my attainment.
This of verse alone, one life allows me;
Verse and nothing else have I to give you.
Other heights in other lives, God willing:
All the gifts from all the heights, your own, Love!

XIII

Yet a semblance of resource avails us—
Shade so finely touched, love's sense must seize it.
Take these lines, look lovingly and nearly,
Lines I write the first time and the last time.
He who works in fresco, steals a hair-brush,
Curbs the liberal hand, subservient proudly,
Cramps his spirit, crowds its all in little,
Makes a strange art of an art familiar,
Fills his lady's missal-marge with flowerets.
He who blows through bronze, may breathe through
      silver,
Fitly serenade a slumbrous princess.
He who writes, may write for once as I do.

XIV

Love, you saw me gather men and women,
Live or dead or fashioned by my fancy,
Enter each and all, and use their service,
Speak from every mouth,—the speech, a poem.
Hardly shall I tell my joys and sorrows,
Hopes and fears, belief and disbelieving:
I am mine and yours—the rest be all men's,
Karshish, Cleon, Norbert, and the fifty.
Let me speak this once in my true person,
Not as Lippo, Roland, or Andrea,

Though the fruit of speech be just this sentence:
Pray you, look on these my men and women,
Take and keep my fifty poems finished;
Where my heart lies, let my brain lie also!
Poor the speech; be how I speak, for all things.

### xv

Not but that you know me! Lo, the moon's self!
Here in London, yonder late in Florence,
Still we find her face, the thrice-transfigured.
Curving on a sky imbrued with color,
Drifted over Fiesole by twilight,
Came she, our new crescent of a hair's-breadth.
Full she flared it, lamping Samminiato,
Rounder 'twixt the cypresses and rounder,
Perfect till the nightingales applauded.
Now, a piece of her old self, impoverished,
Hard to greet, she traverses the house-roofs,
Hurries with unhandsome thrift of silver,
Goes dispiritedly, glad to finish.

### xvi

What, there's nothing in the moon noteworthy?
Nay: for if that moon could love a mortal,
Use, to charm him (so to fit a fancy),
All her magic ('tis the old sweet mythos),
She would turn a new side to her mortal,
Side unseen of herdsman, huntsman, steersman—
Blank to Zoroaster on his terrace,
Blind to Galileo on his turret,
Dumb to Homer, dumb to Keats—him, even!
Think, the wonder of the moonstruck mortal—
When she turns round, comes again in heaven,
Opens out anew for worse or better!

Proves she like some portent of an iceberg
Swimming full upon the ship it founders,
Hungry with huge teeth of splintered crystals?
Proves she as the paved work of a sapphire
Seen by Moses when he climbed the mountain?
Moses, Aaron, Nadab and Abihu
Climbed and saw the very God, the Highest,
Stand upon the paved work of a sapphire.
Like the bodied heaven in his clearness
Shone the stone, the sapphire of that paved work,
When they ate and drank and saw God also!

XVII

What were seen? None knows, none ever shall know.
Only this is sure—the sight were other,
Not the moon's same side, born late in Florence
Dying now impoverished here in London.
God be thanked, the meanest of his creatures
Boasts two soul-sides, one to face the world with,
One to show a woman when he loves her!

XVIII

This I say of me, but think of you, Love!
This to you—yourself my moon of poets!
Ah, but that's the world's side, there's the wonder,
Thus, they see you, praise you, think they know you!
There, in turn I stand with them and praise you—
Out of my own self, I dare to phrase it.
But the best is when I glide from out them,
Cross a step or two of dubious twilight,
Come out on the other side, the novel
Silent silver lights and darks undreamed of,
Where I hush and bless myself with silence.

XIX

Oh, their Rafael of the dear Madonnas,
Oh, their Dante of the dread Inferno,
Wrote one song—and in my brain I sing it,
Drew one angel—borne, see, on my bosom!

R. B.          1855

## MY STAR

ALL that I know
   Of a certain star
Is, it can throw
   (Like the angled spar)
Now a dart of red,
   Now a dart of blue;
Till my friends have said
   They would fain see, too,
My star that dartles the red and the blue!
Then it stops like a bird; like a flower, hangs furled:
   They must solace themselves with the Saturn above it.
What matter to me if their star is a world?
   Mine has opened its soul to me; therefore I love it.

1855

## THE LAST RIDE TOGETHER

I SAID—Then, dearest, since 't is so,
Since now at length my fate I know,
Since nothing all my love avails,
Since all, my life seemed meant for, fails,
   Since this was written and needs must be—
My whole heart rises up to bless
Your name in pride and thankfulness!

Take back the hope you gave,—I claim
Only a memory of the same,
—And this beside, if you will not blame,
   Your leave for one more last ride with me.

My mistress bent that brow of hers;
Those deep dark eyes where pride demurs
When pity would be softening through,
Fixed me a breathing-while or two
   With life or death in the balance: right!
The blood replenished me again;
My last thought was at least not vain:
I and my mistress, side by side
Shall be together, breathe and ride,
So, one day more am I deified.
   Who knows but the world may end to-night?

Hush! if you saw some western cloud
All billowy-bosomed, over-bowed
By many benedictions—sun's
And moon's and evening-star's at once—
   And so, you, looking and loving best,
Conscious grew, your passion drew
Cloud, sunset, moonrise, star-shine too,
Down on you, near and yet more near,
Till flesh must fade for heaven was here!—
Thus leant she and lingered—joy and fear!
   Thus lay she a moment on my breast

Then we began to ride. My soul
Smoothed itself out, a long-cramped scroll
Freshening and fluttering in the wind.
Past hopes already lay behind.
   What need to strive with a life awry?
Had I said that, had I done this,

So might I gain, so might I miss.
Might she have loved me? just as well
She might have hated, who can tell!
Where had I been now if the worst befell?
  And here we are riding, she and I.

Fail I alone, in words and deeds?
Why, all men strive, and who succeeds?
We rode; it seemed my spirit flew,
Saw other regions, cities new,
  As the world rushed by on either side.
I thought,—All labor, yet no less
Bear up beneath their unsuccess.
Look at the end of work, contrast
The petty done, the undone vast,
This present of theirs with the hopeful past!
  I hoped she would love me; here we ride.

What hand and brain went ever paired?
What heart alike conceived and dared?
What act proved all its thought had been?
What will but felt the fleshly screen?
  We ride and I see her bosom heave.
There's many a crown for who can reach.
Ten lines, a statesman's life in each!
The flag stuck on a heap of bones,
A soldier's doing! what atones?
They scratch his name on the Abbey-stones.
  My riding is better, by their leave.

What does it all mean, poet? Well,
Your brains beat into rhythm, you tell
What we felt only; you expressed
You hold things beautiful the best,
  And place them in rhyme so, side by side.

'T is something, nay 't is  much: but then,
Have you yourself what's best for men?
Are you—poor, sick, old ere your time—
Nearer one whit your own sublime
Than we who never have turned a rhyme?
   Sing, riding's a joy! For me, I ride.

And you, great sculptor—so, you gave
A score of years to Art, her slave,
And that's your Venus, whence we turn
To yonder girl that fords the burn!
   You acquiesce, and shall I repine?
What, man of music, you grown gray
With notes and nothing else to say,
Is this your sole praise from a friend,
"Greatly his opera's strains intend,
But in music we know how fashions end!"
   I gave my youth; but we ride, in fine.

Who knows what's fit for us? Had fate
Proposed bliss here should sublimate
My being—had I signed the bond—
Still one must lead some life beyond,
   Have a bliss to die with, dim-descried.
This foot once planted on the goal,
This glory-garland round my soul,
Could I descry such? Try and test!
I sink back shuddering from the quest.
Earth being so good, would heaven seem best?
   Now, heaven and she are beyond this ride.

And yet—she has not spoke so long!
What if heaven be that, fair and strong
At life's best, with our eyes upturned

Whither life's flower is first discerned,
  We, fixed so, ever should so abide?
What if we still ride on, we two,
With life forever old yet new,
Changed not in kind but in degree,
The instant made eternity,—
And heaven just prove that I and she
  Ride, ride together, forever ride?

1855

## A GRAMMARIAN'S FUNERAL

SHORTLY AFTER THE REVIVAL OF LEARNING IN EUROPE

LET us begin and carry up this corpse,
  Singing together.
Leave we the common crofts, the vulgar thorpes
  Each in its tether
Sleeping safe on the bosom of the plain,
  Cared-for till cock-crow:
Look out if yonder be not day again
  Rimming the rock-row!
That's the appropriate country; there, man's thought,
  Rarer, intenser,
Self-gathered for an outbreak, as it ought,
  Chafes in the censer.
Leave we the unlettered plain its herd and crop;
  Seek we sepulture
On a tall mountain, cited to the top,
  Crowded with culture!
All the peaks soar, but one the rest excels;
  Clouds overcome it;
No! yonder sparkle is the citadel's
  Circling its summit.

Thither our path lies; wind we up the heights;
    Wait ye the warning?
Our low life was the level's and the night's;
    He's for the morning.
Step to a tune, square chests, erect each head,
    'Ware the beholders!
This is our master, famous calm and dead,
    Borne on our shoulders.

Sleep, crop and herd! sleep, darkling thorpe and croft,
    Safe from the weather!
He, whom we convoy to his grave aloft,
    Singing together,
He was a man born with thy face and throat,
    Lyric Apollo!
Long he lived nameless: how should spring take note
    Winter would follow?
Till lo, the little touch, and youth was gone!
    Cramped and diminished,
Moaned he, "New measures, other feet anon!
    My dance is finished?"
No, that's the world's way: (keep the mountain-side,
    Make for the city!)
He knew the signal, and stepped on with pride
    Over men's pity;
Left play for work, and grappled with the world
    Bent on escaping:
"What's in the scroll," quoth he, "thou keepest furled?
    Show me their shaping,
Theirs who most studied man, the bard and sage,—
    Give!"—So, he gowned him,
Straight got by heart that book to its last page:
    Learned, we found him.
Yea, but we found him bald too—eyes like lead,
    Accents uncertain:

"Time to taste life," another would have said,
    "Up with the curtain!"
This man said rather, "Actual life comes next?
    Patience a moment!
Grant I have mastered learning's crabbed text,
    Still, there's the comment.
Let me know all! Prate not of most or least,
    Painful or easy!
Even to the crumbs I'd fain eat up the feast,
    Ay, nor feel queasy."
Oh, such a life as he resolved to live,
    When he had learned it,
When he had gathered all books had to give!
    Sooner, he spurned it.
Image the whole, then execute the parts—
    Fancy the fabric
Quite, ere you build, ere steel strike fire from quartz,
    Ere mortar dab brick!

(Here's the town-gate reached: there's the market-place
    Gaping before us.)
Yea, this in him was the peculiar grace
    (Hearten our chorus!)
That before living he'd learn how to live—
    No end to learning:
Earn the means first—God surely will contrive
    Use for our earning.
Others mistrust and say, "But time escapes:
    Live now or never!"
He said, "What's time? leave Now for dogs and apes!
    Man has Forever."
Back to his book then: deeper drooped his head:
    *Calculus* racked him:
Leaden before, his eyes grew dross of lead:
    *Tussis* attacked him.

"Now, Master, take a little rest!"—not he!
    (Caution redoubled,
Step two abreast, the way winds narrowly!)
    Not a whit troubled,
Back to his studies, fresher than at first,
    Fierce as a dragon
He (soul-hydroptic with a sacred thirst)
    Sucked at the flagon.
Oh, if we draw a circle premature,
    Heedless of far gain,
Greedy for quick returns of profit, sure
    Bad is our bargain!
Was it not great? did not he throw on God,
    (He loves the burthen)—
God's task to make the heavenly period
    Perfect the earthen?
Did not he magnify the mind, show clear
    Just what it all meant?
He would not discount life, as fools do here,
    Paid by instalment.
He ventured neck or nothing—heaven's success
    Found, or earth's failure:
"Wilt thou trust death or not?" He answered "Yes:
    Hence with life's pale lure!"
That low man seeks a little thing to do,
    Sees it and does it:
This high man, with a great thing to pursue,
    Dies ere he knows it.
That low man goes on adding one to one,
    His hundred's soon hit:
This high man, aiming at a million,
    Misses an unit.
That, has the world here—should he need the next,
    Let the world mind him!

This, throws himself on God, and unperplexed
    Seeking shall find him.
So, with the throttling hands of death at strife,
    Ground he at grammar;
Still, thro' the rattle, parts of speech were rife:
    While he could stammer
He settled *Hoti's* business—let it be!—
    Properly based *Oun*—
Gave us the doctrine of the enclitic *De,*
    Dead from the waist down.
Well, here's the platform, here's the proper place:
    Hail to your purlieus,
All ye highfliers of the feathered race,
    Swallows and curlews!
Here's the top-peak; the multitude below
    Live, for they can, there:
This man decided not to Live but Know—
    Bury this man there?
Here—here's his place, where meteors shoot, clouds
  form,
    Lightnings are loosened.
Stars come and go! let joy break with the storm,
    Peace let the dew send!
Lofty designs must close in like effects:
    Loftily lying,
Leave him—still loftier than the world suspects,
    Living and dying.

                    1855

## A WOMAN'S LAST WORD

LET's contend no more, Love,
    Strive nor weep:
All be as before, Love,
    —Only sleep!

What so wild as words are?
  I and thou
In debate, as birds are,
  Hawk on bough!

See the creature stalking
  While we speak!
Hush and hide the talking,
  Cheek on cheek!

What so false as truth is,
  False to thee?
Where the serpent's tooth is
  Shun the tree—

Where the apple reddens
  Never pry—
Lest we lose our Edens,
  Eve and I.

Be a god and hold me
  With a charm!
Be a man and fold me
  With thine arm!

Teach me, only teach, Love!
  As I ought
I will speak thy speech, Love,
  Think thy thought—

Meet, if thou require it,
  Both demands,
Laying flesh and spirit
  In thy hands.

That shall be to-morrow,
　　Not to-night:
I must bury sorrow
　　Out of sight:

—Must a little weep, Love,
　　(Foolish me!)
And so fall asleep, Love,
　　Loved by thee.

1855

## LOVE AMONG THE RUINS

Where the quiet-colored end of evening smiles
　　Miles and miles
On the solitary pastures where our sheep
　　Half-asleep
Tinkle homeward through the twilight, stray or stop
　　As they crop—
Was the site once of a city great and gay,
　　(So they say)
Of our country's very capital, its prince
　　Ages since
Held his court in, gathered councils, wielding far
　　Peace or war.

Now,—the country does not even boast a tree,
　　As you see,
To distinguish slopes of verdure, certain rills
　　From the hills
Intersect and give a name to, (else they run
　　Into one)
Where the domed and daring palace shot its spires
　　Up like fires

O'er the hundred-gated circuit of a wall
  Bounding all,
Made of marble, men might march on nor be pressed,
  Twelve abreast.

And such plenty and perfection, see, of grass
  Never was!
Such a carpet as, this summer-time, o'erspreads
  And embeds
Every vestige of the city, guessed alone,
  Stock or stone—
Where a multitude of men breathed joy and woe
  Long ago;
Lust of glory pricked their hearts up, dread of shame
  Struck them tame;
And that glory and that shame alike, the gold
  Bought and sold.

Now,—the single little turret that remains
  On the plains,
By the caper overrooted, by the gourd
  Overscored,
While the patching houseleek's head of blossom winks
  Through the chinks—
Marks the basement whence a tower in ancient time
  Sprang sublime,
And a burning ring, all round, the chariots traced
  As they raced,
And the monarch and his minions and his dames
  Viewed the games.

And I know, while thus the quiet-colored eve
  Smiles to leave

To their folding, all our many-tinkling fleece
    In such peace,
And the slopes and rills in undistinguished gray
    Melt away—
That a girl with eager eyes and yellow hair
    Waits me there
In the turret whence the charioteers caught soul
    For the goal,
When the king looked, where she looks now, breathless,
  dumb
    Till I come.

But he looked upon the city, every side,
    Far and wide,
All the mountains topped with temples, all the glades'
    Colonnades,
All the causeys, bridges, aqueducts,—and then,
    All the men!
When I do come, she will speak not, she will stand,
    Either hand
On my shoulder, give her eyes the first embrace
    Of my face,
Ere we rush, ere we extinguish sight and speech
    Each on each.

In one year they sent a million fighters forth
    South and North,
And they built their gods a brazen pillar high
    As the sky,
Yet reserved a thousand chariots in full force—
    Gold, of course.
Oh heart! oh blood that freezes, blood that burns!
    Earth's returns
For whole centuries of folly, noise and sin!
    Shut them in,

With their triumphs and their glories and the rest!
    Love is best.

1855

## FRA LIPPO LIPPI

I am poor brother Lippo, by your leave!
You need not clap your torches to my face,
Zooks, what's to blame? you think you see a monk!
What, 'tis past midnight, and you go the rounds,
And here you catch me at an alley's end
Where sportive ladies leave their doors ajar?
The Carmine's my cloister: hunt it up,
Do,—harry out, if you must show your zeal,
Whatever rat, there, haps on his wrong hole,
And nip each softling of a wee white mouse,
*Weke, weke,* that's crept to keep him company!
Aha, you know your betters! Then, you'll take
Your hand away that's fiddling on my throat,
And please to know me likewise. Who am I?
Why, one, sir, who is lodging with a friend
Three streets off—he's a certain . . . how d'ye call?
Master—a . . . Cosimo of the Medici,
I' the house that caps the corner. Boh! you were best!
Remember and tell me, the day you're hanged,
How you affected such a gullet's-gripe!
But you, sir, it concerns you that your knaves
Pick up a manner nor discredit you:
Zooks, are we pilchards, that they sweep the streets
And count fair prize what comes into their net?
He's Judas to a tittle, that man is!
Just such a face! Why, sir, you make amends.
Lord, I'm not angry! Bid your hangdogs go
Drink out this quarter-florin to the health
Of the munificent House that harbors me

(And many more beside, lads! more beside!)
And all's come square again. I'd like his face—
His, elbowing on his comrade in the door
With the pike and lantern,—for the slave that holds
John Baptist's head a-dangle by the hair
With one hand ("Look you, now," as who should say)
And his weapon in the other, yet unwiped!
It's not your chance to have a bit of chalk,
A wood-coal or the like? or you should see!
Yes, I'm the painter, since you style me so.
What, brother Lippo's doings, up and down,
You know them and they take you? like enough!
I saw the proper twinkle in your eye—
'Tell you, I liked your looks at very first.
Let's sit and set things straight now, hip to haunch.
Here's spring come, and the nights one makes up bands
To roam the town and sing out carnival,
And I've been three weeks shut within my mew,
A-painting for the great man, saints and saints
And saints again. I could not paint all night—
Ouf! I leaned out of window for fresh air.
There came a hurry of feet and little feet,
A sweep of lute-strings, laughs, and whifts of song,—
*Flower o' the broom,*
*Take away love, and our earth is a tomb!*
*Flower o' the quince,*
*I let Lisa go, and what good in life since?*
*Flower o' the thyme*—and so on. Round they went.
Scarce had they turned the corner when a titter
Like the skipping of rabbits by moonlight,—three slim
          shapes,
And a face that looked up . . . Zooks, sir, flesh and
          blood,
That's all I'm made of! Into shreds it went,
Curtain and counterpane and coverlet,

All the bed-furniture—a dozen knots,
There was a ladder! Down I let myself,
Hands and feet, scrambling somehow, and so dropped,
And after them. I came up with the fun
Hard by Saint Laurence, hail fellow, well met,—
*Flower o' the rose,*
*If I've been merry, what matter who knows?*
And so as I was stealing back again
To get to bed and have a bit of sleep
Ere I rise up to-morrow and go work
On Jerome knocking at his poor old breast
With his great round stone to subdue the flesh,
You snap me of the sudden. Ah, I see!
Though your eye twinkles still, you shake your head—
Mine's shaved—a monk, you say—the sting's in that!
If Master Cosimo announced himself,
Mum's the word naturally; but a monk!
Come, what am I a beast for? tell us, now!
I was a baby when my mother died
And father died and left me in the street.
I starved there, God knows how, a year or two
On fig-skins, melon-parings, rinds and shucks,
Refuse and rubbish. One fine frosty day,
My stomach being empty as your hat,
The wind doubled me up and down I went.
Old Aunt Lapaccia trussed me with one hand,
(Its fellow was a stinger as I knew)
And so along the wall, over the bridge,
By the straight cut to the convent. Six words there,
While I stood munching my first bread that month:
"So, boy, you're minded," quoth the good fat father,
Wiping his own mouth, 'twas refection-time,—
"To quit this very miserable world?
Will you renounce" . . . "the mouthful of bread?"
        thought I;

By no means! Brief, they made a monk of me;
I did renounce the world, its pride and greed,
Palace, farm, villa, shop, and banking-house,
Trash, such as these poor devils of Medici
Have given their hearts to—all at eight years old.
Well, sir, I found in time, you may be sure,
'Twas not for nothing—the good bellyful,
The warm serge and the rope that goes all round,
And day-long blessed idleness beside!
"Let's see what the urchin's fit for"—that came next.
Not overmuch their way, I must confess.
Such a to-do! They tried me with their books;
Lord, they'd have taught me Latin in pure waste!
*Flower o' the clove,*
*All the Latin I construe is "amo," I love!*
But, mind you, when a boy starves in the streets
Eight years together, as my fortune was,
Watching folk's faces to know who will fling
The bit of half-stripped grape-bunch he desires,
And who will curse or kick him for his pains,—
Which gentleman processional and fine,
Holding a candle to the Sacrament,
Will wink and let him lift a plate and catch
The droppings of the wax to sell again,
Or holla for the Eight and have him whipped,—
How say I?—nay, which dog bites, which lets drop
His bone from the heap of offal in the street,—
Why, soul and sense of him grow sharp alike,
He learns the look of things, and none the less
For admonition from the hunger-pinch.
I had a store of such remarks, be sure,
Which, after I found leisure, turned to use.
I drew men's faces on my copy-books,
Scrawled them within the antiphonary's marge,
Joined legs and arms to the long music-notes,

Found eyes and nose and chin for A's and B's,
And made a string of pictures of the world
Betwixt the ins and outs of verb and noun,
On the wall, the bench, the door. The monks looked
    black.
"Nay," quoth the Prior, "turn him out, d'ye say?
In no wise. Lose a crow and catch a lark.
What if at last we get our man of parts,
We Carmelites, like those Camaldolese
And preaching Friars, to do our church up fine
And put the front on it that ought to be!"
And hereupon he bade me daub away.
Thank you! my head being crammed, the walls a blank,
Never was such prompt disemburdening.
First, every sort of monk, the black and white,
I drew them, fat and lean: then, folk at church,
From good old gossips waiting to confess
Their cribs of barrel-droppings, candle-ends,—
To the breathless fellow at the altar-foot,
Fresh from his murder, safe and sitting there
With the little children round him in a row
Of admiration, half for his beard and half
For that white anger of his victim's son
Shaking a fist at him with one fierce arm,
Signing himself with the other because of Christ
(Whose sad face on the cross sees only this
After the passion of a thousand years)
Till some poor girl, her apron o'er her head,
(Which the intense eyes looked through) came at eve
On tiptoe, said a word, dropped in a loaf,
Her pair of earrings and a bunch of flowers
(The brute took growling), prayed, and so was gone.
I painted all, then cried " 'Tis ask and have;
Choose, for more's ready!"—laid the latter flat,
And showed my covered bit of cloister-wall.

The monks closed in a circle and praised loud
Till checked, taught what to see and not to see,
Being simple bodies,—"That's the very man!
Look at the boy who stoops to pat the dog!
That woman's like the Prior's niece who comes
To care about his asthma: it's the life!"
But there my triumph's straw-fire flared and funked;
Their betters took their turn to see and say:
The Prior and the learned pulled a face
And stopped all that in no time. "How? what's here?
Quite from the mark of painting, bless us all!
Faces, arms, legs, and bodies like the true
As much as pea and pea! it's devil's-game!
Your business is not to catch men with show,
With homage to the perishable clay,
But lift them over it, ignore it all,
Make them forget there's such a thing as flesh.
Your business is to paint the souls of men—
Man's soul, and it's a fire, smoke . . . no, it's not . . .
It's vapor done up like a new-born babe—
(In that shape when you die it leaves your mouth)
It's . . . well, what matters talking, it's the soul!
Give us no more of body than shows soul!
Here's Giotto, with his Saint a-praising God,
That sets us praising,—why not stop with him?
Why put all thoughts of praise out of our head
With wonder at lines, colors, and what not?
Paint the soul, never mind the legs and arms!
Rub all out, try at it a second time.
Oh, that white smallish female with the breasts,
She's just my niece . . . Herodias, I would say,—
Who went and danced and got men's heads cut off!
Have it all out!" Now, is this sense, I ask?
A fine way to paint soul, by painting body
So ill, the eye can't stop there, must go further

And can't fare worse! Thus, yellow does for white
When what you put for yellow's simply black,
And any sort of meaning looks intense
When all beside itself means and looks naught.
Why can't a painter lift each foot in turn,
Left foot and right foot, go a double step,
Make his flesh liker and his soul more like,
Both in their order? Take the prettiest face,
The Prior's niece . . . patron-saint—is it so pretty
You can't discover if it means hope, fear,
Sorrow or joy? won't beauty go with these?
Suppose I've made her eyes all right and blue,
Can't I take breath and try to add life's flash,
And then add soul and heighten them threefold?
Or say there's beauty with no soul at all—
(I never saw it—put the case the same—)
If you get simple beauty and naught else,
You get about the best thing God invents:
That's somewhat: and you'll find the soul you have
    missed,
Within yourself, when you return him thanks.
"Rub all out!" Well, well, there's my life, in short
And so the thing has gone on ever since.
I'm grown a man no doubt, I've broken bounds:
You should not take a fellow eight years old
And make him swear to never kiss the girls.
I'm my own master, paint now as I please—
Having a friend, you see, in the Corner-house!
Lord, it's fast holding by the rings in front—
Those great rings serve more purposes than just
To plant a flag in, or tie up a horse!
And yet the old schooling sticks, the old grave eyes
Are peeping o'er my shoulder as I work,
The heads shake still—"It's art's decline, my son!
You're not of the true painters, great and old;

Brother Angelico's the man, you'll find;
Brother Lorenzo stands his single peer:
Fag on a flesh, you'll never make the third!"
*Flower o' the pine,*
*You keep your mistr . . . manners, and I'll stick to*
          *mine!*
I'm not the third, then: bless us, they must know!
Don't you think they're the likeliest to know,
They with their Latin? So, I swallow my rage,
Clench my teeth, suck my lips in tight, and paint
To please them—sometimes do and sometimes don't;
For, doing most, there's pretty sure to come
A turn, some warm eve finds me at my saints—
A laugh, a cry, the business of the world—
(*Flower o' the peach,*
*Death for us all, and his own life for each!*)
And my whole soul revolves, the cup runs over,
The world and life's too big to pass for a dream,
And I do these wild things in sheer despite,
And play the fooleries you catch me at,
In pure rage! The old mill-horse, out at grass
After hard years, throws up his stiff heels so,
Although the miller does not preach to him
The only good of grass is to make chaff.
What would men have? Do they like grass or no—
May they or may n't they? All I want's the thing
Settled forever one way. As it is,
You tell too many lies and hurt yourself:
You don't like what you only like too much,
You do like what, if given you at your word,
You find abundantly detestable.
For me, I think I speak as I was taught;
I always see the garden and God there
A-making man's wife: and, my lesson learned,

The value and significance of flesh,
I can't unlearn ten minutes afterwards.

You understand me: I'm a beast, I know.
But see, now—why, I see as certainly
As that the morning-star's about to shine,
What will hap some day. We've a youngster here
Comes to our convent, studies what I do,
Slouches and stares and lets no atom drop:
His name is Guidi—he'll not mind the monks—
They call him Hulking Tom, he lets them talk—
He picks my practice up—he'll paint apace,
I hope so—though I never live so long,
I know what's sure to follow. You be judge!
You speak no Latin more than I, belike;
However, you're my man, you've seen the world
—The beauty and the wonder and the power,
The shapes of things, their colors, lights and shades,
Changes, surprises,—and God made it all!
—For what? Do you feel thankful, ay or no,
For this fair town's face, yonder river's line,
The mountain round it and the sky above,
Much more the figures of man, woman, child,
These are the frame to? What's it all about?
To be passed over, despised? or dwelt upon,
Wondered at? oh, this last of course!—you say.
But why not do as well as say,—paint these
Just as they are, careless what comes of it?
God's works—paint any one, and count it crime
To let a truth slip. Don't object, "His works
Are here already; nature is complete:
Suppose you reproduce her—(which you can't)
There's no advantage! you must beat her, then."
For, don't you mark? we're made so that we love
First when we see them painted, things we have passed

Perhaps a hundred times nor cared to see;
And so they are better, painted—better to us,
Which is the same thing. Art was given for that;
God uses us to help each other so,
Lending our minds out. Have you noticed, now,
Your cullion's hanging face? A bit of chalk,
And trust me but you should, though! How much more,
If I drew higher things with the same truth!
That were to take the Prior's pulpit-place,
Interpret God to all of you! Oh, oh,
It makes me mad to see what men shall do
And we in our graves! This world's no blot for us,
Nor blank; it means intensely, and means good:
To find its meaning is my meat and drink.
"Ay, but you don't so instigate to prayer!"
Strikes in the Prior: "when your meaning's plain
It does not say to folk—remember matins,
Or, mind you fast next Friday!" Why, for this
What need of art at all? A skull and bones,
Two bits of stick nailed crosswise, or, what's best,
A bell to chime the hour with, does as well.
I painted a Saint Laurence six months since
At Prato, splashed the fresco in fine style:
"How looks my painting, now the scaffold's down?"
I ask a brother: "Hugely," he returns—
"Already not one phiz of your three slaves
Who turn the Deacon off his toasted side,
But's scratched and prodded to our heart's content,
The pious people have so eased their own
With coming to say prayers there in a rage:
We get on fast to see the bricks beneath.
Expect another job this time next year,
For pity and religion grow i' the crowd—
Your painting serves its purpose!" Hang the fools!

—That is—you'll not mistake an idle word
Spoke in a huff by a poor monk, God wot,
Tasting the air this spicy night which turns
The unaccustomed head like Chianti wine!
Oh, the church knows! don't misreport me, now!
It's natural a poor monk out of bounds
Should have his apt word to excuse himself:
And hearken how I plot to make amends.
I have bethought me: I shall paint a piece
. . . There's for you! Give me six months, then go, see
Something in Sant' Ambrogio's! Bless the nuns!
They want a cast o' my office. I shall paint
God in the midst, Madonna and her babe,
Ringed by a bowery, flowery angel-brood,
Lilies and vestments and white faces, sweet
As puff on puff of grated orris-root
When ladies crowd to Church at midsummer.
And then i' the front, of course a saint or two—
Saint John, because he saves the Florentines,
Saint Ambrose, who puts down in black and white
The convent's friends and gives them a long day,
And Job, I must have him there past mistake,
The man of Uz (and Us without the z,
Painters who need his patience). Well, all these
Secured at their devotion, up shall come
Out of a corner when you least expect,
As one by a dark stair into a great light,
Music and talking, who but Lippo! I!—
Mazed, motionless, and moonstruck—I'm the man!
Back I shrink—what is this I see and hear?
I, caught up with my monk's-things by mistake,
My old serge gown and rope that goes all round,
I, in this presence, this pure company!
Where's a hole, where's a corner for escape?
Then steps a sweet angelic slip of a thing

Forward, puts out a soft palm—"Not so fast!"
—Addresses the celestial presence, "nay—
He made you and devised you, after all,
Though he's none of you! Could Saint John there
        draw—
His camel-hair make up a painting-brush?
We come to brother Lippo for all that,
*Iste perfecit opus!*" So, all smile—
I shuffle sideways with my blushing face
Under the cover of a hundred wings
Thrown like a spread of kirtles when you're gay
And play hot cockles, all the doors being shut,
Till, wholly unexpected, in there pops
The hothead husband! Thus I scuttle off
To some safe bench behind, not letting go
The palm of her, the little lily thing
That spoke the good word for me in the nick,
Like the Prior's niece . . . Saint Lucy, I would say.
And so all's saved for me, and for the church
A pretty picture gained. Go, six months hence!
Your hand, sir, and good-bye: no lights, no lights!
The street's hushed, and I know my own way back,
Don't fear me! There's the gray beginning. Zooks!

1855

## ANDREA DEL SARTO

### (CALLED "THE FAULTLESS PAINTER")

But do not let us quarrel any more,
No, my Lucrezia; bear with me for once:
Sit down and all shall happen as you wish.
You turn your face, but does it bring your heart?
I'll work then for your friend's friend, never fear,
Treat his own subject after his own way,

Fix his own time, accept too his own price,
And shut the money into this small hand
When next it takes mine. Will it? tenderly?
Oh, I'll content him,—but to-morrow, Love!
I often am much wearier than you think,
This evening more than usual, and it seems
As if—forgive now—should you let me sit
Here by the window with your hand in mine
And look a half-hour forth on Fiesole,
Both of one mind, as married people use,
Quietly, quietly the evening through,
I might get up to-morrow to my work
Cheerful and fresh as ever. Let us try.
To-morrow, how you shall be glad for this!
Your soft hand is a woman of itself,
And mine the man's bared breast she curls inside.
Don't count the time lost, neither; you must serve
For each of the five pictures we require:
It saves a model. So! keep looking so—
My serpentining beauty, rounds on rounds!
—How could you ever prick those perfect ears,
Even to put the pearl there! oh, so sweet—
My face, my moon, my everybody's moon,
Which everybody looks on and calls his,
And, I suppose, is looked on by in turn,
While she looks—no one's: very dear, no less.
You smile? why, there's my picture ready made,
There's what we painters call our harmony!
A common grayness silvers everything,—
All in a twilight, you and I alike
—You, at the point of your first pride in me
(That's gone you know),—but I, at every point;
My youth, my hope, my art, being all toned down
To yonder sober pleasant Fiesole.
There's the bell clinking from the chapel-top;

That length of convent-wall across the way
Holds the trees safer, huddled more inside;
The last monk leaves the garden; days decrease,
And autumn grows, autumn in everything.
Eh? the whole seems to fall into a shape
As if I saw alike my work and self
And all that I was born to be and do,
A twilight-piece. Love, we are in God's hand.
How strange now looks the life he makes us lead;
So free we seem, so fettered fast we are!
I feel he laid the fetter: let it lie!
This chamber for example—turn your head—
All that's behind us! You don't understand
Nor care to understand about my art,
But you can hear at least when people speak:
And that cartoon, the second from the door
—It is the thing, Love! so such thing should be—
Behold Madonna!—I am bold to say.
I can do with my pencil what I know,
What I see, what at bottom of my heart
I wish for, if I ever wish so deep—
Do easily, too—when I say, perfectly,
I do not boast, perhaps: yourself are judge,
Who listened to the Legate's talk last week,
And just as much they used to say in France.
At any rate 't is easy, all of it!
No sketches first, no studies, that's long past:
I do what many dream of all their lives,
—Dream? strive to do, and agonize to do,
And fail in doing. I could count twenty such
On twice your fingers, and not leave this town,
Who strive—you don't know how the others strive
To paint a little thing like that you smeared
Carelessly passing with your robes afloat,—
Yet do much less, so much less, Someone says,

(I know his name, no matter)—so much less!
Well, less is more, Lucrezia: I am judged.
There burns a truer light of God in them,
In their vexed beating stuffed and stopped-up brain,
Heart, or what'er else, than goes on to prompt
This low-pulsed forthright craftsman's hand of mine,
Their works drop groundward, but themselves, I **know**,
Reach many a time a heaven that's shut to me,
Enter and take their place there sure enough,
Though they come back and cannot tell the world.
My works are nearer heaven, but I sit here.
The sudden blood of these men! at a word—
Praise them, it boils, or blame them, it boils too.
I, painting from myself and to myself,
Know what I do, am unmoved by men's blame
Or their praise either. Somebody remarks
Morello's outline there is wrongly traced,
His hue mistaken; what of that? or else,
Rightly traced and well ordered; what of that?
Speak as they please, what does the mountain care?
Ah, but a man's reach should exceed his grasp,
Or what's a heaven for? All is silver-gray
Placid and perfect with my art: the worse!
I know both what I want and what might gain,
And yet how profitless to know, to sigh
"Had I been two, another and myself,
Our head would have o'erlooked the world!" **No doubt.**
Yonder's a work now, of that famous youth
The Urbinate, who died five years ago.
('T is copied, George Vasari sent it me.)
Well, I can fancy how he did it all,
Pouring his soul, with kings and popes to see,
Reaching, that heaven might so replenish him,
Above and through his art—for it gives way;
That arm is wrongly put—and there again—

A fault to pardon in the drawing's lines,
Its body, so to speak: its soul is right,
He means right—that, a child may understand.
Still, what an arm! and I could alter it:
But all the play, the insight and the stretch—
Out of me, out of me! And wherefore out?
Had you enjoined them on me, given me soul,
We might have risen to Rafael, I and you!
Nay, Love, you did give all I asked, I think—
More than I merit, yes, by many times.
But had you—oh, with the same perfect brow,
And perfect eyes, and more than perfect mouth,
And the low voice my soul hears, as a bird
The fowler's pipe, and follows to the snare—
Had you, with these the same, but brought a mind!
Some women do so. Had the mouth there urged
"God and the glory! never care for gain.
The present by the future, what is that?
Live for fame, side by side with Agnolo!
Rafael is waiting: up to God, all three!"
I might have done it for you. So it seems:
Perhaps not. All is as God overrules.
Beside, incentives come from the soul's self;
The rest avail not. Why do I need you?
What wife had Rafael, or has Agnolo?
In this world, who can do a thing, will not;
And who would do it, cannot, I perceive:
Yet the will's somewhat—somewhat, too, the **power**—
And thus we half-men struggle. At the end,
God, I conclude, compensates, punishes.
'T is safer for me, if the award be strict,
That I am something underrated here,
Poor this long while, despised, to speak the truth.
I dared not, do you know, leave home all day,
For fear of chancing on the Paris lords.

The best is when they pass and look aside;
But they speak sometimes; I must bear it all.
Well may they speak! That Francis, that first time,
And that long festal year at Fontainebleau!
I surely then could sometimes leave the ground,
Put on the glory, Rafael's daily wear,
In that humane great monarch's golden look,—
One finger in his beard or twisted curl
Over his mouth's good mark that made the smile,
One arm about my shoulder, round my neck,
The jingle of his gold chain in my ear,
I painting proudly with his breath on me,
All his court round him, seeing with his eyes,
Such frank French eyes, and such a fire of souls
Profuse, my hand kept plying by those hearts,—
And, best of all, this, this face beyond,
This in the background, waiting on my work,
To crown the issue with a last reward!
A good time, was it not, my kingly days?
And had you not grown restless . . . but I know—
'T is done and past; 't was right, my instinct said;
Too live the life grew, golden and not gray,
And I'm the weak-eyed bat no sun should tempt
Out of the grange whose four walls make his world.
How could it end in any other way?
You called me, and I came home to your heart.
The triumph was—to reach and stay there; since
I reached it ere the triumph, what is lost?
Let my hands frame your face in your hair's gold,
You beautiful Lucrezia that are mine!
"Rafael did this, Andrea painted that;
The Roman's is the better when you pray,
But still the other's Virgin was his wife"—
Men will excuse me. I am glad to judge
Both pictures in your presence; clearer grows

My better fortune, I resolve to think.
For, do you know, Lucrezia, as God lives,
Said one day Agnolo, his very self,
To Rafael . . . I have known it all these years . . .
(When the young man was flaming out his thoughts
Upon a palace-wall for Rome to see,
Too lifted up in heart because of it)
"Friend, there's a certain sorry little scrub
Goes up and down our Florence, none cares how,
Who, were he set to plan and execute
As you are, pricked on by your popes and kings,
Would bring the sweat into that brow of yours!"
To Rafael's!—And indeed the arm is wrong.
I hardly dare . . . yet, only you to see,
Give the chalk here—quick, thus the line should go!
Ay, but the soul! he's Rafael! rub it out!
Still, all I care for, if he spoke the truth,
(What he? why, who but Michel Agnolo?
Do you forget already words like those?)
If really there was such a chance. so lost,—
Is, whether you're—not grateful—but more pleased.
Well, let me think so. And you smile indeed!
This hour has been an hour! Another smile?
If you would sit thus by me every night
I should work better, do you comprehend?
I mean that I should earn more, give you more.
See, it is settled dusk now; there's a star;
Morello's gone, the watch-lights show the wall,
The cue-owls speak the name we call them by.
Come from the window, love,—come in, at last,
Inside the melancholy little house
We built to be so gay with. God is just.
King Francis may forgive me: oft at nights
When I look up from painting, eyes tired out,
The walls become illumined, brick from brick

Distinct, instead of mortar, fierce bright gold,
That gold of his I did cement them with!
Let us but love each other. Must you go?
That Cousin here again? he waits outside?
Must see you—you, and not with me? Those loans?
More gaming debts to pay? you smiled for that?
Well, let smiles buy me! have you more to spend?
While hand and eye and something of a heart
Are left me, work's my ware, and what's it worth?
I'll pay my fancy. Only let me sit
The gray remainder of the evening out,
Idle, you call it, and muse perfectly
How I could paint, were I but back in France,
One picture, just one more—the Virgin's face,
Not yours this time! I want you at my side
To hear them—that is, Michel Agnolo—
Judge all I do and tell you of its worth.
Will you? To-morrow, satisfy your friend.
I take the subjects for his corridor,
Finish the portrait out of hand—there, there,
And throw him in another thing or two
If he demurs; the whole should prove enough
To pay for this same Cousin's freak. Beside,
What's better and what's all I care about,
Get you the thirteen scudi for the ruff!
Love, does that please you? Ah, but what does he,
The Cousin! what does he to please you more?

I am grown peaceful as old age to-night.
I regret little, I would change still less.
Since there my past life lies, why alter it?
The very wrong to Francis!—it is true
I took his coin, was tempted and complied,
And built this house and sinned, and all is said.
My father and my mother died of want.

Well, had I riches of my own? you see
How one gets rich! Let each one bear his lot.
They were born poor, lived poor, and poor they died:
And I have labored somewhat in my time
And not been paid profusely. Some good son
Paint my two hundred pictures—let him try!
No doubt, there's something strikes a balance. Yes,
You loved me quite enough, it seems, to-night.
This must suffice me here. What would one have?
In heaven, perhaps, new chances, one more chance—
Four great walls in the New Jerusalem,
Meted on each side by the angel's reed,
For Leonard, Rafael, Agnolo and me
To cover—the three first without a wife,
While I have mine! So—still they overcome
Because there's still Lucrezia,—as I choose.

Again the Cousin's whistle! Go, my Love.

1855


## RABBI BEN EZRA

Grow old along with me!
The best is yet to be,
The last of life, for which the first was made:
Our times are in his hand
Who saith, "A whole I planned,
Youth shows but half; trust God: see all, nor be afraid!"

Not that, amassing flowers,
Youth sighed, "Which rose make ours,
Which lily leave and then as best recall?"
Not that, admiring stars,
It yearned. "Nor Jove, nor Mars;

Mine be some figured flame which blends, transcends
    them all!"

Not for such hopes and fears
Annulling youth's brief years,
Do I remonstrate: folly wide the mark!
Rather I prize the doubt
Low kinds exist without,
Finished and finite clods, untroubled by a spark.

Poor vaunt of life indeed,
Were man but formed to feed
On joy, to solely seek and find and feast:
Such feasting ended, then
As sure an end to men;
Irks care the crop-full bird? Frets doubt the maw-
    crammed beast?

Rejoice we are allied
To That which doth provide
And not partake, effect and not receive!
A spark disturbs our clod;
Nearer we hold of God
Who gives, than of his tribes that take, I must believe.

Then, welcome each rebuff
That turns earth's smoothness rough,
Each sting that bids nor sit nor stand but go!
Be our joys three-parts pain!
Strive, and hold cheap the strain;
Learn, nor account the pang; dare, never grudge the
    throe!

For thence,—a paradox
Which comforts while it mocks,—

Shall life succeed in that it seems to fail:
What I aspired to be,
And was not, comforts me:
A brute I might have been, but would not sink i' the
  scale.

What is he but a brute
Whose flesh hath soul to suit,
Whose spirit works lest arms and legs want play?
To man, propose this test—
Thy body at its best,
How far can that project thy soul on its lone way?

Yet gifts should prove their use:
I own the Past profuse
Of power each side, perfection every turn:
Eyes, ears took in their dole,
Brain treasured up the whole;
Should not the heart beat once "How good to live and
  learn"?

Not once beat "Praise be thine!
I see the whole design,
I, who saw power, see now Love perfect too:
Perfect I call thy plan:
Thanks that I was a man!
Maker, remake, complete,—I trust what thou shalt do!"

For pleasant is this flesh;
Our soul, in its rose-mesh
Pulled over to the earth, still yearns for rest;
Would we some prize might hold
To match those manifold
Possessions of the brute,—gain most, as we did best!

Let us not always say,
"Spite of this flesh to-day
I strove, made head, gained ground upon the whole!"
As the bird wings and sings,
Let us cry, "All good things
Are ours, nor soul helps flesh more, now, than flesh helps
      soul!"

Therefore I summon age
To grant youth's heritage,
Life's struggle having so far reached its term:
Thence shall I pass, approved
A man, for aye removed
From the developed brute; a God though in the germ.

And I shall thereupon
Take rest, ere I be gone
Once more on my adventure brave and new:
Fearless and unperplexed,
When I wage battle next,
What weapons to select, what armor to indue.

Youth ended, I shall try
My gain or loss thereby;
Leave the fire ashes, what survives is gold:
And I shall weigh the same,
Give life its praise or blame:
Young, all lay in dispute; I shall know, being old.

For note, when evening shuts,
A certain moment cuts
The deed off, calls the glory from the gray:
A whisper from the west
Shoots—"Add this to the rest,
Take it and try its worth: here dies another day."

So, still within this life,
Though lifted o'er its strife,
Let me discern, compare, pronounce at last,
"This rage was right i' the main,
That acquiescence vain:
The Future I may face now I have proved the Past."

For more is not reserved
To man, with soul just nerved
To act to-morrow what he learns to-day:
Here, work enough to watch
The Master work, and catch
Hints of the proper craft, tricks of the tool's true play.

As it was better, youth
Should strive, through acts uncouth,
Toward making, than repose on aught found made:
So, better, age, exempt
From strife, should know, than tempt
Further. Thou waitedst age: wait death nor be afraid!

Enough now, if the Right
And Good and Infinite
Be named here, as thou callest thy hand thine own,
With knowledge absolute,
Subject to no dispute
From fools that crowded youth, nor let thee feel alone.

Be there, for once and all,
Severed great minds from small,
Announced to each his station in the Past!
Was I, the world arraigned,
Were they, my soul disdained,
Right? Let age speak the truth and give us peace at last!

Now, who shall arbitrate?
Ten men love what I hate,
Shun what I follow, slight what I receive;
Ten, who in ears and eyes
Match me: we all surmise,
They this thing, and I that: whom shall my soul believe?

Not on the vulgar mass
Called "work," must sentence pass,
Things done, that took the eye and had the price;
O'er which, from level stand,
The low world laid its hand,
Found straightway to its mind, could value in a trice:

But all, the world's coarse thumb
And finger failed to plumb,
So passed in making up the main account;
All instincts immature,
All purposes unsure,
That weighed not as his work, yet swelled the man's
        amount:

Thoughts hardly to be packed
Into a narrow act,
Fancies that broke through language and escaped;
All I could never be,
All, men ignored in me,
This, I was worth to God, whose wheel the pitcher
        shaped.

Ay, note that Potter's wheel,
That metaphor! and feel
Why time spins fast, why passive lies our clay,—
Thou, to whom fools propound,

When the wine makes its round,
"Since life fleets, all is change; the Past gone, seize
      to-day!"

Fool! All that is, at all,
Lasts ever, past recall;
Earth changes, but thy soul and God stand sure:
What entered into thee,
*That* was, is, and shall be:
Time's wheel runs back or stops: Potter and clay endure.

He fixed thee 'mid this dance
Of plastic circumstance,
This Present, thou, forsooth, would fain arrest:
Machinery just meant
To give thy soul its bent,
Try thee and turn thee forth, sufficiently impressed

What though the earlier grooves
Which ran the laughing loves
Around thy base, no longer pause and press?
What though, about thy rim,
Skull-things in order grim
Grow out, in graver mood, obey the sterner stress?

Look not thou down but up!
To uses of a cup,
The festal board, lamp's flash and trumpet's peal,
The new wine's foaming flow,
The Master's lips aglow!
Thou, heaven's consummate cup, what needst thou with
      earth's wheel?

But I need, now as then,
Thee, God, who mouldest men;

And since, not even while the whirl was worst,
Did I—to the wheel of life
With shapes and colors rife,
Bound dizzily—mistake my end, to slake thy thirst:

So, take and use thy work:
Amend what flaws may lurk,
What strain o' the stuff, what warpings past the aim!
My times be in thy hand!
Perfect the cup as planned!
Let age approve of youth, and death complete the same!

1864

# YOUTH AND ART

IT ONCE might have been, once only:
    We lodged in a street together,
You, a sparrow on the housetop lonely,
    I, a lone she-bird of his feather.

Your trade was with sticks and clay,
    You thumbed, thrust, patted and polished,
Then laughed "They will see some day
    Smith made, and Gibson demolished."

My business was song, song, song;
    I chirped, cheeped, trilled and twittered,
"Kate Brown's on the boards ere long,
    And Grisi's existence embittered!"

I earned no more by a warble
    Than you by a sketch in plaster;

You wanted a piece of marble,
   I needed a music master.

We studied hard in our styles,
   Chipped each at a crust like Hindoos,
For air, looked out on the tiles,
   For fun, watched each other's windows.

You lounged, like a boy of the South,
   Cap and blouse—nay, a bit of beard too;
Or you got it, rubbing your mouth
   With fingers the clay adhered to.

And I—soon managed to find
   Weak points in the flower-fence facing,
Was forced to put up a blind
   And be safe in my corset-lacing.

No harm! It was not my fault
   If you never turned your eyes' tail up
As I shook the E *in alt.,*
   Or ran the chromatic scale up:

For spring bade the sparrows pair,
   And the boys and girls gave guesses,
And stalls in our street looked rare
   With bulrush and watercresses.

Why did not you pinch a flower
   In a pellet of clay and fling it?
Why did not I put a power
   Of thanks in a look, or sing it?

I did look, sharp as a lynx,
   (And yet the memory rankles,)

When models arrived, some minx
   Tripped up-stairs, she and her ankles.

But I think I gave you as good!
   "That foreign fellow,—who can know
How she pays, in a playful mood,
   For his tuning her that piano?"

Could you say so, and never say,
   "Suppose we join hands and fortunes,
And I fetch her from over the way,
   Her, piano, and long tunes and short tunes"?

No, no: you would not be rash,
   Nor I rasher and something over:
You've to settle yet Gibson's hash,
   And Grisi yet lives in clover.

But you meet the Prince at the Board,
   I'm queen myself at *bals-paré,*
I've married a rich old lord,
   And you're dubbed knight and an R. A.

Each life unfulfilled, you see;
   It hangs still, patchy and scrappy:
We have not sighed deep, laughed free,
   Starved, feasted, despaired,—been happy.

And nobody calls you a dunce,
   And people suppose me clever:
This could but have happened once,
   And we missed it, lost it forever.

1864

## CALIBAN UPON SETEBOS;
### OR, NATURAL THEOLOGY IN THE ISLAND

"Thou thoughtest that I was altogether such a one
as thyself."

['WILL sprawl, now that the heat of the day is best,
Flat on his belly in the pit's much mire,
With elbows wide, fists clenched to prop his chin.
And, while he kicks both feet in the cool slush,
And feels about his spine small eft-things course,
Run in and out each arm, and make him laugh:
And while above his head a pompion-plant,
Coating the cave-top as a brow its eye,
Creeps down to touch and tickle hair and beard,
And now a flower drops with a bee inside,
And now a fruit to snap at, catch and crunch,—
He looks out o'er yon sea which sunbeams cross
And recross till they weave a spider-web,
(Meshes of fire, some great fish breaks at times)
And talks to his own self, howe'er he please,
Touching that other, whom his dam called God.
Because to talk about Him, vexes—ha,
Could He but know! and time to vex is now,
When talk is safer than in winter-time.
Moreover Prosper and Miranda sleep
In confidence he drudges at their task,
And it is good to cheat the pair, and gibe,
Letting the rank tongue blossom into speech.]

Setebos, Setebos, and Setebos!
'Thinketh, He dwelleth i' the cold o' the moon.

'Thinketh He made it, with the sun to match,
But not the stars; the stars come otherwise;

Only made clouds, winds, meteors, such as that:
Also this isle, what lives and grows thereon,
And snaky sea which rounds and ends the same.

'Thinketh, it came of being ill at ease:
He hated that He cannot change His cold,
Nor cure its ache. 'Hath spied an icy fish
That longed to 'scape the rock-stream where she lived,
And thaw herself within the luke warm brine
O' the lazy sea her stream thrusts far amid,
A crystal spike 'twixt two warm walls of wave;
Only, she ever sickened, found repulse
At the other kind of water, not her life,
(Green-dense and dim-delicious, bred o' the sun)
Flounced back from bliss she was not born to breathe,
And in her old bounds buried her despair,
Hating and loving warmth alike: so He.

'Thinketh, He made thereat the sun, this isle,
Trees and the fowls here, beast and creeping thing.
Yon otter, sleek-wet, black, lithe as a leech;
Yon auk, one fire-eye in a ball of foam,
That floats and feeds; a certain badger brown
He hath watched hunt with that slant white-wedge eye
By moonlight; and the pie with the long tongue
That pricks deep into oakwarts for a worm,
And says a plain word when she finds her prize,
But will not eat the ants; the ants themselves
That build a wall of seeds and settled stalks
About their hole—He made all these and more,
Made all we see, and us, in spite: how else?
He could not, Himself, make a second self
To be His mate; as well have made Himself:
He would not make what he mislikes or slights,
An eyesore to Him, or not worth His pains:

But did, in envy, listlessness or sport,
Make what Himself would fain, in a manner, be—
Weaker in most points, stronger in a few,
Worthy, and yet mere playthings all the while,
Things He admires and mocks too,—that is it.
Because, so brave, so better though they be,
It nothing skills if He begin to plague.
Look now, I melt a gourd-fruit into mash,
Add honeycomb and pods, I have perceived,
Which bite like finches when they bill and kiss,—
Then, when froth rises bladdery, drink up all,
Quick, quick, till maggots scamper through my brain;
Last, throw me on my back i' the seeded thyme,
And wanton, wishing I were born a bird.
Put case, unable to be what I wish,
I yet could make a live bird out of clay:
Would not I take clay, pinch my Caliban
Able to fly?—for, there, see, he hath wings,
And great comb like the hoopoe's to admire,
And there, a sting to do his foes offence,
There, and I will that he begin to live,
Fly to yon rock-top, nip me off the horns
Of grigs high up that make the merry din,
Saucy through their veined wings, and mind me not.
In which feat, if his leg snapped, brittle clay,
And he lay stupid-like,—why, I should laugh;
And if he, spying me, should fall to weep,
Beseech me to be good, repair his wrong,
Bid his poor leg smart less or grow again,—
Well, as the chance were, this might take or else
Not take my fancy: I might hear his cry,
And give the mankin three sound legs for one,
Or pluck the other off, leave him like an egg,
And lessoned he was mine and merely clay.
Were this no pleasure, lying in the thyme,

Drinking the mash, with brain become alive,
Making and marring clay at will? So He.

'Thinketh, such shows nor right nor wrong in Him,
Nor kind, nor cruel: He is strong and Lord.
'Am strong myself compared to yonder crabs
That march now from the mountain to the sea;
'Let twenty pass, and stone the twenty-first,
Loving not, hating not, just choosing so.
'Say, the first straggler that boasts purple spots
Shall join the file, one pincer twisted off;
'Say, this bruised fellow shall receive a worm,
And two worms he whose nippers end in red;
As it likes me each time, I do: so He.

Well then, 'supposeth He is good i' the main,
Placable if His mind and ways were guessed,
But rougher than His handiwork, be sure!
Oh, He hath made things worthier than Himself,
And envieth that, so helped, such things do more
Than He who made them! What consoles but this?
That they, unless through Him, do nought at all,
And must submit: what other use in things?
'Hath cut a pipe of pithless elder joint
That, blown through, gives exact the scream o' the jay
When from her wing you twitch the feathers blue:
Sound this, and little birds that hate the jay
Flock within stone's throw, glad their foe is hurt:
Put case such pipe could prattle and boast forsooth
"I catch the birds, I am the crafty thing,
I make the cry my maker cannot make
With his great round mouth; he must blow **through**
       mine!"
Would not I smash it with my foot? So He.

But wherefore rough, why cold and ill at ease?
Aha, that is a question! Ask, for that,
What knows,—the something over Setebos
That made Him, or He, may be, found and fought,
Worsted, drove off and did to nothing, perchance.
There may be something quiet o'er His head,
Out of His reach, that feels nor joy nor grief,
Since both derive from weakness in some way.
I joy because the quails come; would not joy
Could I bring quails here when I have a mind:
This Quiet, all it hath a mind to, doth.
'Esteemeth stars the outposts of its couch,
But never spends much thought nor care that way.
It may look up, work up,—the worse for those
It works on! 'Careth but for Setebos
The many-handed as a cuttle-fish,
Who, making Himself feared through what He does,
Looks up, first, and perceives he cannot soar
To what is quiet and hath happy life;
Next looks down here, and out of very spite
Makes this a bauble-world to ape yon real,
These good things to match those as hips do grapes.
'Tis solace making baubles, ay, and sport.
Himself peeped late, eyed Prosper at his books
Careless and lofty, lord now of the isle:
Vexed, 'stiched a book of broad leaves, arrow-shaped,
Wrote thereon, he knows what, prodigious words;
Has peeled a wand and called it by a name;
Weareth at whiles for an enchanter's robe
The eyed skin of a supple oncelot;
And hath an ounce sleeker than youngling mole,
A four-legged serpent he makes cower and couch,
Now snarl, now hold its breath and mind his eye,
And saith she is Miranda and my wife:
'Keeps for his Ariel a tall pouch-bill crane

He bids go wade for fish and straight disgorge;
Also a sea-beast, lumpish, which he snared,
Blinded the eyes of, and brought somewhat tame,
And split its toe-webs, and now pens the drudge
In a hole o' the rock and calls him Caliban;
A bitter heart that bides its time and bites.
'Plays thus at being Prosper in a way,
Taketh his mirth with make-believes: so He.

His dam held that the Quiet made all things
Which Setebos vexed only: 'holds not so.
Who made them weak, meant weakness He might vex.
Had He meant other, while His hand was in,
Why not make horny eyes no thorn could prick,
Or plate my scalp with bone against the snow,
Or overscale my flesh 'neath joint and joint,
Like an orc's armour? Ay,—so spoil His sport!
He is the One now: only He doth all.

'Saith, He may like, perchance, what profits Him.
Ay, himself loves what does him good; but why?
'Gets good no otherwise. This blinded beast
Loves whoso places flesh-meat on his nose,
But, had he eyes, would want no help, but hate
Or love, just as it liked him: He hath eyes.
Also it pleaseth Setebos to work,
Use all His hands, and exercise much craft,
By no means for the love of what is worked.
'Tasteth, himself, no finer good i' the world
When all goes right, in this safe summer-time,
And he wants little, hungers, aches not much,
Than trying what to do with wit and strength.
'Falls to make something: 'piled yon pile of turfs,
And squared and stuck there squares of soft white chalk,
And, with a fish-tooth, scratched a moon on each,

And set up endwise certain spikes of tree,
And crowned the whole with a sloth's skull a-**top**,
Found dead i' the woods, too hard for one to kill.
No use at all i' the work, for work's sole sake;
'Shall some day knock it down again: so He.

'Saith He is terrible: watch His feats in proof!
One hurricane will spoil six good months' hope.
He hath a spite against me, that I know,
Just as He favours Prosper, who knows why?
So it is, all the same, as well I find.
'Wove wattles half the winter, fenced them firm
With stone and stake to stop she-tortoises
Crawling to lay their eggs here: well, one wave,
Feeling the foot of Him upon its neck,
Gaped as a snake does, lolled out its large tongue,
And licked the whole labour flat: so much for spite.

'Saw a ball flame down late (yonder it lies)
Where, half an hour before, I slept i' the shade:
Often they scatter sparkles: there is force!
'Dug up a newt He may have envied once
And turned to stone, shut up inside a stone.
Please Him and hinder this?—What Prosper does?
Aha, if He would tell me how! Not He!
There is the sport: discover how or die!
All need not die, for of the things o' the isle
Some flee afar, some dive, some run up trees;
Those at His mercy,—why, they please Him most
When . . . when . . . well, never try the same **way**
      twice!
Repeat what act has pleased, He may grow wroth.
You must not know His ways, and play Him off,
Sure of the issue. 'Doth the like himself:
'Spareth a squirrel that it nothing fears

But steals the nut from underneath my thumb,
And when I threat, bites stoutly in defence:
'Spareth an urchin that contrariwise,
Curls up into a ball, pretending death
For fright at my approach: the two ways please.
But what would move my choler more than this,
That either creature counted on its life
To-morrow and next day and all days to come,
Saying, forsooth, in the inmost of its heart,
"Because he did so yesterday with me,
And otherwise with such another brute,
So must he do henceforth and always."—Ay?
Would teach the reasoning couple what "must" means!
'Doth as he likes, or wherefore Lord? So He.

'Conceiveth all things will continue thus,
And we shall have to live in fear of Him
So long as He lives, keeps His strength: no change,
If He have done His best, make no new world
To please Him more, so leave off watching this,—
If He surprise not even the Quiet's self
Some strange day,—or, suppose, grow into it
As grubs grow butterflies: else, here we are,
And there is He, and nowhere help at all.

'Believeth with the life, the pain shall stop.
His dam held different, that after death
He both plagued enemies and feasted friends:
Idly! He doth His worst in this our life,
Giving just respite lest we die through pain,
Saving last pain for worst,—with which, an end.
Meanwhile, the best way to escape His ire
Is, not to seem too happy. 'Sees, himself,
Yonder two flies, with purple films and pink,
Bask on the pompion-bell above: kills both.

'Sees two black painful beetles roll their ball
On head and tail as if to save their lives:
Moves them the stick away they strive to clear.

Even so, 'would have Him misconceive, suppose
This Caliban strives hard and ails no less,
And always, above all else, envies Him;
Wherefore he mainly dances on dark nights,
Moans in the sun, gets under holes to laugh,
And never speaks his mind save housed as now:
Outside, 'groans, curses. If He caught me here,
O'erheard this speech, and asked "What chucklest at?"
'Would, to appease Him, cut a finger off,
Or of my three kid yearlings burn the best,
Or let the toothsome apples rot on tree,
Or push my tame beast for the orc to taste:
While myself lit a fire, and made a song
And sung it, *"What I hate, be consecrate
To celebrate Thee and Thy state, no mate
For Thee; what see for envy in poor me?"*
Hoping the while, since evils sometimes mend,
Warts rub away and sores are cured with slime,
That some strange day, will either the Quiet catch
And conquer Setebos, or likelier He
Decrepit may doze, doze, as good as die.

———

[What, what? A curtain o'er the world at once!
Crickets stop hissing; not a bird—or, yes,
There scuds His raven that has told Him all!
It was fool's play, this prattling! Ha! The wind
Shoulders the pillared dust, death's house o' the move,
And fast invading fires begin! White blaze—

A tree's head snaps—and there, there, there, there,
      there,
His thunder follows! Fool to gibe at Him!
Lo! 'Lieth flat and loveth Setebos!
'Maketh his teeth meet through his upper lip,
Will let those quails fly, will not eat this month
One little mess of whelks, so he may 'scape!]

1864

## PROSPICE

Fear death?—to feel the fog in my throat,
    The mist in my face,
When the snows begin, and the blasts denote
    I am nearing the place,
The power of the night, the press of the storm,
    The post of the foe;
Where he stands, the Arch Fear in a visible form,
    Yet the strong man must go:
For the journey is done and the summit attained,
    And the barriers fall,
Though a battle's to fight ere the guerdon be gained,
    The reward of it all.
I was ever a fighter, so—one fight more,
    The best and the last!
I would hate that death bandaged my eyes, and forbore,
    And bade me creep past.
No! let me taste the whole of it, fare like my peers
    The heroes of old,
Bear the brunt, in a minute pay glad life's arrears
    Of pain, darkness and cold.
For sudden the worst turns the best to the brave,
    The black minute's at end,
And the elements' rage, the fiend-voices that rave,
    Shall dwindle, shall blend,

Shall change, shall become first a peace out of pain,
    Then a light, then thy breast,
O thou soul of my soul! I shall clasp thee again,
    And with God be the rest!

1864

## EPILOGUE TO ASOLANDO

AT THE midnight in the silence of the sleep-time,
    When you set your fancies free,
Will they pass to where—by death, fools think, im-
        prisoned—
Low he lies who once so loved you, whom you loved so,
        —Pity me?

Oh to love so, be so loved, yet so mistaken!
    What had I on earth to do
With the slothful, with the mawkish, the unmanly?
Like the aimless, helpless, hopeless, did I drivel
        —Being—who?

One who never turned his back but marched breast for-
        ward,
    Never doubted clouds would break,
Never dreamed, though right were worsted, wrong would
        triumph,
Held we fall to rise, are baffled to fight better,
        Sleep to wake.

No, at noonday in the bustle of man's work-time
    Greet the unseen with a cheer!
Bid him forward, breast and back as either should be,
"Strive and thrive!" cry "Speed,—fight on, fare ever
        There as here!"

1889

ELIZABETH BARRETT BROWNING (1806-1861)

## THE PRISONER

I count the dismal time by months and years
Since last I felt the greensward under foot,
And the great breath of all things summer-mute
Met mine upon my lips. Now earth appears
As strange to me as dreams of distant spheres,
Or thoughts of Heaven we weep at. Nature's lute
Sounds on, behind this door so closely shut,
A strange, wild music to the prisoner's ears,
Dilated by the distance, till the brain
Grows dim with fancies which it feels too fine:
While ever, with a visionary pain,
Past the precluded senses, sweep and shine
Streams, forests, glades, and many a golden train
Of sunlit hills transfigured to Divine.

1843

## THE CRY OF THE CHILDREN

Do ye hear the children weeping, O my brothers,
  Ere the sorrow comes with years?
They are leaning their young heads against their
      mothers,
  And *that* cannot stop their tears.
The young lambs are bleating in the meadows:
  The young birds are chirping in the nest;
The young fawns are playing with the shadows;
  The young flowers are blowing toward the west—
But the young, young children, O my brothers,
  They are weeping bitterly!

They are weeping in the playtime of the others,
  In the country of the free.


Do you question the young children in their sorrow,
  Why their tears are falling so?
The old man may weep for his to-morrow
  Which is lost in Long Ago;
The old tree is leafless in the forest,
  The old year is ending in the frost,
The old wound, if stricken, is the sorest,
  The old hope is hardest to be lost:
But the young, young children, O my brothers,
  Do you ask them why they stand
Weeping sore before the bosoms of their mothers,
  In our happy Fatherland?


They look up with their pale and sunken faces,
  And their looks are sad to see,
For the man's hoary anguish draws and presses
  Down the cheeks of infancy;
"Your old earth," they say, "is very dreary,
  Our young feet," they say, "are very weak;
Few paces have we taken, yet are weary—
  Our grave-rest is very far to seek:
Ask the agèd why they weep, and not the children,
  For the outside earth is cold,
And we young ones stand without, in our bewildering,
  And the graves are for the old.


"True," say the children, "it may happen
  That we die before our time:
Little Alice died last year, her grave is shapen
  Like a snowball, in the rime.
We looked into the pit prepared to take her:
  Was no room for any work in the close clay!

From the sleep wherein she lieth none will wake her,
   Crying, 'Get up, little Alice! it is day.'
If you listen by that grave, in sun and shower,
   With your ear down, little Alice never cries;
Could we see her face, be sure we should not know her,
   For a smile has time for growing in her eyes:
And merry go her moments, lulled and stilled in
   The shroud by the kirk-chime.
It is good when it happens," say the children,
   "That we die before our time."

Alas, alas, the children! they are seeking
   Death in life as best to have:
They are binding up their hearts away from breaking,
   With a cerement from the grave.
Go out, children, from the mine and from the city,
   Sing out, children, as the little thrushes do;
Pluck your handfuls of the meadow-cowslips pretty,
   Laugh aloud, to feel your fingers let them through!
But they answer, "Are your cowslips of the meadows
   Like our weeds anear the mine?
Leave us quiet in the dark of the coal-shadows,
   From your pleasures fair and fine!

"For oh," say the children, "we are weary,
   And we cannot run or leap;
If we cared for any meadows, it were merely
   To drop down in them and sleep.
Our knees tremble sorely in the stooping,
   We fall upon our faces, trying to go;
And, underneath our heavy eyelids drooping
   The reddest flower would look as pale as snow.
For, all day, we drag our burden tiring
   Through the coal-dark, underground;

Or, all day, we drive the wheels of iron
   In the factories, round and round.

"For, all day, the wheels are droning, turning;
   Their wind comes in our faces,
Till our hearts turn, our heads, with pulses burning,
   And the walls turn in their places:
Turns the sky in the high window, blank and reeling,
   Turns the long light that drops adown the wall,
Turn the black flies that crawl along the ceiling:
   All are turning, all the day, and we with all.
And all day the iron wheels are droning,
   And sometimes we could pray,
'O ye wheels' (breaking out in a mad moaning),
   'Stop! be silent for to-day!'"

Ay, be silent! Let them hear each other breathing
   For a moment, mouth to mouth!
Let them touch each other's hands, in a fresh wreathing
   Of their tender human youth!
Let them feel that this cold metallic motion
   Is not all the life God fashions or reveals:
Let them prove their living souls against the notion
   That they live in you, or under you, O wheels!
Still, all day, the iron wheels go onward,
   Grinding life down from its mark;
And the children's souls, which God is calling sunward,
   Spin on blindly in the dark.

Now tell the poor young children, O my brothers,
   To look up to Him and pray;
So the blessèd One who blesseth all the others,
   Will bless them another day.
They answer, "Who is God that He should hear us,
   While the rushing of the iron wheels is stirred?

When we sob aloud, the human creatures near us
  Pass by, hearing not, or answer not a word.
And *we* hear not (for the wheels in their resounding)
  Strangers speaking at the door:
Is it likely God, with angels singing round Him,
  Hears our weeping any more?

"Two words, indeed, of praying we remember,
  And at midnight's hour of harm,
'Our Father,' looking upward in the chamber,
  We say softly for a charm.
We know no other words except 'Our Father,'
  And we think that, in some pause of angels' song,
God may pluck them with the silence sweet to gather,
  And hold both within His right hand which is strong.
'Our Father!' If He heard us, He would surely
  (For they call Him good and mild)
Answer, smiling down the steep world very purely,
  'Come and rest with me, my child.'

"But no!" say the children, weeping faster,
  "He is speechless as a stone:
And they tell us, of His image is the master
  Who commands us to work on.
Go to!" say the children,—"up in Heaven,
  Dark, wheel-like, turning clouds are all we find.
Do not mock us; grief has made us unbelieving:
  We look up for God, but tears have made us blind."
Do you hear the children weeping and disproving,
  O my brothers, what ye preach?
For God's possible is taught by His world's loving,
  And the children doubt of each.

And well may the children weep before you!
  They are weary ere they run;

They have never seen the sunshine, nor the glory
    Which is brighter than the sun.
They know the grief of man, without its wisdom;
    They sink in man's despair, without its calm;
Are slaves, without the liberty in Christdom,
    Are martyrs, by the pang without the palm:
Are worn as if with age, yet unretrievingly
    The harvest of its memories cannot reap,—
Are orphans of the earthly love and heavenly.
    Let them weep! let them weep!

They look up with their pale and sunken faces,
    And their look is dread to see,
For they mind you of their angels in high places,
    With eyes turned on Deity.
"How long," they say, "how long, O cruel nation,
    Will you stand, to move the world, on a child's heart,—
Stifle down with a mailèd heel its palpitation,
    And tread onward to your throne amid the mart?
Our blood splashes upward, O gold-heaper,
    And your purple shows your path!
But the child's sob in the silence curses deeper
    Than the strong man in his wrath."

                                                    1844


## SONNETS FROM THE PORTUGUESE

### III

UNLIKE are we, unlike, O princely Heart!
Unlike our uses and our destinies.
Our ministering two angels look surprise
On one another, as they strike athwart
Their wings in passing. Thou, bethink thee, art

A guest for queens to social pageantries,
With gages from a hundred brighter eyes
Than tears even can make mine, to play thy part
Of chief musician. What hast *thou* to do
With looking from the lattice-lights at me,
A poor, tired, wandering singer, singing through
The dark, and leaning up a cypress tree?
The chrism is on thine head,—on mine, the dew,—
And Death must dig the level where these agree.

### XLIII

How do I love thee? Let me count the ways.
I love thee to the depth and breadth and height
My soul can reach, when feeling out of sight
For the ends of Being and ideal Grace.
I love thee to the level of everyday's
Most quiet need, by sun and candle-light.
I love thee freely, as men strive for Right;
I love thee purely, as they turn from Praise.
I love thee with the passion put to use
In my old griefs, and with my childhood's faith.
I love thee with a love I seemed to lose
With my lost saints,—I love thee with the breath,
Smiles, tears, of all my life!—and, if God choose,
I shall but love thee better after death.

1847

## A MUSICAL INSTRUMENT

WHAT was he doing, the great god Pan,
    Down in the reeds by the river?
Spreading ruin and scattering ban,
Splashing and paddling with hoofs of a goat,

And breaking the golden lilies afloat
  With the dragon-fly on the river.

He tore out a reed, the great god Pan.
  From the deep cool bed of the river:
The limpid water turbidly ran,
And the broken lilies a-dying lay,
And the dragon-fly had fled away,
  Ere he brought it out of the river.

High on the shore sat the great god Pan
  While turbidly flowed the river;
And hacked and hewed as a great god can,
With his hard bleak steel at the patient reed,
Till there was not a sign of the leaf indeed
  To prove it fresh from the river.

He cut it short, did the great god Pan,
  (How tall it stood in the river!)
Then drew the pith, like the heart of a man,
Steadily from the outside ring,
And notched the poor dry empty thing
  In holes, as he sat by the river.

"This is the way," laughed the great god Pan
  (Laughed while he sat by the river),
"The only way, since gods began
To make sweet music, they could suceed."
Then, dropping his mouth to a hole in the reed,
  He blew in power by the river.

Sweet, sweet, sweet, O Pan!
  Piercing sweet by the river!

Blinding sweet, O great god Pan!
The sun on the hill forgot to die,
And the lilies revived, and the dragon-fly
    Came back to dream on the river.

Yet half a beast is the great god Pan,
    To laugh as he sits by the river,
Making a poet out of a man:
The true gods sigh for the cost and pain,—
For the reed which grows nevermore again
    As a reed with the reeds in the river.

1860

## EDWARD FITZGERALD (1809-1883)

## THE RUBÁIYÁT OF OMAR KHAYYÁM

### I

WAKE! For the Sun behind yon Eastern height
Has chased the Session of the Stars from Night;
    And, to the field of Heav'n ascending, strikes
The Sultán's Turret with a Shaft of Light.

### II

Before the phantom of False morning died,
Methought a Voice within the Tavern cried,
    "When all the Temple is prepared within,
Why lags the drowsy Worshipper outside?"

### III

And, as the Cock crew, those who stood before
The Tavern shouted—"Open then the door!

You know how little while we have to stay,
And, once departed, may return no more."

IV

Now the New Year reviving old Desires,
The thoughtful Soul to Solitude retires,
    Where the *White Hand of Moses* on the Bough
Puts out, and Jesus from the ground suspires.

V

Iram indeed is gone with all his Rose,
And Jamshýd's Sev'n-ring'd Cup where no one knows:
    But still a Ruby gushes from the Vine,
And many a Garden by the Water blows.

VI

And David's lips are lockt; but in divine
High-piping Péhleví, with "Wine! Wine! Wine!
    Red Wine!"—the Nightingale cries to the Rose
That sallow cheek of hers to incarnadine.

VII

Come, fill the Cup, and in the fire of Spring
Your Winter-garment of Repentance fling!
    The Bird of Time has but a little way
To flutter—and the Bird is on the Wing.

VIII

Whether at Naishápúr or Babylon,
Whether the Cup with sweet or bitter run,

The Wine of Life keeps oozing drop by drop,
The Leaves of Life keep falling one by one.

IX

Morning a thousand Roses brings, you say;
Yes, but where leaves the Rose of yesterday?
    And this first Summer month that brings the Rose
Shall take Jamshýd and Kaikobád away.

X

Well, let it take them! What have we to do
With Kaikobád the Great, or Kaikhosrú?
    Let Rustum cry "To Battle!" as he likes,
Or Hátim Tai "To Supper!"—heed not you.

XI

With me along the strip of Herbage strown
That just divides the desert from the sown,
    Where name of Slave and Sultán is forgot—
And Peace to Máhmúd on his golden Throne!

XII

Here with a little Bread beneath the Bough,
A Flask of Wine, a Book of Verse—and Thou
    Beside me singing in the Wilderness—
Oh, Wilderness were Paradise enow!

XIII

Some for the Glories of This World; and some
Sigh for the Prophet's Paradise to come;

Ah, take the Cash, and let the Promise go,
Nor heed the music of a distant Drum!

### XIV

Were it not Folly, Spider-like to spin
The Thread of present Life away to win—
    What? for ourselves, who know not if we shall
Breathe out the very Breath we now breathe in!

### XV

Look to the blowing Rose about us—"Lo,
Laughing," she says, "into the world I blow:
    At once the silken tassel of my Purse
Tear, and its Treasure on the Garden throw."

### XVI

For those who husbanded the Golden Grain,
And those who flung it to the winds like Rain,
    Alike to no such aureate Earth are turn'd
As, buried once, Men want dug up again.

### XVII

The Worldly Hope men set their Hearts upon
Turns Ashes—or it prospers; and anon,
    Like Snow upon the Desert's dusty Face,
Lighting a little hour or two—was gone.

### XVIII

Think, in this batter'd Caravanserai,
Whose Portals are alternate Night and Day,

How Sultán after Sultán with his Pomp
Abode his destin'd Hour, and went his way.

### XIX

They say the Lion and the Lizard keep
The Courts where Jamshýd gloried and drank deep;
    And Bahrám, that great Hunter—the Wild Ass
Stamps o'er his Head, but cannot break his Sleep.

### XX

The Palace that to Heav'n his pillars threw,
And Kings the forehead on his threshold drew—
    I saw the solitary Ringdove there,
And "Coo, coo, coo," she cried; and "Coo, coo, coo."

### XXI

Ah, my Belovéd, fill the Cup that clears
To-DAY of past Regret and future Fears:
    To-MORROW!—Why, To-morrow I may be
Myself with Yesterday's Sev'n Thousand Years.

### XXII

For some we loved, the loveliest and the best
That from his Vintage rolling Time has prest,
    Have drunk their Cup a Round or two before,
And one by one crept silently to rest.

### XXIII

And we, that now make merry in the Room
They left, and Summer dresses in new bloom,

Ourselves must we beneath the Couch of Earth
Descend, ourselves to make a Couch—for whom?

### XXIV

I sometimes think that never blows so red
The Rose as where some buried Cæsar bled;
    That every Hyacinth the Garden wears
Dropt in her Lap from some once lovely Head.

### XXV

And this delightful Herb whose living Green
Fledges the River's Lip on which we lean—
    Ah, lean upon it lightly! for who knows
From what once lovely Lip it springs unseen!

### XXVI

Ah, make the most of what we yet may spend,
Before we too into the Dust descend;
    Dust into Dust, and under Dust, to lie,
Sans Wine, sans Song, sans Singer, and—sans End!

### XXVII

Alike for those who for To-DAY prepare,
And those that after some To-MORROW stare,
    A Muezzín from the Tower of Darkness cries,
"Fools! your Reward is neither Here nor There!"

### XXVIII

Another Voice, when I am sleeping, cries,
"The Flower should open with the Morning skies."

And a retreating Whisper, as I wake —
"The Flower that once has blown for ever dies."

### XXIX

Why, all the Saints and Sages who discuss'd
Of the Two Worlds so learnedly, are thrust
    Like foolish Prophets forth; their Words to Scorn
Are scatter'd, and their Mouths are stopt with Dust.

### XXX

Myself when young did eagerly frequent
Doctor and Saint, and heard great argument
    About it and about: but evermore
Came out by the same door as in I went.

### XXXI

With them the seed of Wisdom did I sow,
And with my own hand wrought to make it grow;
    And this was all the Harvest that I reap'd—
"I came like Water, and like Wind I go."

### XXXII

Into this Universe, and *Why* not knowing
Nor *Whence,* like Water willy-nilly flowing;
    And out of it, as Wind along the Waste,
I know not *Whither,* willy-nilly blowing.

### XXXIII

What, without asking, hither hurried *Whence?*
And, without asking, *Whither* hurried hence!

Ah, contrite Heav'n endowed us with the Vine
To drug the memory of that insolence!

### XXXIV

Up from Earth's Centre through the Seventh Gate
I rose, and on the Throne of Saturn sate,
  And many Knots unravel'd by the Road;
But not the Master-knot of Human Fate.

### XXXV

There was the Door to which I found no Key:
There was the Veil through which I could not see:
  Some little talk awhile of ME and THEE
There was—and then no more of THEE and ME.

### XXXVI

Earth could not answer; nor the Seas that mourn
In flowing Purple, of their Lord forlorn;
  Nor Heaven, with those eternal Signs reveal'd
And hidden by the sleeve of Night and Morn.

### XXXVII

Then of the THEE in ME who works behind
The Veil of Universe I cried to find
  A Lamp to guide me through the darkness; and
Something then said—"An Understanding blind."

### XXXVIII

Then to the Lip of this poor earthen Urn
I lean'd, the secret Well of Life to learn:

And Lip to Lip it murmur'd—"While you live,
Drink!—for, once dead, you never shall return."

### XXXIX

I think the Vessel, that with fugitive
Articulation answer'd, once did live,
　　And drink; and that impassive Lip I kiss'd,
How many Kisses might it take—and give!

### XL

For I remember stopping by the way
To watch a Potter thumping his wet Clay:
　　And with its all-obliterated Tongue
It murmur'd—"Gently, Brother, gently, pray!"

### XLI

For has not such a Story from of Old
Down Man's successive generations roll'd
　　Of such a clod of saturated Earth
Cast by the Maker into Human mould?

### XLII

And not a drop that from our Cups we throw
On the parcht herbage but may steal below
　　To quench the fire of Anguish in some Eye
There hidden—far beneath, and long ago.

### XLIII

As then the Tulip for her wonted sup
Of Heavenly Vintage lifts her chalice up,

Do you, twin offspring of the soil, till Heav'n
To Earth invert you like an empty Cup.

### XLIV

Do you, within your little hour of Grace,
The waving Cypress in your Arms enlace,
  Before the Mother back into her arms
Fold, and dissolve you in a last embrace.

### XLV

And if the Cup you drink, the Lip you press,
End in what All begins and ends in—Yes;
  Imagine then you *are* what heretofore
You *were*—hereafter you shall not be less.

### XLVI

So when at last the Angel of the drink
Of Darkness finds you by the river-brink,
  And, proffering his Cup, invites your Soul
Forth to your Lips to quaff it—do not shrink.

### XLVII

And fear not lest Existence closing *your*
Account, should lose, or know the type no more;
  The Eternal Sáki from the Bowl has pour'd
Millions of Bubbles like us, and will pour.

### XLVIII

When You and I behind the Veil are past,
Oh, but the long long while the World shall last,

Which of our Coming and Departure heeds
As much as Ocean of a pebble-cast.

### XLIX

One Moment in Annihilation's Waste,
One Moment, of the Well of Life to taste—
   The Stars are setting, and the Caravan
Draws to the Dawn of Nothing—Oh make haste!

### L

Would you that spangle of Existence spend
About THE SECRET—quick about it, Friend!
   A Hair, they say, divides the False and True—
And upon what, prithee, does Life depend?

### LI

A Hair, they say, divides the False and True;
Yes, and a single Alif were the clue,
   Could you but find it, to the Treasure-house,
And peradventure to THE MASTER too;

### LII

Whose secret Presence, through Creation's veins
Running Quicksilver-like eludes your pains;
   Taking all shapes from Máh to Máhi; and
They change and perish all—but He remains;

### LIII

A moment guess'd—then back behind the Fold
Immerst of Darkness round the Drama roll'd

Which, for the Pastime of Eternity,
He does Himself contrive, enact, behold.

### LIV

But if in vain, down on the stubborn floor
Of Earth, and up to Heav'n's unopening Door,
    You gaze To-day, while You are You—how then
To-morrow, You when shall be You no more?

### LV

Oh, plagued no more with Human or Divine,
To-morrow's tangle to itself resign,
    And lose your fingers in the tresses of
The Cypress-slender Minister of Wine.

### LVI

Waste not your Hour, nor in the vain pursuit
Of This and That endeavour and dispute;
    Better be merry with the fruitful Grape
Than sadden after none, or bitter, Fruit.

### LVII

You know, my Friends, how bravely in my House
For a new Marriage I did make Carouse:
    Divorced old barren Reason from my Bed,
And took the Daughter of the Vine to Spouse.

### LVIII

For "Is" and "Is-not" though with Rule and Line
And "Up-and-down" by Logic I define,

Of all that one should care to fathom, I
Was never deep in anything but—Wine.

### LIX

Ah, but my Computations, People say,
Have squared the Year to Human Compass, eh?
   If so, by striking from the Calendar
Unborn To-morrow, and dead Yesterday.

### LX

And lately, by the Tavern Door agape,
Came shining through the Dusk an Angel Shape
   Bearing a Vessel on his Shoulder; and
He bid me taste of it; and 'twas—the Grape!

### LXI

The Grape that can with Logic absolute
The Two-and-Seventy jarring Sects confute:
   The sovereign Alchemist that in a trice
Life's leaden metal into Gold transmute:

### LXII

The mighty Mahmúd, Allah-breathing Lord,
That all the misbelieving and black Horde
   Of Fears and Sorrows that infest the Soul
Scatters before him with his whirlwind Sword.

### LXIII

Why, be this Juice the growth of God, who dare
Blaspheme the twisted tendril as a Snare?

A Blessing, we should use it, should we not?
And if a Curse—why, then, Who set it there?

### LXIV

I must abjure the Balm of Life, I must,
Scared by some After-reckoning ta'en on trust,
   Or lured with Hope of some Diviner Drink,
When the frail Cup is crumbled into Dust!

### LXV

If but the Vine and Love-abjuring Band
Are in the Prophet's Paradise to stand,
   Alack, I doubt the Prophet's Paradise
Were empty as the hollow of one's Hand.

### LXVI

Oh threats of Hell and Hopes of Paradise!
One thing at least is certain—*This* Life flies;
   One thing is certain and the rest is Lies;
The Flower that once is blown for ever dies.

### LXVII

Strange, is it not? that of the myriads who
Before us pass'd the door of Darkness through,
   Not one returns to tell us of the Road,
Which to discover we must travel too.

### LXVIII

The Revelations of Devout and Learn'd
Who rose before us, and as Prophets burn'd,

Are all but Stories, which, awoke from Sleep
**They** told their fellows, and to Sleep return'd.

### LXIX

Why, if the Soul can fling the Dust aside,
And naked on the Air of Heaven ride,
   Is't not a shame—is't not a shame for **him**
So long in this Clay suburb to abide!

### LXX

But that is but a Tent wherein may rest
A Sultán to the realm of Death addrest;
   The Sultán rises, and the dark Ferrásh
Strikes, and prepares it for another guest.

### LXXI

I sent my Soul through the Invisible,
Some letter of that After-life to spell:
   And after many days my Soul return'd
And said, "Behold, Myself am Heav'n and Hell":

### LXXII

Heav'n but the Vision of fulfill'd Desire,
And Hell the Shadow of a Soul on fire,
   Cast on the Darkness into which Ourselves,
So late emerg'd from, shall so soon expire.

### LXXIII

We are no other than a moving row
Of visionary Shapes that come and go

Round with this Sun-illumin'd Lantern held
In Midnight by the Master of the Show;

### LXXIV

Impotent Pieces of the Game He plays
Upon the Chequer-board of Nights and Days;
    Hither and thither moves, and checks, and slays,
And one by one back in the Closet lays.

### LXXV

The Ball no question makes of Ayes and Noes,
But Right or Left as strikes the Player goes;
    And He that toss'd you down into the Field,
*He* knows about it all—HE knows—HE knows!

### LXXVI

The Moving Finger writes; and, having writ,
Moves on: nor all your Piety nor Wit
    Shall lure it back to cancel half a Line,
Nor all your Tears wash out a Word of it.

### LXXVII

For let Philosopher and Doctor preach
Of what they will, and what they will not—each
    Is but one Link in an eternal Chain
That none can slip, nor break, nor over-reach.

### LXXVIII

And that inverted Bowl we call The Sky,
Whereunder crawling coop'd we live and die

Lift not your hands to *It* for help—for It
As impotently rolls as you or I.

### LXXIX

With Earth's first Clay They did the Last Man knead
And there of the Last Harvest sow'd the Seed:
　　And the first Morning of Creation wrote
What the Last Dawn of Reckoning shall read.

### LXXX

Yesterday *This* Day's Madness did prepare;
To-morrow's Silence, Triumph, or Despair:
　　Drink! for you know not whence you came, nor why:
Drink! for you know not why you go, nor where.

### LXXXI

I tell you this—When, started from the Goal,
Over the flaming shoulders of the Foal
　　Of Heav'n Parwín and Mushtari they flung,
In my predestin'd Plot of Dust and Soul.

### LXXXII

The Vine had struck a fibre: which about
If clings my being—let the Dervish flout:
　　Of my Base metal may be filed a Key,
That shall unlock the Door he howls without.

### LXXXIII

And this I know: whether the one True Light
Kindle to Love, or Wrath-consume me quite,

One Flash of It within the Tavern caught
Better than in the Temple lost outright.

### LXXXIV

What! out of senseless Nothing to provoke
A conscious Something to resent the yoke
  Of unpermitted Pleasure, under pain
Of Everlasting Penalties, if broke!

### LXXXV

What! from his helpless Creature be repaid
Pure Gold for what he lent us dross-allay'd—
  Sue for a Debt we never did contract,
And cannot answer—Oh, the sorry trade!

### LXXXVI

Nay, but, for terror of his wrathful Face,
I swear I will not call Injustice Grace;
  Not one Good Fellow of the Tavern but
Would kick so poor a Coward from the place.

### LXXXVII

Oh Thou, who didst with pitfall and with gin
Beset the Road I was to wander in,
  Thou wilt not with Predestin'd Evil round
Enmesh, and then impute my Fall to Sin?

### LXXXVIII

Oh, Thou, who Man of baser Earth didst make,
And ev'n with Paradise devise the Snake:

For all the Sin the Face of wretched Man
Is black with—Man's Forgiveness give—and take!

\*      \*      \*      \*      \*      \*

### LXXXIX

As under cover of departing Day
Slunk hunger-stricken Ramazán away,
   Once more within the Potter's house alone
I stood, surrounded by the Shapes of Clay.

### XC

And once again there gather'd a scarce heard
Whisper among them; as it were, the stirr'd
   Ashes of some all but extinguisht Tongue,
Which mine ear kindled into living Word.

### XCI

Said one among them—"Surely not in vain,
My Substance from the common Earth was ta'en,
   That He who subtly wrought me into Shape
Should stamp me back to shapeless Earth again?"

### XCII

Another said—"Why, ne'er a peevish Boy
Would break the Cup from which he drank in Joy;
   Shall He that of His own free Fancy made
The Vessel, in an after-rage destroy!"

### XCIII

None answer'd this; but after silence spake
Some Vessel of a more ungainly Make;
    "They sneer at me for leaning all awry:
What! did the Hand then of the Potter shake?"

### XCIV

Thus with the Dead as with the Living, *What?*
And *Why?* so ready, but the *Wherefor* not,
    One on a sudden peevishly exclaim'd,
"Which is the Potter, pray, and which the Pot?"

### XCV

Said one—"Folks of a surly Master tell,
And daub his Visage with the Smoke of Hell:
    They talk of some sharp Trial of us—Pish!
He's a Good Fellow, and 'twill all be well."

### XCVI

"Well," said another, "Whoso will, let try,
My Clay with long Oblivion is gone dry:
    But, fill me with the old familiar Juice,
Methinks I might recover by-and-by!"

### XCVII

So while the Vessels one by one were speaking,
One spied the little Crescent all were seeking:

And then they jogg'd each other, "Brother! Brother!
Now for the Porter's shoulder-knot a-creaking!"

\*　　\*　　\*　　\*　　\*　　\*

### XCVIII

Ah, with the Grape my fading Life provide,
And wash my Body whence the Life has died,
　　And lay me, shrouded in the living Leaf,
By some not unfrequented Garden-side.

### XCIX

Whither resorting from the vernal Heat
Shall Old Acquaintance Old Acquaintance greet,
　　Under the Branch that leans above the Wall
To shed his Blossom over head and feet.

### C

That ev'n my buried Ashes such a snare
Of Vintage shall fling up into the Air,
　　As not a True-believer passing by
But shall be overtaken unaware.

### CI

Indeed the Idols I have loved so long
Have done my credit in Men's eye much wrong:
　　Have drown'd my Glory in a shallow Cup,
And sold my Reputation for a Song.

CII

Indeed, indeed, Repentance oft before
I swore—but was I sober when I swore?
  And then and then came Spring, and Rose-in-hand
My thread-bare Penitence apieces tore.

CIII

And much as Wine has play'd the Infidel,
And robb'd me of my Robe of Honour—Well,
  I often wonder what the Vintners buy
One half so precious as the ware they sell.

CIV

Yet Ah, that Spring should vanish with the Rose!
That Youth's sweet-scented manuscript should close!
  The Nightingale that in the branches sang,
Ah whence, and whither flown again, who knows!

CV

Would but the Desert of the Fountain yield
One glimpse—if dimly, yet indeed, reveal'd,
  Toward which the fainting Traveller might spring,
As springs the trampled herbage of the field!

CVI

Oh if the World were but to re-create,
That we might catch ere closed the Book of Fate,

And make The Writer on a fairer leaf
Inscribe our names, or quite obliterate!

## CVII

Better, oh better, cancel from the Scroll
Of Universe one luckless Human Soul,
    Than drop by drop enlarge the Flood that roils
Hoarser with Anguish as the Ages Roll.

## CVIII

Ah Love! could you and I with Fate conspire
To grasp this sorry Scheme of Things entire,
    Would not we shatter it to bits—and then
Re-mould it nearer to the Heart's Desire!

## CIX

But see! The rising Moon of Heav'n again
Looks for us, Sweet-heart, through the quivering Plane:
    How oft hereafter rising will she look
Among those leaves—for one of us in vain!

## CX

And when Yourself with silver Foot shall pass
Among the Guests Star-scatter'd on the Grass,
    And in your joyous errand reach the spot
Where I made One—turn down an empty Glass!

TAMÁM
Second edition—1868

## ARTHUR HUGH CLOUGH (1819-1861)

### IN A LECTURE-ROOM

Away, haunt thou not me,
Thou vain Philosophy!
Little hast thou bestead,
Save to perplex the head,
And leave the spirit dead.
Unto thy broken cisterns wherefore go,
While from the secret treasure-depths below,
Fed by the skiey shower,
And clouds that sink and rest on hill-tops high,
Wisdom at once, and Power,
Are welling, bubbling forth, unseen, incessantly?
Why labour at the dull mechanic oar,
When the fresh breeze is blowing,
And the strong current flowing,
Right onward to the Eternal Shore?

1840

### QUA CURSUM VENTUS

As ships, becalmed at eve, that lay
  With canvas drooping, side by side,
Two towers of sail at dawn of day
  Are scarce long leagues apart descried;

When fell the night, upsprung the breeze,
  And all the darkling hours they plied,
Nor dreamt but each the self-same seas
  By each was cleaving, side by side:

E'en so—but why the tale reveal
  Of those, whom year by year unchanged,

Brief absence joined anew to feel,
   Astounded, soul from soul estranged?

At dead of night their sails were filled,
   And onward each rejoicing steered—
Ah, neither blame, for neither willed,
   Or wist, what first with dawn appeared!

To veer, how vain! On, onward strain,
   Brave barks! In light, in darkness too,
Through winds and tides one compass guides--
   To that, and your own selves, be true.

But O blithe breeze; and O great seas,
   Though ne'er, that earliest parting past,
On your wide plain they join again,
   Together lead them home at last.

One port, methought, alike they sought,
   One purpose hold where'er they fare,—
O bounding breeze, O rushing seas!
   At last, at last, unite them there!

1849

## SAY NOT THE STRUGGLE NOUGHT
## AVAILETH

Say not the struggle nought availeth,
   The labour and the wounds are vain,
The enemy faints not, nor faileth,
   And as things have been they remain.

If hopes were dupes, fears may be liars;
   It may be, in yon smoke concealed,
Your comrades chase e'en now the fliers,
   And, but for you, possess the field.

For while the tired waves, vainly breaking,
  Seem here no painful inch to gain,
Far back, through creeks and inlets making,
  Comes silent, flooding in, the main.

And not by eastern windows only,
  When daylight comes, come in the light,
In front, the sun climbs slow, how slowly,
  But westward, look, the land is bright.

1849


## WHERE LIES THE LAND

Where lies the land to which the ship would go?
Far, far ahead, is all her seamen know.
And where the land she travels from? Away,
Far, far behind, is all that they can say.

On sunny noons upon the deck's smooth face,
Linked arm in arm, how pleasant here to pace;
Or, o'er the stern reclining, watch below
The foaming wake far widening as we go.

On stormy nights when wild north-westers rave,
How proud a thing to fight with wind and wave!
The dripping sailor on the reeling mast
Exults to bear, and scorns to wish it past.

Where lies the land to which the ship would go?
Far, far ahead, is all her seamen know.
And where the land she travels from? Away,
Far, far behind, is all that they can say.

1862

MATTHEW  ARNOLD  (1822–1888)

## THE FORSAKEN MERMAN

Come, dear children, let us away;
Down and away below.
Now my brothers call from the bay;
Now the great winds shorewards blow;
Now the salt tides seawards flow;
Now the wild white horses play,
Champ and chafe and toss in the spray.
Children dear, let us away.
This way, this way.

Call her once before you go.
Call once yet.
In a voice that she will know:
"Margaret! Margaret!"
Children's voices should be dear
(Call once more) to a mother's ear:
Children's voices, wild with pain.
Surely she will come again.
Call her once and come away.
This way, this way.
"Mother dear, we cannot stay."
The wild white horses foam and fret.
Margaret! Margaret!
Come, dear children, come away down.

Call no more.
One last look at the white-wall'd town,
And the little grey church on the windy shore.
Then come down.

She will not come though you call all day
Come away, come away.

Children dear, was it yesterday
We heard the sweet bells over the bay?
In the caverns where we lay,
Through the surf and through the swell
The far-off sound of a silver bell?
Sand-strewn caverns, cool and deep,
Where the winds are all asleep;
Where the spent lights quiver and gleam;
Where the salt weed sways in the stream;
Where the sea-beasts rang'd all round,
Feed in the ooze of their pasture-ground;
Where the sea-snakes coil and twine,
Dry their mail and bask in the brine;
Where great whales come sailing by,
Sail and sail, with unshut eye,
Round the world forever and aye?
When did music come this way?
Children dear, was it yesterday?

Children dear, was it yesterday
(Call yet once) that she went away?
Once she sate with you and me,
On a gold throne in the heart of the sea,
And the youngest sate on her knee,
She comb'd its bright hair, and she tended it well,
When down swung the sound of the far-off bell.
She sigh'd, she look'd up through the clear green sea.
She said: "I must go, for my kinsfolk pray
In the little grey church on the shore to-day.
'Twill be Easter-time in the world—ah me!
And I lose my poor soul, Merman, here with thee."
I said: "Go up, dear heart, through the waves.

Say thy prayer, and come back to the kind sea-caves."
She smil'd, she went up through the surf in the bay.
Children dear, was it yesterday?

Children dear, were we long alone?
"The sea grows stormy, the little ones moan.
Long prayers," I said, "in the world they say.
Come," I said, and we rose through the surf in the bay.
We went up the beach, by the sandy down
Where the sea-stocks bloom, to the white-wall'd town.
Through the narrow pav'd streets, where all was still,
To the little grey church on the windy hill.
From the church came a murmur of folk at their prayers,
But we stood without in the cold blowing airs.
We climb'd on the graves, on the stones, worn with rains,
And we gaz'd up the aisle through the small leaded
          panes.
She sat by the pillar; we say her clear:
"Margaret, hist! come quick, we are here.
Dear heart," I said, "we are long alone.
The sea grows stormy, the little ones moan."
But, ah, she gave me never a look,
For her eyes were seal'd to the holy book.
Loud prays the priest; shut stands the door.
Come away, children, call no more.
Come away, come down, call no more.

Down, down, down.
    Down to the depths of the sea.
She sits at her wheel in the humming town,
Singing most joyfully.
Hark, what she sings; "O joy, O joy,
For the humming street, and the child with its toy.
For the priest, and the bell, and the holy well.
For the wheel where I spun.

And the blessed light of the sun."
And so she sings her fill,
Singing most joyfully,
Till the shuttle falls from her hand,
And the whizzing wheel stands still.
She steals to the window, and looks at the sand;
And over the sand at the sea;
And her eyes are set in a stare;
And anon there breaks a sigh,
And anon there drops a tear,
From a sorrow-clouded eye,
And a heart sorrow-laden,
A long, long sigh,
For the cold strange eyes of a little Mermaiden,
And the gleam of her golden hair.

Come away, away children.
Come children, come down.
The hoarse wind blows colder;
Lights shine in the town.
She will start from her slumber
When gusts shake the door;
She will hear the winds howling,
Will hear the waves roar.
We shall see, while above us
The waves roar and whirl,
A ceiling of amber,
A pavement of pearl.
Singing, "Here came a mortal,
But faithless was she.
And alone dwell for ever
The kings of the sea."

But, children, at midnight,
When soft the winds blow;

When clear falls the moonlight;
When spring-tides are low:
When sweet airs come seaward
From heaths starr'd with broom;
And high rocks throw mildly
On the blanch'd sands a gloom:
Up the still, glistening beaches,
Up the creeks we will hie;
Over banks of bright seaweed
The ebb-tide leaves dry.
We will gaze, from the sand-hills,
At the white, sleeping town;
At the church on the hill-side—
And then come back down.
Singing, "There dwells a lov'd one,
But cruel is she!
She left lonely for ever
The kings of the sea."

                                        1849

## TO A FRIEND

Who prop, thou ask'st, in these bad days, my mind?
He much, the old man, who, clearest-soul'd of men,
Saw The Wide Prospect, and the Asian Fen,
And Tmolus' hill, and Smyrna's bay, though blind.
Much he, whose friendship I not long since won,
That halting slave, who in Nicopolis
Taught Arrian, when Vespasian's brutal son
Clear'd Rome of what most sham'd him.
        But be his
My special thanks, whose even-balanc'd soul,
From first youth tested up to extreme old age,
Business could not make dull, nor Passion wild:
Who saw life steadily, and saw it whole:

The mellow glory of the Attic stage;
Singer of sweet Colonus, and its child.

1849

## SHAKESPEARE

OTHERS abide our question. Thou art free.
We ask and ask: Thou smilest and art still,
Out-topping knowledge. For the loftiest hill
That to the stars uncrowns his majesty,
Planting his stedfast footsteps in the sea,
Making the Heaven of Heavens his dwelling-place,
Spares but the cloudy border of his base
To the foil'd searching of mortality:
And thou, who didst the stars and sunbeams know,
Self-school'd, self-scann'd, self-honour'd, self-secure,
Didst walk on Earth unguess'd at. Better so!
All pains the immortal spirit must endure,
All weakness that impairs, all griefs that bow,
Find their sole voice in that victorious brow.

1849

## SELF-DEPENDENCE

WEARY of myself, and sick of asking
What I am, and what I ought to be,
At the vessel's prow I stand, which bears me
Forwards, forwards, o'er the starlit sea.

And a look of passionate desire
O'er the sea and to the stars I send:
"Ye who from my childhood up have calm'd me,
Calm me, ah, compose me to the end.

"Ah, once more," I cried, "ye stars, ye waters,
On my heart your mighty charm renew:

Still, still, let me, as I gaze upon you,
Feel my soul becoming vast like you."

From the intense, clear, star-sown vault of heaven,
Over the lit sea's unquiet way,
In the rustling night-air came the answer—
"Wouldst thou *be* as these are? *Live* as they.

"Unaffrighted by the silence round them,
Undistracted by the sights they see,
These demand not that the things without them
Yield them love, amusement, sympathy.

"And with joy the stars perform their shining,
And the sea its long moon-silver'd roll.
For alone they live, nor pine with noting
All the fever of some differing soul.

"Bounded by themselves, and unobservant
In what state God's other works may be,
In their own tasks all their powers pouring,
These attain the mighty life you see."

O air-born Voice! long since, severely clear,
A cry like thine in my own heart I hear.
"Resolve to be thyself: and know, that he
Who finds himself, loses his misery."

1852

## A SUMMER NIGHT

IN THE deserted moon-blanch'd' street
How lonely rings the echo of my feet!
Those windows, which I gaze at, frown,

Silent and white, unopening down,
Repellent as the world;—but see!
A break between the housetops shows
The moon, and, lost behind her, fading dim
Into the dewy dark obscurity
Down at the far horizon's rim,
Doth a whole tract of heaven disclose.

And to my mind the thought
Is on a sudden brought
Of a past night, and a far different scene.
Headlands stood out into the moon-lit deep
As clearly as at noon;
The spring-tide's brimming flow
Heav'd dazzlingly between;
Houses with long white sweep
Girdled the glistening bay:
Behind, through the soft air,
The blue haze-cradled mountains spread away.
That night was far more fair;
But the same restless pacings to and fro
And the same vainly throbbing heart was there,
And the same bright calm moon.

And the calm moonlight seems to say—
*Hast thou then still the old unquiet breast*
*That neither deadens into rest*
*Nor ever feels the fiery glow*
*That whirls the spirit from itself away,*
*But fluctuates to and fro*
*Never by passion quite possess'd,*
*And never quite benumb'd by the world's sway?*
And I, I know not if to pray
Still to be what I am, or yield, and be
Like all the other men I see.

For most men in a brazen prison live,
Where in the sun's hot eye,
With heads bent o'er their toil, they languidly
Their lives to some unmeaning taskwork give,
Dreaming of nought beyond their prison wall.
And as, year after year,
Fresh products of their barren labour fall
From their tired hands, and rest
Never yet comes more near,
Gloom settles slowly down over their breast.
And while they try to stem
The waves of mournful thought by which they are prest,
Death in their prison reaches them,
Unfreed, having seen nothing, still unblest.

And the rest, a few,
Escape their prison, and depart
On the wide Ocean of Life anew.
There the freed prisoner, where'er his heart
Listeth, will sail;
Nor doth he know how there prevail,
Despotic on life's sea,
Trade-winds which cross it from eternity.
Awhile he holds some false way, undebarr'd
By thwarting signs, and braves
The freshening wind and blackening waves
And then the tempest strikes him; and between
The lightning-bursts is seen
Only a driving wreck,
And the pale master on his spar-strewn deck
With anguish'd face and flying hair
Grasping the rudder hard,
Still bent to make some port he knows not where,
Still standing for some false, impossible shore.
And sterner comes the roar

Of sea and wind, and through the deepening gloom
Fainter and fainter wreck and helmsman loom,
And he too disappears, and comes no more.

Is there no life, but these alone?
Madman or slave, must man be one?
Plainness and clearness without shadow of stain!
Clearness divine!
Ye heavens, whose pure dark regions have no sign
Of languor, though so calm, and, though so great,
Are yet untroubled and unpassionate;
Who, though so noble, share in the world's toil,
And, though so task'd, keep free from dust and soil!
I will not say that your mild deeps retain
A tinge, it may be, of their silent pain
Who have long'd deeply once, and long'd in vain—
But I will rather say that you remain
A world above man's head, to let him see
How boundless might his soul's horizons be,
How vast, yet of what clear transparency!
How it were good to abide there, and breathe free;
How fair a lot to fill
Is left to each man still!

1852

## REQUIESCAT

STREW on her roses, roses,
　And never a spray of yew.
In quiet she reposes:
　Ah, would that I did too!

Her mirth the world required:
　She bath'd it in smiles of glee.

But her heart was tired, tired,
  And now they let her be.

Her life was turning, turning,
  In mazes of heat and sound.
But for peace her soul was yearning,
  And now peace laps her round.

Her cabin'd, ample Spirit,
  It flutter'd and fail'd for breath.
To-night it doth inherit
  The vasty Hall of Death.

1853

## STANZAS FROM THE GRANDE CHARTREUSE

THROUGH Alpine meadows soft-suffused
With rain, where thick the crocus blows,
Past the dark forges long disused,
The mule-track from Saint Laurent goes.
The bridge is cross'd, and slow we ride,
Through forest, up the mountain-side.

The autumnal evening darkens round,
The wind is up, and drives the rain;
While, hark! far down, with strangled sound
Doth the Dead Guier's stream complain,
Where that wet smoke, among the woods,
Over his boiling cauldron broods.

Swift rush the spectral vapors white
Past limestone scars with ragged pines,
Showing—then blotting from our sight!—
Halt—through the cloud-drift something shines!

High in the valley, wet and drear,
The huts of Courrerie appear.

*Strike leftward!* cries our guide; and higher
Mounts up the stony forest-way.
At last the encircling trees retire;
Look! through the showery twilight gray
What pointed roofs are these advance?—
A palace of the Kings of France?

Approach, for what we seek is here!
Alight, and sparely sup, and wait
For rest in this outbuilding near;
Then cross the sward and reach that gate.
Knock; pass the wicket! Thou art come
To the Carthusians' world-famed home.

The silent courts, where night and day
Into their stone-carved basins cold
The splashing icy fountains play—
The humid corridors behold!
Where, ghostlike in the deepening night
Cowl'd forms brush by in gleaming white.

The chapel, where no organ's peal
Invests the stern and naked prayer—
With penitential cries they kneel
And wrestle; rising then, with bare
And white uplifted faces stand,
Passing the Host from hand to hand;

Each takes, and then his visage wan
Is buried in his cowl once more.
The cells!—the suffering Son of Man
Upon the wall—the knee-worn floor—

And where they sleep, that wooden bed,
Which shall their coffin be, when dead!

The library, where tract and tome
Not to feed priestly pride are there,
To hymn the conquering march of Rome,
Nor yet to amuse, as ours are!
They paint of souls the inner strife,
Their drops of blood, their death in life.

The garden, overgrown—yet mild,
See, fragrant herbs are flowering there!
Strong children of the Alpine wild
Whose culture is the brethren's care;
Of human tasks their only one,
And cheerful works beneath the sun.

Those halls, too, destined to contain
Each its own pilgrim-host of old,
From England, Germany, or Spain—
All are before me! I behold
The House, the Brotherhood austere!
—And what am I, that I am here?

For rigorous teachers seized my youth,
And purged its faith, and trimm'd its fire,
Show'd me the high, white star of Truth,
There bade me gaze, and there aspire.
Even now their whispers pierce the gloom:
*What dost thou in this living tomb?*

Forgive me, masters of the mind!
At whose behest I long ago
So much unlearnt, so much resign'd—
I come not here to be your foe!

I seek these anchorites, not in ruth,
To curse and to deny your truth;

Not as their friend, or child, I speak!
But as, on some far northern strand,
Thinking of his own Gods, a Greek
In pity and mournful awe might stand
Before some fallen Runic stone—
For both were faiths, and both are gone.

Wandering between two worlds, one dead,
The other powerless to be born,
With nowhere yet to rest my head,
Like these, on earth I wait forlorn.
Their faith, my tears, the world deride—
I come to shed them at their side.

Oh, hide me in your gloom profound,
Ye solemn seats of holy pain!
Take me, cowl'd forms, and fence me round,
Till I possess my soul again;
Till free my thoughts before me roll,
Not chafed by hourly false control!

For the world cries your faith is now
But a dead time's exploded dream;
My melancholy, sciolists say,
Is a pass'd mode, an outworn theme—
As if the world had ever had
A faith, or sciolists been sad!

Ah, if it *be* pass'd, take away,
At least, the restlessness, the pain;
Be man henceforth no more a prey
To these out-dated stings again!

The nobleness of grief is gone—
Ah, leave us not the fret alone!

But—if you cannot give us ease—
Last of the race of them who grieve
Here leave us to die out with these
Last of the people who believe!
Silent, while years engrave the brow;
Silent—the best are silent now.

Achilles ponders in his tent,
The kings of modern thought are dumb;
Silent they are, though not content,
And wait to see the future come.
They have the grief men had of yore,
But they contend and cry no more.

Our fathers water'd with their tears
This sea of time whereon we sail,
Their voices were in all men's ears
We pass'd within their puissant hail.
Still the same ocean round us raves,
But we stand mute, and watch the waves.

For what avail'd it, all the noise
And outcry of the former men?—
Say, have their sons achieved more joys?
Say, is life lighter now than then?
The sufferers died, they left their pain—
The pangs which tortured them remain.

What helps it now, that Byron bore,
With haughty scorn which mock'd the smart,
Through Europe to the Ætolian shore
The pageant of his bleeding heart?

That thousands counted every groan,
And Europe made his woe her own?

What boots it, Shelley! that the breeze
Carried thy lovely wail away,
Musical through Italian trees
Which fringe thy soft blue Spezzian bay?
Inheritors of thy distress
Have restless hearts one throb the less?

Or are we easier, to have read,
O Obermann! the sad, stern page,
Which tells us how thou hidd'st thy head
From the fierce tempest of thine age
In the lone brakes of Fontainebleau,
Or chalets near the Alpine snow?

Ye slumber in your silent grave!—
The world, which for an idle day
Grace to your mood of sadness gave,
Long since hath flung her weeds away.
The eternal trifler breaks your spell;
But we—we learned your lore too well!

Years hence, perhaps, may dawn an age,
More fortunate, alas! than we,
Which without hardness will be sage,
And gay without frivolity.
Sons of the world, oh, speed those years;
But, while we wait, allow our tears!

Allow them! We admire with awe
The exulting thunder of your race;
You give the universe your law,
You triumph over time and space.

Your pride of life, your tireless powers,
We mark them, but they are not ours.

We are like children rear'd in shade
Beneath some old-world abbey wall
Forgotten in a forest-glade
And secret from the eyes of all;
Deep, deep the greenwood round them waves,
Their abbey, and its close of graves.

But, where the road runs near the stream,
Oft through the trees they catch a glance
Of passing troops in the sun's beam—
Pennon, and plume, and flashing lance!
Forth to the world those soldiers fare,
To life, to cities, and to war.

And through the woods, another way,
Faint bugle-notes from far are borne,
Where hunters gather, staghounds bay,
Round some old forest-lodge at morn;
Gay dames are there in sylvan green;
Laughter and cries—those notes between!

The banners flashing through the trees
Make their blood dance and chain their eyes;
That bugle-music on the breeze
Arrests them with a charm'd surprise.
Banner by turns and bugle woo:
*Ye shy recluses, follow too!*

O children, what do ye reply?—
"Action and pleasure, will ye roam
Through these secluded dells to cry
And call us? but too late ye come!

Too late for us your call ye blow
Whose bent was taken long ago.

"Long since we pace this shadow'd nave;
We watch those yellow tapers shine,
Emblems of hope over the grave,
In the high altar's depth divine;
The organ carries to our ear
Its accents of another sphere.

"Fenced early in this cloistral round
Of reverie, of shade, of prayer,
How should we grow in other ground?
How should we flower in foreign air?
Pass, banners, pass, and bugles, cease!
And leave our desert to its peace."

1855

## DOVER BEACH

THE sea is calm to-night.
The tide is full, the moon lies fair
Upon the Straits;—on the French coast, the light
Gleams, and is gone; the cliffs of England stand,
Glimmering and vast, out in the tranquil bay.
Come to the window, sweet is the night air!
Only, from the long line of spray
Where the sea meets the moon-blanch'd sand,
Listen! you hear the grating roar
Of pebbles which the waves suck back, and fling,
At their return, up the high strand,
Begin, and cease, and then again begin,
With tremulous cadence slow, and bring
The eternal note of sadness in.

Sophocles long ago
Heard it on the Ægæan, and it brought
Into his mind the turbid ebb and flow
Of human misery; we
Find also in the sound a thought,
Hearing it by this distant northern sea.

The sea of faith
Was once, too, at the full, and round earth's shore
Lay like the folds of a bright girdle furl'd;
But now I only hear
Its melancholy, long, withdrawing roar,
Retreating to the breath
Of the night-wind down the vast edges drear
And naked shingles of the world.

Ah, love, let us be true
To one another! for the world, which seems
To lie before us like a land of dreams,
So various, so beautiful, so new,
Hath really neither joy, nor love, nor light,
Nor certitude, nor peace, nor help for pain;
And we are here as on a darkling plain
Swept with confused alarms of struggle and flight,
Where ignorant armies clash by night.

1867

## RUGBY CHAPEL

COLDLY, sadly descends
The autumn evening. The field
Strewn with its dank yellow drifts
Of wither'd leaves, and the elms,
Fade into dimness apace,
Silent;—hardly a shout

From a few boys late at their play!
The lights come out in the street,
In the school-room windows; but cold,
Solemn, unlighted, austere,
Through the gathering darkness, arise
The chapel-walls, in whose bound
Thou, my father! art laid.

There thou dost lie, in the gloom
Of the autumn evening. But ah!
That word, *gloom*, to my mind
Brings thee back in the light
Of thy radiant vigour again!
In the gloom of November we pass'd
Days not dark at thy side;
Seasons impair'd not the ray
Of thine even cheerfulness clear.
Such thou wast! and I stand
In the autumn evening, and think
Of bygone autumns with thee.

Fifteen years have gone round
Since thou arosest to tread,
In the summer morning, the road
Of death, at a call unforeseen,
Sudden. For fifteen years,
We who till then in thy shade
Rested as under the boughs
Of a mighty oak, have endured
Sunshine and rain as we might,
Bare, unshaded, alone,
Lacking the shelter of thee.

O strong soul, by what shore
Tarriest thou now? For that force,

Surely, has not been left vain!
Somewhere, surely, afar,
In the sounding labour-house vast
Of being, is practised that strength,
Zealous, beneficent, firm!

Yes, in some far-shining sphere,
Conscious or not of the past,
Still thou performest the word
Of the Spirit in whom thou dost live,
Prompt, unwearied, as here!
Still thou upraisest with zeal
The humble good from the ground,
Sternly repressest the bad!
Still, like a trumpet, dost rouse
Those who with half-open eyes
Tread the border-land dim
'Twixt vice and virtue; reviv'st,
Succourest!—this was thy work,
This was thy life upon earth.

What is the course of the life
Of mortal men on the earth?
Most men eddy about
Here and there—eat and drink,
Chatter and love and hate,
Gather and squander, are raised
Aloft, are hurl'd in the dust,
Striving blindly, achieving
Nothing; and then they die—
Perish; and no one asks
Who or what they have been,
More than he asks what waves
In the moonlit solitudes mild

Of the midmost Ocean, have swell'd,
Foam'd for a moment, and gone.

And there are some, whom a thirst
Ardent, unquenchable, fires,
Not with the crowd to be spent,
Not without aim to go round
In an eddy of purposeless dust
Effort unmeaning and vain.
Ah yes! some of us strive
Not without action to die
Fruitless, but something to snatch
From dull oblivion, nor all
Glut the devouring grave!
We, we have chosen our path—
Path to a clear-purposed goal,
Path of advance!—but it leads
A long, steep journey, through sunk
Gorges, o'er mountains in snow.
Cheerful, with friends, we set forth;
Then, on the height, comes the storm.
Thunder crashes from rock
To rock; the cataracts reply;
Lightnings dazzle our eyes;
Roaring torrents have breach'd
The track; the stream-bed descends
In the place where the wayfarer once
Planted his footstep; the spray
Boils o'er its borders; aloft,
The unseen snow-beds dislodge
Their hanging ruin. Alas,
Havoc is made in our train!
Friends who set forth at our side
Falter, are lost in the storm!

We, we only, are left!
With frowning foreheads, with lips
Sternly compress'd, we strain on,
On—and at nightfall, at last,
Come to the end of our way,
To the lonely inn 'mid the rocks;
Where the gaunt and taciturn host
Stands on the threshold, the wind
Shaking his thin white hairs—
Holds his lantern to scan
Our storm-beat figures, and asks:
Whom in our party we bring?
Whom we have left in the snow?

Sadly we answer: We bring
Only ourselves; we lost
Sight of the rest in the storm.
Hardly ourselves we fought through,
Stripp'd, without friends, as we are.
Friends, companions, and train
The avalanche swept from our side.

But thou would'st not *alone*
Be saved, my father! *alone*
Conquer and come to thy goal,
Leaving the rest in the wild.
We were weary, and we
Fearful, and we, in our march,
Fain to drop down and to die.
Still thou turnedst, and still
Beckonedst the trembler, and still
Gavest the weary thy hand.
If, in the paths of the world,
Stones might have wounded thy feet,
Toil or dejection have tried
Thy spirit, of that we saw

Nothing!—to us thou wert still
Cheerful, and helpful, and firm!
Therefore to thee it was given
Many to save with thyself;
And, at the end of thy day,
O faithful shepherd! to come,
Bringing thy sheep in thy hand.


And through thee I believe
In the noble and great who are gone;
Pure souls honour'd and blest
By former ages, who else—
Such, so soulless, so poor,
Is the race of men whom I see—
Seem'd but a dream of the heart,
Seem'd but a cry of desire.
Yes! I believe that there lived
Others like thee in the past,
Not like the men of the crowd
Who all round me to-day
Bluster or cringe, and make life
Hideous, and arid, and vile;
But souls temper'd with fire,
Fervent, heroic, and good,
Helpers and friends of mankind.


Servants of God!—or sons
Shall I not call you? because
Not as servants ye knew
Your Father's innermost mind,
His, who unwillingly sees
One of his little ones lost—
Yours is the praise, if mankind

Hath not as yet in its march
Fainted, and fallen, and died!

See! In the rocks of the world
Marches the host of mankind,
A feeble, wavering line.
Where are they tending?—A God
Marshall'd them, gave them their goal.
Ah, but the way is so long!
Years they have been in the wild!
Sore thirst plagues them; the rocks,
Rising all round, overawe;
Factions divide them; their host
Threatens to break, to dissolve.
Ah, keep, keep them combined!
Else, of the myriads who fill
That army, not one shall arrive;
Sole they shall stray; in the rocks
Labour for ever in vain,
Die one by one in the waste.

Then, in such hour of need
Of your fainting, dispirited race,
Ye, like angels, appear,
Radiant with ardour divine.
Beacons of hope, ye appear!
Languor is not in your heart,
Weakness is not in your word,
Weariness not on your brow.
Ye alight in our van; at your voice,
Panic, despair, flee away.
Ye move through the ranks, recall
The stragglers, refresh the outworn,
Praise, re-inspire the brave.
Order, courage, return.

Eyes rekindling, and prayers,
Follow your steps as ye go.
Ye fill up the gaps in our files,
Strengthen the wavering line,
Stablish, continue our march,
On, to the bound of the waste,
On, to the City of God.

1867

# DANTE GABRIEL ROSSETTI (1828-1882)

## THE BLESSED DAMOZEL

THE blessed damozel leaned out
    From the gold bar of Heaven;
Her eyes were deeper than the depth
    Of waters stilled at even;
She had three lilies in her hand,
    And the stars in her hair were seven.

Her robe, ungirt from clasp to hem,
    No wrought flowers did adorn,
But a white rose of Mary's gift,
    For service meetly worn;
Her hair that lay along her back
    Was yellow like ripe corn.

Herseemed she scarce had been a day
    One of God's choristers;
The wonder was not yet quite gone
    From that still look of hers;
Albeit, to them she left, her day
    Had counted as ten years.

(To one, it is ten years of years.
  . . . Yet now, and in this place,
Surely she leaned o'er me—her hair
  Fell all about my face. . . .
Nothing: the autumn fall of leaves.
  The whole year sets apace.)

It was the rampart of God's house
  That she was standing on;
By God built over the sheer depth
  The which is Space begun;
So high, that looking downward thence
  She scarce could see the sun.

It lies in Heaven, across the flood
  Of ether, as a bridge.
Beneath, the tides of day and night
  With flame and darkness ridge
The void, as low as where this earth
  Spins like a fretful midge.

Around her, lovers, newly met
  'Mid deathless love's acclaims,
Spoke evermore among themselves
  Their heart-remembered names;
And the souls mounting up to God
  Went by her like thin flames.

And still she bowed herself and stooped
  Out of the circling charm;
Until her bosom must have made
  The bar she leaned on warm,
And the lilies lay as if asleep
  Along her bended arm.

From the fixed place of Heaven she saw
    Time like a pulse shake fierce
Through all the world. Her gaze still strove
    Within the gulf to pierce
Its path; and now she spoke as when
    The stars sang in their spheres.

The sun was gone now; the curled moon
    Was like a little feather
Fluttering far down the gulf; and now
    She spoke through the still weather.
Her voice was like the voice the stars
    Had when they sang together.

(Ah sweet! Even now, in that bird's song,
    Strove not her accents there,
Fain to be hearkened? When those bells
    Possessed the mid-day air,
Strove not her steps to reach my side
    Down all the echoing stair?)

"I wish that he were come to me,
    For he will come," she said.
"Have I not prayed in Heaven?—on earth,
    Lord, Lord, has he not pray'd?
Are not two prayers a perfect strength?
    And shall I feel afraid?

"When round his head the aureole clings.
    And he is clothed in white,
I'll take his hand and go with him
    To the deep wells of light;
As unto a stream we will step down,
    And bathe there in God's sight.

"We two will stand beside that shrine,
   Occult, withheld, untrod,
Whose lamps are stirred continually
   With prayer sent up to God;
And see our old prayers, granted, melt
   Each like a little cloud.

"We two will lie i' the shadow of
   That living mystic tree
Within whose secret growth the Dove
   Is sometimes felt to be,
While every leaf that His plumes touch
   Saith His Name audibly.

"And I myself will teach to him,
   I myself, lying so,
The songs I sing here; which his voice
   Shall pause in, hushed and slow,
And find some knowledge at each pause,
   Or some new thing to know."

(Alas! We two, we two, thou say'st!
   Yea, one wast thou with me
That once of old. But shall God lift
   To endless unity
The soul whose likeness with thy soul
   Was but its love for thee?)

"We two," she said, "will seek the groves
   Where the lady Mary is,
With her five handmaidens, whose names
   Are five sweet symphonies,
Cecily, Gertrude, Magdalen,
   Margaret and Rosalys.

"Circlewise sit they, with bound locks
  And foreheads garlanded;
Into the fine cloth white like flame
  Weaving the golden thread,
To fashion the birth-robes for them
  Who are just born, being dead.

"He shall fear, haply, and be dumb;
  Then will I lay my cheek
To his, and tell about our love,
  Not once abashed or weak;
And the dear Mother will approve
  My pride, and let me speak.

"Herself shall bring us, hand in hand,
  To Him round whom all souls
Kneel, the clear-ranged unnumbered heads
  Bowed with their aureoles:
And angels meeting us shall sing
  To their citherns and citoles.

"There will I ask of Christ the Lord
  Thus much for him and me:—
Only to live as once on earth
  With Love, only to be,
As then awhile, for ever now
  Together, I and he."

She gazed and listened and then said,
  Less sad of speech than mild,—
"All this is when he comes." She ceased.
  The light thrilled towards her, fill'd
With angels in strong level flight.
  Her eyes prayed, and she smil'd.

(I saw her smile.) But soon their path
   Was vague in distant spheres:
And then she cast her arms along
   The golden barriers,
And laid her face between her hands,
   And wept. (I heard her tears.)

1847

## SISTER HELEN

"Why did you melt your waxen man,
                     Sister Helen?
To-day is the third since you began."
"The time was long, yet the time ran,
                     Little brother."
          *(O Mother, Mary Mother,*
*Three days to-day, between Hell and Heaven!)*

"But if you have done your work aright,
                     Sister Helen,
You'll let me play, for you said I might."
"Be very still in your play to-night,
                     Little brother."
          *(O Mother, Mary Mother,*
*Third night, to-night, between Hell and Heaven!)*

"You said it must melt ere vesper-bell,
                     Sister Helen;
If now it be molten, all is well."
"Even so,—nay, peace! you cannot tell,
                     Little brother."
          *(O Mother, Mary Mother,*
*O what is this, between Hell and Heaven?)*

"Oh the waxen knave was plump to-day,
                     Sister Helen;
How like dead folk he has dropped away!"

"Nay now, of the dead what can you say,
               Little brother?"
                    (*O Mother, Mary Mother,*
*What of the dead, between Hell and Heaven?*)


"See, see, the sunken pile of wood,
               Sister Helen,
Shines through the thinned wax red as blood!"
"Nay now, when looked you yet on blood,
               Little brother?"
                    (*O Mother, Mary Mother,*
*How pale she is, between Hell and Heaven!*)


"Now close your eyes, for they're sick and sore,
               Sister Helen,
And I'll play without the gallery door."
"Aye, let me rest,—I'll lie on the floor,
               Little brother."
                    (*O Mother, Mary Mother,*
*What rest to-night between Hell and Heaven?*)


"Here high up in the balcony,
               Sister Helen,
The moon flies face to face with me."
"Aye, look and say whatever you see,
               Little brother."
                    (*O Mother, Mary Mother,*
*What sight to-night, between Hell and Heaven?*)


"Outside it's merry in the wind's wake,
               Sister Helen;
In the shaken trees the chill stars shake."
"Hush, heard you a horse-tread as you spake,
               Little brother?"

*(O Mother, Mary Mother,*
*What sound to-night, between Hell and Heaven?)*

"I hear a horse-tread, and I see,
                    Sister Helen,
Three horsemen that ride terribly."
"Little brother, whence come the three,
                    Little brother?"
                    *(O Mother, Mary Mother,*
*Whence should they come, between Hell and*
        *Heaven?)*

"They come by the hill-verge from Boyne Bar,
                    Sister Helen,
And one draws nigh, but two are afar."
"Look, look, do you know them who they are,
                    Little brother?"
                    *(O Mother, Mary Mother,*
*Who should they be, between Hell and Heaven?)*

"Oh, it's Keith of Eastholm rides so fast,
                    Sister Helen,
For I know the white mane on the blast."
"The hour has come, has come at last,
                    Little brother!"
                    *(O Mother, Mary Mother,*
*Her hour at last, between Hell and Heaven!)*

"He has made a sign and called Halloo!
                    Sister Helen,
And he says that he would speak with you."
"Oh tell him I fear the frozen dew,
                    Little brother."
                    *(O Mother, Mary Mother,*
*Why laughs she thus, between Hell and Heaven?)*

"The wind is loud, but I hear him cry,
      *Sister Helen,*
That Keith of Ewern's like to die."
"And he and thou, and thou and I,
       *Little brother.*"
     *(O Mother, Mary Mother,*
*And they and we, between Hell and Heaven!)*

"Three days ago, on his marriage-morn,
       *Sister Helen,*
He sickened, and lies since then forlorn."
"For bridegroom's side is the bride a thorn,
       *Little brother?*"
     *(O Mother, Mary Mother,*
*Cold bridal cheer, between Hell and Heaven!)*

"Three days and nights he has lain abed,
       *Sister Helen,*
And he prays in torment to be dead."
"The thing may chance, if he have prayed,
       *Little brother!*"
     *(O Mother, Mary Mother,*
*If he have prayed, between Hell and Heaven!)*

"But he has not ceased to cry to-day,
       *Sister Helen,*
That you should take your curse away."
"*My* prayer was heard,—he need but pray,
       *Little brother!*"
     *(O Mother, Mary Mother,*
*Shall God not hear, between Hell and Heaven?)*

"But he says, till you take back your ban,
       *Sister Helen,*
His soul would pass, yet never can."

"Nay then, shall I slay a living man,
                Little brother?"
           *(O Mother, Mary Mother,*
*A living soul, between Hell and Heaven!)*

"But he calls for ever on your name,
                Sister Helen,
And says that he melts before a flame."
"My heart for his pleasure fared the same,
                Little brother."
           *(O Mother, Mary Mother,*
*Fire at the heart, between Hell and Heaven!)*

"Here's Keith of Westholm riding fast,
                Sister Helen;
For I know the white plume on the blast."
"The hour, the sweet hour I forecast,
                Little brother!"
           *(O Mother, Mary Mother,*
*Is the hour sweet, between Hell and Heaven?)*

"He stops to speak, and he stills his horse,
                Sister Helen;
But his words are drowned in the wind's course."
"Nay hear, nay hear, you must hear perforce,
                Little brother!"
           *(O Mother, Mary Mother,*
*What word now heard, between Hell and Heaven?)*

"Oh, he says that Keith of Ewern's cry,
                Sister Helen,
Is ever to see you ere he die."
"In all that his soul sees, there am I,
                Little brother!"

*(O Mother, Mary Mother,*
*The soul's one sight, between Hell and Heaven!)*


"He sends a ring and a broken coin,
                    **Sister Helen,**
And bids you mind the banks of Boyne."
"What else he broke will he ever join,
                    Little brother?"
                    *(O Mother, Mary Mother,*
*No, never joined, between Hell and Heaven!)*


"He yields you these and craves full fain,
                    **Sister Helen,**
You pardon him in his mortal pain."
"What else he took will he give again,
                    Little brother?"
                    *(O Mother, Mary Mother,*
*Not twice to give, between Hell and Heaven!)*


"He calls your name in an agony,
                    **Sister Helen,**
That even dead Love must weep to see."
"Hate, born of Love, is blind as he,
                    Little brother!"
                    *(O Mother, Mary Mother,*
*Love turned to hate, between Hell and Heaven!)*


"Oh it's Keith of Keith now that rides fast,
                    **Sister Helen,**
For I know the white hair on the blast."
"The short, short hour will soon be past,
                    Little brother!"
                    *(O Mother, Mary Mother,*
*Will soon be past, between Hell and Heaven!)*

"He looks at me and he tries to speak,
     Sister Helen,
But oh! his voice is sad and weak!"
"What here should the mighty Baron seek,
      Little brother?"
    *(O Mother, Mary Mother,*
*Is this the end, between Hell and Heaven?)*

"Oh his son still cries, if you forgive,
     Sister Helen,
The body dies, but the soul shall live."
"Fire shall forgive me as I forgive,
      Little brother!"
    *(O Mother, Mary Mother,*
*As she forgives, between Hell and Heaven!)*

"Oh he prays you, as his heart would rive,
     Sister Helen,
To save his dear son's soul alive."
"Fire cannot slay it, it shall thrive,
      Little brother!"
    *(O Mother, Mary Mother,*
*Alas, alas, between Hell and Heaven!)*

"He cries to you, kneeling in the road,
     Sister Helen,
To go with him for the love of God!"
"The way is long to his son's abode,
      Little brother."
    *(O Mother, Mary Mother,*
*The way is long, between Hell and Heaven!)*

"A lady's here, by a dark steed brought,
     Sister Helen,
So darkly clad, I saw her not."

"See her now or never see aught,
                    Little brother!"
                    *(O Mother, Mary Mother,*
*What more to see, between Hell and Heaven!)*


"Her hood falls back, and the moon shines fair,
                    Sister Helen,
On the Lady of Ewern's golden hair."
"Blest hour of my power and her despair,
                    Little brother!"
                    *(O Mother, Mary Mother,*
*Hour blest and bann'd, between Hell and Heaven!)*


"Pale, pale her cheeks, that in pride did glow,
                    Sister Helen,
'Neath the bridal-wreath three days ago."
"One morn for pride and three days for woe,
                    Little brother!"
                    *(O Mother, Mary Mother,*
*Three days, three nights, between Hell and*
*    Heaven!)*


"Her clasped hands stretch from her bending head,
                    Sister Helen,
With the loud wind's wail her sobs are wed."
"What wedding-strains hath her bridal-bed,
                    Little brother?"
                    *(O Mother, Mary Mother,*
*What strain but death's, between Hell and*
*    Heaven?)*


"She may not speak, she sinks in a swoon,
                    Sister Helen,
She lifts her lips and gasps on the moon."

"Oh! might I but hear her soul's blithe tune,
     Little brother!"
    *(O Mother, Mary Mother,*
*Her woe's dumb cry, between Hell and Heaven!)*

"They've caught her to Westholm's saddle-bow,
     Sister Helen,
And her moonlit hair gleams white in its flow."
"Let it turn whiter than winter snow,
     Little brother!"
    *(O Mother, Mary Mother,*
*Woe-withered gold, between Hell and Heaven!)*

"O Sister Helen, you heard the bell,
     Sister Helen!
More loud than the vesper-chime it fell."
"No vesper-chime, but a dying knell,
     Little brother!"
    *(O Mother, Mary Mother,*
*His dying knell, between Hell and Heaven!)*

"Alas! but I fear the heavy sound,
     Sister Helen;
Is it in the sky or in the ground?"
"Say, have they turned their horses round,
     Little brother?"
    *(O Mother, Mary Mother,*
*What would she more, between Hell and Heaven?)*

"They have raised the old man from his knee,
     Sister Helen,
And they ride in silence hastily."
"More fast the naked soul doth flee,
     Little brother!"

*(O Mother, Mary Mother,*
*The naked soul, between Hell and Heaven!)*

"Flank to flank are the three steeds gone,
                                    Sister Helen,
But the lady's dark steed goes alone."
"And lonely her bridegroom's soul hath flown,
                                    Little brother."
                          *(O Mother, Mary Mother,*
*The lonely ghost, between Hell and Heaven!)*

"Oh the wind is sad in the iron chill,
                                    Sister Helen,
And weary sad they look by the hill."
"But he and I are sadder still,
                                    Little brother!"
                          *(O Mother, Mary Mother,*
*Most sad of all, between Hell and Heaven!)*

"See, see, the wax has dropped from its place,
                                    Sister Helen,
And the flames are winning up apace!"
"Yet here they burn but for a space,
                                    Little brother!"
                          *(O Mother, Mary Mother,*
*Here for a space, between Hell and Heaven!)*

"Ah! what white thing at the door has cross'd,
                                    Sister Helen?
Ah! what is this that sighs in the frost?"
"A soul that's lost as mine is lost,
                                    Little brother!"
                          *(O Mother, Mary Mother,*
*Lost, lost, all lost, between Hell and Heaven!)*

                                              1853, 1870

## THE HOUSE OF LIFE

### XV.   THE BIRTH-BOND

HAVE you not noted, in some family
   Where two were born of a first marriage-bed,
   How still they own their gracious bond, though fed
And nursed on the forgotten breast and knee?—
How to their father's children they shall be
   In act and thought of one goodwill; but each
   Shall for the other have, in silence speech,
And in a word complete community?

Even so, when first I saw you, seemed it, love,
   That among souls allied to mine was yet
One nearer kindred than life hinted of.
   O born with me somewhere that men forget,
   And though in years of sight and sound unmet,
Known for my soul's birth-partner well enough!

### XXIII.   LOVE'S BAUBLES

I stood where Love in brimming armfuls bore
   Slight wanton flowers and foolish toys of fruit:
   And round him ladies thronged in warm pursuit,
Fingered and lipped and proffered the strange store.
And from one hand the petal and the core
   Savoured of sleep; and cluster and curled shoot
   Seemed from another hand like shame's salute,—
Gifts that I felt my cheek was blushing for.

At last Love bade my Lady give the same:
   And as I looked, the dew was light thereon;
   And as I took them, at her touch they shone
With inmost heaven-hue of the heart of flame.

And then Love said: "Lo! when the hand is hers,
Follies of love are love's true ministers."

### LXXXVI.   LOST DAYS

The lost days of my life until to-day,
   What were they, could I see them on the street
   Lie as they fell? Would they be ears of wheat
Sown once for food but trodden into clay?
Or golden coins squandered and still to pay?
   Or drops of blood dabbling the guilty feet?
   Or such spilt water as in dreams must cheat
The undying throats of Hell, athirst alway?

I do not see them here; but after death
   God knows I know the faces I shall see,
Each one a murdered self, with low last breath.
   "I am thyself,—what hast thou done to me?"
"And I—and I—thyself," (lo! each one saith,)
   "And thou thyself to all eternity!"

### XCVII.   A SUPERSCRIPTION

Look in my face; my name is Might-have-been;
   I am also called No-more, Too-late, Farewell;
   Unto thine ear I hold the dead-sea shell
Cast up thy Life's foam-fretted feet between;
Unto thine eyes the glass where that is seen
   Which had Life's form and Love's, but by my spell
   Is now a shaken shadow intolerable,
Of ultimate things unuttered the frail screen.

Mark me, how still I am! But should there dart
   One moment through thy soul the soft surprise

Of that winged Peace which lulls the breath of
  sighs,—
Then shalt thou see me smile, and turn apart
Thy visage to mine ambush at thy heart
  Sleepless with cold commemorative eyes.

### CI. THE ONE HOPE

When vain desire at last and vain regret
  Go hand in hand to death, and all is vain,
  What shall assuage the unforgotten pain
And teach the unforgetful to forget?
Shall Peace be still a sunk stream long unmet,—
  Or may the soul at once in a green plain
  Stoop through the spray of some sweet life-fountain
And cull the dew-drenched flowering amulet?

Ah! when the wan soul in that golden air
  Between the scriptured petals softly blown
  Peers breathless for the gift of grace unknown,—
Ah! let none other alien spell soe'er
But only the one Hope's one name be there,—
  Not less nor more, but even that word alone.

1869

# THOMAS CHATTERTON

With Shakespeare's manhood at a boy's wild heart,—
  Through Hamlet's doubt to Shakespeare near allied,
  And kin to Milton through his Satan's pride,—
At Death's sole door he stooped, and craved a dart;
And to the dear new bower of England's art,—
  Even to that shrine Time else had deified,
  The unuttered heart that soared against his side,—
Drove the fell point, and smote life's seals apart.

Thy nested home-loves, noble Chatterton;
  The angel-trodden stair thy soul could trace
  Up Redcliffe's spire: and in the world's armed space
Thy gallant sword-play:—these to many an one
Are sweet for ever; as thy grave unknown
  And love-dream of thine unrecorded face.

1881

## WINTER

How large that thrush looks on the bare thorn-tree!
  A swarm of such, three little months ago,
  Had hidden in the leaves and let none know
Save by the outburst of their minstrelsy.
A white flake here and there—a snow-lily
  Of last night's frost—our naked flower-beds hold;
  And for a rose-flower on the darkling mould
The hungry redbreast gleams. No bloom, no bee.

The current shudders to its ice-bound sedge:
  Nipped in their bath, the stark reeds one by one
  Flash each its clinging diamond in the sun:
'Neath winds which for this winter's sovereign pledge
Shall curb great king-masts to the ocean's edge
  And leave memorial forest-kings o'erthrown.

1881

## GEORGE MEREDITH (1828-1909)

## LOVE IN THE VALLEY

Under yonder beech-tree single on the green-sward,
  Couched with her arms behind her golden head,

Knees and tresses folded to slip and ripple idly,
  Lies my young love sleeping in the shade.
Had I the heart to slide an arm beneath her,
  Press her parting lips as her waist I gather slow,
Waking in amazement she could not but embrace me:
  Then would she hold me and never let me go?

\*     \*     \*

Shy as the squirrel and wayward as the swallow,
  Swift as the swallow along the river's light
Circleting the surface to meet his mirrored winglets,
  Fleeter she seems in her stay than in her flight.
Shy as the squirrel that leaps among the pine-tops,
  Wayward as the swallow overhead at set of sun,
She whom I love is hard to catch and conquer,
  Hard, but O the glory of the winning were she won!

\*     \*     \*

When her mother tends her before the laughing mirror,
  Tying up her laces, looping up her hair,
Often she thinks, were this wild thing wedded,
  More love should I have, and much less care.
When her mother tends her before the lighted mirror,
  Loosening her laces, combing down her curls,
Often she thinks, were this wild thing wedded,
  I should miss but one for many boys and girls.

\*     \*     \*

Heartless she is as the shadow in the meadows
  Flying to the hills on a blue and breezy noon.
No, she is athirst and drinking up her wonder:
  Earth to her is young as the slip of the new moon.
Deals she an unkindness, 't is but her rapid measure,
  Even as in a dance; and her smile can heal no less:

Like the swinging May-cloud that pelts the flowers with
      hailstones
  Off a sunny border, she was made to bruise and bless.

*          *          *

Lovely are the curves of the white owl sweeping
  Wavy in the dusk lit by one large star.
Lone on the fir-branch, his rattle-note unvaried,
  Brooding o'er the gloom, spins the brown eve-jar,
Darker grows the valley, more and more forgetting:
  So were it with me if forgetting could be willed.
Tell the grassy hollow that holds the bubbling well-
      spring,
  Tell it to forget the source that keeps it filled.

*          *          *

Stepping down the hill with her fair companions,
  Arm in arm, all against the raying West,
Boldly she sings, to the merry tune she marches,
  Brave in her shape, and sweeter unpossessed.
Sweeter, for she is what my heart first awaking
  Whispered the world was; morning light is she.
Love that so desires would fain keep her changeless;
  Fain would fling the net, and fain have her free.

*          *          *

Happy happy time, when the white star hovers
  Low over dim fields fresh with bloomy dew,
Near the face of dawn, that draws athwart the darkness,
  Threading it with colour, like yewberries the yew.
Thicker crowd the shades as the grave East deepens
  Glowing, and with crimson a long cloud swells.
Maiden still the morn is; and strange she is, and secret;
  Strange her eyes; her cheeks are cold as cold sea-
      shells.

*          *          *

Sunrays, leaning on our southern hills and lighting
   Wild cloud-mountains that drag the hills along,
Oft ends the day of your shifting brilliant laughter
   Chill as a dull face frowning on a song.
Ay, but shows the South-West a ripple-feathered bosom
   Blown to silver while the clouds are shaken and ascend
Scaling the mid-heavens as they stream, there comes a
      sunset
   Rich, deep like love in beauty without end.

*     *     *

When at dawn she sighs, and like an infant to the
   window
   Turns grave eyes craving light, released from dreams,
Beautiful she looks, like a white water-lily
   Bursting out of bud in havens of the streams.
When from bed she rises clothed from neck to ankle
   In her long nightgown sweet as boughs of May,
Beautiful she looks, like a tall garden lily
   Pure from the night, and splendid for the day.

*     *     *

Mother of the dews, dark eye-lashed twilight,
   Low-lidded twilight, o'er the valley's brim,
Rounding on thy breast sings the dew-delighted skylark,
   Clear as though the dewdrops had their voice in him.
Hidden where the rose-flush drinks the rayless planet,
   Fountain-full he pours the spraying fountain-showers.
Let me hear her laughter, I would have her ever
   Cool as dew in twilight, the lark above the flowers.

*     *     *

All the girls are out with their baskets for the primrose;
   Up lanes, woods through, they troop in joyful bands.
My sweet leads: she knows not why, but now she loiters,
   Eyes the bent anemones, and hangs her hands.
Such a look will tell that the violets are peeping,

Coming the rose: and unaware a cry
Springs in her bosom for odours and for colour,
   Covert and the nightingale; she knows not why.

      *        *        *

Kerchiefed head and chin she darts between her tulips,
   Streaming like a willow grey in arrowy rain:
Some bend beaten cheek to gravel, and their angel
   She will be; she lifts them, and on she speeds again.
Black the driving raincloud breasts the iron gateway:
   She is forth to cheer a neighbour lacking mirth.
So when sky and grass met rolling dumb for thunder
   Saw I once a white dove, sole light of earth.

      *        *        *

Prim little scholars are the flowers of her garden,
   Trained to stand in rows, and asking if they please.
I might love them well but for loving more the wild ones:
   O my wild ones! they tell me more than these.
You, my wild one, you tell of honied field-rose
   Violet, blushing eglantine in life; and even as they,
They by the wayside are earnest of your goodness,
   You are of life's, on the banks that line the way.

      *        *        *

Peering at her chamber the white crowns the red rose,
   Jasmine winds the porch with stars two and three.
Parted is the window; she sleeps; the starry jasmine
   Breathes a falling breath that carries thoughts of me.
Sweeter unpossessed, have I said of her my sweetest?
   Not while she sleeps: while she sleeps the jasmine
      breathes,
Luring her to love; she sleeps; the starry jasmine
   Bears me to her pillow under white rose-wreaths.

      *        *        *

Yellow with birdfoot-trefoil are the grass-glades;
   Yellow with cinquefoil of the dew-grey leaf;

Yellow with stonecrop; the moss-mounds are yellow;
  Blue-necked the wheat sways, yellowing to the sheaf.
Green-yellow bursts from the copse the laughing yaffle;
  Sharp as a sickle is the edge of shade and shine:
Earth in her heart laughs looking at the heavens,
  Thinking of the harvest: I look and think of mine.

\* \* \*

This I may know: her dressing and undressing
  Such a change of light shows as when the skies in
    sport
Shift from cloud to moonlight; or edging over thunder
  Slips a ray of sun; or sweeping into port
White sails furl; or on the ocean borders
  White sails lean along the waves leaping green.
Visions of her shower before me, but from eyesight
  Guarded she would be like the sun were she seen.

\* \* \*

Front door and back of the mossed old farmhouse
  Open with the morn, and in a breezy link
Freshly sparkles garden to stripe-shadow'd orchard,
  Green across a rill where on sand the minnows wink.
Busy in the grass the early sun of summer
  Swarms, and the blackbird's mellow fluting notes
Call my darling up with round and roguish challenge:
  Quaintest, richest carol of all the singing throats!

\* \* \*

Cool was the woodside; cool as her white dairy
  Keeping sweet the cream-pan; and there the boys from
    school,
Cricketing below, rush'd brown and red with sunshine;
  O the dark translucence of the deep-eyed cool!
Spying from the farm, herself she fetched a pitcher
  Full of milk, and tilted for each in turn the beak.

Then a little fellow, mouth up and on tiptoe,
　Said, "I will kiss you": she laughed and leaned her
　　cheek.

\* \* \*

Doves of the fir-wood walling high our red roof
　Through the long noon coo, crooning through the coo.
Loose droop the leaves, and down the sleepy roadway
　Sometimes pipes a chaffinch; loose droops the blue.
Cows flap a slow tail knee-deep in the river,
　Breathless, given up to sun and gnat and fly.
Nowhere is she seen; and if I see her nowhere,
　Lightning may come, straight rains and tiger sky.

\* \* \*

O the golden sheaf, the rustling treasure-armful!
　O the nutbrown tresses nodding interlaced!
O the treasure-tresses one another over
　Nodding! O the girdle slack about the waist!
Slain are the poppies that shot their random scarlet
　Quick amid the wheat-ears: wound about the waist,
Gathered, see these brides of Earth one blush of ripe-
　　ness!
　O the nutbrown tresses nodding interlaced!

\* \* \*

Large and smoky red the sun's cold disk drops,
　Clipped by naked hills, on violet shaded snow:
Eastward large and still lights up a bower of moonrise,
　Whence at her leisure steps the moon aglow.
Nightlong on black print-branches our beech-tree
　Gazes in this whiteness: nightlong could I.
Here may life on death or death on life be painted.
　Let me clasp her soul to know she cannot die!

\* \* \*

Gossips count her faults; they scour a narrow chamber
　　Where there is no window, read not heaven or her.
"When she was a tiny," one agèd woman quavers,
　　Plucks at my heart and leads me by the ear.
Faults she had once as she learned to run and tumbled:
　　Faults of feature some see, beauty not complete.
Yet, good gossips, beauty that makes holy
　　Earth and air, may have faults from head to feet.

*　　　　*　　　　*

Hither she comes; she comes to me; she lingers,
　　Deepens her brown eyebrows, while in new surpris
High rise the lashes in wonder of a stranger;
　　Yet am I the light and living of her eyes.
Something friends have told her fills her heart to brim-
　　　　ming,
　　Nets her in her blushes, and wounds her, and tames.—
Sure of her haven, O like a dove alighting
　　Arms up, she dropped: our souls were in our names.

*　　　　*　　　　*

Soon will she lie like a white frost sunrise.
　　Yellow oats and brown wheat, barley pale as rye.
Long since your sheaves have yielded to the thresher,
　　Felt the girdle loosened, seen the tresses fly.
Soon will she lie like a blood-red sunset.
　　Swift with the to-morrow, green-winged Spring!
Sing from the South-West, bring her back the truants,
　　Nightingale and swallow, song and dipping wing.

*　　　　*　　　　*

Soft new beech-leaves, up to beamy April
　　Spreading bough on bough a primrose mountain, you
Lucid in the moon, raise lilies to the skyfields,
　　Youngest green transfused in silver shining through:
Fairer than the lily, than the wild white cherry:
　　Fair as in image my seraph love appears

Borne to me by dreams when dawn is at my eyelids:
  Fair as in the flesh she swims to me on tears.

\*          \*          \*

Could I find a place to be alone with heaven,
  I would speak my heart out: heaven is my need.
Every woodland tree is flushing like the dogwood,
  Flashing like the whitebeam, swaying like the reed.
Flushing like the dogwood crimson in October;
  Streaming like the flag-reed South-West blown;
Flashing as in gusts the sudden-lighted whitebeam:
  All seem to know what is for heaven alone.

1862


## JUGGLING JERRY

### I

PITCH here the tent, while the old horse grazes:
  By the old hedge-side we'll halt a stage.
It's nigh my last above the daisies:
  My next leaf'll be man's blank page.
Yes, my old girl! and it's no use crying:
  Juggler, constable, king, must bow.
One that outjuggles all's been spying
  Long to have me, and he has me now.

### II

We've travelled times to this old common:
  Often we've hung our pots in the gorse.
We've had a stirring life, old woman!
  You, and I, and the old grey horse.
Races, and fairs, and royal occasions,
  Found us coming to their call:

Now they'll miss us at our stations:
  There's a Juggler outjuggles all!

### III

Up goes the lark, as if all were jolly!
  Over the duck-pond the willow shakes.
Easy to think that grieving's folly,
  When the hand's firm as driven stakes!
Ay, when we're strong, and braced, and manful,
  Life's a sweet fiddle: but we're a batch
Born to become the Great Juggler's han'ful:
  Balls he shies up, and is safe to catch.

### IV

Here's where the lads of the village cricket:
  I was a lad not wide from here:
Couldn't I whip off the bale from the wicket?
  Like an old world those days appear!
Donkey, sheep, geese, and thatched ale-house—I know
      them!
  They are old friends of my halts, and seem,
Somehow, as if kind thanks I owe them:
  Juggling don't hinder the heart's esteem.

### V

Juggling's no sin, for we must have victual:
  Nature allows us to bait for the fool.
Holding one's own makes us juggle no little;
  But, to increase it, hard juggling's the rule.
You that are sneering at my profession,
  Haven't you juggled a vast amount?

There's the Prime Minister, in one Session,
　Juggles more games than my sins'll count.

### VI

I've murdered insects with mock thunder:
　Conscience, for that, in men don't quail.
I've made bread from the bump of wonder:
　That's my business, and there's my tale.
Fashion and rank all praised the professor:
　Ay! and I've had my smile from the Queen:
Bravo, Jerry! she meant: God bless her!
　Ain't this a sermon on that scene?

### VII

I've studied men from my topsy-turvy
　Close, and I reckon, rather true.
Some are fine fellows: some, right scurvy:
　Most, a dash between the two.
But it's a woman, old girl, that makes me
　Think more kindly of the race:
And it's a woman, old girl, that shakes me
　When the Great Juggler I must face.

### VIII

We two were married, due and legal:
　Honest we've lived since we've been one.
Lord! I could then jump like an eagle:
　You danced bright as a bit o' the sun.
Birds in a May-bush, we were! right merry!
　All night we kiss'd, we juggled all day.
Joy was the heart of Juggling Jerry!
　Now from his old girl he's juggled away.

## IX

It's past parsons to console us:
  No, nor no doctor fetch for me:
I can die without my bolus;
  Two of a trade, lass, never agree!
Parson and Doctor!—don't they love rarely,
  Fighting the devil in other men's fields!
Stand up yourself and match him fairly:
  Then see how the rascal yields!

## X

I, lass, have lived no gypsy, flaunting
  Finery while his poor helpmate grubs:
Coin I've stored, and you won't be wanting:
  You shan't beg from the troughs and tubs.
Nobly you've stuck to me, though in his kitchen
  Many a Marquis would hail you Cook!
Palaces you could have ruled and grown rich in,
  But your old Jerry you never forsook.

## XI

Hand up the chirper! ripe ale winks in it;
  Let's have comfort and be at peace.
Once a stout draught made me light as a linnet.
  Cheer up! the Lord must have his lease.
May be—for none see in that black hollow—
  It's just a place where we're held in pawn,
And when the Great Juggler makes as to swallow,
  It's just the sword-trick—I ain't quite gone!

### XII

Yonder came smells of the gorse, so nutty,
  Gold-like and warm: it's the prime of May.
Better than mortar, brick and putty,
  Is God's house on a blowing day.
Lean me more up the mound; now I feel it:
  All the old heath-smells! Ain't it strange?
There's the world laughing, as if to conceal it,
  But He's by us, juggling the change.

### XIII

I mind it well, by the sea-beach lying,
  Once—it's long gone—when two gulls we beheld,
Which, as the moon got up, were flying
  Down a big wave that sparkled and swelled.
Crack, went a gun: one fell: the second
  Wheeled round him twice, and was off for new luck:
There in the dark her white wing beckoned:—
  Drop me a kiss—I'm the bird dead-struck!

                                        1862

## LUCIFER IN STARLIGHT

On a starred night Prince Lucifer uprose.
Tired of his dark dominion swung the fiend
Above the rolling ball in cloud part screened,
Where sinners hugged their spectre of repose.
Poor prey to his hot fit of pride were those.
And now upon his western wing he leaned,
Now his huge bulk o'er Afric's sands careened,
Now the black planet shadowed Arctic snows.

Soaring through wider zones that pricked his scars
With memory of the old revolt from Awe,
He reached a middle height, and at the stars,
Which are the brain of heaven, he looked, and sank.
Around the ancient track marched, rank on rank,
The army of unalterable law.

1883

## DIRGE IN WOODS

A wind sways the pines,
          And below
Not a breath of wild air;
Still as the mosses that glow
On the flooring and over the lines
Of the roots here and there.
The pine-tree drops its dead;
They are quiet, as under the sea.
Overhead, overhead
Rushes life in a race,
As the clouds the clouds chase;
          And we go,
And we drop like the fruits of the tree,
          Even we.
          Even so.

1888

## SONG IN THE SONGLESS

They have no song, the sedges dry,
And still they sing.
It is within my breast they sing,
As I pass by.
Within my breast they touch a spring,
They wake a sigh.

There is but sound of sedges dry;
In me they sing.

1900

## YOUTH IN AGE

Once I was part of the music I heard
  On the boughs or sweet between earth and sky,
  For joy of the beating of wings on high
My heart shot into the breast of the bird.

I hear it now and I see it fly,
  And a life in wrinkles again is stirred,
  My heart shoots into the breast of the bird,
As it will for sheer love still the last long sigh.

1908

## WILLIAM MORRIS (1834-1896)

### AN APOLOGY

#### PROLOGUE TO THE EARTHLY PARADISE

Of Heaven or Hell I have no power to sing,
I cannot ease the burden of your fears,
Or make quick-coming death a little thing,
Or bring again the pleasure of past years,
Nor for my words shall ye forget your tears,
Or hope again for aught that I can say,
The idle singer of an empty day.

But rather when aweary of your mirth,
From full hearts still unsatisfied ye sigh,
And, feeling kindly unto all the earth,
Grudge every minute as it passes by,

Made the more mindful that the sweet days die—
Remember me a little then I pray,
The idle singer of an empty day.

The heavy trouble, the bewildering care
That weighs us down who live and earn our bread,
These idle verses have no power to bear;
So let us sing of names rememberèd,
Because they, living not, can ne'er be dead,
Or long time take their memory quite away
From us poor singers of an empty day.

Dreamer of dreams, born out of my due time,
Why should I strive to set the crooked straight?
Let it suffice me that my murmuring rhyme
Beats with light wing against the ivory gate,
Telling a tale not too importunate
To those who in the sleepy region stay,
Lulled by the singer of an empty day.

Folk say, a wizard to a northern king
At Christmas-tide such wondrous things did show,
That through one window men beheld the spring,
And through another saw the summer glow,
And through a third the fruited vines a-row,
While still, unheard, but in its wonted way,
Piped the drear wind of that December day.

So with this Earthly Paradise it is,
If ye will read aright and pardon me,
Who strive to build a shadowy isle of bliss
Midmost the beating of a steely sea,
Where tossed about all hearts of men must be;

Whose ravening monsters men of might shall slay,
Not the poor singer of an empty day.

1868

## THE HAYSTACK IN THE FLOODS

Had she come all the way for this,
To part at last without a kiss?
Yea, had she borne the dirt and rain
That her own eyes might see him slain
Beside the haystack in the floods?

Along the dripping leafless woods,
The stirrup touching either shoe,
She rode astride as troopers do;
With kirtle kilted to her knee,
To which the mud splash'd wretchedly;
And the wet dripp'd from every tree
Upon her head and heavy hair,
And on her eyelids broad and fair;
The tears and rain ran down her face.

By fits and starts they rode apace,
And very often was his place
Far off from her; he had to ride
Ahead, to see what might betide
When the roads cross'd; and sometimes, when
There rose a murmuring from his men,
Had to turn back with promises.
Ah me! she had but little ease;
And often for pure doubt and dread
She sobb'd, made giddy in the head
By the swift riding; while, for cold,
Her slender fingers scarce could hold

The wet reins; yea, and scarcely, too,
She felt the foot within her shoe
Against the stirrup: all for this,
To part at last without a kiss
Beside the haystack in the floods.

For when they near'd that old soak'd hay,
They saw across the only way
That Judas, Godmar, and the three
Red running lions dismally
Grinn'd from his pennon, under which
In one straight line along the ditch,
They counted thirty heads.
                              So then
While Robert turn'd round to his men,
She saw at once the wretched end,
And, stooping down, tried hard to rend
Her coif the wrong way from her head,
And hid her eyes; while Robert said:
"Nay, love, 'tis scarcely two to one;
At Poictiers where we made them run
So fast—why, sweet my love, good cheer,
The Gascon frontier is so near,
Nought after this."
                        But, "O," she said,
"My God! my God! I have to tread
The long way back without you; then
The court at Paris; those six men;
The gratings of the Chatelet;
The swift Seine on some rainy day
Like this, and people standing by,
And laughing, while my weak hands try
To recollect how strong men swim.
All this, or else a life with him,

For which I should be damned at last,
Would God that this next hour were past!"


He answer'd not, but cried his cry,
"St. George for Marny!" cheerily;
And laid his hand upon her rein.
Alas! no man of all his train
Gave back that cheery cry again;
And, while for rage his thumb beat fast
Upon his sword-hilt, some one cast
About his neck a kerchief long,
And bound him.
           Then they went along
To Godmar; who said: "Now, Jehane,
Your lover's life is on the wane
So fast, that, if this very hour
You yield not as my paramour,
He will not see the rain leave off—
Nay, keep your tongue from gibe and scoff
Sir Robert, or I slay you now."


She laid her hand upon her brow,
Then gazed upon the palm, as though
She thought her forehead bled, and—"No!"
She said, and turn'd her head away,
As there was nothing else to say,
And everything was settled: red
Grew Godmar's face from chin to head:
"Jehane, on yonder hill there stands
My castle, guarding well my lands:
What hinders me from taking you,
And doing that I list to do
To your fair wilful body, while

Your knight lies dead?"

      A wicked smile
Wrinkled her face, her lips grew thin,
A long way out she thrust her chin:
"You know that I should strangle you
While you were sleeping; or bite through
Your throat, by God's help—ah!" she said,
"Lord Jesus, pity your poor maid!
For in such wise they hem me in,
I cannot choose but sin and sin,
Whatever happens: yet I think
They could not make me eat or drink,
And so should I just reach my rest."
"Nay, if you do not my behest,
O Jehane! though I love you well,"
Said Godmar, "would I fail to tell
All that I know?" "Foul lies," she said.
"Eh? lies, my Jehane? by God's head,
At Paris folks would deem them true!
Do you know, Jehane, they cry for you:
'Jehane the brown! Jehane the brown!
Give us Jehane to burn or drown!'
Eh!—gag me Robert!—sweet my friend,
This were indeed a piteous end
For those long fingers, and long feet,
And long neck, and smooth shoulders sweet;
An end that few men would forget
That saw it.  So, an hour yet:
Consider, Jehane, which to take
Of life or death!"

      So, scarce awake,
Dismounting, did she leave that place,
And totter some yards: with her face
Turn'd upward to the sky she lay,

Her head on a wet heap of hay,
And fell asleep: and while she slept,
And did not dream, the minutes crept
Round to the twelve again; but she,
Being waked at last, sigh'd quietly,
And strangely childlike came, and said:
"I will not." Straightway Godmar's head,
As though it hung on strong wires, turn'd
Most sharply round, and his face burn'd.

For Robert—both his eyes were dry,
He could not weep, but gloomily
He seem'd to watch the rain; yea, too,
His lips were firm; he tried once more
To touch her lips; she reach'd out, sore
And vain desire so tortured them,
The poor gray lips, and now the hem
Of his sleeve brush'd them.

                              With a start
Up Godmar rose, thrust them apart;
From Robert's throat he loosed the bands
Of silk and mail; with empty hands
Held out, she stood and gazed, and saw,
The long bright blade without a flaw
Glide out from Godmar's sheath, his hand
In Robert's hair; she saw him bend
Back Robert's head; she saw him send
The thin steel down; the blow told well,
Right backward the knight Robert fell,
And moaned as dogs do, being half dead,
Unwitting, as I deem: so then
Godmar turn'd grinning to his men,

Who ran, some five or six, and beat
His head to pieces at their feet.

Then Godmar turn'd again and said:
"So, Jehane, the first fitte is read!
Take note, my lady, that your way
Lies backward to the Chatelet!"
She shook her head and gazed awhile
At her cold hands with a rueful smile,
As though this thing had made her mad.

This was the parting that they had
Beside the haystack in the floods.

1858

# SIGURD THE VOLSUNG

## REGIN

### OF THE FORGING OF THE SWORD THAT IS CALLED THE WRATH OF SIGURD

Now again came Sigurd to Regin, and said: "Thou hast
taught me a task
Whereof none knoweth the ending: and a gift at thine
hands I ask."

Then answered Regin the Master: "The world must be
wide indeed
If my hand may not reach across it for aught thine heart
may need."

"Yea wide is the world," said Sigurd, "and soon spoken
is thy word;

But this gift thou shalt nought gainsay me: for I bid
  thee forge me a sword."

Then spake the Master of Masters, and his voice was
  sweet and soft,
"Look forth abroad, O Sigurd, and note in the heavens
  aloft
How the dim white moon of the daylight hangs round
  as the Goth-god's shield:
Now for thee first rang mine anvil when she walked the
  heavenly field
A slim and lovely lady, and the old moon lay on her arm:
Lo, here is a sword I have wrought thee with many a
  spell and charm
And all the craft of the Dwarf-kind; be glad thereof
  and sure;
Mid many a storm of battle full well shall it endure."

Then Sigurd looked on the slayer, and never a word
  would speak:
Gemmed were the hilts and golden, and the blade was
  blue and bleak,
And runes of the Dwarf-kin's cunning each side the
  trench were scored:
But soft and sweet spake Regin: "How likest thou the
  sword?"

Then Sigurd laughed and answered: "The work is
  proved by the deed;
See now if this be a traitor to fail me in my need."

Then Regin trembled and shrank, so bright his eyes outshone
As he turned about to the anvil, and smote the sword
  thereon.

But the shards fell shivering earthward, and Sigurd's
    heart grew wroth
As the steel-flakes tinkled about him: "Lo, there the
    right-hand's troth;
Lo, there the golden glitter, and the word that soon is
    spilt."
And down amongst the ashes he cast the glittering hilt,
And turned his back on Regin and strode out through
    the door
And for many a day of spring-tide came back again no
    more.
But at last he came to the stithy and again took up the
    word:
"What hast thou done, O Master, in the forging of the
    sword?"


Then sweetly Regin answered: "Hard task-master art
    thou,
But lo, a blade of battle that shall surely please thee
    now!
Two moons are clean departed since thou lookedst to-
    ward the sky
And sawest the dim white circle amid the cloud-flecks
    lie;
And night and day have I laboured; and the cunning or
    old days
Hath surely left my right-hand if this sword thou shalt
    not praise."
And indeed the hilts gleamed glorious with many a
    dear-bought stone,
And down the fallow edges the light of battle shone;
Yet Sigurd's eyes shone brighter, nor yet might Regin
    face

Those eyes of the heart of the Volsungs; but trembled
　　in his place
As Sigurd cried: "O Regin, thy kin of the days of old
Were an evil and treacherous folk, and they lied and
　　murdered for gold;
And now if thou wouldst bewray me, of the ancient curse
　　beware,
And set thy face as the flint the bale and the shame to
　　bear:
For he that would win to the heavens, and be as the
　　Gods on high
Must tremble nought at the road, and the place where
　　men-folk die."
White leaps the blade in his hand and gleams in the gear
　　of the wall,
And he smites, and the oft-smitten edges on the beaten
　　anvil fall:
But the life of the sword departed, and dull and broken
　　it lay
On the ashes and flaked-off iron, and no word did Sigurd
　　say,
But strode off through the door of the stithy and went to
　　the Hall of Kings,
And was merry and blithe that even mid all imaginings.

But when the morrow was come he went to his mother
　　and spake:
"The shards, the shards of the sword, that thou glean-
　　edst for my sake
In the night on the field of slaughter, in the tide when
　　my father fell,
Hast thou kept them through sorrow and joyance? hast
　　thou warded them trusty and well?
Where hast thou laid them, my mother?"
　　　　　　　　Then she looked upon him and said:

"Art thou wroth, O Sigurd my son, that such eyes are
     in thine head?
And wilt thou be wroth with thy mother? do I with-
     stand thee at all?"

"Nay," said he, "nought am I wrathful, but the days rise
     up like a wall
Betwixt my soul and the deeds, and I strive to rend them
     through.
And why wilt thou fear mine eyen? as the sword lies
     baleful and blue
E'en 'twixt the lips of lovers, when they swear their
     troth thereon,
So keen are the eyes ye have fashioned, ye folk of the
     days agone;
For therein is the light of battle, though whiles it lieth
     asleep.
Now give me the sword, my mother, that Sigmund gave
     thee to keep."

She said: "I shall give it thee gladly, for fain shall I be
     of thy praise
When thou knowest my careful keeping of that hope of
     the earlier days."

So she took his hand in her hand, and they went their
     ways, they twain,
Till they came to the treasure of queen-folk, the guarded
     chamber of gain:
They were all alone with its riches, and she turned the
     key in the gold,
And lifted the sea-born purple, and the silken web un-
     rolled,
And lo, 'twixt her hands and her bosom the shards of
     Sigmund's sword;

No rust-fleck stained its edges, and the gems of the
    ocean's hoard
Were as bright in the hilts and glorious, as when in the
    Volsungs' hall
It shone in the eyes of the earl-folk and flashed from the
    shielded wall.

But Sigurd smiled upon it, and he said: "O Mother of
    Kings,
Well hast thou warded the war-glaive for a mirror of
    many things,
And a hope of much fulfilment: well has thou given to
    me
The message of my fathers, and the word of things to
    be:
Trusty hath been thy warding, but its hour is over now:
These shards shall be knit together, and shall hear the
    war-wind blow.
They shall shine through the rain of Odin, as the sun
    come back to the world,
When the heaviest bolt of the thunder amidst the storm
    is hurled:
They shall shake the thrones of Kings, and shear the
    walls of war,
And undo the knot of treason when the world is darken-
    ing o'er.
They have shone in the dusk and the night-tide, they
    shall shine in the dawn and the day;
They have gathered the storm together, they shall chase
    the clouds away;
They have sheared red gold asunder, they shall gleam
    o'er the garnered gold;
They have ended many a story, they shall fashion a tale
    to be told:

They have lived in the wrack of the people; they shall
      live in the glory of folk:
They have stricken the Gods in battle, for the Gods
      shall they strike the stroke."


Then she felt his hands about her as he took the fateful
      sword,
And he kissed her soft and sweetly; but she answered
      never a word:
So great and fair was he waxen, so glorious was his face,
So young, as the deathless Gods are, that long in the
      golden place
She stood when he was departed: as some for-travailed
      one
Comes over the dark fell-ridges on the birth-tide of the
      sun,
And his gathering sleep falls from him mid the glory and
      the blaze;
And he sees the world grow merry and looks on the
      lightened ways,
While the ruddy streaks are melting in the day-flood
      broad and white;
Then the morn-dusk he forgetteth, and the moon-lit
      waste of night,
And the hall whence he departed with its yellow candles'
      flare:
So stood the Isle-king's daughter in that treasure-
      chamber fair.


But swift on his ways went Sigurd, and to Regin's house
      he came,
Where the Master stood in the doorway and behind him
      leapt the flame,
And dark he looked and little: no more his speech was
      sweet,

No words on his lip were gathered the Volsung child to
      greet,
Till he took the sword from Sigurd and the shards of
      the days of old;
Then he spake:
    "Will nothing serve thee save this blue steel and cold,
The bane of thy father's father, the fate of all his kin,
The baleful blade I fashioned, the Wrath that the Gods
      would win?"

Then answered the eye-bright Sigurd: "If thou thy craft
      wilt do
Nought save these battle-gleanings shall be my helper
      true:
And what if thou begrudgest, and my battle-blade be
      dull,
Yet the hand of the Norns is lifted and the cup is over-
      full.
Repent'st thou ne'er so sorely that thy kin must lie
      alow,
How much soe'er thou longest the world to overthrow,
And, doubting the gold and the wisdom, wouldst even
      now appease
Blind hate and eyeless murder, and win the world with
      these;
O'er-late is the time for repenting the word thy lips
      have said:
Thou shalt have the gold and the wisdom and take its
      curse on thine head.

I say that thy lips have spoken, and no more with thee
      it lies
To do the deed or leave it: since thou hast shown mine
      eyes
The world that was aforetime, I see the world to be:

And woe to the tangling thicket, or the wall that hinder-
eth me!

And short is the space I will tarry; for how if the
Worm should die

Ere the first of my strokes be stricken? Wilt thou get
to thy mastery

And knit these shards together that once in the Bran-
stock stood?

But if not and a smith's hands fail me, a King's hand
yet shall be good;

And the Norns have doomed thy brother. And yet I deem
this sword

Is the slayer of the Serpent, and the scatterer of the
Hoard."

Great waxed the gloom of Regin, and he said: "Thou
sayest sooth,

For none may turn him backward: the sword of a very
youth

Shall one day end my cunning, as the Gods my joyance
slew,

When nought thereof they were deeming, and another
thing would do.

But this sword shall slay the Serpent, and do another
deed,

And many an one thereafter till it fail thee in thy need.

But as fair and great as thou standest, yet get thee from
mine house,

For in me too might ariseth, and the place is perilous

With the craft that was aforetime, and shall never be
again,

When the hands that have taught thee cunning have
failed from the world of men.

Thou art wroth; but thy wrath must slumber till fate
its blossom bear;

Not thus were the eyes of Odin when I held him in the
snare.
Depart! lest the end overtake us ere thy work and mine
be done,
But come again in the night-tide and the slumber of
the sun,
When the sharded moon of April hangs round in the
undark May."

Hither and thither awhile did the heart of Sigurd sway;
For he feared no craft of the Dwarf-kind, nor heeded
the ways of Fate,
But his hand wrought e'en as his heart would: and now
was he weary with hate
Of the hatred and scorn of the Gods, and the greed of
gold and of gain,
And the weaponless hands of the stripling of the wrath
and the rending were fain.
But there stood Regin the Master, and his eyes were on
Sigurd's eyes,
Though nought belike they beheld him, and his brow
was sad and wise;
And the greed died out of his visage and he stood like
an image of old.

So the Norns drew Sigurd away, and the tide was an
even of gold,
And sweet in the April even were the fowl-kind singing
their best;
And the light of life smote Sigurd, and the joy that
knows no rest,
And the fond unnamed desire, and the hope of hidden
things;
And he wended fair and lovely to the house of the feasting Kings.

But now when the moon was at full and the undark May
        begun,
Went Sigurd unto Regin mid the slumber of the sun,
And amidst the fire-hall's pavement the King of the
        Dwarf-kind stood
Like an image of deeds departed and days that once
        were good;
And he seemed but faint and weary, and his eyes were
        dim and dazed
As they met the glory of Sigurd where the fitful candles
        blazed.
Then he spake:
            "Hail, Son of the Volsungs, the corner-
                stone is laid,
I have toiled and thou hast desired, and, lo, the fateful
        blade!"

Then Sigurd saw it lying on the ashes slaked and pale
Like the sun and the lightning mingled mid the even's
        cloudy bale;
For ruddy and great were the hilts, and the edges fine
        and wan,
And all adown to the blood-point a very flame there ran
That swallowed the runes of wisdom wherewith its sides
        were scored.
No sound did Sigurd utter as he stooped adown for his
        sword,
But it seemed as his lips were moving with speech of
        strong desire.
White leapt the blade o'er his head, and he stood in the
        ring of its fire
As hither and thither it played, till it fell on the anvil's
        strength,
And he cried aloud in his glory, and held out the sword
        full length,

As one who would show it the world; for the edges were
    dulled no whit,
And the anvil was cleft to the pavement with the dread-
    ful dint of it.


But Regin cried to his harp-strings: "Before the days
    of men
I smithied the Wrath of Sigurd, and now is it smithied
    again:
And my hand alone hath done it, and my heart alone
    hath dared
To bid that man to the mountain, and behold his glory
    bared.
Ah, if the Son of Sigmund might wot of the thing I
    would,
Then how were the ages bettered, and the world all
    waxen good!
Then how were the past forgotten and the weary days of
    yore,
And the hope of man that dieth and the waste that never
    bore!
How should this one live through the winter and know
    of all increase!
How should that one spring to the sunlight and bear the
    blossom of peace!
No more should the long-lived wisdom o'er the waste of
    the wilderness stray;
Nor the clear-eyed hero hasten to the deedless ending
    of day.
And what if the hearts of the Volsungs for this deed of
    deeds were born,
How then were their life-days evil and the end of their
    lives forlorn?"

There stood Sigurd the Volsung, and heard how the
    harp-strings rang,
But of other things they told him than the hope that
    the Master sang;
And his world lay far away from the Dwarf-king's
    eyeless realm
And the road that leadeth nowhere, and the ship without
    a helm:
But he spake: "How oft shall I say it, that I shall work
    thy will?
If my father hath made me mighty, thine heart shall I
    fulfil
With the wisdom and gold thou wouldest, before I wend
    on my ways;
For now hast thou failed me nought, and the sword is
    the wonder of days."

No word for a while spake Regin; but he hung his head
    adown
As a man that pondereth sorely, and his voice once more
    was grown
As the voice of the smithying-master as he spake: "This
    Wrath of thine
Hath cleft the hard and the heavy; it shall shear the
    soft and the fine:
Come forth to the night and prove it."

                      So they twain
    went forth abroad,
And the moon lay white on the river and lit the sleep-
    less ford,
And down to its pools they wended, and the stream was
    swift and full;
Then Regin cast against it a lock of fine-spun wool,
And it whirled about on the eddy till it met the edges
    bared,

And as clean as the careless water the laboured fleece
 was sheared.

Then Regin spake: "It is good, what the smithying-carl
 hath wrought:
Now the work of the King beginneth, and the end that
 my soul hath sought.
Thou shalt toil and I shall desire, and the deed shall be
 surely done:
For thy Wrath is alive and awake and the story of bale
 is begun."

Therewith was the Wrath of Sigurd laid soft in a golden
 sheath
And the peace-strings knit around it; for that blade was
 fain of death;
And 'tis ill to show such edges to the broad blue light of
 day,
Or to let the hall-glare light them, if ye list not play the
 play.

1877

## THE DAY IS COMING

Come hither, lads, and harken, for a tale there is to tell,
Of the wonderful days a-coming, when all shall be better
 than well.

And the tale shall be told of a country, a land in the
 midst of the sea,
And folk shall call it England in the days that are going
 to be.

There more than one in a thousand in the days that are
 yet to come,

Shall have some hope of the morrow, some joy of the
    ancient home.

For then, laugh not, but listen to this strange tale of
    mine,
All folk that are in England shall be better lodged than
    swine.

Then a man shall work and bethink him, and rejoice in
    the deeds of his hand,
Nor yet come home in the even too faint and weary to
    stand.

Men in that time a-coming shall work and have no fear
For to-morrow's lack of earning and the hunger-wolf
    anear.

1885

## ALGERNON CHARLES SWINBURNE (1837-1909)

### A SONG IN TIME OF ORDER

Push hard across the sand,
    For the salt wind gathers breath;
Shoulder and wrist and hand,
    Push hard as the push of death.

The wind is as iron that rings,
    The foam-heads loosen and flee;
It swells and welters and swings,
    The pulse of the tide of the sea.

And up on the yellow cliff
    The long corn flickers and shakes;
Push, for the wind holds stiff,
    And the gunwale dips and rakes.

Good hap to the fresh fierce weather,
  The quiver and beat of the sea!
While three men hold together,
  The kingdoms are less by three.

Out to the sea with her there,
  Out with her over the sand,
Let the kings keep the earth for their share!
  We have done with the sharers of land.

They have tied the world in a tether,
  They have bought over God with a fee;
While three men hold together,
  The kingdoms are less by three.

We have done with the kisses that sting,
  The thief's mouth red from the feast,
The blood on the hands of the king,
  And the lie at the lips of the priest.

Will they tie the winds in a tether,
  Put a bit in the jaws of the sea?
While three men hold together,
  The kingdoms are less by three.

Let our flag run out straight in the wind!
  The old red shall be floated again
When the ranks that are thin shall be thinned,
  When the names that were twenty are ten;

When the devil's riddle is mastered,
  And the galley-bench creaks with a Pope,
We shall see Buonaparte the bastard
  Kick heels with his throat in a rope.

While the shepherd sets wolves on his sheep,
    And the emperor halters his kine,
While Shame is a watchman asleep,
    And Faith is a keeper of swine,—

Let the wind shake our flag like a feather,
    Like the plumes of the foam of the sea!
While three men hold together,
    The kingdoms are less by three.

All the world has its burdens to bear,
    From Cayenne to the Austrian whips;
Forth, with the rain in our hair
    And the salt sweet foam in our lips;

In the teeth of the hard glad weather,
    In the blown wet face of the sea;
While three men hold together,
    The kingdoms are less by three.

1862


# WHEN THE HOUNDS OF SPRING

### CHORUS FROM ATALANTA IN CALYDON

When the hounds of spring are on winter's traces,
    The mother of months in meadow or plain
Fills the shadows and windy places
    With lisp of leaves and ripple of rain;
And the brown bright nightingale amorous
Is half assuaged for Itylus,
For the Thracian ships and the foreign faces,
    The tongueless vigil, and all the pain.

Come with bows bent and with emptying of quivers,
   Maiden most perfect, lady of light,
With a noise of winds and many rivers,
   With a clamour of waters, and with might;
Bind on thy sandals, O thou most fleet,
Over the splendour and speed of thy feet;
For the faint east quickens, the wan west shivers,
   Round the feet of the day and the feet of the night.

Where shall we find her, how shall we sing to her,
   Fold our hands round her knees, and cling?
O that man's heart were as fire and could spring to her,
   Fire, or the strength of the streams that spring!
For the stars and the winds are unto her
As raiment, as songs of the harp-player;
For the risen stars and the fallen cling to her,
   And the southwest-wind and the west-wind sing.

For winter's rains and ruins are over,
   And all the season of snows and sins;
The days dividing lover and lover,
   The light that loses, the night that wins;
And time remembered is grief forgotten,
And frosts are slain and flowers begotten,
And in green underwood and cover
   Blossom by blossom the spring begins.

The full streams feed on flower of rushes,
   Ripe grasses trammel a travelling foot,
The faint fresh flame of the young year flushes
   From leaf to flower and flower to fruit;
And fruit and leaf are as gold and fire,
And the oat is heard above the lyre,
And the hoofèd heel of a satyr crushes
   The chestnut-husk at the chestnut-root.

And Pan by noon and Bacchus by night,
   Fleeter of foot than the fleet-foot kid,
Follows with dancing and fills with delight
   The Mænad and the Bassarid;
And soft as lips that laugh and hide
The laughing leaves of the trees divide,
And screen from seeing and leave in sight
   The god pursuing, the maiden hid.

The ivy falls with the Bacchanal's hair
   Over her eyebrows hiding her eyes;
The wild vine slipping down leaves bare
   Her bright breast shortening into sighs;
The wild vine slips with the weight of its leaves,
But the berried ivy catches and cleaves
To the limbs that glitter, the feet that scare
   The wolf that follows, the fawn that flies.

1865

## BEFORE THE BEGINNING OF YEARS

### CHORUS FROM ATALANTA IN CALYDON

BEFORE the beginning of years
   There came to the making of man
Time, with a gift of tears;
   Grief, with a glass that ran;
Pleasure, with pain for leaven;
   Summer, with flowers that fell;
Remembrance fallen from heaven,
   And madness risen from hell;
Strength without hands to smite;
   Love that endures for a breath
Night, the shadow of light,
   And life, the shadow of death.

And the high gods took in hand
　　Fire, and the falling of tears,
And a measure of sliding sand
　　From under the feet of the years;
And froth and drift of the sea;
　　And dust of the labouring earth;
And bodies of things to be
　　In the houses of death and of birth;
And wrought with weeping and laughter,
　　And fashioned with loathing and love,
With life before and after
　　And death beneath and above,
For a day and a night and a morrow,
　　That his strength might endure for a span
With travail and heavy sorrow,
　　The holy spirit of man.

From the winds of the north and the south
　　They gathered as unto strife;
They breathed upon his mouth,
　　They filled his body with life;
Eyesight and speech they wrought
　　For the veils of the soul therein,
A time for labour and thought,
　　A time to serve and to sin;
They gave him light in his ways,
　　And love, and a space for delight,
And beauty and length of days,
　　And night, and sleep in the night.
His speech is a burning fire;
　　With his lips he travaileth;
In his heart is a blind desire,
　　In his eyes foreknowledge of death;
He weaves, and is clothed with derision;
　　Sows, and he shall not reap;

His life is a watch or a vision
  Between a sleep and a sleep.

1865

## A LEAVE-TAKING

LET us go hence, my songs: she will not hear.
Let us go hence together without fear;
Keep silence now, for singing-time is over,
And over all old things and all things dear.
She loves not you nor me as all we love her.
Yea, though we sang as angels in her ear,
      She would not hear.

Let us rise up and part; she will not know.
Let us go seaward as the great winds go,
Full of blown sand and foam; what help is here?
There is no help, for all these things are so,
And all the world is bitter as a tear.
And how these things are, though ye strove to show,
      She would not know.

Let us go home and hence: she will not weep.
We gave love many dreams and days to keep,
Flowers without scent, and fruits that would not grow,
Saying, "If thou wilt, thrust in thy sickle, and reap."
All is reaped now; no grass is left to mow:
And we that sowed, though all we fell on sleep,
      She would not weep.

Let us go hence and rest: she will not love,
She shall not hear us if we sing hereof,
Nor see love's ways, how sore they are and steep.
Come hence, let be, lie still; it is enough.
Love is a barren sea, bitter and deep;

And though she saw all heaven in flower above,
  She would not love.

Let us give up, go down: she will not care.
Though all the stars made gold of all the air,
And the sea moving saw before it move
One moon-flower making all the foam-flowers fair;
Though all those waves went over us, and drove
Deep down the stifling lips and drowning hair,
  She would not care.

Let us go hence, go hence: she will not see.
Sing all once more together; surely she,
She too, remembering days and words that were,
Will turn a little toward us, sighing; but we,
We are hence, we are gone, as though we had not
  been there.
Nay, and though all men seeing had pity on me,
  She would not see.

                                        1866


## THE GARDEN OF PROSERPINE

Here, where the world is quiet;
  Here, where all trouble seems
Dead winds' and spent waves' riot
  In doubtful dreams of dreams;
I watch the green field growing
For reaping folk and sowing,
For harvest-time and mowing,
  A sleepy world of streams.

I am tired of tears and laughter,
  And men that laugh and weep;

Of what may come hereafter
    For men that sow to reap:
I am weary of days and hours,
Blown buds of barren flowers,
Desires and dreams and powers
    And everything but sleep.


Here life has death for neighbour,
    And far from eye or ear
Wan waves and wet winds labour,
    Weak ships and spirits steer;
They drive adrift, and whither
They wot not who make thither;
But no such winds blow hither,
    And no such things grow here.


No growth of moor or coppice,
    No heather-flower or vine,
But bloomless buds of poppies,
    Green grapes of Proserpine,
Pale beds of blowing rushes
Where no leaf blooms or blushes
Save this whereout she crushes
    For dead men deadly wine.


Pale, without name or number,
    In fruitless fields of corn,
They bow themselves and slumber
    All night till light is born;
And like a soul belated,
In hell and heaven unmated,
By cloud and mist abated
    Comes out of darkness morn.

Though one were strong as seven,
　He too with death shall dwell,
Nor wake with wings in heaven,
　Nor weep for pains in hell;
Though one were fair as roses,
His beauty clouds and closes;
And well though love reposes,
　In the end it is not well.

Pale, beyond porch and portal,
　Crowned with calm leaves, she stands
Who gathers all things mortal
　With cold immortal hands;
Her languid lips are sweeter
Than love's who fears to greet her
To men that mix and meet her
　From many times and lands.

She waits for each and other,
　She waits for all men born;
Forgets the earth her mother,
　The life of fruits and corn;
And spring and seed and swallow
Take wing for her and follow
Where summer song rings hollow
　And flowers are put to scorn.

There go the loves that wither,
　The old loves with wearier wings;
And all dead years draw thither,
　And all disastrous things;
Dead dreams of days forsaken,
Blind buds that snows have shaken,
Wild leaves that winds have taken,
　Red strays of ruined springs.

We are not sure of sorrow,
  And joy was never sure;
To-day will die to-morrow;
  Time stoops to no man's lure;
And love, grown faint and fretful,
With lips but half regretful
Sighs, and with eyes forgetful
  Weeps that no loves endure.

From too much love of living,
  From hope and fear set free,
We thank with brief thanksgiving
  Whatever gods may be
That no life lives for ever;
That dead men rise up never;
That even the weariest river
  Winds somewhere safe to sea.

Then star nor sun shall waken,
  Nor any change of light:
Nor sound of waters shaken,
  Nor any sound or sight:
Nor wintry leaves nor vernal,
Nor days nor things diurnal;
Only the sleep eternal
  In an eternal night.

**1866**


## A VISION OF SPRING IN WINTER

### 1

O TENDER time that love thinks long to see,
  Sweet foot of spring that with her football sows
  Late snow-like flowery leavings of the snows,

Be not too long irresolute to be!
O mother-month, where have they hidden thee?
  Out of the pale time of the flowerless rose,
I reach my heart out toward the springtime lands.
 I stretch my spirit forth to the fair hours,
    The purplest of the prime;
I lean my soul down over them, with hands
  Made wide to take the ghostly growths of flowers;
    I send my love back to the lovely time.


2


Where has the greenwood hid thy gracious head?
  Veiled with what visions while the gray world grieves,
  Or muffled with what shadows of green leaves,
With warm intangible green shadows spread
To sweeten the sweet twilight for thy bed?
  What sleep enchants thee? what delight deceives?
Where the deep dreamlike dew before the dawn
  Feels not the fingers of the sunlight yet
    Its silver web unweave,
Thy footless ghost on some unfooted lawn
  Whose air the unrisen sunbeams fear to fret
    Lives a ghost's life of daylong dawn and eve.


3


Sunrise it sees not, neither set of star,
  Large nightfall, nor imperial plenilune,
  Nor strong sweet shape of the full-breasted noon;
But where the silver-sandalled shadows are,
Too soft for arrows of the sun to mar,
  Moves with the mild gait of an ungrown moon.

Hard overhead the half-lit crescent swims,
  The tender-colored night draws hardly breath,
    The light is listening;
They watch the dawn of slender-shapen limbs,
  Virginal, born again of doubtful death,
    Chill foster-father of the weanling spring.


4


As sweet desire of day before the day,
  As dreams of love before the true love born,
  From the outer edge of winter overworn
The ghost arisen of May before the May
Takes through dim air her unawakened way,
  The gracious ghost of morning risen ere morn.
With little unblown breasts and child-eyed looks
  Following, the very maid, the girl-child spring,
    Lifts windward her bright brows,
Dips her light feet in warm and moving brooks,
  And kindles with her own mouth's coloring
    The fearful firstlings of the plumeless boughs.


5


I seek thee sleeping, and awhile I see,
  Fair face that art not, how thy maiden breath
  Shall put at last the deadly days to death,
And fill the fields and fire the woods with thee,
And seaward hollows where my feet would be
  When heaven shall hear the word that April saith
To change the cold heart of the weary time,
  To stir and soften all the time to tears,
    Tears joyfuller than mirth:

As even to May's clear height the young days climb
  With feet not swifter than those fair first years
    Whose flowers revive not with thy flowers on earth.

### 6

I would not bid thee, though I might, give back
  One good thing youth has given and borne away:
  I crave not any comfort of the day
That is not, nor on time's re-trodden track
Would turn to meet the white-robed hours or black
  That long since left me on their mortal way;
Nor light nor love that has been, nor the breath
  That comes with morning from the sun to be,
    And sets light hope on fire;
No fruit, no flower thought once too fair for death,
  No flower nor hour once fallen from life's green tree,
    No leaf once plucked, or once fulfilled desire.

### 7

The morning song beneath the stars that fled
  With twilight through the moonless mountain air,
  While youth with burning lips and wreathless hair
Sang toward the sun that was to crown his head,
Rising; the hopes that triumphed and fell dead,
  The sweet swift eyes and songs of hours that were,—
These may'st thou not give back forever; these,
  As at the sea's heart all her wrecks lie waste,
    Lie deeper than the sea;
But flowers thou may'st, and winds, and hours of ease,
  And all its April to the world thou may'st
    Give back, and half my April back to me.

                                         1866

## A FORSAKEN GARDEN

In a coign of the cliff between lowland and highland,
  At the sea-down's edge between windward and lee,
Walled round with rocks as an inland island,
  The ghost of a garden fronts the sea.
A girdle of brushwood and thorn encloses
  The steep square slope of the blossomless bed
Where the weeds that grew green from the graves of
      its roses
          Now lie dead.

The fields fall southward, abrupt and broken,
  To the low last edge of the long lone land.
If a step should sound or a word be spoken,
  Would a ghost not rise at the strange guest's hand?
So long have the gray bare walks lain guestless,
  Through branches and briers if a man make way,
He shall find no life but the sea-wind's restless
          Night and day.

The dense hard passage is blind and stifled
  That crawls by a track none turn to climb
To the strait waste place that the years have rifled
  Of all but the thorns that are touched not of time.
The thorns he spares when the rose is taken;
  The rocks are left when he wastes the plain;
The wind that wanders, the weeds wind-shaken,
          These remain.

Not a flower to be pressed of the foot that falls not;
  As the heart of a dead man the seed-plots are dry;
From the thicket of thorns whence the nightingale calls
      not,

Could she call, there were never a rose to reply.
Over the meadows that blossom and wither
  Rings but the note of a sea-bird's song;
Only the sun and the rain come hither
      All year long.

The sun burns sere and the rain dishevels
  One gaunt bleak blossom of scentless breath.
Only the wind here hovers and revels
  In a round where life seems barren as death.
Here there was laughing of old, there was weeping,
Haply, of lovers none ever will know,
Whose eyes went seaward a hundred sleeping
      Years ago.

Heart handfast in heart as they stood, "Look thither,"
  Did he whisper? "look forth from the flowers to the
    sea;
For the foam-flowers endure when rose-blossoms wither,
  And men that love lightly may die—but we?"
And the same wind sang and the same waves whitened,
  And or ever the garden's last petals were shed,
In the lips that had whispered, the eyes that had light-
    ened,
      Love was dead.

Or they loved their life through, and then went whither?
  And were one to the end—but what end who knows?
Love deep as the sea as a rose must wither,
  As the rose-red seaweed that mocks the rose.
Shall the dead take thought for the dead to love them?
  What love was ever as deep as a grave?
They are loveless now as the grass above them
      Or the wave.

All are at one now, roses and lovers,
   Not known of the cliffs and the fields and the sea.
Not a breath of the time that has been hovers
   In the air now soft with a summer to be.
Not a breath shall there sweeten the seasons hereafter
   Of the flowers or the lovers that laugh now or weep,
When as they that are free now of weeping and laughter,
        We shall sleep.

Here death may deal not again for ever:
   Here change may come not till all change end.
From the graves they have made they shall rise up
      never,
   Who have left nought living to ravage and rend.
Earth, stones, and thorns of the wild ground growing,
   While the sun and the rain live, these shall be:
Till a last wind's breath upon all these blowing
        Roll the sea.

Till the slow sea rise and the sheer cliff crumble,
   Till terrace and meadow the deep gulfs drink,
Till the strength of the waves of the high tides humble
   The fields that lessen, the rocks that shrink,
Here now in his triumph where all things falter,
   Stretched out on the spoils that his own hand spread,
As a god self-slain on his own strange altar,
        Death lies dead.

                   1878

## ON THE DEATHS OF THOMAS CARLYLE AND GEORGE ELIOT

Two souls diverse out of our human sight
   Pass, followed one with love and each with wonder:
   The stormy sophist with his mouth of thunder,

Clothed with loud words and mantled in the might
Of darkness and magnificence of night;
    And one whose eye could smite the night in sunder,
    Searching if light or no light were thereunder,
And found in love of loving-kindness light.
Duty divine and Thought with eyes of fire
Still following Righteousness with deep desire
    Shone sole and stern before her and above—
Sure stars and sole to steer by; but more sweet
Shone lower the loveliest lamp for earthly feet,—
    The light of little children, and their love.

1881

## WILLIAM SHAKESPEARE

Not if men's tongues and angels' all in one
    Spake, might the word be said that might speak Thee.
    Streams, winds, woods, flowers, fields, mountains, yea,
        the sea,
What power is in them all to praise the sun?
His praise is this,—he can be praised of none.
    Man, woman, child, praise God for him; but he
    Exults not to be worshipped, but to be.
He is; and, being, beholds his work well done.
All joy, all glory, all sorrow, all strength, all mirth,
Are his: without him, day were night on earth.
    Time knows not his from time's own period.
All lutes, all harps, all viols, all flutes, all lyres,
Fall dumb before him ere one string suspires.
    All stars are angels; but the sun is God.

1882

## ON A COUNTRY ROAD

Along these low pleached lanes, on such a day,
So soft a day as this, through shade and sun,

With glad grave eyes that scanned the glad wild way,
And heart still hovering o'er a song begun,
And smile that warmed the world with benison,
Our father, lord long since of lordly rhyme,
Long since hath haply ridden, when the lime
Bloomed broad above him, flowering where he came.
Because thy passage once made warm this clime,
Our father Chaucer, here we praise thy name.

Each year that England clothes herself with May,
She takes thy likeness on her.  Time hath spun
Fresh raiment all in vain and strange array
For earth and man's new spirit, fain to shun
Things past for dreams of better to be won,
Through many a century since thy funeral chime
Rang, and men deemed it death's most direful crime
To have spared not thee for very love or shame;
And yet, while mists round last year's memories climb,
Our father Chaucer, here we praise thy name.

Each turn of the old wild road whereon we stray,
Meseems, might bring us face to face with one
Whom seeing we could not but give thanks, and pray
For England's love our father and her son
To speak with us as once in days long done
With all men, sage and churl and monk and mime,
Who knew not as we know the soul sublime
That sang for song's love more than lust of fame.
Yet, though this be not, yet, in happy time,
Our father Chaucer, here we praise thy name.

Friend, even as bees about the flowering thyme,
Years crowd on years, till hoar decay begrime
Names once beloved; but seeing the sun the same,

As birds of autumn fain to praise the prime,
Our father Chaucer, here we praise thy name.

1884

## A JACOBITE'S FAREWELL

THERE's nae mair lands to tyne, my dear,
  And nae mair lives to gie:
Though a man think sair to live nae mair,
  There's but one day to die.

For a' things come and a' days gane,
  What needs ye rend your hair?
But kiss me till the morn's morrow,
  Then I'll kiss ye nae mair.

O lands are lost and life's losing,
  And what were they to gie?
Fu' mony a man gives all he can,
  But nae man else gives ye.

Our king wons ower the sea's water,
  And I in prison sair:
But I'll win out the morn's morrow,
  And ye'll see me nae mair.

1889

## DICKENS

CHIEF in thy generation born of men
  Whom English praise acclaimed as English-born,
  With eyes that matched the world-wide eyes of morn
For gleam of tears or laughter, tenderest then

When thoughts of children warmed their light, or when
　Reverence of age with love and labour worn,
　Or godlike pity fired with godlike scorn,
Shot through them flame that winged thy swift live
　　pen:
Where stars and suns that we behold not burn,
　Higher even than here, though highest was here thy
　　　place,
　　Love sees thy spirit laugh and speak and shine
With Shakespeare, and the soft bright soul of Sterne,
　And Fielding's kindliest might, and Goldsmith's grace;
　　Scarce one more loved or worthier love than thine.

　　　　　　　　　　　　　　　　　　　　1904

## THOMAS HARDY (1840-1928)

### (From *Wessex Poems and Other Verses,* 1898)

### HAP

If but some vengeful god would call to me
　From up the sky, and laugh: "Thou suffering thing,
Know that thy sorrow is my ecstasy,
　That thy love's loss is my hate's profiting!"

Then would I bear it, clench myself, and die,
　Steeled by the sense of ire unmerited;
Half-eased, too, that a Powerfuller than I
　Had willed and meted me the tears I shed.

But not so. How arrives it joy lies slain,
　And why unblooms the best hope ever sown?
—Crass Casualty ɔbstructs the sun and rain,
　And dicing Time for gladness casts a moan. . . .
　　These purblind Doomsters had as readily strown
Blisses about my pilgrimage as pain.

## HER INITIALS

UPON a poet's page I wrote
  Of old two letters of her name;
Part seemed she of the effulgent thought
  Whence that high singer's rapture came.
—When now I turn the leaf the same
  Immortal light illumes the lay,
But from the letters of her name
  The radiance has died away!

(From *Poems of the Past and the Present,* 1902)

## ROME

(At the pyramid of Cestius near the graves of Shelley
and Keats)

WHO, then, was Cestius,
  And what is he to me?—
Amid thick thoughts and memories multitudinous
  One thought alone brings he.

I can recall no word
  Of anything he did;
For me he is a man who died and was interred
  To leave a pyramid

Whose purpose was exprest
  Not with its first design,
Nor till, far down in Time, beside it found their rest
  Two countrymen of mine.

Cestius in life, maybe,
Slew, breathed out threatening;
I know not. This I know: in death all silently
He does a finer thing,

In beckoning pilgrim feet
With marble finger high
To where, by shadowy wall and history-haunted street,
Those matchless singers lie. . . .

—Say, then, he lived and died
That stones which bear his name
Should mark, through Time, where two immortal Shades
abide;
It is an ample fame.

## A CHRISTMAS GHOST-STORY

SOUTH of the Line, inland from far Durban,
A moldering soldier lies—your countryman.
Awry and doubled up are his gray bones,
And on the breeze his puzzled phantom moans
Nightly to clear Canopus: "I would know
By whom and when the All-Earth-gladdening Law
Of Peace, brought in by that Man Crucified,
Was ruled to be inept, and set aside?
And what of logic or of truth appears
In tacking 'Anno Domini' to the years?
Near twenty-hundred liveried thus have hied,
But tarries yet the Cause for which He died."

## "I SAID TO LOVE"

I SAID to Love,
"It is not now as in old days

When men adored thee and thy ways
    All else above;
Named thee the Boy, the Bright, the One
Who spread a heaven beneath the sun,"
    I said to Love.

    I said to him,
"We now know more of thee than then;
We were but weak in judgment when,
    With hearts abrim,
We clamored thee that thou would'st please
Inflict on us thine agonies,"
    I said to him.

    I said to Love,
"Thou art not young, thou art not fair,
No elfin darts, no cherub air,
    Nor swan, nor dove,
Are thine; but features pitiless,
And iron daggers of distress,"
    I said to Love.

    "Depart then, Love! . . .
—Man's race shall perish, threatenest thou,
Without thy kindling coupling-vow?
The age to come the man of now
    Know nothing of?—
We fear not such a threat from thee;
We are too old in apathy!
*Mankind shall cease.*—So let it be,"
    I said to Love.

## ON A FINE MORNING

WHENCE comes Solace?—Not from seeing
What is doing, suffering, being,

Not from noting Life's conditions,
Nor from heeding Time's monitions;
But in cleaving to the Dream,
And in gazing at the gleam
Whereby gray things golden seem.

Thus do I this heyday, holding
Shadows but as lights unfolding,
As no specious show this moment
With its iris-hued embowment;
    But as nothing other than
    Part of a benignant plan;
    Proof that earth was made for man.


## AN AUGUST MIDNIGHT

### 1

A SHADED lamp and a waving blind,
And the beat of a clock from a distant floor:
On this scene enter—winged, horned, and spined—
A longlegs, a moth, and a dumbledore;
While 'mid my page there idly stands
A sleepy fly, that rubs its hands. . . .

### 2

Thus meet we five, in this still place,
At this point of time, at this point in space.
—My guests besmear my new-penned line,
Or bang at the lamp and fall supine.
"God's humblest, they!" I muse. Yet why?
They know Earth-secrets that know not I.

## TO LIFE

O LIFE with the sad seared face,
    I weary of seeing thee,
And thy draggled cloak, and thy hobbling pace,
    And thy too-forced pleasantry!

I know what thou would'st tell
    Of Death, Time, Destiny—
I have known it long, and know, too, well
    What it all means for me.

But canst thou not array
    Thyself in rare disguise,
And feign like truth, for one mad day,
    That Earth is Paradise?

I'll tune me to the mood,
    And mumm with thee till eve;
And maybe what as interlude
    I feign, I shall believe!

(From *Time's Laughing-stocks and Other Verses,* 1909)

## TO SINCERITY

O SWEET sincerity!—
Where modern methods be
What scope for thine and thee?

Life may be sad past saying,
Its greens for ever graying,
Its faiths to dust decaying;

And youth may have foreknown it,
And riper seasons shown it,
But custom cries: "Disown it:

"Say ye rejoice, though grieving,
Believe, while unbelieving,
Behold, without perceiving!"

—Yet, would men look at true things,
And unilluded view things,
And count to bear undue things,

The real might mend the seeming,
Facts better their foredeeming,
And Life its disesteeming.

## MISCONCEPTION

I BUSIED myself to find a sure
        Snug hermitage
That should preserve my Love secure
        From the world's rage;
Where no unseemly saturnals,
        Or strident traffic-roars,
Or hum of intervolved cabals
        Should echo at her doors.

I labored that the diurnal spin
        Of vanities
Should not contrive to suck her in
        By dark degrees,
And cunningly operate to blur
        Sweet teachings I had begun;
And then I went full-heart to her
        To expound the glad deeds done.

She looked at me, and said thereto
    With a pitying smile,
"And *this* is what has busied you
    So long a while?
O poor exhausted one, I see
    You have worn you old and thin
For naught! Those moils you fear for me
    I find most pleasure in!"

(From *Satires of Circumstance*, 1914)


## "AH, ARE YOU DIGGING ON MY GRAVE?"

"Ah, are you digging on my grave
    My loved one?—planting rue?"
—"No: yesterday he went to wed
One of the brightest wealth has bred
'It cannot hurt her now,' he said,
    'That I should not be true.'"

"Then who is digging on my grave
    My nearest dearest kin?"
—"Ah, no: they sit and think, 'What use!
What good will planting flowers produce?
No tendance of her mound can loose
    Her spirit from Death's gin.'"

"But some one digs upon my grave?
    My enemy?—prodding sly?"
—"Nay: when she heard you had passed the Gate
That shuts on all flesh soon or late,
She thought you no more worth her hate,
    And cares not where you lie."

"Then who is digging on my grave?
   Say—since I have not guessed!"
—"O it is I, my mistress dear,
Your little dog, who still lives near,
And much I hope my movements here
   Have not disturbed your rest?"

"Ah, yes! *You* dig upon my grave . . .
   Why flashed it not on me
That one true heart was left behind!
What feeling do we ever find
To equal among human kind
   A dog's fidelity!"

"Mistress, I dug upon your grave
   To bury a bone, in case
I should be hungry near this spot
When passing on my daily trot.
I am sorry, but I quite forgot
   It was your resting-place."

(From *Moments of Vision and Miscellaneous Verses,*
          1917)

## LIFE LAUGHS ONWARD

RAMBLING I looked for an old abode
Where, years back, one had lived I knew;
Its site a dwelling duly showed,
    But it was new.

I went where, not so long ago,
The sod had riven two breasts asunder;
Daisies throve gayly there, as though
    No grave were under.

ì walked along a terrace where
Loud children gamboled in the sun;
The figure that had once sat there
     Was missed by none.

Life laughed and moved on unsubdued,
I saw that Old succumbed to Young:
'Twas well. My too regretful mood
     Died on my tongue.

## THOMAS BABINGTON MACAULAY (1800-1859)

### BOSWELL

(From Review of *Croker's Boswell's Johnson*)

THE Life of Johnson is assuredly a great, a very great work. Homer is not more decidedly the first of heroic poets, Shakespeare is not more decidedly the first of dramatists, Demosthenes is not more decidedly the first of orators, than Boswell is the first of biographers. He has no second. He has distanced all his competitors so decidedly that it is not worth while to place them. Eclipse is first, and the rest nowhere.

We are not sure that there is in the whole history of the human intellect so strange a phenomenon as this book. Many of the greatest men that ever lived have written biography. Boswell was one of the smallest men that ever lived, and he has beaten them all. He was, if we are to give any credit to his own account or to the united testimony of all who knew him, a man of the meanest and feeblest intellect. Johnson described him as a fellow who had missed his only chance of immortality by not having been alive when the Dunciad was written. Beauclerk used his name as a proverbial expression for a bore. He was the laughing-stock of the whole of that brilliant society which has owed to him the greater part of its fame. He was always laying himself at the feet of some eminent man, and begging to be spit upon and trampled upon. He was always earning some ridiculous nickname, and the "binding it as a crown unto him," not merely in metaphor, but literally. He exhibited himself, at the Shakespeare Jubilee, to all the crowd which filled Stratford-on-Avon, with a placard round his hat bearing the inscription of Corsica Boswell. In his Tour, he proclaimed to all the world that at Edinburgh he was known by the appellation of Paoli Boswell. Servile and impertinent, shallow and pedantic, a bigot and a sot, bloated with family pride, and eternally blustering about the dignity of a born gentleman, yet stooping to be a talebearer, and eavesdropper, a common butt in the taverns of London, so curious to know everybody that was talked about, that, Tory and High Churchman as he was, he manœuvered, as we have been told, for an introduction to Tom Paine; so vain of the most childish distinctions, that when he had been to court, he drove to the office where his book was printing without changing his clothes, and summoned all the printer's devils to admire his new ruffles and sword; such was this man, and such he was content and proud to be. Everything which another man would have hidden, everything the publication of which would have made another man hang himself, was matter of gay and clamorous exultation to his weak and diseased mind. What silly things he said, what bitter retorts he provoked, how at one place he was troubled with evil presentiments which came to nothing, how at another place, on waking from a drunken doze, he read the prayer-book and took a hair of the dog that had bitten him, how he went to see men hanged and came away maudlin, how he added five hundred pounds to the fortune of one of his babies because she was not scared at Johnson's ugly face, how he was frightened out of his wits at sea, and how the sailors quieted him as they would have quieted a child, how tipsy he was at Lady Cork's one evening and how much his merriment annoyed the ladies, how impertinent he was to the Duchess of Argle and with what stately contempt she put down his impertinence, how Colonel Macleod sneered to his face at his impudent obtrusiveness, how his father, and the very wife of his bosom laughed and fretted at his fooleries—all these things he proclaimed to all the world, as if they had been subjects for pride and ostentatious rejoicing. All caprices of his temper, all the illusions of his vanity, all his hypochondriac whimsies, all his castles in the air, he displayed with a cool self-complacency, a perfect unconsciousness that he was making a fool of himself, to which it is impossible to find a parallel in the whole history of mankind. He had used many people ill; but assuredly he has used nobody so ill as himself.

That such a man should have written one of the best books in the world is strange enough. But this is not all. Many persons who have conducted themselves foolishly in active life, and whose conversation has indicated no superior powers of mind, have left us valuable works. Goldsmith was very justly described by one of his contemporaries as an inspired idiot, and by another as a being

"Who wrote like an angel, and talked like poor Poll."

La Fontaine was in society a mere simpleton. His blunders would not come in amiss among the stories of Hierocles. But these men attained literary eminence in spite of their weaknesses. Boswell attained it by reason of his weaknesses. If he had not been a great fool,

he would never have been a great writer. Without all
the qualities which made him the jest and the torment
of those among whom he lived, without the officiousness,
the inquisitiveness, the effrontery, the toad-eating, the
insensibility to all reproof, he never could have produced so excellent a book. He was a slave proud of his
servitude, a Paul Pry, convinced that his own curiosity
and garrulity were virtues, an unsafe companion who
never scrupled to repay the most liberal hospitality by
the basest violation of confidence, a man without delicacy, without shame, without sense enough to know
when he was hurting the feelings of others or when he
was exposing himself to derision; and because he was all
this, he has, in an important department of literature,
immeasurably surpassed such writers as Tacitus, Claren-
don, Alfieri, and his own idol Johnson.

Of the talents which ordinarily raise men to eminence as writers, Boswell had absolutely none. There
is not in all his books a single remark of his own on
literature, politics, religion, or society, which is not either
commonplace or absurd. His dissertations on hereditary
gentility, on the slave-trade, and on the entailing of
landed estates, may serve as examples. To say that these
passages are sophistical would be to pay them an ex-
travagant compliment. They have no pretense to argument, or even to meaning. He has reported innumerable
observations made by himself in the course of conversation. Of those observations we do not remember one
which is above the intellectual capacity of a boy of
fifteen. He has printed many of his own letters, and in
these letters he is always ranting or twaddling. Logic,
eloquence, wit, taste, all those things which are generally considered as making a book valuable were utterly
wanting to him. He had, indeed, a quick observation and
a retentive memory. These qualities, if he had been a

man of sense and virtue would scarcely of themselves have sufficed to make him conspicuous; but because he was a dunce, a parasite, and a coxcomb, they have made him immortal.

Those parts of his book which, considered abstractedly, are most utterly worthless, are delightful when we read them as illustrations of the character of the writer. Bad in themselves, they are good dramatically, like the nonsense of Justice Shallow, the clipped English of Dr. Caius, or the misplaced consonants of Fluellen. Of all confessors, Boswell is the most candid. Other men who have pretended to lay open their own hearts, Rousseau, for example, and Lord Byron, have evidently written with a constant view to effect, and are to be then most distrusted when they seem to be most sincere. There is scarcely any man who would not rather accuse himself of great crimes and of dark and tempestuous passions than proclaim all his little vanities and wild fancies. It would be easier to find a person who would avow actions like those of Cæsar Borgia or Danton, than one who would publish a daydream like those of Alnaschar and Malvolio. Those weaknesses which most men keep covered up in the most secret places of the mind, not to be disclosed to the eye of friendship or of love, were precisely the weaknesses which Boswell paraded before all the world. He was perfectly frank, because the weakness of his understanding and the tumult of his spirits prevented him from knowing when he made himself ridiculous. His book resembles nothing so much as the conversation of the inmates of the Palace of Truth.

His fame is great; and it will, we have no doubt, be lasting; but it is fame of a peculiar kind, and indeed marvellously resembles infamy. We remember no other case in which the world has made so great a distinction between a book and its author. In general, the book and the author are considered as one. To admire the book is to admire the author. The case of Boswell is an exception, we think the only exception, to this rule. His work is universally allowed to be interesting, instructive, eminently original; yet it has brought him nothing but contempt. All the world reads it; all the world delights in it; yet we do not remember ever to have read or ever to have heard any expression of respect and admiration for the man to whom we owe so much instruction and amusement. While edition after edition of his book was coming forth, his son, as Mr. Croker tells us, was ashamed of it, and hated to hear it mentioned. This feeling was natural and reasonable. Sir Alexander saw that, in proportion to the celebrity of the work, was the degradation of the author. The very editors of this unfortunate gentleman's books have forgotten their allegiance, and, like those Puritan casuists who took arms by the authority of the king against his person, have attacked the writer while doing homage to his writings. Mr. Croker, for example, has published two thousand five hundred notes on the life of Johnson, and yet scarcely ever mentions the biographer whose performance he has taken such pains to illustrate without some expression of contempt.

An ill-natured man Boswell certainly was not; yet the malignity of the most malignant satirist could scarcely cut deeper than his thoughtless loquacity. Having himself no sensibility to derision and contempt, he took it for granted that all others were equally callous. He was not ashamed to exhibit himself to the whole world as a common spy, a common tattler, a humble companion without the excuse of poverty, and to tell a hundred stories of his own pertness and folly, and of the insults which his pertness and folly brought upon him.

It was natural that he should show little discretion in cases in which the feelings or the honour of others might be concerned. No man, surely, ever published such stories respecting persons whom he professed to love and revere. He would infallibly have made his hero as contemptible as he has made himself, had not his hero really possessed some moral and intellectual qualities of a very high order. The best proof that Johnson was really an extraordinary man is that his character, instead of being degraded, has, on the whole, been decidedly raised by a work in which all his vices and weaknesses are exposed more unsparingly than they ever were exposed by Churchill or by Kenrick.

Johnson grown old, Johnson in the fulness of his fame and in the enjoyment of a competent fortune, is better known to us than any other man in history. Everything about him, his coat, his wig, his figure, his face, his scrofula, his St. Vitus's dance, his rolling walk, his blinking eye, the outward signs which too clearly marked his approbation of his dinner, his insatiable appetite for fish-sauce and veal-pie with plums, his inextinguishable thirst for tea, his trick of touching the posts as he walked, his mysterious practice of treasuring up scraps of orange-peel, his morning slumbers, his midnight disputations, his contortions, his mutterings, his gruntings, his puffings, his vigorous, acute, and ready eloquence, his sarcastic wit, his vehemence, his insolence, his fits of tempestuous rage, his queer inmates, old Mr. Levett and blind Mrs. Williams, the cat Hodge and the negro Frank, all are as familiar to us as the objects by which we have been surrounded from childhood. But we have no minute information respecting those years of Johnson's life during which his character and his manners became immutably fixed. We know him, not as he was known to the men of his own generation, but as he was known to men whose father he might have been. That celebrated club of which he was the most distinguished member contained few persons who could remember a time when his fame was not fully established and his habits completely formed. He had made himself a name in literature while Reynolds and the Wartons were still boys. He was about twenty years older than Burke, Goldsmith, and Gerard Hamilton, about thirty years older than Gibbon, Beauclerk, and Langton, and about forty years older than Lord Stowell, Sir William Jones, and Windham. Boswell and Mrs. Thrale, the two writers from whom we derive most of our knowledge respecting him, never saw him till long after he was fifty years old, till most of his great works had become classical, and till the pension bestowed on him by the Crown had placed him above poverty. Of those eminent men who were his most intimate associates toward the close of his life, the only one, as far as we remember, who knew him during the first ten or twelve years of his residence in the capital, was David Garrick; and it does not appear that, during those years, David Garrick saw much of his fellow-townsman.                                    1831

# THE COFFEE-HOUSE

## (From the *History of England*)

THE coffee-house must not be dismissed with a cursory mention. It might indeed, at that time, have been not improperly called a most important political institution. No Parliament had sate for years. The municipal council of the City had ceased to speak the sense of the citizens. Public meetings, harangues, resolutions, and the rest of the modern machinery of agitation had not yet come into fashion. Nothing resembling the modern newspaper existed. In such circumstances the coffeehouses were the chief organs through which the public opinion of the metropolis vented itself.

The first of these establishments had been set up, in the time of the Commonwealth, by a Turkey merchant, who had acquired among the Mahometans a taste for their favorite beverage. The convenience of being able to make appointments in any part of the town, and of being able to pass evenings socially at a very small charge, was so great that the fashion spread fast. Every man of the upper or middle class went daily to his coffee-house to learn the news and to discuss it. Every coffee-house had one or more orators to whose eloquence the crowd listened with admiration, and who soon became, what the journalists of our time have been called, a Fourth Estate of the realm. The Court had long seen with uneasiness the growth of this new power in the state. An attempt had been made, during Danby's administration, to close the coffee-houses. But men of all parties missed their usual places of resort so much that there was an universal outcry. The government did not venture, in opposition to a feeling so strong and general, to enforce a regulation of which the legality might well be questioned. Since that time ten years had elapsed, and, during those years, the number and influence of the coffee-houses had been constantly increasing. Foreigners remarked that the coffee-house was that which especially distinguished London from all other cities; that the coffeehouse was the Londoner's home, and that those who wished to find a gentleman commonly asked, not whether he lived in Fleet Street or Chancery Lane, but whether he frequented the Grecian or the Rainbow. Nobody was excluded from these places who laid down his penny at the bar. Yet every rank and profession, and every shade of religious and political opinion, had its own headquarters. There were houses near St. James's Park where fops congregated, their heads and shoulders covered with black or flaxen wigs, not less ample than those which are now worn by the Chancellor and by the Speaker of the House of Commons. The wig came from Paris and so did the rest of the fine gentleman's ornaments, his embroidered coat, his fringed gloves, and the tassel which upheld his pantaloons. The conversation was in that dialect which, long after it had ceased to be spoken in fashionable circles, continued in the mouth of Lord Foppington, to excite the mirth of theatres. The atmosphere was like that of a perfumer's shop. Tobacco in any other form than that of richly scented snuff was held in abomination. If any clown, ignorant of the usages of the house, called for a pipe, the sneers of the whole assembly and the short answers of the waiters soon convinced him that he had better go somewhere else. Nor, indeed, would he have had far to go. For, in general, the coffee-rooms reeked with tobacco like a guard room; and strangers sometimes expressed their surprise that so many people should leave their own firesides to sit in the midst of eternal fog and stench. Nowhere was the smoking more constant than at Will's. That celebrated house, situated between Covent Garden and Bow Street, was sacred to polite letters. There the talk was about poetical justice and the unities of place and time. There was a faction for Perrault and the moderns, a faction for Boileau and the ancients. One group debated whether Paradise Lost ought not to have been in rhyme. To another an envious poetaster demonstrated that Venice Preserved ought to have been hooted from the stage. Under no roof was a greater variety of figures to be seen,—earls in stars and garters, clergymen in cassocks and bands, pert Templars, sheepish lads from the Universities, translators and index-makers in ragged coats of frieze. The great press was to get near the chair where John Dryden sate. In winter, that chair was always in the warmest nook by the fire; in summer, it stood in the balcony. To bow to the Laureate, and to hear his opinion of Racine's last tragedy or of Bossu's treatise on epic poetry, was thought a privilege. A pinch from his snuff-box was an honour sufficient to turn the head of a young enthusiast. There were coffee-houses where the first medical men might be consulted. Doctor John Radcliffe, who, in the year 1685, rose to the largest practice in London, came daily, at the hour when the Exchange was full, from his house in Bow Street, then a fashionable part of the capital, to Garraway's, and was to be found, surrounded by surgeons and apothecaries, at a particular table. There were Puritan coffee-houses where no oath was heard and where lank-haired men discussed election, and reprobation through their noses; Jew coffee-houses where dark-eyed money changers from Venice and Amsterdam greeted each other; and Popish coffee-houses where, as good Protestants believed, Jesuits planned, over their cups, another great fire, and cast silver bullets to shoot the King.

These gregarious habits had no small share in forming the character of the Londoner of that age. He was, indeed, a different being from the rustic Englishman. There was not then the intercourse which now exists between the two classes. Only very great men were in the habit of dividing the year between town and country. Few esquires came to the capital thrice in their lives. Nor was it yet the practice of all citizens in easy circumstances to breathe the fresh air of the fields and woods during some weeks of every summer.

A cockney, in a rural village, was stared at as much as if he had intruded into a Kraal of Hottentots. On the other hand, when the lord of a Lincolnshire or Shropshire manor appeared in Fleet Street, he was as easily distinguished from the resident population as a Turk or a Lascar. His dress, his gait, his accent, the manner in which he gazed at the shops, stumbled into the gutters, ran against the porters, and stood under the waterspouts, marked him out as an excellent subject for the operations of swindlers and banterers. Bullies jostled him into the kennel. Hackney coachmen splashed him from head to foot. Thieves explored with perfect security the huge pockets of his horseman's coat, while he stood entranced by the splendour of the Lord Mayor's show. Moneydroppers, sore from the cart's tail, introduced themselves to him, and appeared to him the most honest friendly gentlemen he had ever seen. Painted women, the refuse of Lewkner Lane and Whetstone Park, passed themselves on him for countesses and maids of honour. If he asked his way to St. James's, his informants sent him to Mile End. If he went into a shop, he was instantly discerned to be a fit purchaser of everything that nobody else would buy, of second-hand embroidery, copper rings, and watches that would not go. If he rambled into any fashionable coffee-house, he became a mark for the insolent derision of fops and the grave waggery of Templars. Enraged and mortified, he soon returned to his mansion, and there, in the homage of his tenants and the conversation of his boon companions, found consolation for the vexations and humiliations which he had undergone. There he was once more a great man, and saw nothing above himself except when at the assizes he took his seat on the bench near the Judge, or when at the muster of the militia he saluted the Lord Lieutenant.                    1848

## THOMAS CARLYLE (1795-1881)

## BOSWELL THE HERO-WORSHIPPER

(From *Boswell's Life of Johnson*)

WE HAVE a next word to say of James Boswell. Boswell has already been much commented upon; but rather in the way of censure and vituperation than of true recognition. He was a man that brought himself much before the world; confessed that he eagerly coveted fame, or if that were not possible, notoriety; of which latter as he gained far more than was his due, the public were incited, not only by their natural love of scandal, but by a special ground of envy, to say whatever ill of him could be said. Out of the fifteen millions that then lived, and had bed and board, in the British islands, this man has provided us a greater *pleasure* than any other individual, at whose cost we now enjoy ourselves; perhaps has done us a greater *service* than can be especially attributed to more than two or three: yet, ungrateful that we are, no written or spoken eulogy of James Boswell anywhere exists; his recompense in solid pudding (so far as copyright went) was not excessive; and as for the empty praise, it has altogether been denied him. Men are unwiser than children; they do *not* know the hand that feeds them.

Boswell was a person whose mean or bad qualities lay open to the general eye; visible, palpable to the dullest. His good qualities, again, belonged not to the Time he lived in; were far from common then; indeed, in such a degree, were almost unexampled; not recognizable therefore by every one; nay, apt even (so strange had they grown) to be confounded with the very vices they lay contiguous to and had sprung out of. That he was a winebibber and gross liver; gluttonously fond of whatever would yield him a little solacement, were it only of a stomachic character, is undeniable enough. That he was vain, heedless, a babbler; had much of the sycophant, alternating with the braggadocio, curiously spiced too with an all-pervading dash of the coxcomb; that he gloried much when the Tailor, by a court-suit, had made a new man of him; that he appeared at the Shakespeare Jubilee with a ribbon, imprinted "Corsica Boswell," round his hat; and in short, if you will, lived no day of his life without doing and saying more than one pretentious ineptitude: all this unhappily is evident as the sun at noon. The very look of Boswell seems to have signified so much. In that cocked nose, cocked partly in triumph over his weaker fellow-creatures, partly to snuff up the smell of coming pleasure, and scent it from afar; in those bag-cheeks, hanging like half-filled wine-skins, still able to contain more; in that coarsely protruded shelf-mouth, that fat dew-lapped chin: in all this, who sees not sensuality, pretension, boisterous imbecility enough; much that could not have been ornamental in the temper of a great man's overfed great man (what the Scotch name *flunky*), though it had been more natural there? The under part of Boswell's face is of a low, almost brutish character.

Unfortunately, on the other hand, what great and genuine good lay in him was nowise so self-evident. That Boswell was a hunter after spiritual Notabilities, that he loved such, and longed, and even crept and crawled to be near them; that he first (in old Touchwood Auchinleck's phraseology) "took on with Paoli;" and then being off with "the Corsican landlouper," took on with a schoolmaster, "ane that keeped a schule, and ca'd it an academy:" that he did all this, and could not help doing it, we count a very singular merit. The man, once for all, had an "open sense," an open loving heart, which so few have: where Excellence existed, he was compelled to acknowledge it; was drawn towards it, and (let the old sulphur-brand of a Laird say what he liked) *could not but* walk with it—if not as superior, if not as equal, then as inferior and lackey, better so than not at all. If we reflect now that this love of Excellence had not only *such* an evil *nature* to triumph over; but also what an *education* and social position withstood it and weighed it down, its innate strength, victorious over all these things, may astonish us. Consider what an inward impulse there must have been, how many mountains of impediment hurled aside, before the Scottish Laird could, as humble servant, embrace the knees (the bosom was not permitted him) of the English Dominie! "Your Scottish Laird," says an English naturalist of these days, "may be defined as the hungriest and vainest of all bipeds yet known." Boswell too was a Tory; of quite peculiarly feudal, genealogical, pragmatical temper; had been nurtured in an atmosphere of Heraldry, at the feet of a very Gamaliel in that kind; within bare walls, adorned only with pedigrees, amid serving-men in threadbare livery; all things teaching him, from birth upwards, to remember that a Laird was a Laird. Perhaps there was a special vanity in his very blood: old Auchinleck had, if not the gay, tail-spreading, peacock vanity of his son, no little of the slow-stalking, contentious, hissing vanity of the gander; a still more fatal species. Scottish Advocates will tell you how the ancient man, having chanced to be the first sheriff appointed (after the abolition of "hereditary jurisdiction") by royal authority, was wont, in dull-snuffling pompous tone, to preface many a deliverance from the bench with these words: "I, the first King's Sheriff in Scotland."

And now behold the worthy Bozzy, so prepossessed and held back by nature and by art, fly nevertheless like iron to its magnet, whither his better genius called! You may surround the iron and the magnet with what enclosures and encumbrances you please—with wood, with rubbish, with brass: it matters not, the two feel each other, they struggle restlessly towards each other, they *will* be together. The iron may be a Scottish squirelet, full of gulosity and "gigmanity;" the magnet an English plebeian, and moving rag-and-dust mountain, coarse, proud, irascible, imperious: nevertheless, behold how they embrace, and inseparably cleave to one another! It is one of the strangest phenomena of the past century, that at a time when the old reverent feeling of discipleship (such as brought men from far countries with rich gifts, and prostrate soul, to the feet of the Prophets) had passed utterly away from men's practical experience, and was no longer surmised to exist (as it does), perennial, indestructible, in man's inmost heart—James Boswell should have been the individual, of all others, predestined to recall it, in such singular guise, to the wondering, and for a long while, laughing and unrecognizing world.

It has been commonly said, The man's vulgar vanity was all that attached him to Johnson; he delighted to be seen near him, to be thought connected with him. Now let it be at once granted that no consideration springing out of vulgar vanity could well be absent from the mind of James Boswell, in this his intercourse with Johnson, or in any considerable transaction of his life. At the same time, ask yourself; whether such vanity, and nothing else, actuated him therein; whether this was the true essence and moving principle of the phenomenon, or not rather its outward vesture, and the accidental environment (and defacement) in which it came to light? The man was, by nature and habit, vain; a sycophant-coxcomb, be it granted: but had there been nothing more than vanity in him, was Samuel Johnson the man of men to whom he must attach himself? At the date when Johnson was a poor rusty-coated "scholar," dwelling in Temple-lane, and indeed throughout their whole intercourse afterwards, were there not chancellors and prime ministers enough; graceful gentlemen, the glass of fashion; honor-giving noblemen; dinner-giving rich men; renowned fire-eaters, swordsmen, gownmen; Quacks and Realities of all hues —any one of whom bulked much larger in the world's eye than Johnson ever did? To any one of whom, by half that submissiveness and assiduity, our Bozzy might have recommended himself; and sat there, the envy of surrounding lickspittles; pocketing now solid emolument, swallowing now well-cooked viands and wines of rich red vintage; in each case, also, shone-on by some glittering reflex of Renown or Notoriety, so as to be the observed of innumerable observers. To no one of whom, however, though otherwise a most diligent solicitor and purveyor, did he so attach himself: such vulgar courtierships were his paid drudgery, or leisure-amusement; the worship of Johnson was his grand, ideal, voluntary business. Does not the frothy-hearted, yet enthusiastic man, doffing his Advocate's wig, regularly take post, and hurry up to London, for the sake of his sage chiefly; as to a feast of tabernacles, the Sabbath of his whole year? The plate-licker and wine-bibber dives into Bolt Court, to sip muddy coffee with a cynical old man and a sour-tempered blind old woman (feeling the cups, whether they are full, with her finger); and patiently endures contradictions without end; too happy so he may be but allowed to listen and live. Nay, it does not appear that vulgar vanity could ever have been much flattered by Boswell's relation to Johnson. Mr. Croker says, Johnson was, to the last, little regarded by the great world; from which, for a vulgar vanity, all honor, as from its fountain, descends. Bozzy, even among Johnson's friends and special admirers, seems rather to have been laughed at than envied: his officious, whisking, consequential ways, the daily reproofs and rebuffs he underwent, could gain from the world no golden, but only leaden opinions. His devout Discipleship seemed nothing more than a mean Spanielship, in the general eye. His mighty "constellation," or sun, round whom he, as satellite, observantly gyrated, was, for the mass of men, but a huge ill-snuffed tallow-light, and he a weak night-moth, circling foolishly, dangerously about it, not knowing what he wanted. If he enjoyed Highland dinners and toasts, as henchman to a new sort of chieftain, Henry Erskine, in the domestic "Outer-House," could hand him a shilling "for the sight of his Bear." Doubtless the man was laughed at, and often heard himself laughed at for his Johnsonism. To be envied is the grand and sole aim of vulgar vanity; to be filled with good things is that of sensuality: for Johnson perhaps no man living *envied* poor Bozzy; and of good things (except himself paid for them) there was no vestige in that acquaintanceship. Had nothing other or better than vanity and sensuality been there, Johnson and Boswell had never come together, or had soon and finally separated again.

In fact, the so copious terrestrial Dross that welters chaotically, as the outer sphere of this man's character, does but render for us more remarkable, more touching, the celestial spark of goodness, of light, and Reverence for Wisdom which dwelt in the interior, and could struggle through such encumbrances, and in some degree illuminate and beautify them. There *is* much lying yet undeveloped in the love of Boswell for Johnson. A cheering proof, in a time which else utterly wanted and still wants such, that living Wisdom is quite *infinitely* precious to man, is the symbol of the God-like to him, which even weak eyes may discern; that Loyalty, Discipleship, all that was ever meant by *Hero-worship,* lives perennially in the human bosom, and waits, even in these dead days, only for occasions to unfold it, and inspire all men with it, and again make the world alive! James Boswell we can regard as a practical witness, or real *martyr,* to this high everlasting truth. A wonderful martyr, if you will; and in a time which made such martyrdom doubly wonderful: yet the time and its martyr perhaps suited each other. For a decrepit, death-sick Era, when CANT had first decisively opened her poison-breathing lips to proclaim that God-worship and Mammon-worship were one and the same, that Life was a *Lie,* and the Earth Beelzebub's, which the *Supreme Quack* should inherit; and so all things were fallen into the yellow leaf, and fast hastening to noisome corruption: for such an Era, perhaps no better Prophet than a parti-colored Zany-Prophet, concealing, from himself and others, his prophetic significance in such unexpected vestures,—was deserved, or would have been in place. A precious medicine lay hidden in floods of coarsest, most composite treacle; the world swallowed the treacle, for it suited the world's palate; and now, after half a century, may the medicine also begin to show itself! James Boswell belonged, in his corruptible part, to the lowest classes of mankind; a foolish, inflated creature, swimming in an element of self-conceit: but in his corruptible there dwelt an incorruptible, all the more impressive and indubitable for the strange lodging it had taken.

Consider, too, with what force, diligence, and vivacity

he has rendered back all this which, in Johnson's neighborhood, his "open sense" had so eagerly and freely taken in. That loose-flowing, careless-looking Work of his is as a picture by one of Nature's own Artists; the best possible remembrance of a Reality; like the very image thereof in a clear mirror. Which indeed it was: let but the mirror be *clear,* this is the great point; the picture must and will be genuine. How the babbling Bozzy, inspired only by love, and the recognition and vision which love can lend, epitomizes nightly the words of Wisdom, the deeds and aspects of Wisdom, and so, by little and little, unconsciously works together for us a whole *Johnsoniad;* a more free, perfect, sunlit and spirit-speaking likeness than for many centuries had been drawn by man of man! Scarcely since the days of Homer has the feat been equalled; indeed, in many senses, this also is a kind of heroic poem. The fit *Odyssey* of our unheroic age was to be written, not sung; of a Thinker, not of a Fighter; and (for want of a Homer) by the first open soul that might offer—looked such even through the organs of a Boswell. We do the man's intellectual endowment great wrong, if we measure it by its mere logical outcome; though, here too, there is not wanting a light ingenuity, a figurativeness and fanciful sport, with glimpses of insight far deeper than the common. But Boswell's grand intellectual talent was, as such ever is, an *unconscious* one, of far higher reach, and significance than Logic; and showed itself in the whole, not in parts. Here again we have that old saying verified, "The heart sees further than the head."

Thus does poor Bozzy stand out to us an ill-assorted, glaring mixture of the highest and the lowest. What, indeed, is man's life generally but a kind of beast-godhood; the god in us triumphing in us more and more over the beast; striving more and more to subdue it under his feet? Did not the Ancients, in their wise, perennially-significant way, figure nature itself, in their sacred ALL, or PAN, as a portentous commingling of these two discords; as musical, humane, oracular in its upper part, yet ending below in the cloven hairy feet of a goat? The union of melodious, celestial Free-will and Reason with foul Irrationality and Lust; in which, nevertheless, dwelt a mysterious unspeakable Fear and half mad *panic* Awe; as for mortals there well might! And is not man a microcosm, or epitomized mirror of that same universe; or rather, is not that universe even himself, the reflex of his own fearful and wonderful being, "the waste fantasy of his own dream?" No wonder that man, that each man, and James Boswell like the others, should resemble it! The peculiarity in his case was the unusual defect of amalgamation and subordination: the highest lay side by side with the lowest; not morally combined with it and spiritually transfiguring it, but tumbling in half-mechanical juxtaposition with it, and from time to time, as the mad alternation chanced, irradiating it, or eclipsed by it.

The world, as we said, has been but unjust to him; discerning only the outer terrestrial and often sordid mass; without eye, as it generally is, for his inner divine secret; and thus figuring him nowise as a god Pan, but simply of the bestial species, like the cattle on a thousand hills. Nay, sometimes a strange enough hypothesis has been started of him; as if it were in virtue even of these same bad qualities that he did his good work; as if it were the very fact of his being among the worst men in this world that had enabled him to write one of the best books therein! Falser hypothesis, we may venture to say, never rose in human soul. *Bad* is by its nature negative, and can do *nothing;* whatsoever enables us to do anything is by its **very nature** *good.*

Alas, that there should be teachers in Israel, or even
learners, to whom this world-ancient fact is still prob-
lematical, or even deniable! Boswell wrote a good Book
because he had a heart and an eye to discern Wisdom,
and an utterance to render it forth; because of his free
insight, his lively talent—above all, of his Love and
childlike Open-mindedness. His sneaking sycophancies,
his greediness and forwardness, whatever was bestial
and earthy in him, are so many blemishes in his Book,
which still disturb us in its clearness; wholly hindrances,
not helps. Towards Johnson, however, his feeling was
not Sycophancy, which is the lowest, but Reverence,
which is the highest of human feelings. None but a
*reverent* man (which so unspeakably few are) could
have found his way from Boswell's environment to Johnson's: if such worship for real God-made superiors,
showed itself also as worship for apparent, Tailor-made
superiors, even as hollow interested mouth-worship for
such—the case, in this composite human nature of ours,
was not miraculous, the more was the pity! But for ourselves, let every one of us cling to this last article of
faith, and know it as the beginning of all knowledge
worth the name: That neither James Boswell's good
Book, nor any other good thing, in any time or in any
place, was, is, or can be performed by any man in virtue
of his *badness,* but always and solely in spite thereof.

                                                    1832

## SARTOR RESARTUS
### SELECTIONS

#### THE CLOTHES METAPHOR

"WELL sang the Hebrew Psalmist: 'If I take the
wings of the morning and dwell in the uttermost parts
of the universe, God is there.' Thou thyself, O culti-

vated reader, who too probably art no Psalmist, but a Prosaist, knowing God only by tradition, knowest thou any corner of the world where at least Force is not? The drop which thou shakest from thy wet hand, rests not where it falls, but tomorrow thou findest it swept away; already, on the wings of the North-wind, it is nearing the Tropic of Cancer. How came it to evaporate, and not lie motionless? Thinkest thou there is aught motionless; without Force, and utterly dead?

"As I rode through the Schwarzwald, I said to myself: That little fire which glows star-like across the dark growing (*nachtende*) moor, where the sooty smith bends over his anvil, and thou hopest to replace thy lost horse-shoe,—it is a detached, separated speck, cutoff from the whole Universe; or indissolubly joined to the whole? Thou fool, that smithy-fire was (primarily) kindled at the Sun; is fed by air that circulates from before Noah's Deluge, from beyond the Dog-star; therein, with Iron Force, and Coal Force, and the far stranger Force of Man, are cunning affinities and battles and victories of Force brought about: it is a little ganglion, or nervous centre, in the great vital system of Immensity. Call it, if thou will, an unconscious Altar, kindled on the bosom of the All; whose iron sacrifice, whose iron smoke and influence, reach quite through the All; whose Dingy Priest, not by word, yet by brain and sinew, preaches forth the mystery of Force; nay, preaches forth (exoterically enough) one little textlet from the Gospel of Freedom, the Gospel of Man's Force, commanding, and one day to be all-commanding.

"Detached, separated! I say there is no such separation: nothing hitherto was ever stranded, cast aside; but all, were it only a withered leaf, works together with all; is borne forward on the bottomless, shoreless flood of Action, and lives through perpetual metamorphoses. The withered leaf is not dead and lost, there are Forces in it and around it, though working in inverse order; else how could it *rot?* Despise not the rag from which man makes Paper, or the little from which the Earth makes Corn. Rightly viewed no meanest object is insignificant; all objects are as windows, through which the philosophic eye looks into Infinitude itself."

Again leaving that wondrous Schwarzwald Smithy-Altar, what vacant, high-sailing airships are these, and whither will they sail with us?

"All visible things are emblems; what thou seest is not there on its own account; strictly taken, is not there at all: Matter exists only spiritually, and to represent some Idea, and *body* it forth. Hence Clothes, as despicable as we think them, are so unspeakably significant. Clothes, from the King's mantle downwards, are Emblematic, not of want only, but of a manifold cunning Victory over Want. On the other hand, all Emblematic things are properly Clothes, thought-woven or hand-woven: must not the Imagination weave Garments, visible Bodies, wherein the else invisible creations and inspirations of our Reason, are, like Spirits, revealed, and first become all-powerful;—the rather if, as we often see, the Hand too aid her, and (by wool Clothes or otherwise) reveal such even to the outward eye?

"Men are properly said to be clothed with Authority, clothed with Beauty, with Curses, and the like. Nay, if you consider it, what is Man himself, and his whole terrestrial Life, but an Emblem; a Clothing or visible Garment for that divine ME of his, cast hither, like a light-particle, down from Heaven? Thus is he said also to be clothed with a Body.

"Language is called the Garment of Thought: however, it should rather be, Language is the Flesh-Garment, the Body of Thought. I said that Imagination wove this Flesh-Garment; and does not she? Metaphors are her stuff: examine Language; what, if you except some few primitive elements (of natural sound), what is it all but Metaphors, recognized as such, or no longer recognized: still fluid and florid, or now solid-grown and colorless? If those same primitive elements are the osseous fixtures in the Flesh-Garment, Language,— then are Metaphors its muscles and tissues, and living integuments. An unmetaphorical style you shall in vain seek for; is not your very *Attention* a *Stretching-to*? The difference lies here: some styles are lean, adust, wiry, the muscle itself seems osseous; some are even quite pallid, hunger-bitten, and dead-looking; while others again glow in the flush of health and vigorous self-growth, sometimes (as in my own case) not without an apoplectic tendency. Moreover, there are sham Metaphors, which overhanging that same Thought's Body (best naked), and deceptively bedizening, or bolstering it out, may be called its false stuffings, superfluous show-cloaks (*Putz-Mantel*), and tawdry woolen rags: whereof he that runs and reads may gather whole hampers,— and burn them."

Than which paragraph on Metaphors did the reader ever chance to see a more surprisingly metaphorical? However, that is not our chief grievance; the Professor continues:

"Why multiply instances? It is written, the Heavens and the Earth shall fade away like a Vesture: which indeed they are: the Time-vesture of the Eternal. What-soever sensibly exists, whatsoever represents Spirit to Spirit, is properly a Clothing, a suit of Raiment, put on for a season, and to be laid off. Thus in this one pregnant subject of CLOTHES, rightly understood, is included all that men have thought, dreamed, done, and been: the whole External Universe and what it holds is but Clothing; and the essence of all Science lies in the PHILOSOPHY OF CLOTHES."

## THE EVERLASTING YEA

"BEAUTIFUL it was to sit there, as in my skyey Tent, musing and meditating; on the high table-land, in front of the Mountains; over me, as roof, the azure Dome, and around me, for walls, four azure-flowing curtains,—namely, of the Four azure Winds, on whose bottom-fringes also I have seen gilding. And then to fancy the fair Castles, that stood sheltered in these Mountain hollows; with their green flower-lawns, and white dames and damosels, lovely enough: or better still, the straw-roofed Cottages, wherein stood many a Mother baking bread, with her children round her:—all hidden and protectingly folded-up in the valley-folds; yet there and alive, as sure as if I beheld them. Or to see, as well as fancy, the nine Towns and Villages, that lay round my mountain-seat, which, in still weather, were wont to speak to me (by their steeple-bells) with metal tongue; and, in almost all weather, proclaimed their vitality by repeated Smoke-clouds; whereon, as on a culinary horologe, I might read the hour of the day. For it was the smoke of cookery, as kind housewives at morning, midday, eventide, were boiling their husbands' kettles; and ever a blue pillar rose up into the air, successively or simultaneously, from each of the nine, saying, as plainly as smoke could say: Such and such a meal is getting ready here. Not uninteresting! For you have the whole Borough, with all its love-makings and scandal-mongeries, contentions and contentments, as in miniature, and could cover it all with your hat.—If, in my wide Wayfarings, I had learned to look into the business of the World in its details, here perhaps was the place for combining it into general propositions, and deducing inferences therefrom.

"Often also could I see the black Tempest marching in anger through the Distance: round some Schreckhorn, as yet grim-blue, would the eddying vapour gather, and there tumultuously eddy, and flow down like a mad witch's hair; till, after a space, it vanished, and, in the clear sunbeam, your Schreckhorn stood smiling grim-white, for the vapour had held snow. How thou fermentest and elaboratest, in thy great fermenting-vat and laboratory of an Atmosphere, of a World, O Nature!— Or what is Nature? Ha! why do I not name thee GOD? Art thou not the 'Living Garment of God'? O Heavens, is it, in very deed, HE, then, that ever speaks through thee; that lives and loves in thee, that lives and loves in me?

"Fore-shadows, call them rather fore-splendors, of that Truth, and Beginning of Truths, fell mysteriously over my soul. Sweeter than Dayspring to the Shipwrecked in Nova Zembla; ah, like the mother's voice to her little child that strays bewildered, weeping, in unknown tumults; like soft streamings of celestial music to my too-exasperated heart, came that Evangel. The Universe is not dead and demoniacal, a charnel-house with specters; but godlike, and my Father's!

"So true it is, what I then said, that *the Fraction of Life can be increased in value not so much by increasing your Numerator as by lessening your Denominator.* Nay, unless my Algebra deceive me, *Unity* itself divided by *Zero* will give *Infinity.* Make thy claim of wages a zero, then; thou hast the world under thy feet. Well did the Wisest of our time write: 'It is only with Renunciation (*Entsagen*) that Life, properly speaking, can be said to begin.'

"I asked myself: What is this that, ever since earliest

years, thou hast been fretting and fuming, and lamenting and self-tormenting, on account of? Say it in a word: is it not because thou art not HAPPY? Because the THOU (sweet gentleman) is not sufficiently honoured, nourished, soft-bedded, and lovingly cared-for? Foolish soul! What Act of Legislature was there that *thou* shouldst be Happy? A little while ago thou hadst no right to *be* at all. What if thou wert born and predestined not to be Happy, but to be Unhappy! Art thou nothing other than a Vulture, then, that fliest through the Universe seeking after somewhat to *eat;* and shrieking dolefully because carrion enough is not given thee? Close thy *Byron;* open thy *Goethe.*"

"*Es leuchtet mir ein,* I see a glimpse of it!" cries he elsewhere: "there is in man a HIGHER than Love of Happiness: he can do without Happiness, and instead thereof find Blessedness! Was it not to preach-forth this same HIGHER that sages and martyrs, the Poet and the Priest, in all times, have spoken and suffered; bearing testimony, through life and through death, of the Godlike that is in Man, and how in the Godlike only has he Strength and Freedom? Which God-inspired Doctrine art thou also honoured to be taught; O Heavens! and broken with manifold merciful Afflictions, even till thou become contrite, and learn it! O, thank thy Destiny for these; thankfully bear what yet remain: thou hadst need of them; the Self in thee needed to be annihilated. By benignant fever-paroxysms is Life rooting out the deep-seated chronic Disease, and triumphs over Death. On the roaring billows of Time, thou art not engulfed, but borne aloft into the azure of Eternity. Love not Pleasure; love God. This is the EVERLASTING YEA, wherein all contradiction is solved: wherein whoso walks and works, it is well with him."     1833-34

## HERO-WORSHIP

### (From *Heroes and Hero-Worship*)

But now if all things whatsoever that we look upon are emblems to us of the Highest God, I add that more so than any of them is man such an emblem. You have heard of St. Chrysostom's celebrated saying in reference to the Shekinah, or Ark of Testimony, visible Revelation of God, among the Hebrews: "The true Shekinah is Man!" Yes, it is even so: this is no vain phrase, it is veritably so. The essence of our being, the mystery in us that calls itself "I,"—ah, what words have we for such things?—is a breath of Heaven; the Highest Being reveals himself in man. This body, these faculties, this life of ours, is it not all as a vesture for that Unnamed? "There is but one Temple in the Universe," says the devout Novalis, "and that is the Body of Man. Nothing is holier than that high form. Bending before men is a reverence done to this Revelation in the Flesh. We touch heaven when we lay our hand on a human body." This sounds much like a mere flourish of rhetoric; but it is not so. If well meditated, it will turn out to be a scientific fact; the expression, in such words as can be had, of the actual truth of the thing. *We* are the miracle of miracles,—the great inscrutable mystery of God. We cannot understand it, we know not how to speak of it; but we may feel and know it, if we like, that it is verily so.

Well, these truths were once more readily felt than now. The young generations of the world, who had in them the freshness of young children, and yet the depth of earnest men, who did not think that they had finished off all things in Heaven and Earth by merely giving them scientific names, but had to gaze direct at them there, with awe and wonder: they felt better what of divinity is in man and Nature;—they, without being mad, could *worship* Nature, and man more than anything else in Nature. Worship, that is, as I said above, admire without limit: this, in the full use of their faculties, with all sincerity of heart, they could do. I consider Hero-worship to be the grand modifying element in that ancient system of thought. What I called the perplexed jungle of Paganism sprang, we may say, out of many roots: every admiration, adoration of a star or natural object, was a root, or fibre of a root; but Hero-worship is the deepest root of all; the tap-root, from which in a great degree all the rest were nourished and grown.

And now if worship even of a star had some meaning in it, how much more might that of a Hero! Worship of a Hero is transcendent admiration of a great Man! I say great men are still admirable; I say, there is at bottom, nothing else admirable! No nobler feeling than this of admiration for one higher than himself dwells in the breast of man. It is to this hour, and at all hours, the vivifying influence in man's life. Religions I find stand upon it; not paganism only, but far higher and truer religions,—all religion hitherto known. Hero-worship, heartfelt prostrate admiration, submission, burning, boundless, for a noblest godlike Form of Man, —is not that the germ of Christianity itself? The greatest of all Heroes is One—whom we do not name here! Let sacred silence meditate that sacred matter; you will find it the ultimate perfection of a principle extant throughout man's history on earth.

Or coming into lower, less unspeakable provinces, is not all Loyalty akin to religious Faith also? Faith is loyalty to some inspired Teacher, some spiritual Hero.

And what therefore is loyalty proper, the life-breath of all society, but an effluence of Hero-worship, submissive admiration for the truly great? Society is founded on Hero-worship. All dignities of rank, on which human association rests, are what we may call a *Hero*archy (Government of Heroes),—or a Hierarchy, for it is "sacred" enough withal! The Duke means *Dux*, Leader; King is *Kon-ning, Kan-ning,* Man that *knows* or *cans*. Society everywhere is some representation, not *in*supportably inaccurate, of a graduated Worship of Heroes:—reverence and obedience done to men really great and wise. Not *in*supportably inaccurate, I say! They are all as bank-notes, these social dignitaries, all representing gold;—and several of them alas, always are forged notes. We can do with some forged false notes; with a good many even; but not with all, or the most of them forged! No: there have to come revolutions then; cries of Democracy, Liberty and Equality, and I know not what:—the notes being all false, and no gold to be had for *them,* people take to crying in their despair that there is no gold, that there never was any!—"Gold," Hero-worship, *is* nevertheless, as it was always and everywhere, and cannot cease till man himself ceases.

I am well aware that in these days Hero-worship, the thing I call Hero-worship, professes to have gone out, and finally ceased. This, for reasons which it will be worth while sometime to inquire into, is an age that as it were denies the existence of great men; denies the desirableness of great men. Show our critics a great man, a Luther for example, they begin to what they call "account" for him; not to worship him, but take the dimensions of him,—and bring him out to be a little kind of man! He was the "creature of the Time," they say; the Time called him forth, the Time did everything, he nothing—but what we the little critic could have done too! This seems to me but melancholy work. The Time call forth? Alas, we have known Times *call* loudly enough for their great man; but not find him when they called! He was not there; Providence had not sent him; the Time, *calling* its loudest, had to go down to confusion and wreck because he would not come when called.

For if we think of it, no Time need have gone to ruin, could it have found a man great enough, a man wise and good enough; wisdom to discern truly what the Time wanted, valour to lead it on the right road thither; these are the salvation of any Time. But I liken common languid Times, with their unbelief, distress, perplexity, with their languid doubting characters and embarrassed circumstances, impotently crumbling down into ever worse distress towards final ruin:—all this I liken to dry dead fuel, waiting for the lightning out of Heaven that shall kindle it. The great man, with his free force direct out of God's own hand, is the lightning. His word is the wise healing word which all can believe in. All blazes round him now, when he has once struck on it, into fire like his own. The dry mouldering sticks are thought to have called him forth. They did want him greatly; but as to calling him forth—! Those are critics of small vision, I think, who cry: "See, is it not the sticks that made the fire?" No sadder proof can be given by a man of his own littleness than disbelief in great men. There is no sadder symptom of a generation than such general blindness to the spiritual lightning, with faith only in the heap of barren dead fuel. It is the last consummation of unbelief. In all epochs of the world's history, we shall find the Great Man to have been the indispensable saviour of his epoch:—the lightning, without which the fuel never would have burnt. The His-

tory of the World, I said already, was the Biography
of Great Men.                                    1841

## BURNS

### (From *Heroes and Hero-Worship*)

It was a curious phenomenon, in the withered, unbelieving, secondhand Eighteenth Century, that of a hero
starting up, among the artificial pasteboard figures and
productions, in the guise of a Robert Burns. Like a
little well in the rocky desert places,—like a sudden
splendour of Heaven in the artificial Vauxhall! People
knew not what to make of it. They took it for a piece
of the Vauxhall firework; alas, it *let* itself be so taken,
though struggling half-blindly, as in bitterness of death,
against that! Perhaps no man had such a false reception from his fellowmen. Once more a very wasteful life-
drama was enacted under the sun.

The tragedy of Burns's life is known to all of you.
Surely we may say if discrepancy between place held
and place merited constituted perverseness of lot for a
man, no lot could be more perverse than Burns's. Among
those secondhand acting-figures, *mimes* for most part,
of the Eighteenth Century, once more a giant Original
Man; one of those men who reach down to the perennial Deeps, who take rank with the Heroic among men:
and he was born in a poor Ayrshire hut. The largest soul
of all the British lands came among us in the shape
of a hard-handed Scottish Peasant.

His Father, a poor toiling man, tried various things;
did not succeed in any; was involved in continual difficulties. The Steward, Factor as the Scotch call him,
used to send letters and threatenings, Burns says, "which

threw us all into tears." The brave, hard-toiling, hard-suffering Father, his brave heroine of a wife; and those children, of whom Robert was one! In this Earth, so wide otherwise, no shelter for *them*. The letters "threw us all into tears:" figure it. The brave Father, I say always;—a *silent* Hero and Poet; without whom the son had never been a speaking one! Burns's schoolmaster came afterwards to London, learnt what good society was; but declares that in no meeting of men did he ever enjoy better discourse than at the hearth of this peasant. And his poor "seven acres of nursery-ground,"—not that, nor the miserable patch of clay-farm, nor anything he tried to get a living by, would prosper with him; he had a sore unequal battle all his days. But he stood to it valiantly; a wise, faithful, unconquerable man;—swallowing down how many sore sufferings daily into silence; fighting like an unseen Hero,—nobody publishing newspaper paragraphs about his nobleness; voting pieces of plate to him! However, he was not lost; nothing is lost. Robert is there; the outcome of him,—and indeed of many generations of such as him.

This Burns appeared under every disadvantage; uninstructed, poor, born only to hard manual toil; and writing, when it came to that, in a rustic special dialect, known only to a small province of the country he lived in. Had he written, even what he did write, in the general language of England, I doubt not he had already become universally recognized as being, or capable to be, one of our greatest men. That he should have tempted so many to penetrate through the rough husk of that dialect of his, is proof that there lay something far from common within it. He has gained a certain recognition, and is continuing to do so over all quarters of our wide Saxon world: wheresoever a Saxon dialect is spoken, it begins to be understood, by personal inspection of this and the other, that one of the most considerable Saxon men of the Eighteenth Century was an Ayrshire Peasant named Robert Burns. Yes, I will say, here too was a piece of the right Saxon stuff: strong as the Harz-rock, rooted in the depths of the world;—rock, yet with wells of living softness in it! A wild impetuous whirlwind of passion and faculty slumbered quiet there; such heavenly melody dwelling in the heart of it. A noble rough genuineness; homely, rustic, honest; true simplicity of strength; with its lightning-fire, with its soft dewy pity;—like the old Norse Thor, the Peasant-god!

Burns's brother Gilbert, a man of much sense and worth, has told me that Robert, in his young days, in spite of their hardship, was usually the gayest of speech; a fellow of infinite frolic, laughter, sense and heart; far pleasanter to hear there, stript, cutting peats in the bog, or suchlike, than he ever afterwards knew him. I can well believe it. The basis of mirth (*"fond gaillard,"* as old Marquis Mirabeau calls it), a primal-element of sunshine and joyfulness, coupled with his other deep and earnest qualities, is one of the most attractive characteristics of Burns. A large fund of Hope dwells in him; spite of his tragical history, he is not a mourning man. He shakes his sorrows gallantly aside; bounds forth victorious over them. It is as the lion shaking "dew-drops from his mane;" as the swift-bounding horse, that laughs at the shaking of the spear.—But indeed, Hope, Mirth, of the sort like Burns's, are they not the outcome properly of warm generous affection,—such as is the beginning of all to every man?

You would think it strange if I called Burns the most gifted British soul we had in all that century of his: and yet I believe the day is coming when there will

be little danger in saying so. His writings, all that he
*did* under such obstructions are only a poor fragment
of him. Professor Stewart remarked very justly, what
indeed is true of all Poets good for much, that his
poetry was not any particular faculty; but the general
result of a naturally vigorous original mind expressing
itself in that way. Burns's gifts, expressed in conversation, are the theme of all that ever heard him. All kinds
of gifts: from the gracefulest utterances of courtesy,
to the highest fire of passionate speech; loud floods of
mirth, soft wailings of affection, laconic emphasis, clear
piercing insight; all was in him. Witty duchesses celebrate him as a man whose speech "led them off their
feet." This is beautiful: but still more beautiful that
which Mr. Lockhart has recorded, which I have more
than once alluded to, How the waiters and ostlers at
inns would get out of bed, and come crowding to hear
this man speak! Waiters and ostlers:—they too were
men, and here was a man! I have heard much about
his speech; but one of the best things I ever heard of
it was, last year, from a venerable gentleman long
familiar with him. That it was speech distinguished by
*always having something in it.* "He spoke rather little
than much," this old man told me; "sat rather silent
in those early days, as in the company of persons
above him; and always when he did speak, it was to
throw new light on the matter." I know not why any
one should ever speak otherwise!—But if we look at
his general force of soul, his healthy *robustness* every
way, the rugged downrightness, penetration, generous
valour and manfulness that was in him,—where shall
we readily find a better-gifted man?

Among the great men of the Eighteenth Century, I
sometimes feel as if Burns might be found to resemble

Mirabeau more than any other. They differ widely in
vesture; yet look at them intrinsically. There is the
same burly thick-necked strength of body as of soul;—
built, in both cases, on what the old Marquis calls a
*fond gaillard*. By nature, by course of breeding, indeed
by nation, Mirabeau has much more of bluster; a noisy,
forward, unresting man. But the characteristic of Mirabeau too is veracity and sense, power of true *insight*,
superiority of vision. The thing that he says is worth
remembering. It is a flash of insight into some object
or other: so do both these men speak. The same raging
passions; capable too in both of manifesting themselves
as the tenderest noble affections. Wit, wild laughter,
energy, directness, sincerity: these were in both. The
types of the two men are not dissimilar. Burns too
could have governed, debated in National Assemblies;
policised, as few could. Alas, the courage which had to
exhibit itself in capture of smuggling schooners in the
Solway Frith, in keeping *silence* over so much, where
no good speech, but only inarticulate rage was possible:
this might have bellowed forth Ushers de Brézé and
the like; and made itself visible to all men, in managing
of kingdoms, in ruling of great, ever-memorable epochs!
But they said to him reprovingly, his Official Superiors
said, and wrote: "You are to work, not to think." Of
your *thinking*-faculty, the greatest in this land, we have
no need; you are to gauge beer there; for that only are
*you* wanted. Very notable;—and worth mentioning,
though we know what is to be said and answered! As if
thought, Power of Thinking, were not at all times, in
all places and situations of the world, precisely the
thing that *was* wanted. The fatal man, is he not always
the *un*thinking man, the man who cannot think and *see;*
but only grope, and hallucinate; and *mis*see the nature
of the thing he works with? He misses it, *mi*stakes it

as we say; takes it for one thing, and it *is* another thing, —and leaves him standing like a Futility there! He is the fatal man; unutterably fatal, put in the high places of men.—"Why complain of this?" say some: "Strength is mournfully denied its arena; that was true from of old." Doubtless; and the worse for the *arena,* answer I! *Complaining* profits little; stating of the truth may profit. That a Europe, with its French Revolution just breaking out, finds no need of a Burns except for gauging beer,—is a thing I, for one, cannot *rejoice* at.

Once more we have to say here, that the chief quality of Burns is the *sincerity* of him. So in his Poetry, so in his life. The Song he sings is not of fantasticalities; it is of a thing felt, really there; the prime merit of this, as of all in him, and of his life generally, is truth. The life of Burns is what we may call a great tragic sincerity. A sort of savage sincerity,—not cruel, far from that; but wild, wrestling naked with the truth of things. In that sense, there is something of the savage in all great men.

Hero-worship,—Odin, Burns? Well: These Men of Letters too were not without a kind of Hero-worship; but what a strange condition has that got into now! The waiters and ostlers of Scotch inns, prying about the door, eager to catch any words that fell from Burns, were doing unconscious reverence to the Heroic. Johnson had his Boswell for worshipper; Rousseau had worshippers enough—princes calling on him in his mean garret; the great, the beautiful doing reverence to the poor moonstruck man. For himself a most portentous contradiction; the two ends of his life not to be brought into harmony. He sits at the tables of grandees; and has to copy music for his own living. He cannot even get his music copied: "By dint of dining out," says he, "I run the risk of dying by starvation at home." For his worshippers too a most questionable thing! If doing Hero-worship well or badly be the test of vital wellbeing or illbeing to a generation, can we say that these generations are very first-rate?—And yet our heroic Men of Letters do teach, govern, are kings, priests, or what you like to call them; intrinsically there is no preventing it by any means whatever. The world *has* to obey him who thinks and sees in the world. The world can alter the manner of that; can either have it as blessed continuous summer sunshine, or as unblessed black thunder and tornado,—with unspeakable difference of profit for the world! The manner of it is very alterable; the matter and fact of it is not alterable by any power under the sky. Light; or, failing that, lightning: the world can take its choice. Not whether we call an Odin god, prophet, priest, or what we call him; but whether we believe the word he tells us: there it all lies. If it be a true word, we shall have to believe it; believing it, we shall have to do it. What *name* or welcome we give him or it, is a point that concerns ourselves mainly. *It,* the new Truth, new deeper revealing of the Secret of this Universe, is verily of the nature of a message from on high; and must and will have itself obeyed.

My last remark is on that notablest phasis of Burns's history,—his visit to Edinburgh. Often it seems to me as if his demeanour there were the highest proof he gave of what a fund of worth and genuine manhood was in him. If we think of it, few heavier burdens could be laid on the strength of a man. So sudden; all common *Lionism,* which ruins innumerable men, was as nothing to this. It is as if Napoleon had been made a King of, not gradually, but at once from the Artillery Lieutenantcy in the Regiment La Fère. Burns, still only in his twenty-seventh year, is no longer even a ploughman; he is flying to the West Indies to escape disgrace and jail. This

month he is a ruined peasant, his wages seven pounds
a year, and these gone from him: next month he is in the
blaze of rank and beauty, handing down jewelled
Duchesses to dinner; the cynosure of all eyes! Adversity
is sometimes hard upon a man; but for one man who can
stand prosperity, there are a hundred that will stand
adversity. I admire much the way in which Burns met
all this. Perhaps no man one could point out, was ever
so sorely tried, and so little forgot himself. Tranquil,
unastonished; not abashed, not inflated, neither awk-
wardness nor affectation: he feels that *he* there is the
man Robert Burns; that the "rank is but the guinea-
stamp;" that the celebrity is but the candle-light, which
will show *what* man, not in the least make him a better
or other man! Alas, it may readily, unless he look to
it, make him a *worse* man; a wretched inflated wind-
bag,—inflated till he *burst,* and become a *dead* lion; for
whom, as some one has said, "there is no resurrection
of the body;" worse than a living dog!—Burns is admirable here.

And yet, alas, as I have observed elsewhere, these
Lion-hunters were the ruin and death of Burns. It was
they that rendered it impossible for him to live! They
gathered round him in his Farm; hindered his industry;
no place was remote enough from them. He could not get
his Lionism forgotten, honestly as he was disposed to
do so. He falls into discontents, into miseries, faults;
the world getting ever more desolate for him; health,
character, peace of mind, all gone;—solitary enough
now. It is tragical to think of! These men came but to *see*
him; it was out of no sympathy with him, nor no hatred
to him. They came to get a little amusement: they got
their amusement;—and the Hero's life went for it!

## PAST AND PRESENT
### SELECTIONS

#### GOSPEL OF WORK

THE only happiness a brave man ever troubled himself with asking much about was, happiness enough to get his work done. Not "I can't eat!" but "I can't work!" That was the burden of all wise complaining among men. It is, after all, the one unhappiness of a man, That he cannot work; that he cannot get his destiny as a man fulfilled. Behold, the day is passing swiftly over, our life is passing swiftly over; and the night cometh, wherein no man can work. The night once come, our happiness, our unhappiness,—it is all abolished, vanished, clean gone; a thing that has been: "not of the slightest consequence" whether we were happy as eupeptic Curtis, as the fattest pig of Epicurus, or unhappy as Job with potsherds, as musical Byron with Giaours and sensibilities of the heart; as the unmusical Meatjack with hard labor and rust! But our work,—behold, that is not abolished, that has not vanished: our work, behold, it remains, or the want of it remains;—for endless Times and Eternities, remains; and that is now the sole question with us for evermore! Brief brawling Day, with its noisy phantasms, its poor papercrowns tinsel-gilt, is gone; and divine everlasting Night, with her star-diadems, with her silences and her veracities, is come! What hast thou done, and how? Happiness, unhappiness: all that was but the *wages* thou hadst; thou hast spent all that, in sustaining thyself hitherward; not a coin of it remains with thee, it is all spent, eaten: and now thy work, where is thy work? Swift, out with it; let us see thy work!

Of a truth, if man were not a poor hungry dastard, and even much of a blockhead withal, he would cease criticising his victuals to such extent; and criticise himself rather, what he does with his victuals!

\* \* \* \* \* \* \*

For there is a perennial nobleness, and even sacredness, in Work. Were he never so benighted, forgetful of his high calling, there is always hope in a man that actually and earnestly works: in Idleness alone is there perpetual despair. Work, never so Mammonish, mean, *is* in communication with Nature; the real desire to get Work done will itself lead one more and more to truth, to Nature's appointments and regulations, which are truth.

The latest Gospel in this world is, Know thy work and do it. "Know thyself": long enough has that poor "self" of thine tormented thee; thou wilt never get to "know" it, I believe! Think it not thy business, this of knowing thyself; thou art an unknowable individual: know what thou canst work at; and work at it, like a Hercules! That will be thy better plan.

It has been written, "an endless significance lies in Work"; a man perfects himself by working. Foul jungles are cleared away, fair seedfields rise instead, and stately cities; and withal the man himself first ceases to be a jungle and foul unwholesome desert thereby. Consider how, even in the meanest sorts of Labor, the whole soul of a man is composed into a kind of real harmony, the instant he sets himself to work! Doubt, Desire, Sorrow, Remorse, Indignation, Despair itself, all these like helldogs lie beleaguering the soul of the poor day-worker, as of every man: but he bends himself with free valor against his task, and all these are stilled, all these shrink murmuring far off into their caves. The man is now a man. The blessed glow of Labor in him, is it not as purifying fire, wherein all poison is burnt up, and of sour smoke itself there is made bright blessed flame!

Destiny, on the whole, has no other way of cultivating us. A formless Chaos, once set it *revolving,* grows round and ever rounder; ranges itself, by mere force of gravity, into strata, spherical courses; is no longer a Chaos, but a round compacted World. What would become of the Earth, did she cease to revolve? In the poor old Earth, so long as she revolves, all inequalities, irregularities disperse themselves; all irregularities are incessantly becoming regular. Hast thou looked on the Potter's wheel,—one of the venerablest objects; old as the Prophet Ezechiel and far older? Rude lumps of clay, how they spin themselves up, by mere quick whirling, into beautiful circular dishes. And fancy the most assiduous Potter, but without his wheel; reduced to make dishes, or rather amorphous botches, by mere kneading and baking! Even such a Potter were Destiny, with a human soul that would rest and lie at ease, that would not work and spin! Of an idle unrevolving man the kindest Destiny, like the most assiduous Potter without wheel, can bake and knead nothing other than a botch; let her spend on him what expensive coloring, what gilding and enamelling she will, he is but a botch. Not a dish; no, a bulging, kneaded, crooked, shambling, squint-cornered, amorphous botch,—a mere enamelled vessel of dishonor! Let the idle think of this.

Blessed is he who has found his work; let him ask no other blessedness. He has a work, a life-purpose; he has found it, and will follow it! How, as a free-flowing channel, dug and torn by noble force through the sour mud-swamp of one's existence, like an ever-deepening river there, it runs and flows;—draining-off the sour festering water, gradually from the root of the remotest grass-blade; making, instead of pestilential swamp, a green fruitful meadow with its clear-flowing stream. How blessed for the meadow itself, let the stream and *its* value be great or small! Labor is Life: from the inmost heart of the Worker rises his God-given Force, the sacred celestial Life-essence breathed into him by Almighty God; from his inmost heart awakens him to all nobleness,—to all knowledge, "self-knowledge" and much else, so soon as Work fitly begins. Knowledge? The knowledge that will hold good in working, cleave thou to that; for Nature herself accredits that, says Yea to that. Properly thou hast no other knowledge but what thou hast got by working: the rest is yet all a hypothesis of knowledge; a thing to be argued of in schools, a thing floating in the clouds, in endless logic-vortices, till we try it and fix it. "Doubt, of whatever kind, can be ended by Action alone."

## GOSPEL OF MAMMONISM

"The word Hell," says Sauerteig, "is still frequently in use among the English people: but I could not without difficulty ascertain what they meant by it. Hell generally signifies the Infinite Terror, the thing a man *is* infinitely afraid of, and shudders and shrinks from, struggling with his whole soul to escape from it. There is a Hell therefore, if you will consider, which accompanies man, in all stages of his history, and religious or other development: but the Hells of men and Peoples differ notably. With Christians it is the infinite terror of being found guilty before the Just Judge. With old Romans, I conjecture, it was the terror not of Pluto, for whom probably they cared little, but of doing unworthily, doing unvirtuously, which was their word for un*man*fully. And now what is it, if you pierce through his Cants, his oft-repeated Hearsays, what he calls his Worships and so forth,—what is it that the modern English soul does, in very truth, dread infinitely, and contemplate with entire despair? What *is* his Hell, after all these reputable, oft-repeated Hearsays, what is it? With hesitation, with astonishment, I pronounce it to be: The terror of 'Not succeeding'; of not making money, fame, or some other figure in the world,—chiefly of not making money! Is not that a somewhat singular Hell?"

Yes, O Sauerteig, it is very singular. If we do not "succeed," where is the use of us? We had better never have been born. "Tremble intensely," as our friend the Emperor of China says: *there* is the black Bottomless of Terror; what Sauerteig calls the "Hell of the English"!—But indeed this Hell belongs naturally to the Gospel of Mammonism, which also has its corresponding Heaven. For there *is* one Reality among so many Phantasms; about one thing we are entirely in earnest: The making of money. Working Mammonism does divide the world with idle game-preserving Dilettantism:—thank Heaven that there is even a Mammonism, *any*thing we are in earnest about! Idleness is worst, Idleness alone is without hope: work earnestly at anything, you will by degrees learn to work at almost all things. There is endless hope in work, were it even work at making money.

True, it must be owned, we for the present, with our Mammon-Gospel, have come to strange conclusions. We call it a Society; and go about professing openly the totalest separation, isolation. Our life is not a mutual helpfulness; but rather, cloaked under due laws-of-war, named "fair competition" and so forth, it is a mutual hostility. We have profoundly forgotten everywhere that

*Cash-payment* is not the sole relation of human beings; we think, nothing doubting, that *it* absolves and liquidates all engagements of man. "My starving workers?" answers the rich mill-owner: "Did I not hire them fairly in the market? Did I not pay them, to the last sixpence, the sum covenanted for? What have I to do with them more?"—Verily Mammon-worship is a melancholy creed. When Cain, for his own behoof, had killed Abel, and was questioned, "Where is thy brother?" he too made answer, "Am I my brother's keeper?" Did I not pay my brother *his* wages, the thing he had merited from me?

## GOSPEL OF DILETTANTISM

BUT after all, the Gospel of Dilettantism, producing a Governing Class who do not govern, nor understand in the least that they are bound or expected to govern, is still mournfuler than that of Mammonism. Mammonism, as we said, at least works; this goes idle. Mammonism has seized some portion of the message of Nature to man; and seizing that, and following it, will seize and appropriate more and more of Nature's message: but Dilettantism has missed it wholly. "Make money": that will mean withal, "Do work in order to make money." But, "Go gracefully idle in Mayfair," what does or can that mean? An idle, game-preserving and even corn-lawing Aristocracy, in such an England as ours: has the world, if we take thought of it, ever seen such a phenomenon till very lately? Can it long continue to see such?

## CAPTAINS OF INDUSTRY

THE Leaders of Industry, if Industry is ever to be led, are virtually the Captains of the World! if there be no nobleness in them, there will never be an Aristocracy more. But let the Captains of Industry consider: once again, are they born of other clay than the old Captains of Slaughter; doomed forever to be no Chivalry, but a mere gold-plated *Doggery*,—what the French well name *Canaille*, "Doggery" with more or less gold carrion at its disposal? Captains of Industry are the true Fighters, henceforth recognizable as the only true ones: Fighters against Chaos, Necessity and the Devils and Jötuns; and lead on Mankind in that great, and alone true, and universal warfare; the stars in their courses fighting for them, and all Heaven and all Earth saying audibly, Well done! Let the Captains of Industry retire into their own hearts, and ask solemnly, If there is nothing but vulturous hunger, for fine wines, valet reputation and gilt carriages, discoverable there? Of hearts made by the Almighty God I will not believe such a thing. Deep-hidden under wretchedest god-forgetting Cants, Epicurisms, Dead-Sea Apisms; forgotten as under foulest fat Lethe mud and weeds, there is yet, in all hearts born into this God's-World, a spark of the Godlike slumbering. Awake, O nightmare sleepers; awake, arise, or be forever fallen! This is not playhouse poetry; it is sober fact. Our England, our world cannot live as it is. It will connect itself with a God again, or go down with nameless throes and fire-consummation to the Devils. Thou who feelest aught of such a Godlike stirring in thee, any faintest intimation of it as through heavy-laden dreams, follow *it*, I conjure thee. Arise, save thyself, be one of those that save thy country.

Bucaniers, Chactaw Indians, whose supreme aim in fighting is that they may get the scalps, the money, that they may amass scalps and money: out of such came no Chivalry, and never will! Out of such came only gore and wreck, infernal rage and misery; desperation quenched in annihilation. Behold it, I bid thee, behold there, and consider! What is it that thou have a hundred thousand-pound bills laid-up in thy strong-room, a hundred scalps hung-up in thy wigwam? I value not them or thee. Thy scalps and thy thousand-pound bills are as yet nothing, if no nobleness from within ir-radiate them; if no Chivalry, in action, or in embryo ever struggling toward birth and action, be there.

Love of men cannot be bought by cash-payment; and without love men cannot endure to be together. You cannot lead a Fighting World without having it regimented, chivalried: the thing, in a day, becomes impossible; all men in it, the highest at first, the very lowest at last, discern consciously, or by a noble instinct, this necessity. And can you any more continue to lead a working World unregimented, anarchic? I answer, and the Heavens and Earth are now answering, No! The thing becomes not "in a day" impossible; but in some two generations it does. Yes, when fathers and mothers, in Stockport hunger-cellars, begin to eat their children, and Irish widows have to prove their relationship by dying of typhus-fever; and amid Governing "Corporations of the Best and Bravest," busy to preserve their game by "bush-ing," dark millions of God's human creatures start up in mad Chartisms, impracticable Sacred-Months, and Man-chester Insurrections;—and there is a virtual Industrial Aristocracy as yet only half-alive, spell-bound amid money-bags and ledgers; and an actual Idle Aristocracy seemingly near dead in somnolent delusions, in tres-passes and double-barrels; "sliding," as on inclined-planes, which every new year they *soap* with new Hansard's-jargon under God's sky, and so are "sliding," ever faster, toward a "scale" and balance-scale whereon is written *Thou art found Wanting:*—in such days, after a generation or two, I say, it does become, even to the low and simple, very palpably impossible! No Working

World, any more than a Fighting World, can be led on
without a noble Chivalry of Work, and laws and fixed
rules which follow out of that,—far nobler than any
Chivalry of Fighting was. As an anarchic multitude on
mere Supply-and-demand, it is becoming inevitable that
we dwindle in horrid suicidal convulsion and self-abra-
sion, frightful to the imagination, into *Chactaw* Workers.
With wigwams and scalps,—with palaces and thousand-
pound bills; with savagery, depopulation, chaotic deso-
lation! Good Heavens, will not one French Revolution
and Reign of Terror suffice us, but must there be two?
There will be two if needed; there will be twenty if
needed; there will be precisely as many as are needed.
The Laws of Nature will have themselves fulfilled.
That is a thing certain to me.

Your gallant battle-hosts and work-hosts, as the others
did, will need to be made loyally yours; they must and
will be regulated, methodically secured in their just
share of conquest under you;—joined with you in veri-
table brotherhood, sonhood, by quite other and deeper
ties than those of temporary day's wages! How would
mere red-coated regiments, to say nothing of chivalries,
fight for you, if you could discharge them on the evening
of the battle, on payment of the stipulated shillings,—
and they discharge you on the morning of it!

                                                    1843


## JOHN HENRY NEWMAN (1801-1890)

## KNOWLEDGE VIEWED IN RELATION TO LEARNING

### (From *The Idea of a University*)

KNOWLEDGE then is the indispensable condition of
expansion of mind, and the instrument of attaining to

it; this cannot be denied, it is ever to be insisted on; I begin with it as a first principle; however, the very truth of it carries men too far, and confirms to them the notion that it is the whole of the matter. A narrow mind is thought to be that which contains little knowledge; and an enlarged mind, that which holds a great deal; and what seems to put the matter beyond dispute is, the fact of the great number of studies which are pursued in a University, by its very profession. Lectures are given on every kind of subject; examinations are held; prizes awarded. There are moral, metaphysical, physical Professors; Professors of languages, of history, of mathematics, of experimental science. Lists of questions are published, wonderful for their range and depth, variety and difficulty; treatises are written, which carry upon their very face the evidence of extensive reading or multifarious information; what then is wanting for mental culture to a person of large reading and scientific attainments? what is grasp of mind but acquirement? where shall philosophical repose be found, but in the consciousness and enjoyment of large intellectual possessions?

And yet this notion is, I conceive, a mistake, and my present business is to show that it is one, and that the end of a Liberal Education is not mere knowledge, or knowledge considered in its *matter;* and I shall best attain my object, by actually setting down some cases, which will be generally granted to be instances of the process of enlightenment or enlargement of mind, and others which are not, and thus, by the comparison, you will be able to judge for yourselves, Gentlemen, whether Knowledge, that is, acquirement, is after all the real principle of the enlargement, or whether that principle is not rather something beyond it.

For instance, let a person, whose experience has hitherto been confined to the more calm and unpretending scenery of these islands, whether here or in England, go for the first time into parts where physical nature puts on her wilder and more awful forms, whether at home or abroad, as into mountainous districts; or let one, who has ever lived in a quiet village, go for the first time to a great metropolis,—then I suppose he will have a sensation which perhaps he never had before. He has a feeling not in addition or increase of former feelings, but of something different in its nature. He will perhaps be borne forward, and find for a time that he has lost his bearings. He has made a certain progress, and he has a consciousness of mental enlargement; he does not stand where he did, he has a new centre, and a range of thoughts to which he was before a stranger.

Again, the view of the heavens which the telescope opens upon us, if allowed to fill and possess the mind, may almost whirl it round and make it dizzy. It brings in a flood of ideas, and is rightly called an intellectual enlargement, whatever is meant by the term.

And so again, the sight of beasts of prey and other foreign animals, their strangeness, the originality (if I may use the term) of their forms and gestures and habits, and their variety and independence of each other, throw us out of ourselves into another creation, and as if under another Creator, if I may so express the temptation which may come on the mind. We seem to have new faculties, or a new exercise for our faculties, by this addition to our knowledge; like a prisoner, who, having been accustomed to wear manacles or fetters, suddenly finds his arms and legs free.

Hence Physical Science generally, in all its departments, as bringing before us the exuberant riches and resources, yet the orderly course, of the Universe, elevates and excites the student, and at first, I may say, almost takes away his breath, while in time it exercises a tranquillizing influence upon him.

Again, the study of history is said to enlarge and enlighten the mind, and why? because, as I conceive, it gives it a power of judging of passing events, and of all events, and a conscious superiority over them, which before it did not possess.

And in like manner, what is called seeing the world, entering into active life, going into society, travelling, gaining acquaintance with the various classes of the community, coming into contact with the principles and modes of thought of various parties, interests, and races, their views, aims, habits and manners, their religious creeds and forms of worship,—gaining experience how various yet how alike men are, how lowminded, how bad, how opposed, yet how confident in their opinions; all this exerts a perceptible influence upon the mind, which it is impossible to mistake, be it good or be it bad, and is popularly called its enlargement.

And then again, the first time the mind comes across the arguments and speculations of unbelievers, and feels what a novel light they cast upon what he has hitherto accounted sacred; and still more, if it gives in to them and embraces them, and throws off as so much prejudice what it has hitherto held, and, as if waking from a dream, begins to realize to its imagination that there is now no such thing as law and the transgression of law, that sin is a phantom, and punishment a bugbear. that it is free to sin, free to enjoy the world and the flesh; and still further, when it does enjoy them, and reflects that it may think and hold just what it will, that "the world is all before it where to choose," and what system to build up as its own private persuasion; when this torrent of wilful thoughts rushes over and inundates it, who will deny that the fruit of the tree of knowledge, or what the mind takes for knowledge, has made it one of the gods, with a sense of expansion and elevation,—an intoxication in reality, still, so far as the subjective state of the mind goes, an illumination? Hence the fanaticism of individuals or nations, who suddenly cast off their Maker. Their eyes are opened; and, like the judgment-stricken king in the Tragedy, they see two suns, and a magic universe, out of which they look back upon their former state of faith and innocence with a sort of contempt and indignation, as if they were then but fools, and the dupes of imposture.

On the other hand, Religion has its own enlargement, and an enlargement, not of tumult, but of peace. It is often remarked of uneducated persons, who have hitherto thought little of the unseen world, that, on their turning to God, looking into themselves, regulating their hearts, reforming their conduct, and meditating on death and judgment, heaven and hell, they seem to become, in point of intellect, different beings from what they were. Before, they took things as they came, and thought no more of one thing than another. But now every event has a meaning; they have their own estimate of whatever happens to them; they are mindful of times and seasons, and compare the present with the past; and the world, no longer dull, monotonous, unprofitable, and hopeless, is a various and complicated drama, with parts and an object, and an awful moral.

Now from these instances, to which many more might be added, it is plain, first, that the communication of knowledge certainly is either a condition or the means of that sense of enlargement, or enlightenment of which at this day we hear so much in certain quarters: this cannot be denied; but next, it is equally plain, that such communication is not the whole of the process

The enlargement consists, not merely in the passive reception into the mind of a number of ideas hitherto unknown to it, but in the mind's energetic and simultaneous action upon and towards and among those new ideas, which are rushing in upon it. It is the action of a formative power, reducing to order and meaning the matter of our acquirements; it is a making the objects of our knowledge subjectively our own, or, to use a familiar word, it is a digestion of what we receive, into the substance of our previous state of thought; and without this no enlargement is said to follow.   There is no enlargement, unless there be a comparison of ideas one with another, as they come before the mind, and a systematizing of them. We feel our minds to be growing and expanding *then,* when we not only learn, but refer what we learn to what we know already. It is not the mere addition to our knowledge that is the illumination; but the locomotion, the movement onwards, of that mental centre, to which both what we know, and what we are learning, the accumulating mass of our acquirements, gravitates. And therefore a truly great intellect, and recognized to be such by the common opinion of mankind, such as the intellect of Aristotle, or of St. Thomas, or of Newton, or of Goethe (I purposely take instances within and without the Catholic pale, when I would speak of the intellect as such), is one which takes a connected view of old and new, past and present, far and near, and which has an insight into the influence of all these one on another; without which there is no whole, and no centre. It possesses the knowledge, not only of things, but also of their mutual and true relations; knowledge, not merely considered as acquirement but as philosophy.

Accordingly, when this analytical, distributive, harmonizing process is away, the mind experiences no enlargement, and is not reckoned as enlightened **or** comprehensive, whatever it may add to its knowledge. For instance, a great memory, as I have already said, does not make a philosopher, any more than a dictionary can be called a grammar. There are men who embrace in their minds a vast multitude of ideas, but with little sensibility about their real relations towards each other. These may be antiquarians, annalists, naturalists; they may be learned in the law; they may be versed in statistics; they are most useful in their own place; I should shrink from speaking disrespectfully of them; still, there is nothing in such attainments to guarantee the absence of narrowness of mind. If they are nothing more than well-read men, or men of information, they have not what specially deserves the name of culture of mind, or fulfils the type of Liberal Education.

In like manner, we sometimes fall in with persons who have seen much of the world, and of the men who, in their day, have played a conspicuous part in it, but who generalize nothing, and have no observation, in the true sense of the word. They abound in information in detail, curious and entertaining, about men and things; and, having lived under the influence of no very clear or settled principles, religious or political, they speak of every one and every thing, only as so many phenomena, which are complete in themselves, and lead to nothing, not discussing them, or teaching any truth, or instructing the hearer, but simply talking. No one would say that these persons, well informed as they are, had attained to any great culture of intellect or to philosophy.

The case is the same still more strikingly where the persons in question are beyond dispute men of inferior powers and deficient education. Perhaps they have been much in foreign countries, and they receive, in a passive, otiose, unfruitful way, the various facts which are forced upon them there. Seafaring men, for example, range from one end of the earth to the other; but the multiplicity of external objects, which they have encountered, forms no symmetrical and consistent picture upon their imagination; they see the tapestry of human life, as it were on the wrong side, and it tells no story. They sleep, and they rise up, and they find themselves, now in Europe, now in Asia; they see visions of great cities and wild regions; they are in the marts of commerce, or amid the islands of the South; they gaze on Pompey's Pillar, or on the Andes; and nothing which meets them carries them forward or backward, to any idea beyond itself. Nothing has a drift or relation; nothing has a history or a promise. Every thing stands by itself, and comes and goes in its turn, like the shifting scenes of a show, which leave the spectator where he was. Perhaps you are near such a man on a particular occasion, and expect him to be shocked or perplexed at something which occurs; but one thing is much the same to him as another, or, if he is perplexed, it is as not knowing what to say, whether it is right to admire, or to ridicule, or to disapprove, while conscious that some expression of opinion is expected from him; for in fact he has no standard of judgment at all, and no landmarks to guide him to a conclusion. Such is mere acquisition, and, I repeat, no one would dream of calling it philosophy.

Instances, such as these, confirm, by the contrast, the conclusion I have already drawn from those which preceded them. That only is true enlargement of mind which is the power of viewing many things at once as one whole, of referring them severally to their true place in the universal system, of understanding their respective values, and determining their mutual dependence. Thus is that form of Universal Knowledge, of which I have on a former occasion spoken, set up in the individual intellect, and constitutes its perfection. Possessed of this real illumination, the mind never views any part of the extended subject-matter of Knowledge without recollecting that it is but a part, or without the associations which spring from this recollection. It makes everything in some sort lead to everything else; it would communicate the image of the whole to every separate portion, till that whole becomes in imagination like a spirit, everywhere pervading and penetrating its component parts, and giving them one definite meaning. Just as our bodily organs, when mentioned, recall their function in the body, as the word "creation" suggests the Creator, and "subjects" a sovereign, so, in the mind of the Philosopher, as we are abstractedly conceiving of him, the elements of the physical and moral world, sciences, arts, pursuits, ranks, offices, events, opinions, individualities, are all viewed as one, with correlative functions, and as gradually by successive combinations converging, one and all, to the true centre.

To have even a portion of this illuminative reason and true philosophy is the highest state to which nature can aspire, in the way of intellect; it puts the mind above the influences of chance and necessity, above anxiety, suspense, unsettlement, and superstition, which is the lot of the many. Men, whose minds are possessed with some one object, take exaggerated views of its importance, are feverish in the pursuit of it, make it the measure of things which are utterly foreign to it, and are startled and despond if it happens to fail them. They are ever in alarm or in transport. Those on the other hand who have no object or principle whatever to hold by, lose their way every step they take. They are thrown out, and do not know what to think or say, at every fresh juncture; they have no view of persons, or occurrences, or facts, which come suddenly upon them, and they hang upon the opinion of others for want of internal resources. But the intellect, which has been disciplined to the perfection of its powers, which knows, and thinks while it knows, which has learned to leaven the dense mass of facts and events with the elastic force of reason, such an intellect cannot be partial, cannot be exclusive, cannot be impetuous, cannot be at a loss, cannot but be patient, collected, and majestically calm, because it discerns the end in every beginning, the origin in every end, the law in every interruption, the limit in each delay; because it ever knows where it stands, and how its path lies from one point to another. It is the τετράγωνος of the Peripatetic, and has the "nil admirari" of the Stoic,—

> Felix qui potuit rerum cognoscere causas,
> Atque metus omnes, et inexorabile fatum
> Subjecit pedibus, strepitumque Acherontis avari.

There are men who, when in difficulties, originate at the moment vast ideas or dazzling projects; who, under the influence of excitement, are able to cast a light, almost as if from inspiration, on a subject or course of action which comes before them; who have a sudden presence of mind equal to any emergency, rising with the occasion, and an undaunted magnanimous bearing, and an energy and keenness which is but made intense by opposition. This is genius, this is heroism; it is the exhibition of a natural gift, which no culture can teach, at which no Institution can aim: here, on the contrary, we are concerned, not with mere nature, but with training and teaching. That perfection of the Intellect, which is the result of Education, and its *beau ideal*, to be imparted to individuals in their respective measures, is the clear, calm, accurate vision and comprehension of all things, as far as the finite mind can embrace them, each in its place, and with its own characteristics upon it. It is almost prophetic from its knowledge of history; it is almost heart-searching from its knowledge of human nature; it has almost supernatural charity from its freedom from littleness and prejudice; it has almost the repose of faith, because nothing can startle it; it has almost the beauty and harmony of heavenly contemplation, so intimate is it with the eternal order of things and the music of the spheres.

And now, if I may take for granted that the true and adequate end of intellectual training and of a University is not Learning or Acquirement, but rather, is Thought or Reason exercised upon Knowledge, or what may be called Philosophy, I shall be in a position to explain the various mistakes which at the present day beset the subject of University Education.

\*　　\*　　\*　　\*　　\*　　\*　　\*

I will tell you, Gentlemen, what has been the practical error of the last twenty years,—not to load the memory of the student with a mass of undigested knowledge, but to force upon him so much that he has rejected all. It has been the error of distracting and enfeebling the mind by an unmeaning profusion of subjects; of implying that a smattering in a dozen branches of study is not shallowness, which it really is, but enlargement, which it is not; of considering an acquaintance with the learned names of things and persons, and the possession of clever duodecimos, and attendance on eloquent lecturers, and membership with scientific institutions, and the sight of the experiments of a platform and the specimens of a museum, that all this was not dissipation of mind, but progress. All things now are to be learned at once, not first one thing, then another, not one well, but many badly. Learning is to be without exertion, without attention, without toil; without grounding, without advance, without finishing. There is to be nothing individual in it; and this, forsooth, is the wonder of the age. What the steam engine does with matter, the printing-press is to do with mind; it is to act mechanically, and the population is to be passively, almost unconsciously enlightened, by the mere multiplication and dissemination of volumes. Whether it be the school-boy, or the school-girl, or the youth at college, or the mechanic in the town, or the politician in the senate, all have been the victims in one way or other of this most preposterous and pernicious of delusions. Wise men have lifted up their voices in vain; and at length, lest their own institutions should be outshone and should disappear in the folly of the hour, they have been obliged, as far as they could with a good conscience, to humour a spirit which they could not withstand, and make temporizing concessions at which they could not but inwardly smile.

\* \* \* \* \* \* \*

I protest to you, Gentlemen, that if I had to choose between a so-called University, which dispensed with residence and tutorial superintendence, and gave its degrees to any person who passed an examination in a wide range of subjects, and a University which had no professors or examinations at all, but merely brought a number of young men together for three or four years, and then sent them away as the University of Oxford is said to have done some sixty years since, if I were asked which of these two methods was the better discipline of the intellect,—mind, I do not say which is *morally* the better, for it is plain that compulsory study must be a good and idleness an intolerable mischief,—but if I must determine which of the two courses was the more successful in training, moulding, enlarging the mind, which sent out men the more fitted for their secular duties, which produced better public men, men of the world, men whose names would descend to posterity, I have no hesitation in giving the preference to that University which did nothing, over that which exacted of its members an acquaintance with every science under the sun. And, paradox as this may seem, still if results be the test of systems, the influence of the public schools and colleges of England, in the course of the last century, at least will bear out one side of the contrast as I have drawn it. What would come, on the other hand, of the ideal systems of education which have fascinated the imagination of this age, could they ever take effect, and whether they would not produce a generation frivolous, narrow-minded, and resourceless, intellectually considered, is a fair subject for debate; but so far is certain, that the Universities and scholastic establishments, to which I refer, and which did little more than bring together first boys and then youths in large numbers, these institutions, with miserable deformities on the side of morals, with a hollow profession of Christianity, and a heathen code of ethics,—I say, at least they can boast of a succession of heroes and statesmen, of literary men and philosophers, of men conspicuous for great natural virtues, for habits of business, for knowledge of life, for practical judgment, for cultivated tastes, for accomplishments, who have made England what it is,—able to subdue the earth, able to domineer over Catholics.

How is this to be explained? I suppose as follows: When a multitude of young men, keen, open-hearted, sympathetic, and observant, as young men are, come together and freely mix with each other, they are sure to learn one from another, even if there be no one to teach them; the conversation of all is a series of lectures to each, and they gain for themselves new ideas and views, fresh matter of thought, and distinct principles for judging and acting, day by day. An infant has to learn the meaning of the information which its senses convey to it, and this seems to be its employment. It fancies all that the eye presents to it to be close to it, till it actually learns the contrary, and thus by practice does it ascertain the relations and uses of those first elements of knowledge which are necessary for its animal existence. A parallel teaching is necessary for our social being, and it is secured by a large school or a college; and this effect may be fairly called in its own department an enlargement of mind. It is seeing the world on a small field with little trouble; for the pupils or students come from very different places, and with widely different notions, and there is much to generalize, much to adjust, much to eliminate, there are inter-relations to be defined, and conventional rules to be established, in the process, by which the whole assemblage is moulded together, and gains one tone and one character.

Let it be clearly understood, I repeat it, that I am not taking into account moral or religious considerations; I am but saying that that youthful community will constitute a whole, it will embody a specific idea, it will represent a doctrine, it will administer a code of conduct, and it will furnish principles of thought and action. It will give birth to a living teaching, which in course of time will take the shape of a self-perpetuating tradition, or a *genius loci,* as it is sometimes called; which haunts the home where it has been born, and which imbues and forms, more or less, and one by one, every individual who is successively brought under its shadow. Thus it is that, independent of direct instruction on the part of Superiors, there is a sort of self-education in the academic institutions of Protestant England; a characteristic tone of thought, a recognized standard of judgment is found in them, which as developed in the individual who is submitted to it, becomes a twofold source of strength to him, both from the distinct stamp it impresses on his mind, and from the bond of union which it creates between him and others,—effects which are shared by the authorities of the place, for they themselves have been educated in it, and at all times are exposed to the influence of its ethical atmosphere. Here then is a real teaching, whatever be its standards and principles, true or false; and it at least tends towards cultivation of the intellect; it at least recognizes that knowledge is something more than a sort of passive reception of scraps and details; it is a something, and it does a something, which never will issue from the most strenuous efforts of a set of teachers, with no mutual sympathies and no intercommunion, of a set of examiners with no opinions which they dare profess, and with no common principles, who are teaching or questioning a set of youths who do not know them, and do not know each other, on a large number of subjects, different in kind, and connected by no wide philosophy, three times a week, or three times a year, or once in three years, in chill lecture-rooms or on a pompous anniversary.                                          1852

# WILLIAM MAKEPEACE THACKERAY
## (1811-1863)

## ON A PEAL OF BELLS

### (From *Roundabout Papers*)

As SOME bells in a church hard by are making a great holiday clanging in the summer afternoon, I am reminded somehow of a July day, a garden, and a great clanging of bells years and years ago, on the very day when George IV was crowned. I remember a little boy lying in that garden reading his first novel. It was called the "Scottish Chiefs." The little boy (who is now ancient and not little) read this book in the summer-house of his great-grandmamma. She was eighty years of age then. A most lovely and picturesque old lady, with a long tortoise-shell cane, with a little puff, or tour of snow white (or was it powdered?) hair under her cap, with the prettiest little black-velvet slippers and high heels you ever saw. She had a grandson, a lieutenant in the navy; son of her son, a captain in the navy; grandson of her husband, a captain in the navy. She lived for scores and scores of years in a dear little old Hampshire town inhabited by the wives, widows, daughters of navy captains, admirals, lieutenants. Dear me! Don't I remember Mrs. Duval, widow of Admiral Duval; and the Miss Dennets, at the Great house at the other end of the town, Admiral Dennet's daughters; and the Miss Barrys, the late Captain Barry's daughters; and the good old Miss Maskews, Admiral Maskews' daughters; and that dear little Miss Norval, and the kind Miss Bookers, one of whom married Captain, now Admiral Sir Henry Excellent, K. C. B.? Far, far away into the past I look and see the little town with its friendly glimmer. That town was so like a novel of Miss Austen's that I wonder was she born and bred there? No, we should have known, and the good old ladies would have pronounced her to be a little idle thing, occupied with her silly books and neglecting her housekeeping. There were other towns in England, no doubt, where dwelt the widows and wives of other navy captains; where they tattled, loved each other, and quarreled; talked about Betty the maid, and her fine ribbons indeed! Took their dish of tea at six, played at quadrille every night till ten, when there was a little bit of supper, after which Betty came with the lanthorn; and the next day came, and next, and next, and so forth, until a day arrived when the lanthorn was out, when Betty came no more: all that little company sank to rest under the daisies, whither some folks will presently follow them.

\*    \*    \*    \*    \*

How do these rich historical and personal reminiscences come out of the subject at present in hand? What is that subject, by the way? My dear friend, if you look at the last essaykin (though you may leave it alone, and I shall not be in the least surprised or offended), if you look at the last paper, where the writer imagines Athos and Porthos, Dalgetty and Ivanhoe, Amelia and Sir Charles Grandison, Don Quixote, and Sir Roger, walking in at the garden window, you will at once perceive that NOVELS and their heroes and heroines are our present subject of discourse, into which we will presently plunge. Are you one of us, dear sir, and do you love novel-reading? To be reminded of your first novel will surely be a pleasure to you. Hush! I never read quite to the end of my first, the "Scottish Chiefs." I couldn't. I peeped in an alarmed furtive manner at some of the closing pages. Miss Porter, like a kind dear tenderhearted creature, would not have Wallace's head chopped off at the end of Vol. V. She made him die in prison, and if I remember right (protesting I have not read the book for forty-two or three years), Robert Bruce made a speech to his soldiers, in which he said, "And Bannockburn shall equal Cambuskenneth." But I repeat I could not read the end of the fifth volume of that dear delightful book for crying. Good heavens! It was as sad, as sad as going back to school.

The glorious Scott cycle of romances came to me some four or five years afterwards; and I think boys of our year were specially fortunate in coming upon those delightful books at that special time when we could best enjoy them. Oh, that sunshiny bench on half-holidays, with Claverhouse or Ivanhoe for a companion! I have remarked of very late days some little men in a great state of delectation over the romances of Captain Mayne Reid, and Gustave Aimard's Prairie and Indian Stories, and during occasional holiday visits, lurking off to bed with the volume under their arms. But are those Indians and warriors so terrible as our Indians and warriors were? (I say, are they? Young gentlemen, mind, I do not say they are not.) But as an oldster I can be heartily thankful for the novels of the I-10 Geo. IV., let us say, and so downward to a period not unremote. Let us see; there is, first, our dear Scott. Whom do I love in the works of that dear old master? Amo—

The Baron of Bradwardine and Fergus. (Captain Waverly is certainly very mild.)

Amo Ivanhoe; LOCKSLEY; the Templar.

Amo Quentin Durwald, and especially Quentin's uncle, who brought the boar to bay. I forget the gentleman's name.

I have never cared for the Master of Ravenswood, or fetched his hat out of the water since he dropped it there when I last met him (circa 1825).

Amo SALADIN and the Scotch Knight in the "Talisman." The Sultan best.

Amo CLAVERHOUSE.

Amo MAJOR DALGETTY. Delightful Major. To think of him is to desire to jump up, run to the book, and get the volume down from the shelf. About all those heroes of Scott, what a manly bloom there is, and honorable modesty! They are not at all heroic. They seem to blush somehow in their position of hero, and as it were to say, "Since it must be done, here goes!" They are handsome, modest, upright, simple, courageous, not too clever. If I were a mother (which is absurd), I should like to be mother-in-law to several young men of the Walter-Scott-hero sort.

Much as I like those most unassuming, manly, unpretending gentlemen, I have to own that I think the heroes of another writer, viz.:—

LEATHER-STOCKING,

UNCAS,

HARDHEART,

TOM COFFIN,

are quite the equals of Scott's men; perhaps Leather-stocking is better than any one in "Scott's lot." La Longue Carabine is one of the great prize men of fiction. He ranks with your Uncle Toby, Sir Roger de Coverley, Falstaff—heroic figures, all—American or British, and the artist has deserved well of his country who devised them.

At school, in my time, there was a public day, when the boys' relatives, an examining bigwig or two from the universities, old school-fellows, and so forth, came to the place. The boys were all paraded; prizes were administered; each lad being in a new suit of clothes— and magnificent dandies, I promise you, some of us were. Oh, the chubby cheeks, clean collars, glossy new raiment, beaming faces, glorious in youth—*fit tueri cœlum*— bright with truth, and mirth, and honor! To see a hundred boys marshaled in a chapel or old hall; to hear their sweet fresh voices when they chant, and look in their brave calm faces; I say, does not the sight and sound of them smite you, somehow, with a pang of exquisite kindness? . . . Well. As about boys, so about Novelists. I fancy the boys of Parnassus School all

paraded. I am a lower boy myself in that academy. I
like our fellows to look well, upright, gentlemanlike.
There is Master Fielding—he with the black eye. What
a magnificent build of a boy! There is Master Scott, one
of the heads of the school. Did you ever see the fellow
more hearty and manly? Yonder lean, shambling, cadav-
erous lad, who is always borrowing money, telling lies,
leering after the housemaids, is Master Laurence Sterne
—a bishop's grandson, and himself intended for the
Church; for shame, you little reprobate! But what a
genius the fellow has! Let him have a sound flogging,
and as soon as the young scamp is out of the whipping
room give him a gold medal. Such would be my practice
if I were Doctor Birch, and master of the school.

Let us drop this school metaphor, this birch and all
pertaining thereto. Our subject, I beg leave to remind
the reader's humble servant, is novel heroes and heroines.
How do you like your heroes, ladies? Gentlemen, what
novel heroines do you prefer? When I set this essay
going, I sent the above question to two of the most
inveterate novel-readers of my acquaintance. The gentleman refers me to Miss Austen; the lady says Athos,
Guy Livingston, and (pardon my rosy blushes) Colonel
Esmond, and owns that in youth she was very much in
love with Valancourt.

"Valancourt? and who was he?" cry the young people.
Valancourt, my dears, was the hero of one of the most
famous romances which ever was published in this country. The beauty and elegance of Valancourt made your
young grandmammas' gentle hearts to beat with respect-
ful sympathy. He and his glory have passed away. Ah,
woe is me that the glory of novels should ever decay;
that dust should gather round them on the shelves; that
the annual checks from Messieurs the publishers should
dwindle, dwindle! Inquire at Mudie's, or the London

Library, who asks for the "Mysteries of Udolpho" now? Have not even the "Mysteries of Paris" ceased to frighten? Alas, our novels are but for a season; and I know characters whom a painful modesty forbids me to mention, who shall go to limbo along with "Valancourt" and "Doricourt" and "Thaddeus of Warsaw."

A dear old sentimental friend, with whom I discoursed on the subject of novels yesterday, said that her favorite hero was Lord Orville, in "Evelina," that novel which Dr. Johnson loved so. I took down the book from a dusty old crypt at a club, where Mrs. Barbauld's novelists repose: and this is the kind of thing, ladies and gentlemen, in which your ancestors found pleasure:—

"And here, whilst I was looking for the books, I was followed by Lord Orville. He shut the door after he came in, and, approaching me with a look of anxiety, said, 'Is this true, Miss Anville—are you going?'

"'I believe so, my lord,' said I, still looking for the books.

"'So suddenly, so unexpectedly: must I lose you?'

"'No great loss, my lord,' said I, endeavoring to speak cheerfully.

"'Is it possible,' said he, gravely, 'Miss Anville can doubt my sincerity?'

"'I can't imagine,' cried I, 'what Mrs. Selwyn has done with those books.'

"'Would to heaven,' continued he, 'I might flatter myself you would allow me to prove it!'

"'I must run upstairs,' cried I, greatly confused, 'and ask what she has done with them.'

"'You are going then,' cried he, taking my hand, 'and you give me not the smallest hope of any return! Will you not, my too lovely friend, will you not teach me, with fortitude like your own, to support your absence?

" 'My lord,' cried I, endeavoring to disengage my hand, 'pray let me go!'

" 'I will,' cried he, to my inexpressible confusion, dropping on one knee, 'if you wish me to leave you.'

" 'Oh, my lord,' exclaimed I, 'rise, I beseech you; rise. Surely your lordship is not so cruel as to mock me.'

" 'Mock you!' repeated he earnestly, 'no, I revere you. I esteem and admire you above all human beings! You are the friend to whom my soul is attached, as to its better half. You are the most amiable, the most perfect of women; and you are dearer to me than language has the power of telling.'

"I attempt not to describe my sensations at that moment; I scarce breathed; I doubted if I existed; the blood forsook my cheeks, and my feet refused to sustain me. Lord Orville hastily rising supported me to a chair upon which I sank almost lifeless.

"I cannot write the scene that followed, though every word is engraven on my heart; but his protestations, his expressions, were too flattering for repetition; nor would he, in spite of my repeated efforts to leave him, suffer me to escape; in short, my dear sir, I was not proof against his solicitations, and he drew from me the most sacred secret of my heart!"

Other people may not much like this extract, madam, from your favorite novel, but when you come to read it, you will like it. I suspect that when you read that book which you so love, you read it à deux. Did you not yourself pass a winter at Bath, when you were the belle of the assembly? Was there not a Lord Orville in your case too? As you think of him eleven lusters pass away. You look at him with the bright eyes of those days, and your hero stands before you, the brave, the accomplished, the simple, the true gentleman; and makes the most elegant of bows to one of the most beautiful young women the world ever saw: and he leads you out to the cotillon, to the dear unforgotten music. Hark to the horns of Elfland, blowing, blowing! *Bonne vieille,* you remember their melody, and your heartstrings thrill with it still.

Of your heroic heroes, I think our friend Monseigneur Athos, Count de la Fere, is my favorite. I have read about him from sunrise to sunset with the utmost contentment of mind. He has passed through how many volumes? Forty? Fifty? I wish for my part there were a hundred more, and would never tire of him rescuing prisoners, punishing ruffians, and running scoundrels through the midriff with his most graceful rapier. Ah, Athos, Porthos, and Aramis, you are a magnificent trio. I think I like d'Artagnan in his own memoirs best. I bought him years and years ago, price fivepence, in a little parchment-covered Cologne-printed volume, at a stall in Gray's Inn Lane. Dumas glorifies him and makes a Marshal of him; if I remember rightly, the original d'Artagnan was a needy adventurer, who died in exile very early in Louis XIV.'s reign.

*     *     *     *     *

The editor of the Cornhill Magazine (no soft and yielding character like his predecessor, but a man of stern resolution) will only allow these harmless papers to run to a certain length. But for this veto I should gladly have prattled over a half a sheet more, and have discoursed on many heroes and heroines of novels whom fond memory brings back to me. Of these books I have been a diligent student from those early days, which are recorded at the commencement of this little essay. Oh, delightful novels, well remembered! Oh, novels, sweet and delicious as the raspberry open-tarts of bud-

ding boyhood! Do I forget one night after prayers
(when we under-boys were sent to bed) lingering at my
cupboard to read one little half-page more of my dear
Walter Scott—and down came the monitor's dictionary
upon my head! Rebecca, daughter of Isaac of York, I
have loved thee faithfully for forty years! Thou wert
twenty years old (say) and I but twelve, when I knew
thee. At sixty odd, love, most of the ladies of thy Oriental race have lost the bloom of youth, and bulged beyond
the line of beauty; but to me thou art ever young and
fair, and I will do battle with any felon Templar who
assails thy fair name.                          1860-1862

## JOHN RUSKIN (1819-1900)

## AUTOBIOGRAPHY

### (From *Præterita*)

#### THE SPRINGS OF WANDEL

I AM, and my father was before me, a violent Tory
of the old school;—Walter Scott's school, that is to say,
and Homer's. I name these two out of the numberless
great Tory writers, because they were my own two
masters. I had Walter Scott's novels, and the *Iliad*
(Pope's translation), for constant reading when I was
a child, on week-days: on Sunday, their effect was tempered by *Robinson Crusoe* and the *Pilgrim's Progress;*
my mother having it deeply in her heart to make an
evangelical clergyman of me. Fortunately, I had an aunt
more evangelical than my mother; and my aunt gave me
cold mutton for Sunday's dinner, which—as I much preferred it hot—greatly diminished the influence of the
*Pilgrim's Progress;* and the end of the matter was,
that I got all the noble imaginative teaching of Defoe
and Bunyan, and yet—am not an evangelical clergyman.

I had, however, still better teaching than theirs, and that compulsorily, and every day of the week.

Walter Scott and Pope's Homer were reading of my own election, and my mother forced me, by steady daily toil, to learn long chapters of the Bible by heart; as well as to read it every syllable through, aloud, hard names and all, from Genesis to the Apocalypse, about once a year: and to that discipline—patient, accurate, and resolute—I owe, not only a knowledge of the book, which I find occasionally serviceable, but much of my general power of taking pains, and the best part of my taste in literature. From Walter Scott's novels I might easily, as I grew older, have fallen to other people's novels; and Pope might, perhaps, have led me to take Johnson's English, or Gibbon's, as types of language; but once knowing the 32nd of Deuteronomy, the 119th Psalm, the 15th of 1st Corinthians, the Sermon on the Mount, and most of the Apocalypse, every syllable by heart, and having always a way of thinking with myself what words meant, it was not possible for me, even in the foolishest times of youth, to write entirely superficial or formal English; and the affectation of trying to write like Hooker and George Herbert was the most innocent I could have fallen into.

From my own chosen masters, then, Scott and Homer, I learned the Toryism which my best after-thought has only served to confirm.

That is to say, a most sincere love of kings, and dislike of everybody who attempted to disobey them. Only, both by Homer and Scott, I was taught strange ideas about kings, which I find for the present much obsolete; for, I perceived that both the author of the *Iliad* and the author of *Waverley* made their kings, or king-loving persons, do harder work than anybody else. Tydides or

Idomeneus always killed twenty Trojans to other people's one, and Redgauntlet speared more salmon than any of the Solway fishermen; and—which was particularly a subject of admiration to me—I observed that they not only did more, but in proportion to their doings *got* less, than other people—nay, that the best of them were even ready to govern for nothing! and let their followers divide any quantity of spoil or profit. Of late it has seemed to me that the idea of a king has become exactly the contrary of this, and that it has been supposed the duty of superior persons generally to govern less, and get more, than anybody else. So that it was, perhaps, quite as well that in those early days my contemplation of existent kingship was a very distant one.

The aunt who gave me cold mutton on Sundays was my father's sister: she lived at Bridge-end, in the town of Perth, and had a garden full of gooseberry-bushes, sloping down to the Tay, with a door opening to the water, which ran past it, clear-brown over the pebbles three or four feet deep; a swift-eddying,—an infinite thing for a child to look down into.

My father began business as a wine-merchant, with no capital, and a considerable amount of debts bequeathed him by my grandfather. He accepted the bequest, and paid them all before he began to lay by anything for himself,—for which his best friends called him a fool, and I, without expressing any opinion as to his wisdom, which I knew in such matters to be at least equal to mine, have written on the granite slab over his grave that he was "an entirely honest merchant." As days went on he was able to take a house in Hunter Street, Brunswick Square, No. 54 (the windows of it, fortunately for me, commanded a view of a marvellous iron post, out of which the water-carts were filled

through beautiful little trapdoors, by pipes like boa-
constrictors; and I was never weary of contemplating
that mystery, and the delicious dripping consequent);
and as years went on, and I came to be four or five years
old, he could command a postchaise and pair for two
months in the summer, by help of which, with my
mother and me, he went the round of his country cus-
tomers (who liked to see the principal of the house his
own traveller); so that, at a jog-trot pace, and through
the panoramic opening of the four windows of a postchaise, made more panoramic still to me because my
seat was a little bracket in front (for we used to hire
the chaise regularly for the two months out of Long
Acre, and so could have it bracketed and pocketed as
we liked), I saw all the high-roads, and most of the
cross ones, of England and Wales; and every part of
lowland Scotland, as far as Perth, where every other
year we spent the whole summer: and I used to read
the *Abbot* at Kinross, and the *Monastery* in Glen Farg,
which I confused with "Glendearg," and thought that
the White Lady had as certainly lived by the streamlet
in that glen of the Ochils, as the Queen of Scots in
the island of Loch Leven.

To my farther great benefit, as I grew older, I thus
saw nearly all the noblemen's houses in England; in
reverent and healthy delight of uncovetous admiration,
—perceiving, as soon as I could perceive any political
truth at all, that it was probably much happier to live
in a small house, and have Warwick Castle to be astonished at, than to live in Warwick Castle and have nothing
to be astonished at; but that, at all events, it would not
make Brunswick Square in the least more pleasantly
habitable, to pull Warwick Castle down. And at this
day, though I have kind invitations enough to visit

America, I could not, even for a couple of months, live in a country so miserable as to possess no castles.

Nevertheless, having formed my notion of kinghood chiefly from the FitzJames of the *Lady of the Lake,* and of noblesse from the Douglas there, and the Douglas in *Marmion,* a painful wonder soon arose in my child-mind, why the castles should now be always empty. Tantallon was there; but no Archibald of Angus:—Stirling, but no Knight of Snowdoun. The galleries and gardens of England were beautiful to see—but his Lordship and her Ladyship were always in town, said the housekeepers and gardeners. Deep yearning took hold of me for a kind of "Restoration," which I began slowly to feel that Charles the Second had not altogether effected, though I always wore a gilded oak-apple very piously in my button-hole on the 29th of May. It seemed to me that Charles the Second's Restoration had been, as compared with the Restoration I wanted, much as that gilded oak-apple to a real apple. And as I grew wiser, the desire for sweet pippins instead of bitter ones, and Living Kings instead of dead ones, appeared to me rational as well as romantic; and gradually it has become the main purpose of my life to grow pippins, and its chief hope, to see Kings.

### CONSECRATION

DIFFICULT enough for you to imagine, that old travellers' time when Switzerland was yet the land of the Swiss, and the Alps had never been trod by foot of man. Steam, never heard of yet, but for short fair weather crossing at sea (were there paddle-packets across Atlantic! I forget). Any way, the roads by land were safe; and entered once into this mountain Para-

dise, we wound on through its balmy glens past cottage
after cottage on their lawns, still glistering in the dew.

The road got into more barren heights by the mid-day,
the hills arduous; once or twice we had to wait for
horses, and we were still twenty miles from Schaffhausen
at sunset; it was past midnight when we reached her
closed gates. The disturbed porter had the grace to open
them—not quite wide enough; we carried away one of
our lamps in collision with the slanting bar as we drove
through the arch. How much happier the privilege of
dreamily entering a mediæval city, though with the loss
of a lamp, than the free ingress of being jammed between a dray and a tramcar at a railroad station!

It is strange that I but dimly recollect the following
morning; I fancy we must have gone to some sort of
church or other; and certainly, part of the day went
in admiring the bow-windows projecting into the clean
streets. None of us seem to have thought the Alps would
be visible without profane exertion in climbing hills. We
dined at four, as usual, and the evening being entirely
fine, went out to walk, all of us,—my father and mother
and Mary and I.

We must have still spent some time in town-seeing,
for it was drawing toward sunset, when we got up to
some sort of garden promenade—west of the town, I
believe; and high above the Rhine, so as to command
the open country across it to the south and west. At
which open country of low undulation, far into blue,—
gazing as at one of our own distances from Malvern of
Worcestershire, or Dorking of Kent,—suddenly—behold
—beyond!

There was no thought in any of us for a moment of
their being clouds. They were clear as crystal, sharp on
the pure horizon sky, and already tinged with rose by

the sinking sun. Infinitely beyond all that we had ever thought or dreamed,—the seen walls of lost Eden could not have been more beautiful to us; not more awful, round heaven, the walls of sacred Death.

It is not possible to imagine, in any time of the world, a more blessed entrance into life, for a child of such a temperament as mine. True, the temperament belonged to the age: a very few years,—within the hundred,— before that, no child could have been born to care for mountains, or for the men that lived among them, in that way. Till Rousseau's time, there had been no "sentimental" love of nature; and till Scott's, no such apprehensive love of "all sorts and conditions of men," not in the soul merely, but in the flesh. St. Bernard of La Fontaine, looking out to Mont Blanc with his child's eyes, sees above Mont Blanc the Madonna; St. Bernard of Talloires, not the Lake of Annecy, but the dead between Martigny and Aosta. But for me, the Alps and their people were alike beautiful in their snow, and their humanity; and I wanted, neither for them nor myself, sight of any thrones in heaven but the rocks, or of any spirits in heaven but the clouds.

Thus, in perfect health of life and fire of heart, not wanting to be anything but the boy I was, not wanting to have anything more than I had; knowing of sorrow only just so much as to make life serious to me, not enough to slacken in the least its sinews; and with so much of science mixed with feeling as to make the sight of the Alps not only the revelation of the beauty of the earth, but the opening of the first page of its volume,— I went down that evening from the garden-terrace of Schaffhausen with my destiny fixed in all of it that was to be sacred and useful. To that terrace, and the shore of the Lake of Geneva, my heart and faith return to this day, in every impulse that is yet nobly alive in them, and every thought that has in it help or peace.    1887

## NATURE

### INFLUENCE OF NATURE

#### (*Modern Painters,* Vol. III, Ch. 17.)

THE first thing which I remember, as an event in life, was being taken by my nurse to the brow of Friar's Crag on Derwent Water; the intense joy, mingled with awe, that I had in looking through the hollows in the mossy roots, over the crag, into the dark lake, has associated itself more or less with all twining roots of trees ever since. Two other things I remember as, in a sort, beginnings of life;—crossing Shapfells (being let out of the chaise to run up the hills), and going through Glenfarg, near Kinross, in a winter's morning, when the rocks were hung with icicles; these being culminating points in an early life of more travelling than is usually indulged to a child. In such journeyings, whenever they brought me near hills, and in all mountain ground and scenery, I had a pleasure, as early as I can remember, and continuing till I was eighteen or twenty, infinitely greater than any which has been since possible to me in anything; comparable for intensity only to the joy of a lover in being near a noble and kind mistress, but no more explicable or definable than that feeling of love itself. Only thus much I can remember, respecting it, which is important to our present subject.

First: it was never independent of associated thought. Almost as soon as I could see or hear, I had got reading enough to give me associations with all kinds of scenery; and mountains, in particular, were always partly confused with those of my favorite book, Scott's *Monastery;* so that Glenfarg and all other glens were more or less enchanted to me, filled with forms of hesitating creed about Christie of the Clint Hill, and the monk Eustace; and with a general presence of White Lady everywhere. I also generally knew, or was told by my father and mother, such simple facts of history as were necessary to give more definite and justifiable association to other scenes which chiefly interested me, such as the ruins of Lochleven and Kenilworth; and thus my pleasure in mountains or ruins was never, even in earliest childhood, free from a certain awe and melancholy, and general sense of the meaning of death, though, in its principal influence, entirely exhilarating and gladdening.

Secondly: it was partly dependent on contrast with a very simple and unamused mode of general life; I was born in London, and accustomed, for two or three years, to no other prospect than that of the brick walls over the way; had no brothers nor sisters, nor companions; and though I could always make myself happy in a quiet way, the beauty of the mountains had an additional charm of change and adventure which a country-bred child would not have felt.

Thirdly: there was no definite religious feeling mingled with it. I partly believed in ghosts and fairies; but supposed that angels belonged entirely to the Mosaic dispensation, and cannot remember any single thought or feeling connected with them. I believed that God was in heaven, and could hear me and see me; but this gave me neither pleasure nor pain, and I seldom thought of it at all. I never thought of nature as God's work, but as a separate fact or existence.

Fourthly: it was entirely unaccompanied by powers of reflection or invention. Every fancy that I had about nature was put into my head by some book; and I never reflected about anything till I grew older; and then, the more I reflected, the less nature was precious to me: I could then make myself happy, by thinking, in the dark, or in the dullest scenery; and the beautiful scenery became less essential to my pleasure.

Fifthly: it was, according to its strength, inconsistent with every evil feeling, with spite, anger, covetousness, discontent, and every other hateful passion; but would associate itself deeply with every just and noble sorrow, joy, or affection. It had not, however, always the power to repress what was inconsistent with it; and, though only after stout contention, might at last be crushed by what it had partly repressed. And as it only acted by setting one impulse against another, though it had much power in moulding the character, it had hardly any in strengthening it; it formed temperament but never instilled principle; it kept me generally good-humored and kindly, but could not teach me perseverance or self-denial: what firmness or principle I had was quite independent of it; and it came itself nearly as often in the form of a temptation as of a safeguard, leading me to ramble over hills when I should have been learning lessons, and lose days in reveries which I might have spent in doing kindnesses.

Lastly: although there was no definite religious sentiment mingled with it, there was a continual perception of Sanctity in the whole of nature, from the slightest thing to the vastest;—an instinctive awe, mixed with delight; an indefinable thrill, such as we sometimes imagine to indicate the presence of a disembodied spirit. I could only feel this perfectly when I was alone; and then it would often make me shiver from head to foot with the joy and fear of it, when after being some time away from hills, I first got to the shore of a mountain river, where the brown water circled among the pebbles, or when I first saw the swell of distant land against the sunset, or the first low broken wall, covered with mountain moss. I cannot in the least *describe* the feeling; but I do not think this is my fault, nor that of the English language, for I am afraid, no feeling *is* describable. If we had to explain even the sense of bodily hunger to a person who had never felt it, we should be hard put to it for words; and the joy in nature seemed to me to come of a sort of heart-hunger, satisfied with the presence of a Great and Holy Spirit. These feelings remained in their full intensity till I was eighteen or twenty, and then, as the reflective and practical power increased, and the "cares of this world" gained upon me, faded gradually away, in the manner described by Wordsworth in his *Intimations of Immortality*.

I cannot, of course, tell how far I am justified in supposing that these sensations may be reasoned upon as common to children in general. In the same degree they are not of course common, otherwise children would be, most of them, very different from what they are in their choice of pleasures. But, as far as such feelings exist, I apprehend they are more or less similar in their nature and influence; only producing different characters according to the elements with which they are mingled. Thus, a very religious child may give up many pleasures to which its instincts lead it, for the sake of irksome duties; and an inventive child would mingle its love of nature with watchfulness of human sayings and doings; but I believe the feelings I have endeavored to describe are the pure landscape-instinct; and the likelihoods of good or evil resulting from them may be reasoned upon as generally indicating the usefulness or danger of the modern love and study of landscape.            1856

## STUDIES

### AIR AND CLOUDS

THE deep of air that surrounds the earth enters into union with the earth at its surface, and with its waters; so as to be the apparent cause of their ascending into life. First, it warms them, and shades, at once, staying the heat of the sun's rays in its own body, but warding their force with its clouds. It warms and cools at once, with traffic of balm and frost; so that the white wreaths are withdrawn from the field of the Swiss peasant by the glow of Libyan rock. It gives its own strength to the sea; forms and fills every cell of its foam; sustains the precipices, and designs the valleys of its waves; gives the gleam to their moving under the night, and the white fire to their plains under sunrise; lifts their voices along the rocks, bears above them the spray of birds, pencils through them the dimpling of unfooted sands. It gathers out of them a portion in the hollow of its hand; dyes, with that, the hills into dark blue, and their glaciers with dying rose; inlays with that, for sapphire, the dome in which it has to set the cloud; shapes out of that the heavenly flocks; divides them, numbers, cherishes, bears them on its bosom, calls them to their journeys, waits by their rest; feeds from them the brooks that cease not, and strews with them the dews that cease. It spins and weaves their fleece into wild tapestry, rends it, and renews; and flits and flames, and whispers, among the golden threads, thrilling them with a plectrum of strange fire that traverses them to and fro, and is enclosed in them like life.

It enters into the surface of the earth, subdues it, and falls together with it into fruitful dust, from which can be moulded flesh; it joins itself, in dew, to the substance of adamant; and becomes the green leaf out of the dry ground; it enters into the separated shapes of the earth it has tempered, commands the ebb and flow of the current of their life, fills their limbs with its own lightness, measures their existence by its indwelling pulse, moulds upon their lips the words by which one soul can be known to another; is to them the hearing of the ear, and the beating of the heart; and, passing away, leaves them to the peace that hears and moves no more. —*The Queen of the Air*, sec. 98. 1869

WE HAVE next to ask what colour from sunshine can the white cloud receive, and what the black?

You won't expect me to tell you all that, or even the little that is accurately known about that, in a quarter of an hour; yet note these main facts on the matter.

On any pure white, and practically opaque, cloud, or thing like a cloud, as an Alp, or Milan Cathedral, you can have cast by rising or setting sunlight, any tints of amber, orange, or moderately deep rose—you can't have lemon yellows, or any kind of green except in negative hue by opposition; and though by storm-light you may sometimes get the reds cast very deep, beyond a certain limit you cannot go,—the Alps are never vermilion colour, nor flamingo colour, nor canary colour; nor did you ever see a full scarlet cumulus of thundercloud.

On opaque white vapour, then, remember, you can get a glow or a blush of colour, never a flame of it.

But when the cloud is transparent, as well as pure, and can be filled with light through all the body of it, you then can have by the light reflected from its atoms any force conceivable by human mind of the entire group

of the golden and ruby colours, from intensely burnished
gold colour, through a scarlet for whose brightness there
are no words, into any depth and any hue of Tyrian
crimson and Byzantine purple. These with full blue
breathed between them at the zenith, and green blue
nearer the horizon, form the scales and chords of colour
possible to the morning and evening sky in pure and
fine weather; the keynote of the opposition being vermilion against green blue, both of equal tone, and at
such a height and acme of brilliancy that you cannot see
the line where their edges pass into each other.—*The
Storm-Cloud of the Nineteenth Century,* lect. i.    1884

It is to be remembered that although clouds of course
arrange themselves more or less into broad masses, with
a light side and dark side, both their light and shade
are invariably composed of a series of divided masses,
each of which has in its outline as much variety and
character as the great outline of the cloud. . . . Nor
are these multitudinous divisions a truth of slight importance in the character of sky, for they are dependent
on, and illustrative of, a quality which is usually in a
great degree overlooked,—the enormous retiring spaces
of solid clouds. Between the illumined edge of a heaped
cloud, and that part of its body which turns into shadow,
there will generally be a clear distance of several miles,
more or less of course, according to the general size
of the cloud, but in such large masses as in Poussin and
others of the old masters, occupy the fourth or fifth of
the visible sky; the clear illumined breadth of vapour,
from the edge to the shadow, involves at least a distance
of five or six miles. We are little apt, in watching the
changes of a mountainous range of cloud, to reflect
that the masses of vapour which compose it, are huger
and higher than any mountain range of the earth; and

the distances between mass and mass are not yards of air traversed in an instant by the flying form, but valleys of changing atmosphere leagues over; that the slow motions of ascending curves, which we can scarcely trace, is a boiling energy of exulting vapour rushing into the heaven a thousand feet in a minute; and that the toppling angle whose sharp edge almost escapes notice in the multitudinous forms around it, is a nodding precipice of storms, 3000 feet from base to summit. It is not until we have actually compared the forms of the sky with the hill ranges of the earth, and seen the soaring Alp overtopped and buried in one surge of the sky, that we begin to conceive or appreciate the colossal scale of the phenomena of the latter. But of this there can be no doubt in the mind of any one accustomed to trace the forms of clouds among hill ranges—as it is there a demonstrable and evident fact, that the space of vapour visibly extended over an ordinarily cloudy sky, is not less, from the point nearest to the observer to the horizon, than twenty leagues; that the size of every mass of separate form, if it be at all largely divided, is to be expressed in terms of *miles;* and that every boiling heap of illuminated mist in the nearer sky, is an enormous mountain, fifteen or twenty thousand feet in height, six or seven miles over in illuminated surface, furrowed by a thousand colossal ravines, torn by local tempests into peaks and promontories, and changing its features with the majestic velocity of the volcano.— *Modern Painters,* vol. i, part ii, sec. iii, chap. iii.

1843

### WATER

OF ALL inorganic substances, acting in their own proper nature, and without assistance or combination, water is the most wonderful. If we think of it as the source of all the changefulness and beauty which we have seen in clouds; then as the instrument by which the earth we have contemplated was modelled into symmetry, and its crags chiselled into grace; then as, in the form of snow, it robes the mountains it has made with that transcendent light which we could not have conceived if we had not seen; then as it exists in the foam of the torrent, in the iris which spans it, in the morning mist which rises from it, in the deep crystalline pools which mirror its hanging shore, in the broad lake and glancing river; finally, in that which is to all human minds the best emblem of unwearied unconquerable power, the wild, various, fantastic, tameless unity of the sea; what shall we compare to this mighty, this universal element, for glory and for beauty? or how shall we follow its eternal changefulness of feeling? It is like trying to paint a soul. . . .

To suggest the ordinary appearance of calm water, to lay on canvas as much evidence of surface and reflection as may make us understand that water is meant, is, perhaps, the easiest task of art; and even ordinary running or falling water may be sufficiently rendered, by observing careful curves of projection with a dark ground, and breaking a little white over it, as we see done with judgment and truth by Ruysdael. But to paint the actual play of hue on the reflective surface, or to give the forms and fury of water when it begins to show itself; to give the flashing and rocket-like velocity of a noble cataract, or the precision and grace of the sea wave, so exquisitely modelled, though so mockingly transient, so mountainous in its form, yet so cloud-like in its motion, with its variety and delicacy of colour, when every ripple and wreath has some peculiar passage of reflection upon itself alone, and the radiating and scintillating sunbeams are mixed with the dim hues of transparent depth and dark rock below; to do this perfectly is beyond the power of man; to do it even partially has been granted to but one or two, even of those few who have dared to attempt it. . . .

Now, the fact is, that there is hardly a road-side pond or pool which has not as much landscape *in* it as above it. It is not the brown, muddy, dull thing we suppose it to be; it has a heart like ourselves, and in the bottom of that there are the boughs of the tall trees, and the blades of the shaking grass, and all manner of hues of variable pleasant light out of the sky. Nay, the ugly gutter, that stagnates over the drain-bars in the heart of the foul city, is not altogether base; down in that, if you will look deep enough, you may see the dark serious blue of far-off sky, and the passing of pure clouds. It is at your own will that you see in that despised stream, either the refuse of the street, or the image of the sky. So it is with almost all other things that we unkindly despise.—*Modern Painters,* vol. i, part ii, sec. v, chap. i.                    1843

## MOUNTAINS

MOUNTAINS are to the rest of the body of the earth what violent muscular action is to the body of man. The muscles and tendons of its anatomy are, in the mountain, brought out with fierce and convulsive energy, full of expression, passion, and strength; the plains and the lower hills are the repose and the effortless motion of the frame, when its muscles lie dormant and concealed beneath the lines of its beauty, yet ruling those lines in their every undulation. This, then, is the first grand principle of the truth of the earth. The spirit of the hills is action; that of the lowlands, repose; and between these there is to be found every variety of motion and of rest; from the inactive plain, sleeping like the firmament, with cities for stars, to the fiery peaks, which, with heaving bosoms and exulting limbs, with the clouds drifting like hair from their bright foreheads, lift up their Titan hands to Heaven, saying, "I live forever!"

But there is this difference between the action of the earth, and that of a living creature, that while the exerted limb marks its bones and tendons through the flesh, the excited earth casts off the flesh altogether, and its bones come out from beneath. Mountains are the bones of the earth, their highest peaks are invariably those parts of its anatomy which in the plains lie buried under five and twenty-thousand feet of solid thickness of superincumbent soil, and which spring up in the mountain ranges in vast pyramids or wedges, flinging their garment of earth away from them on each side. The masses of the lower hills are laid over and against their sides, like the masses of lateral masonry against the skeleton arch of an unfinished bridge, except that they slope up to and lean against the central ridge: and, finally, upon the slopes of these lower hills are strewed the level beds of sprinkled gravel, sand, and clay, which form the extent of the champaign. Here then is another grand principle of the truth of earth, that the mountains must come from under all, and be the support of all; and that everything else must be laid in their arms, heap above heap, the plains being the uppermost. Opposed to this truth is every appearance of the hills being laid upon the plains, or built upon them. Nor is this a truth only of the earth on a large scale, for every minor rock (in position) comes out from the soil about it as an island out of the sea, lifting the earth near it like waves beating on its sides.—*Modern Painters,* vol. i, part ii, sec. iv, chap. i.                                    1843

EXAMINE the nature of your own emotion (if you feel it) at the sight of the Alp, and you find all the brightness of that emotion hanging, like dew on gossamer, on a curious web of subtle fancy and imperfect knowledge. First, you have a vague idea of its size, coupled with wonder at the work of the great Builder of its walls and foundations, then an apprehension of its eternity, a pathetic sense of its perpetualness, and your own transientness, as of the grass upon its sides; then, and in this very sadness, a sense of strange companionship with past generations in seeing what they saw. They did not see the clouds that are floating over your head; nor the cottage wall on the other side of the field; nor the road by which you are travelling. But they saw *that*. The wall of granite in the heavens was the same to them as to you. They have ceased to look upon it; you will soon cease to look also, and the granite wall will be for others. Then, mingled with these more solemn imaginations, come the understandings of the gifts and glories of the Alps, the fancying forth of all the fountains that well from its rocky walls and strong rivers that are born out of its ice, and of all the pleasant valleys that wind between its cliffs, and all the chalets that gleam among its clouds, and happy farmsteads couched upon its pastures; while together with the thoughts of these, rise strange sympathies with all the unknown of human life, and happiness, and death, signified by that narrow white flame of the everlasting snow, seen so far in the morning sky.—*Modern Painters,* vol. iii, part iv, chap. x.                      1856

INFERIOR hills ordinarily interrupt, in some degree, the richness of the valleys at their feet; the gray downs of Southern England, and treeless coteaux of central France, and gray swells of Scottish moor, whatever peculiar charms they may possess in themselves, are at least destitute of those which belong to the woods and fields of the lowlands. But the great mountains *lift* the lowlands *on their sides*. Let the reader imagine, first, the appearance of the most varied plain of some richly cultivated country; let him imagine it dark with graceful woods, and soft with deepest pastures; let him fill the space of it, to the utmost horizon, with innumerable and changeful incidents of scenery and life; leading pleasant streamlets through its meadows, strewing clusters of cottages beside their banks, tracing sweet footpaths through its avenues, and animating its fields with happy flocks, and slow wandering spots of cattle; and when he has wearied himself with endless imagining, and left no space without some loveliness of its own, let him conceive all this great plain, with its infinite treasures of natural beauty and happy human life, gathered up in God's hands from one edge of the horizon to the other, like a woven garment; and shaken into deep, falling folds, as the robes droop from a king's shoulders; all its bright rivers leaping into cataracts along the hollows of its fall, and all its forests rearing themselves aslant against its slopes, as a rider rears himself back when his horse plunges; and all its villages nestling themselves into the new windings of its glens; and all its pastures thrown into steep waves of greensward, dashed with dew along the edges of their folds, and sweeping down into endless slopes, with a cloud here and there lying quietly, half on the grass, half in the air; and he will have as yet, in all this lifted world, only the foundation of one of the great Alps. And what-

ever is lovely in the lowland scenery becomes lovelier in
this change: the trees which grew heavily and stiffly
from the level line of the plain assume strange lines of
strength and grace as they bend themselves against the
mountain side; they breathe more freely, and toss their
branches more carelessly as each climbs higher, looking
to the clear light above the topmost leaves of its brother
tree: the flowers which on the arable plain fell before
the plough, now find out for themselves unapproachable
places, where year by year they gather into happier fellowship, and fear no evil; and the streams which in the
level land crept in dark eddies by unwholesome banks,
now move in showers of silver, and are clothed with
rainbows and bring health and life wherever the glance
of their waves can reach.—*Modern Painters*, vol. iv,
part v, chap. vii.                                    1856

## THE MISSION OF NATURE

THE great mechanical impulses of the age, of which
most of us are so proud, are a mere passing fever, half
speculative, half childish. People will discover at last
that royal roads to anything can no more be laid in iron
than they can in dust; that there are, in fact, no royal
roads to anywhere worth going to; that if there were, it
would that instant cease to be worth going to, I mean
so far as the things to be obtained are in any way esti-
mable in terms of *price*. For there are two classes of
precious things in the world: those that God gives us
for nothing—sun, air, and life (both mortal life and
immortal); and the secondarily precious things which
He gives us for a price: these secondarily precious
things, worldly wine and milk, can only be bought for
definite money; they never can be cheapened. No cheat-
ing nor bargaining will ever get a single thing out of

nature's "establishment" at half-price. Do we want to be strong?—we must work. To be hungry?—we must starve. To be happy?—we must be kind. To be wise? —we must look and think. No changing of place at a hundred miles an hour, nor making of stuffs a thousand yards a minute, will make us one whit stronger, happier, or wiser. There was always more in the world than men could see, walked they ever so slowly; they will see it no better for going fast. And they will at last, and soon, too, find out that their grand inventions for conquering (as they think) space and time do in reality conquer nothing; for space and time are, in their own essence, unconquerable, and besides did not want any sort of conquering; they wanted *using*. A fool always wants to shorten space and time: a wise man wants to lengthen both. A fool wants to kill space and kill time: a wise man, first to gain them, then to animate them. Your railroad, when you come to understand it, is only a device for making the world smaller: and as for being able to talk from place to place, that is, indeed, well and convenient; but suppose you have, originally, nothing to say. We shall be obliged at last to confess, what we should long ago have known, that the really precious things are thought and sight, not pace. It does a bullet no good to go fast; and a man, if he be truly a man, no harm to go slow; for his glory is not at all in going, but in being. . . .

And I am Utopian and enthusiastic enough to believe, that the time will come when the world will discover this. It has now made its experiments in every possible direction but the right one; and it seems that it must, at last, try the right one, in a mathematical necessity. It has tried fighting, and preaching, and fasting, buying and selling, pomp and parsimony, pride and humiliation, —every possible manner of existence in which it could conjecture there was any happiness or dignity; and all the while, as it bought, sold, and fought, and fasted, and wearied itself with policies, and ambitions, and self-denials, God had placed its real happiness in the keeping of the little mosses of the wayside, and of the clouds of the firmament. Now and then a weary king, or a tormented slave, found out where the true kingdoms of the world were, and possessed himself, in a furrow or two of garden ground, of a truly infinite dominion. But the world would not believe their report, and went on trampling down the mosses, and forgetting the clouds, and seeking happiness in its own way, until, at last, blundering and late, came natural science; and in natural science not only the observation of things, but the finding out of new uses for them. Of course the world, having a choice left to it, went wrong, as usual, and thought that these mere material uses were to be the sources of its happiness. It got the clouds packed into iron cylinders, and made it carry its wise self at their own cloud pace. It got weavable fibres out of the mosses, and made clothes for itself, cheap and fine,—here was happiness at last. To go as fast as the clouds, and manufacture everything out of anything,—here was paradise, indeed!

And now, when, in a little while, it is unparadised again, if there were any other mistake that the world could make, it would of course make it. But I see not that there is any other; and, standing fairly at its wits' ends, having found that going fast, when it is used to it, is no more paradisaical than going slow; and that all the prints and cottons in Manchester cannot make it comfortable in its mind, I do verily believe it will come, finally, to understand that God paints the clouds and shapes the moss-fibres, that men may be happy in seeing Him at His work, and that in resting quietly beside

Him, and watching His working, and—according to the power He has communicated to ourselves, and the guidance He grants,—in carrying out His purposes of peace and charity among all His creatures, are the only real happinesses that ever were, or ever will be, possible to mankind.—*Modern Painters,* vol. iii, part iv, chap. xvii.

1856

# ART

### THE GROUNDS OF ART

Here let me finally and firmly enunciate the great principle to which all that has hitherto been stated is subservient:—that art is valuable or otherwise, only as it expresses the personality, activity, and living perception of a good and great human soul; that it may express and contain this with little help from execution, and less from science; and that if it have not this, if it show not the vigor, perception, and invention of a mighty human spirit, it is worthless. Worthless, I mean, as *art;* it may be precious in some other way, but, as art, it is nugatory. Once let this be well understood among us, and magnificent consequences will soon follow. . . . By work of the soul, I mean the reader always to understand the work of the entire immortal creature, proceeding from a quick, perceptive, and eager heart perfected by the intellect, and finally dealt with by the hands, under the direct guidance of these higher powers. . . .

Whatever may be the means, or whatever the more immediate end of any kind of art, all of it that is good agrees in this, that it is the expression of one soul talking to another, and is precious according to the greatness of the soul that utters it. And consider what mighty consequences follow from our acceptance of this truth! what a key we have herein given us for the interpretation of the art of all time! For, as long as we held art to consist in any high manual skill, or successful imitation of natural objects, or any scientific and legalized manner of performance whatever, it was necessary for us to limit our admiration to narrow periods and to few men. . . .

But let us once comprehend the holier nature of the art of man, and begin to look for the meaning of the spirit however syllabled, and the scene is changed; and we are changed also. Those small and dexterous creatures whom we once worshipped, those fur-capped divinities with sceptres of camel's hair, peering and poring in their one-windowed chambers over the minute preciousness of the labored canvas; how are they swept away and crushed into unnoticeable darkness! And in their stead, as the walls of the dismal rooms that enclosed them and us are struck by the four winds of Heaven, and rent away, and as the world opens to our sight, lo! far back into all the depths of time, and forth from all the fields that have been sown with human life, how the harvest of the dragon's teeth is springing! how the companies of the gods are ascending out of the earth! The dark stones that have so long been the sepulchres of the thoughts of nations, and the forgotten ruins wherein their faith lay charnelled, give up the dead that were in them; and beneath the Egyptian ranks of sultry and silent rock, and amidst the dim golden lights of the Byzantine dome, and out of the confused and cold shadows of the Northern cloister, behold, the multitudinous souls come forth with singing, gazing on us with the soft eyes of newly comprehended sympathy, and stretching their white arms to us across the grave, in the solemn gladness of everlasting brotherhood.— *Stones of Venice*, vol. iii, chap. iv.          1851-1853

WHEREVER art is practised for its own sake, and the delight of the workman is in what he *does* and *produces*, instead of in what he *interprets* or *exhibits*,—there art has an influence of the most fatal kind on brain and heart, and it issues, if long so pursued, in the *destruction both of intellectual power and moral principle;* whereas art, devoted humbly and self-forgetfully to the clear statement and record of the facts of the universe, is always helpful and beneficent to mankind, full of comfort, strength, and salvation.

Now, when you were once well assured of this, you might logically infer another thing; namely, that when Art was occupied in the function in which she was serviceable, she would herself be strengthened by the service; and when she was doing what Providence without doubt intended her to do, she would gain in vitality and dignity just as she advanced in usefulness. On the other hand, you might gather that when her agency was distorted to the deception or degradation of mankind, she would herself be equally misled and degraded—that she would be checked in advance, or precipitated in decline.

And this is the truth also; and holding this clew, you will easily and justly interpret the phenomena of history. So long as Art is steady in the contemplation and exhibition of natural facts, so long she herself lives and grows; and in her own life and growth partly implies, partly secures, that of the nation in the midst of which she is practised. But a time has always hitherto come, in which, having thus reached a singular perfection, she begins to contemplate that perfection, and to imitate it, and deduce rules and forms from it; and thus to forget her duty and ministry as the interpreter and discoverer of Truth. And in the very instant when this diversion of her purpose and forgetfulness of her function take place—forgetfulness generally coincident with her apparent perfection—in that instant, I say, begins her actual catastrophe; and by her own fall—so far as she has influence—she accelerates the ruin of the nation by which she is practised. . . .

But I will ask your patience with me while I try to illustrate, in some farther particulars, the dependence of the healthy state and power of art itself upon the exercise of its appointed function in the interpretation of fact.

You observe that I always say *interpretation,* never *imitation.* My reason for doing so is, first, that good art rarely imitates; it usually only describes or explains. But my second and chief reason is that good art always consists of two things. First, the observation of fact; secondly, the manifesting of human design and authority in the way the fact is told. Great and good art must unite the two; it cannot exist for a moment but in their unity; it consists of the two as essentially as water consists of oxygen and hydrogen, or marble of lime and carbonic acid.

Let us inquire a little into the nature of each of the elements. The first element, we say, is the love of Nature, leading to the effort to observe and report her truly. And this is the first and leading element. Review for yourselves the history of art, and you will find this to be a manifest certainty, that no *great school ever yet existed which had not for primal aim the representation of some natural fact as truly as possible.* . . .

Wheresoever the search after truth begins, there life begins; wheresoever that search ceases, there life ceases. As long as a school of art holds any chain of natural facts, trying to discover more of them and express them better daily, it may play hither and thither as it likes on this side of the chain or that; it may design grotesques and conventionalisms, build the simplest

buildings, serve the most practical utilities, yet all
it does will be gloriously designed and gloriously done;
but let it once quit hold of the chain of natural fact,
cease to pursue that as the clew to its work; let it propose to itself any other end than preaching this living
word, and think first of showing its own skill or its
own fancy, and from that hour its fall is precipitate
—its destruction sure; nothing that it does or designs
will ever have life or loveliness in it more; its hour has
come, and there is no work, nor device, nor knowledge,
nor wisdom in the grave whither it goeth.—*The Two
Paths,* secs. 17-23.                                1860


## SOCIETY

### LIBERTY AND OBEDIENCE

It is true that there are liberties and liberties. Yonder
torrent, crystal-clear, and arrow-swift, with its spray
leaping into the air like white troops of fawns, is free
enough. Lost, presently, amidst bankless, boundless
marsh—soaking in slow shallowness, as it will, hither
and thither, listless, among the poisonous reeds and
unresisting slime—it is free also. We may choose which
liberty we like,—the restraint of voiceful rock, or the
dumb and edgeless shore of darkened sand. Of that
evil liberty, which men are now glorifying, and pro-
claiming as essence of gospel to all the earth, and will
presently, I suppose, proclaim also to the stars, with
invitation to them *out* of their courses,—and of its op-
posite continence, which is the clasp and $\chi\rho\upsilon\sigma\acute{\epsilon}\eta$ $\pi\epsilon\rho\acute{o}\nu\eta$
of Aglaia's cestus, we must try to find out something
true. For no quality of Art has been more powerful in
its influence on public mind; none is more frequently
the subject of popular praise, or the end of vulgar effort,

than what we call "Freedom." It is necessary to determine the justice or injustice of this popular praise.

I said, a little while ago, that the practical teaching of the masters of Art was summed by the O of Giotto. "You may judge my masterhood of craft," Giotto tells us, "by seeing that I can draw a circle unerringly." And we may safely believe him, understanding him to mean, that—though more may be necessary to an artist than such a power—at least *this* power is necessary. The qualities of hand and eye needful to do this are the first conditions of artistic craft.

Try to draw a circle yourself with the "free" hand, and with a single line. You cannot do it if your hand trembles, nor if it hesitates, nor if it is unmanageable, nor if it is in the common sense of the word "free." So far from being free, it must be under a control as absolute and accurate as if it were fastened to an inflexible bar of steel. And yet it must move, under this necessary control, with perfect, untormented serenity of ease.

That is the condition of all good work whatsoever. All freedom is error. Every line you lay down is either right or wrong: it may be timidly and awkwardly wrong, or fearlessly and impudently wrong: the aspect of the impudent wrongness is pleasurable to vulgar persons; and what is commonly called "free" execution: the timid, tottering, hesitating wrongness is rarely so attractive; yet sometimes, if accompanied with good qualities, and right aims in other directions, it becomes in a manner charming, like the inarticulateness of a child: but, whatever the charm or manner of the error, there is but one question ultimately to be asked respecting every line you draw, Is it right or wrong? If right, it most assuredly is not a "free" line, but an intensely continent, restrained, and considered line; and the action of the hand in laying it is just as decisive, and just as "free,"

as the hand of a first-rate surgeon in a critical incision.
A great operator told me that his hand could check itself
within about the two-hundredth of an inch, in penetrating a membrane; and this, of course, without the help
of sight, by sensation only. With help of sight, and in
action on a substance which does not quiver nor yield,
a fine artist's line is measurable in its proposed direction
to considerably less than the thousandth of an inch.

A wide freedom, truly! . . .

I believe we can nowhere find a better type of a perfectly free creature than in the common house fly. Nor
free only, but brave; and irreverent to a degree which
I think no human republican could by any philosophy
exalt himself to. There is no courtesy in him; he does
not care whether it is king or clown whom he teases;
and in every step of his swift mechanical march, and in
every pause of his resolute observation, there is one and
the same expression of perfect egotism, perfect independence and self-confidence, and conviction of the
world's having been made for flies. Strike at him with
your hand; and to him, the mechanical fact and external
aspect of the matter is, what to you it would be, if an
acre of red clay, ten feet thick, tore itself up from
the ground in one massive field, hovered over you in
the air for a second, and came crashing down with an
aim. That is the external aspect of it; the inner aspect,
to his fly's mind, is of quite natural and unimportant
occurrence—one of the momentary conditions of his
active life. He steps out of the way of your hand, and
alights on the back of it. You cannot terrify him, nor
govern him, nor persuade him, nor convince him. He
has his own positive opinion on all matters; not an
unwise one, usually for his own ends; and will ask no
advice of yours. He has no work to do—no tyrannical
instinct to obey. The earthworm has his digging; the

bee, her gathering and building; the spider, her cunning net-work; the ant, her treasury and accounts. All these are comparative slaves, or people of vulgar business. But your fly, free in the air, free in the chamber—a black incarnation of caprice—wandering, investigating, flitting, flirting, feasting at his will, with rich variety of choice in feast, from the heaped sweets in the grocer's window to those of the butcher's back-yard, and from the galled place on your cab-horse's back to the brown spot in the road, from which as the hoof disturbs him, he rises with angry republican buzz—what freedom is like his?

For captivity again, perhaps your poor watch-dog is as sorrowful a type as you will easily find. Mine certainly is. The day is lovely, but I must write this, and cannot go out with him. He is chained in the yard, because I do not like dogs in rooms, and the gardener does not like dogs in gardens. He has no books,—nothing but his own weary thoughts for company, and a group of those free flies, whom he snaps at, with sullen ill success. Such dim hope as he may have that I may yet take him out with me, will be, hour by hour, wearily disappointed; or, worse, darkened at once into a leaden despair by an authoritative "No"—too well understood. His fidelity only seals his fate; if he would not watch for me, he would be sent away, and go hunting with some happier master: but he watches, and is wise, and faithful, and miserable: and his high animal intellect only gives him the wistful powers of wonder, and sorrow, and desire, and affection, which embitter his captivity! Yet of the two, would we rather be watch-dog, or fly?

Indeed, the first point we have all to determine is not how free we are, but what kind of creatures we are. It is of small importance to any of us whether we get liberty; but of the greatest that we deserve it. Whether we can win it, fate must determine; but that we may be worthy of it, we may ourselves determine; and the sorrowfullest fate, of all that we can suffer, is to have it, *without* deserving it.

I have hardly patience to hold my pen and go on writing, as I remember (I would that it were possible for a few consecutive instants to forget) the infinite follies of modern thought in this matter, centred in the notion that liberty is good for a man, irrespectively of the use he is likely to make of it. Folly unfathomable! unspeakable! unendurable to look in the full face of, as the laugh of a cretin. You will send your child, will you, into a room where the table is loaded with sweet wine and fruit—some poisoned, some not?—you will say to him, "Choose freely, my little child! It is so good for you to have freedom of choice: it forms your character—your individuality! If you take the wrong cup, or the wrong berry, you will die before the day is over, but you will have acquired the dignity of a Free child"?

You think that puts the case too sharply? I tell you, lover of liberty, there is no choice offered to you, but it is similarly between life and death. There is no act, nor option of act, possible, but the wrong deed or option has poison in it which will stay in your veins thereafter forever. Never more to all eternity can you be as you might have been, had you not done that—chosen that. You have "formed your character," forsooth! No; if you have chosen ill, you have De-formed it, and that forever! In some choices, it had been better for you that a red-hot iron bar had struck you aside, scarred and helpless, than that you had so chosen. "You will know better next time!" No. Next time will never come. Next time the choice will be in quite another aspect—between quite different things,—you, weaker than you were by the evil into which you have fallen; it, more doubtful than it was, by the increased dimness of your sight. No one ever gets wiser by doing wrong, nor stronger. You will get wiser and stronger only by doing right, whether forced or not; the prime, the one need is to do *that,* under whatever compulsion, until you can do it without compulsion. And then you are a Man.

"What!" a wayward youth might perhaps answer, incredulously; "no one ever gets wiser by doing wrong? Shall I not know the world best by trying the wrong of it, and repenting? Have I not, even as it is, learned much by many of my errors?" Indeed, the effort by which partially you recovered yourself was precious; that part of your thought by which you discerned the error was precious. What wisdom and strength you kept, and rightly used, are rewarded; and in the pain and the repentance, and in the acquaintance with the aspects of folly and sin, you have learned *something;* how much less than you would have learned in right paths, can never be told, but that it *is* less is certain. Your liberty of choice has simply destroyed for you so much life and strength, never regainable. It is true you now know the habits of swine, and the taste of husks: do you think your father could not have taught you to know better habits and pleasanter tastes, if you had stayed in his house; and that the knowledge you have lost would not have been more, as well as sweeter, than that you have gained? But "it so forms my individuality to be free!" Your individuality was given you by God, and in your race; and if you have any to speak of, you will want no liberty. You will want a den to work in, and peace, and light—no more,—in absolute need; if more in any wise, it will still not be liberty, but direction, instruction, reproof, and sympathy. But if you have no individuality, if there is no true character nor true desire in you, then you will indeed want to be free. You will begin early; and, as a boy, desire to be a man; and, as a man, think yourself as good as every other. You will choose freely to eat, freely to drink, freely to stagger and fall, freely, at last, to curse yourself and die. Death is the only real freedom possible to us: and that is consummate freedom,—permission for every particle in the rotting body to leave its neighbour particle, and shift for itself. You call it "corruption" in the flesh; but before it comes to that, all liberty is an equal corruption in mind. You ask for freedom of thought; but if you have not sufficient grounds for thought, you have no business to think; and if you have sufficient grounds, you have no business to think wrong. Only one thought is possible to you, if you are wise—your liberty is geometrically proportionate to your folly.

"But all this glory and activity of our age; what are they owing to, but to our freedom of thought?" In a measure, they are owing—what good is in them—to the discovery of many lies, and the escape from the power of evil. Not to liberty, but to the deliverance from evil or cruel masters. Brave men have dared to examine lies which had long been taught, not because they were *free*-thinkers, but because they were such stern and close thinkers that the lie could no longer escape them. Of course the restriction of thought, or of its expression, by persecution, is merely a form of violence, justifiable or not, as other violence is, according to the character of the persons against whom it is exercised, and the divine and eternal laws which it vindicates or violates. We must not burn a man alive for saying that the Athanasian creed is ungrammatical, nor stop a bishop's salary because we are getting the worst of an argument with him; neither must we let drunken men howl in the public streets at night. There is much that is true in the part of Mr. Mill's essay on Liberty which treats of freedom of thought; some important truths are there beautifully expressed, but many, quite vital, are omitted; and the balance, therefore, is wrongly struck. The liberty of expression, with a great nation, would become like that in a well-educated company, in which there is indeed freedom of speech, but not of clamour; or like that in an orderly senate, in which men who deserve to be heard, are heard in due time, and under determined restrictions. The degree of liberty you can rightly grant to a number of men is in the inverse ratio of their desire for it; and a general hush, or call to order, would be often very desirable in this England of ours. For the rest, of any good or evil extant, it is impossible to say what measure is owing to restraint, and what to licence, where the right is balanced between them. . . .

In fine, the arguments for liberty may in general be summed in a few very simple forms as follows:—

Misguiding is mischievous: therefore, guiding is.

If the blind lead the blind, both fall into the ditch: therefore, nobody should lead anybody.

Lambs and fawns should be left free in the fields; much more bears and wolves.

If a man's gun and shot are his own, he may fire in any direction he pleases.

A fence across a road is inconvenient; much more, one at the side of it.

Babes should not be swaddled with their hands bound down at their sides: therefore, they should be thrown out to roll in the kennels naked.

None of these arguments are good, and the practical issues of them are worse. For there are certain eternal laws for human conduct which are quite clearly discernible by human reason. So far as these are discovered and obeyed, by whatever machinery or authority the obedience is procured, there follow life and strength. So far as they are disobeyed, by whatever good intention the disobedience is brought about, there follow ruin and sorrow. And the first duty of every man in the world is to find his true master, and, for his own good, submit to him; and to find his true inferior, and, for that inferior's good, conquer him. The punishment is sure, if we either refuse the reverence, or are too cowardly and indolent to enforce the compulsion. A base nation crucifies or poisons its wise men, and lets its fools rave and rot in its streets. A wise nation obeys the one, restrains the other, and cherishes all.—*The Queen of the Air*, secs. 143-156.                                         **1869**

## MATTHEW ARNOLD (1822-1888)

## SWEETNESS AND LIGHT

### (From *Culture and Anarchy*)

THE disparagers of culture make its motive curiosity; sometimes, indeed, they make its motive mere exclusiveness and vanity. The culture which is supposed to plume itself on a smattering of Greek and Latin is a culture which is begotten by nothing so intellectual as curiosity; it is valued either out of sheer vanity and ignorance or else as an engine of social and class distinction, separating its holder, like a badge or title, from other people who have not got it. No serious man would call this *culture*, or attach any value to it, as culture, at all. To find the real ground for the very different estimate which serious people will set upon culture, we must find some motive for culture in the terms of which may lie a real ambiguity; and such a motive the word *curiosity* gives us.

I have before now pointed out that we English do

not, like the foreigners, use this word in a good sense as well as in a bad sense. With us the word is always used in a somewhat disapproving sense. A liberal and intelligent eagerness about the things of the mind may be meant by a foreigner when he speaks of curiosity, but with us the word always conveys a certain notion of frivolous and unedifying activity. In the *Quarterly Review*, some little time ago, was an estimate of the celebrated French critic, M. Sainte-Beuve, and a very inadequate estimate it in my judgment was. And its inadequacy consisted chiefly in this: that in our English way it left out of sight the double sense really involved in the word *curiosity*, thinking enough was said to stamp M. Sainte-Beuve with blame if it was said that he was impelled in his operations as a critic by curiosity, and omitting either to perceive that M. Sainte-Beuve himself, and many other people with him, would consider that this was praiseworthy and not blameworthy, or to point out why it ought really to be accounted worthy of blame and not of praise. For as there is a curiosity about intellectual matters which is futile, and merely a disease, so there is certainly a curiosity,—a desire after the things of the mind simply for their own sakes and for the pleasure of seeing them as they are,—which is, in an intelligent being, natural and laudable. Nay, and the very desire to see things as they are implies a balance and regulation of mind which is not often attained without fruitful effort, and which is the very opposite of the blind and diseased impulse of mind which is what we mean to blame when we blame curiosity. Montesquieu says: "The first motive which ought to impel us to study is the desire to augment the excellence of our nature, and to render an intelligent being yet more intelligent." This is the true ground to assign for the genuine scientific passion, however manifested, and for culture, viewed simply as a fruit of this passion; and it is a worthy ground, even though we let the term *curiosity* stand to describe it.

But there is of culture another view, in which not solely the scientific passion, the sheer desire to see things as they are, natural and proper in an intelligent being, appears as the ground of it. There is a view in which all the love of our neighbour, the impulses towards action, help, and beneficence, the desire for removing human error, clearing human confusion, and diminishing human misery, the noble aspiration to leave the world better and happier than we found it,—motives eminently such as are called social,—come in as part of the grounds of culture, and the main and pre-eminent part. Culture is then properly described not as having its origin in curiosity, but as having its origin in the love of perfection; it is *a study of perfection*. It moves by the force, not merely or primarily of the scientific passion for pure knowledge, but also of the moral and social passion for doing good. As, in the first view of it, we took for its worthy motto Montesquieu's words: "To render an intelligent being yet more intelligent!" so, in the second view of it, there is no better motto which it can have than these words of Bishop Wilson: "To make reason and the will of God prevail!"

Only, whereas the passion for doing good is apt to be overhasty in determining what reason and the will of God say, because its turn is for acting rather than thinking and it wants to be beginning to act; and whereas it is apt to take its own conceptions, which proceed from its own state of development and share in all the imperfections and immaturities of this, for a basis of action; what distinguishes culture is, that it is possessed by the scientific passion as well as by the passion of doing good; that it demands worthy notions of reason and the will of God, and does not readily suffer its own crude conceptions to substitute themselves for them. And knowing that no action or institution can be salutary and stable which is not based on reason and the will of God, it is not so bent on acting and instituting, even with the great aim of diminishing human error and misery ever before its thoughts, but that it can remember that acting and instituting are of little use, unless we know how and what we ought to act and to institute.

This culture is more interesting and more far-reaching than that other, which is founded solely on the scientific passion for knowing. But it needs times of faith and ardour, times when the intellectual horizon is opening and widening all round us, to flourish in. And is not the close and bounded intellectual horizon within which we have long lived and moved now lifting up, and are not new lights finding free passage to shine in upon us? For a long time there was no passage for them to make their way in upon us, and then it was of no use to think of adapting the world's action to them. Where was the hope of making reason and the will of God prevail among people who had a routine which they had christened reason and the will of God, in which they were inextricably bound, and beyond which they had no power of looking? But now the iron force of adhesion to the old routine,—social, political, religious,—has wonderfully yielded; the iron force of exclusion of all which is new has wonderfully yielded. The danger now is, not that people should obstinately refuse to allow anything but their old routine to pass for reason and the will of God, but either that they should allow some novelty or other to pass for these too easily, or else that they should underrate the importance of them altogether, and think it enough to follow action for its own sake, without troubling themselves to make reason and the will of

God prevail therein. Now, then, is the moment for culture to be of service, culture which believes in making reason and the will of God prevail, believes in perfection, is the study and pursuit of perfection, and is no longer debarred, by a rigid invincible exclusion of whatever is new, from getting acceptance for its ideas, simply because they are new.

The moment this view of culture is seized, the moment it is regarded not solely as the endeavour to see things as they are, to draw towards a knowledge of the universal order which seems to be intended and aimed at in the world, and which it is a man's happiness to go along with or his misery to go counter to,—to learn, in short, the will of God,—the moment, I say, culture is considered not merely as the endeavour to *see* and *learn* this, but as the endeavour, also, to make it *prevail,* the moral, the social, and beneficent character of culture becomes manifest. The mere endeavour to see and learn the truth for our own personal satisfaction is indeed a commencement for making it prevail, a preparing the way for this, which always serves this, and is wrongly, therefore, stamped with blame absolutely in itself and not only in its caricature and degeneration. But perhaps it has got stamped with blame, and disparaged with the dubious title of curiosity, because in comparison with this wider endeavour of such great and plain utility it looks selfish, petty, and unprofitable.

And religion, the greatest and most important of the efforts by which the human race has manifested its impulse to perfect itself,—religion, that voice of the deepest human experience,—does not only enjoin and sanction the aim which is the great aim of culture, the aim of setting ourselves to ascertain what perfection is and to make it prevail; but also, in determining generally in what human perfection consists, religion comes to a conclusion identical with that which culture,—culture seeking the determination of this question through *all* the voices of human experience which have been heard upon it, of art, science, poetry, philosophy, history, as well as of religion, in order to give a greater fulness and certainty to its solution,—likewise reaches. Religion says: *The kingdom of God is within you;* and culture, in like manner, places human perfection in an *internal* condition, in the growth and predominance of our humanity proper, as distinguished from our animality. It places it in the ever-increasing efficacy and in the general harmonious expansion of those gifts of thought and feeling, which make the peculiar dignity, wealth, and happiness of human nature. As I have said on a former occasion: "It is in making endless additions to itself, in the endless expansion of its powers, in endless growth in wisdom and beauty, that the spirit of the human race finds its ideal. To reach this ideal, culture is an indispensable aid, and that is the true value of culture." Not a having and a resting, but a growing and a becoming, is the character of perfection as culture conceives it; and here, too, it coincides with religion.

And because men are all members of one great whole, and the sympathy which is in human nature will not allow one member to be indifferent to the rest or to have a perfect welfare independent of the rest, the expansion of our humanity, to suit the idea of perfection which culture forms, must be a *general* expansion. Perfection, as culture conceives it, is not possible while the individual remains isolated. The individual is required, under pain of being stunted and enfeebled in his own development if he disobeys, to carry others along with him in his march towards perfection, to be continually doing all he can to enlarge and increase the volume of the human stream sweeping thitherward. And here, once more, culture lays on us the same obligation as religion, which says, as Bishop Wilson has admirably put it, that "to promote the kingdom of God is to increase and hasten one's own happiness."

But, finally, perfection,—as culture from a thorough disinterested study of human nature and human experience learns to conceive it —is a harmonious expansion of *all* the powers which make the beauty and worth of human nature, and is not consistent with the over-development of any one power at the expense of the rest. Here culture goes beyond religion, as religion is generally conceived by us.

If culture, then, is a study of perfection, and of harmonious perfection, general perfection, and perfection which consists in becoming something rather than in having something, in an inward condition of the mind and spirit, not in an outward set of circumstances,—it is clear that culture, instead of being the frivolous and useless thing which Mr. Bright, and Mr. Frederic Harrison, and many other Liberals are apt to call it, has a very important function to fulfil for mankind. And this function is particularly important in our modern world, of which the whole civilisation is, to a much greater degree than the civilisation of Greece and Rome, mechanical and external, and tends constantly to become more so. But above all in our own country has culture a weighty part to perform, because here that mechanical character, which civilisation tends to take everywhere, is shown in the most eminent degree. Indeed nearly all the characters of perfection, as culture teaches us to fix them, meet in this country with some powerful tendency which thwarts them and sets them at defiance. The idea of perfection as an *inward* condition of the mind and spirit is at variance with the mechanical and material civilisation in esteem with us; and nowhere, as I have said, so much in esteem as with us. The idea of perfection as a *general* expansion of the human family is at variance with our strong individualism, our hatred of all limits to the unrestrained swing of the individual's personality, our maxim of "every man for himself." Above all, the idea of perfection as a *harmonious* expansion of human nature is at variance with our want of flexibility, with our inaptitude for seeing more than one side of a thing, with our intense energetic absorption in the particular pursuit we happen to be following. So culture has a rough task to achieve in this country. Its preachers have, and are likely long to have, a hard time of it, and they will much oftener be regarded, for a great while to come, as elegant or spurious Jeremiahs than as friends and benefactors. That, however, will not prevent their doing in the end good service if they persevere. And, meanwhile, the mode of action they have to pursue, and the sort of habits they must fight against, ought to be made quite clear for every one to see, who may be willing to look at the matter attentively and dispassionately.

Faith in machinery is, I said, our besetting danger; often in machinery most absurdly disproportioned to the end which this machinery, if it is to do any good at all, is to serve; but always in machinery, as if it had a value in and for itself. What is freedom but machinery? what is population but machinery? what is coal but machinery? what are railroads but machinery? what is wealth but machinery? what are, even, religious organisations but machinery? Now almost every voice in England is accustomed to speak of these things as if they were precious ends in themselves, and therefore had some of the characters of perfection indisputably joined to them. I have before now noticed Mr. Roebuck's stock argument for proving the greatness and happiness of England as she is, and for quite stopping the mouths of all gainsayers. Mr. Roebuck is never weary of reiterating this argument of his, so I do not know why I should be weary of noticing it. "May not every man in England say what he likes?"—Mr. Roebuck perpetually asks; and that, he thinks, is quite sufficient, and when every man may say what he likes, our aspirations ought to be satisfied. But the aspirations of culture, which is the study of perfection, are not satisfied, unless what men say, when they may say what they like, is worth saying,—has good in it, and more good than bad. In the same way the *Times,* replying to some foreign strictures on the dress, looks, and behaviour of the English abroad, urges that the English ideal is that every one should be free to do and to look just as he likes. But culture indefatigably tries, not to make what each raw person may like the rule by which he fashions himself; but to draw ever nearer to a sense of what is indeed beautiful, graceful, and becoming, and to get the raw person to like that.

And in the same way with respect to railroads and coal. Every one must have observed the strange language current during the late discussions as to the possible failures of our supplies of coal. Our coal, thousands of people were saying, is the real basis of our national greatness; if our coal runs short, there is an end of the greatness of England. But what *is* greatness?—culture makes us ask. Greatness is a spiritual condition worthy to excite love, interest, and admiration; and the outward proof of possessing greatness is that we excite love, interest, and admiration. If England were swallowed up by the sea tomorrow, which of the two, a hundred years hence, would most excite the love, interest, and admiration of mankind,—would most, therefore, show the evidences of having possessed greatness,—the England of the last twenty years, or the England of Elizabeth, of a time of splendid spiritual effort, but when our coal, and our industrial operations depending on coal, were very little developed? Well, then, what an unsound habit of mind it must be which makes us talk of things like coal or iron as constituting the greatness of England, and how salutary a friend is culture, bent on seeing things as they are, and thus dissipating delusions of this kind and fixing standards of perfection that are real!

Wealth, again, that end to which our prodigious works for material advantage are directed,—the commonest of commonplaces tells us how men are always apt to regard wealth as a precious end in itself; and certainly they have never been so apt thus to regard it as they are in England at the present time. Never did people believe anything more firmly than nine Englishmen out of ten at the present day believe that our greatness and welfare are proved by our being so very rich. Now, the use of culture is that it helps us, by means of its spiritual standard of perfection, to regard wealth as but machinery, and not only to say, as a matter of words that we regard wealth as but machinery, but really to perceive and feel that it is so. If it were not for this purging effect wrought upon our minds by culture, the whole world, the future as well as the present, would inevitably belong to the Philistines. The people who believe most that our greatness and welfare are proved by our being very rich, and who most give their lives and thoughts to becoming rich, are just the very people whom we call Philistines. Culture says: "Consider these people, then, their way of life, their habits, their manners, the very tones of their voice; look at them attentively; observe the literature they read, the things which give them pleasure, the words which come forth out of their mouths, the thoughts which make the furniture of their minds; would any amount of wealth be worth having with the condition that one was to become just like these people by having it?" And thus culture begets a dissatisfaction which is of the highest possible value in stemming the common tide of men's thoughts in a wealthy and industrial community, and which saves the future, as one may hope, from being vulgarised, even if it cannot save the present.

Population, again, and bodily health and vigour, are things which are nowhere treated in such an unintelligent, misleading, exaggerated way as in England. Both are really machinery; yet how many people all around us do we see rest in them and fail to look beyond them! Why, one has heard people, fresh from reading certain articles of the *Times* on the Registrar-General's returns of marriages and births in this country, who would talk of our large English families in quite a solemn strain, as if they had something in itself beautiful, elevating, and meritorious in them; as if the British Philistine would have only to present himself before the Great Judge with his twelve children, in order to be received among the sheep as a matter of right!

But bodily health and vigour, it may be said, are not to be classed with wealth and population as mere machinery; they have a more real and essential value. True; but only as they are more intimately connected with a perfect spiritual condition than wealth or population are. The moment we disjoin them from the idea of a perfect spiritual condition, and pursue them, as we do pursue them, for their own sake and as ends in themselves, our worship of them becomes as mere worship of machinery, as our worship of wealth or population, and as unintelligent and vulgarising a worship as that is. Every one with anything like an adequate idea of human perfection has distinctly marked this subordination to higher and spiritual ends of the cultivation of bodily vigour and activity. "Bodily exercise profiteth little; but godliness is profitable unto all things," says the author of the Epistle to Timothy. And the utilitarian Franklin says just as explicitly: "Eat and drink such an exact quantity as suits the constitution of thy body, *in reference to the services of the mind.*" But the point of view of culture, keeping the mark of human perfection simply and broadly in view, and not assigning to this perfection, as religion or utilitarianism assigns to it, a special and limited character, this point of view, I say, of culture is best given by these words of Epictetus:—"It is a sign of ἀφυΐα," says he,—that is, of a nature not finely tempered,—"to give yourselves up to things which relate to the body; to make, for instance, a great fuss about exercise, a great fuss about eating, a great fuss about drinking, a great fuss about walking, a great fuss about riding. All these things ought to be done merely by the way: the formation of the spirit and character must be our real concern." This is admirable; and, indeed, the Greek word εὐφυΐα, a finely tempered nature, gives exactly the notion of perfection as culture brings us to conceive it: a harmonious perfection, a perfection in which the characters of beauty and intelligence are both present, which unites "the two noblest of things,"—as Swift, who of one of the two, at any rate, had himself all too little, most happily calls them in his *Battle of the Books,*—"the two noblest of things, *sweetness and light.*" The εὐφυής is the man who tends towards sweetness and light; the ἀφυής on the other hand, is our Philistine. The immense spiritual significance of the Greeks is due to their having been inspired with this central and happy idea of the essential character of human perfection; and Mr. Bright's misconception of culture, as a smattering of Greek and Latin, comes itself, after all, from this wonderful significance of the Greeks having affected the very machinery of our education, and is in itself a kind of homage to it.

In thus making sweetness and light to be characters of perfection, culture is of like spirit with poetry, follows one law with poetry. Far more than on our freedom, our population, and our industrialism, many amongst us rely upon our religious organisations to save us. I have called religion a yet more important manifestation of human nature than poetry, because it has worked on a broader scale for perfection, and with greater masses of men. But the idea of beauty and of a human nature perfect on all its sides, which is the dominant idea of poetry, is a true and invaluable idea, though it has not yet had the success that the idea of conquering the obvious faults of our animality, and of a human nature perfect on the moral side,—which is the dominant idea of religion,—has been enabled to have; and it is destined, adding to itself the religious idea of a devout energy, to transform and govern the other.

The best art and poetry of the Greeks, in which religion and poetry are one, in which the idea of beauty and of a human nature perfect on all sides adds to itself a religious and devout energy, and works in the strength of that, is on this account of such surpassing interest and instructiveness for us, though it was,—as, having regard to the human race in general, and, indeed, having regard to the Greeks themselves, we must own,—a premature attempt, an attempt which for success needed the moral and religious fibre in humanity to be more braced and developed than it had yet been. But Greece did not err in having the idea of beauty, harmony, and complete human perfection, so present and paramount. It is impossible to have this idea too present and paramount; only, the moral fibre must be braced too. And we, because we have braced the moral fibre, are not on that

account in the right way, if at the same time the idea
of beauty, harmony, and complete human perfection, is
wanting or misapprehended amongst us; and evidently it
*is* wanting or misapprehended at present. And when we
rely as we do on our religious organisations, which in
themselves do not and cannot give us this idea, and think
we have done enough if we make them spread and prevail, then I say, we fall into our common fault of over-
valuing machinery.

Nothing is more common than for people to confound
the inward peace and satisfaction which follows the
subduing of the obvious faults of our animality with
what I may call absolute inward peace and satisfaction,
—the peace and satisfaction which are reached as we
draw near to complete spiritual perfection, and not
merely to moral perfection, or rather to relative moral
perfection. No people in the world have done more and
struggled more to attain this relative moral perfection
than our English race has. For no people in the world
has the command to *resist the devil*, to *overcome the
wicked one*, in the nearest and most obvious sense of
those words, had such a pressing force and reality. And
we have had our reward, not only in the great worldly
prosperity which our obedience to this command has
brought us, but also, and far more, in great inward
peace and satisfaction. But to me few things are more
pathetic than to see people, on the strength of the
inward peace and satisfaction which their rudimentary
efforts towards perfection have brought them, employ,
concerning their incomplete perfection and the religious
organisations within which they have found it, language
which properly applies only to complete perfection, and
is a far-off echo of the human soul's prophecy of it.
Religion itself, I need hardly say, supplies them in
abundance with this grand language. And very freely do

they use it; yet it is really the severest possible criticism of such an incomplete perfection as alone we have yet reached through our religious organisations.

The impulse of the English race towards moral development and self-conquest has nowhere so powerfully manifested itself as in Puritanism. Nowhere has Puritanism found so adequate an expression as in the religious organisation of the Independents. The modern Independents have a newspaper, the *Nonconformist*, written with great sincerity and ability. The motto, the standard, the profession of faith which this organ of theirs carries aloft, is: "The Dissidence of Dissent and the Protestantism of the Protestant religion." There is sweetness and light, and an ideal of complete harmonious human perfection! One need not go to culture and poetry to find language to judge it. Religion, with its instinct for perfection, supplies language to judge it, language, too, which is in our mouths every day. "Finally, be of one mind, united in feeling," says St. Peter. There is an ideal which judges the Puritan ideal: "The Dissidence of Dissent and the Protestantism of the Protestant religion!" And religious organisations like this are what people believe in, rest in, would give their lives for! Such, I say, is the wonderful virtue of even the beginnings of perfection, of having conquered even the plain faults of our animality, that the religious organisation which has helped us to do it can seem to us something precious, salutary, and to be propagated, even when it wears such a brand of imperfection on its forehead as this. And men have got such a habit of giving to the language of religion a special application, of making it a mere jargon, that for the condemnation which religion itself passes on the shortcomings of their religious organisations they have no ear; they are sure to cheat themselves and to explain this condemnation away.

They can only be reached by the criticism which culture, like poetry, speaking a language not to be sophisticated, and resolutely testing these organisations by the ideal of a human perfection complete on all sides, applies to them.

But men of culture and poetry, it will be said, are again and again failing, and failing conspicuously, in the necessary first stage to a harmonious perfection, in the subduing of the great obvious faults of our animality, which it is the glory of these religious organisations to have helped us to subdue. True, they do often so fail. They have often been without the virtues as well as the faults of the Puritan; it has been one of their dangers that they so felt the Puritan's faults that they too much neglected the practice of his virtues. I will not, however, exculpate them at the Puritan's expense. They have often failed in morality, and morality is indispensable. And they have been punished for their failure, as the Puritan has been rewarded for his performance. They have been punished wherein they erred; but their ideal of beauty, of sweetness and light, and a human nature complete on all its sides, remains the true ideal of perfection still; just as the Puritan's ideal of perfection remains narrow and inadequate, although for what he did well he has been richly rewarded. Notwithstanding the mighty results of the Pilgrim Fathers' voyage, they and their standard of perfection are rightly judged when we figure to ourselves Shakespeare or Virgil,—souls in whom sweetness and light, and all that in human nature is most humane, were eminent,—accompanying them on their voyage, and think what intolerable company Shakespeare and Virgil would have found them! In the same way let us judge the religious organisations which we see all around us. Do not let us deny the good and the happiness which they have accomplished; but do not let us fail to see clearly that their idea of human perfection is narrow and inadequate, and that the Dissidence of Dissent and the Protestantism of the Protestant religion will never bring humanity to its true goal. As I said with regard to wealth: Let us look at the life of those who live in and for it,—so I say with regard to the religious organisations. Look at the life imaged in such a newspaper as the *Nonconformist,*—a life of jealousy of the Establishment, disputes, tea-meetings, openings of chapels, sermons; and then think of it as an ideal of a human life completing itself on all sides, and aspiring with all its organs after sweetness, light, and perfection!

Another newspaper, representing, like the *Nonconformist,* one of the religious organisations of this country, was a short time ago giving an account of the crowd at Epsom on the Derby day, and of all the vice and hideousness which was to be seen in that crowd; and then the writer turned suddenly round upon Professor Huxley, and asked him how he proposed to cure all this vice and hideousness without religion. I confess I felt disposed to ask the asker this question: and how do you propose to cure it with such a religion as yours? How is the ideal of a life so unlovely, so unattractive, so incomplete, so narrow, so far removed from a true and satisfying ideal of human perfection, as is the life of your religious organisation as you yourself reflect it, to conquer and transform all this vice and hideousness? Indeed, the strongest plea for the study of perfection as pursued by culture, the clearest proof of the actual inadequacy of the idea of perfection held by the religious organisations,—expressing, as I have said, the most widespread effort which the human race has yet made after perfection,—is to be found in the state of our life and society with these in possession of it, and having

been in possession of it I know not how many hundred
years. We are all of us included in some religious organisation or other; we all call ourselves, in the sublime and
aspiring language of religion which I have before noticed, *children of God*. Children of God;—it is an immense pretension!—and how are we to justify it? By
the works which we do, and the words which we speak.
And the work which we collective children of God do,
our grand centre of life, our *city* which we have builded
for us to dwell in, is London! London, with its unutter-
able external hideousness, and with its internal canker
of *publicè egestas, privatim opulentia,*—to use the words
which Sallust puts into Cato's mouth about Rome,—
unequalled in the world! The word, again, which we
children of God speak, the voice which most hits our
collective thought, the newspaper with the largest circulation in England, nay, with the largest circulation in
the whole world, is the *Daily Telegraph!* I say that
when our religious organisations,—which I admit to
express the most considerable effort after perfection that
our race has yet made,—land us in no better result than
this, it is high time to examine carefully their idea of
perfection, to see whether it does not leave out of account sides and forces of human nature which we might
turn to great use; whether it would not be more operative if it were more complete. And I say that the English
reliance on our religious organisations and on their ideas
of human perfection just as they stand, is like our reliance on freedom, on muscular Christianity, on population, on coal, on wealth,—mere belief in machinery, and
unfruitful; and that it is wholesomely counteracted by
culture, bent on seeing things as they are, and on drawing the human race onwards to a more complete, a harmonious perfection.

Culture, however, shows its single-minded love of perfection, its desire simply to make reason and the will of God prevail, its freedom from fanaticism, by its attitude towards all this machinery, even while it insists that it *is* machinery. Fanatics, seeing the mischief men do themselves by their blind belief in some machinery or other, —whether it is wealth and industrialism, or whether it is the cultivation of bodily strength and activity, or whether it is a political organisation,—or whether it is a religious organisation,—oppose with might and main the tendency to this or that political and religious organisation, or to games and athletic exercises, or to wealth and industrialism, and try violently to stop it. But the flexibility which sweetness and light give, and which is one of the rewards of culture pursued in good faith, enables a man to see that a tendency may be necessary, and even, as a preparation for something in the future, salutary, and yet that the generations or individuals who obey this tendency are sacrificed to it, that they fall short of the hope of perfection by following it; and that its mischiefs are to be criticised, lest it should take too firm a hold and last after it has served its purpose.

Mr. Gladstone well pointed out, in a speech at Paris, —and others have pointed out the same thing,—how necessary is the present great movement towards wealth and industrialism, in order to lay broad foundations of material well-being for the society of the future. The worst of these justifications is, that they are generally addressed to the very people engaged, body and soul, in the movement in question; at all events, that they are always seized with the greatest avidity by these people, and taken by them as quite justifying their life; and that thus they tend to harden them in their sins. Now, culture admits the necessity of the movement towards fortune-making and exaggerated industrialism, readily follows that the future may derive benefit from it; but insists, at the same time, that the passing generations of industrialists,—forming, for the most part, the stout main body of Philistinism,—are sacrificed to it. In the same way, the result of all the games and sports which occupy the passing generation of boys and young men may be the establishment of a better and sounder physical type for the future to work with. Culture does not set itself against the games and sports; it congratulates the future, and hopes it will make a good use of its improved physical basis; but it points out that our passing generation of boys and young men is, meantime, sacrificed. Puritanism was perhaps necessary to develop the moral fibre of the English race, Nonconformity to break the yoke of ecclesiastical domination over men's minds and to prepare the way for freedom of thought in the distant future; still, culture points out that the harmonious perfection of generations of Puritans and Nonconformists have been, in consequence, sacrificed. Freedom of speech may be necessary for the society of the future, but the young lions of the *Daily Telegraph* in the meanwhile are sacrificed. A voice for every man in his country's government may be necessary for the society of the future, but meanwhile Mr. Beales and Mr. Bradlaugh are sacrificed.

Oxford, the Oxford of the past, has many faults; and she has heavily paid for them in defeat, in isolation, in want of hold upon the modern world. Yet we in Oxford, brought up amidst the beauty and sweetness of that beautiful place, have not failed to seize one truth,—the truth that beauty and sweetness are essential characters of a complete human perfection. When I insist on this, I am all in the faith and tradition of Oxford. I say boldly that this our sentiment for beauty and sweetness, our sentiment against hideousness and rawness, has

been at the bottom of our attachment to so many beaten
causes, of our opposition to so many triumphant movements. And the sentiment is true, and has never been
wholly defeated, and has shown its power even in its
defeat. We have not won our political battles, we have
not carried our main points, we have not stopped our
adversaries' advance, we have not marched victoriously
with the modern world; but we have told silently upon
the mind of the country, we have prepared currents of
feeling which sap our adversaries' position when it
seems gained, we have kept up our own communications
with the future. Look at the course of the great movement which shook Oxford to its centre some thirty years
ago! It was directed, as any one who reads Dr. Newman's *Apology* may see, against what in one word may
be called "Liberalism." Liberalism prevailed; it was the
appointed force to do the work of the hour; it was
necessary, it was inevitable that it should prevail. The
Oxford movement was broken, it failed; our wrecks are
scattered on every shore:—

Quæ regio in terris nostri non plena laboris?

But what was it, this liberalism, as Dr. Newman saw
it, and as it really broke the Oxford movement? It was
the great middle-class liberalism, which had for the
cardinal points of its belief the Reform Bill of 1832,
and local self-government, in politics; in the social
sphere, free-trade, unrestricted competition, and the
making of large industrial fortunes; in the religious
sphere, the Dissidence of Dissent and the Protestantism
of the Protestant religion. I do not say that other and
more intelligent forces than this were not opposed to
the Oxford movement: but this was the force which
really beat it; this was the force which Dr. Newman

felt himself fighting with; this was the force which till only the other day seemed to be the paramount force in this country, and to be in possession of the future; this was the force whose achievements fill Mr. Lowe with such inexpressible admiration, and whose rule he was so horror-struck to see threatened. And where is this great force of Philistinism now? It is thrust into the second rank, it is become a power of yesterday, it has lost the future. A new power has suddenly appeared, a power which it is impossible yet to judge fully, but which is certainly a wholly different force from middle-class liberalism; different in its cardinal points of belief, different in its tendencies in every sphere. It loves and admires neither the legislation of middle-class Parliaments, nor the local self-government of middle-class vestries, nor the unrestricted competition of middle-class industrialists, nor the Dissidence of middle-class Dissent and the Protestantism of middle-class Protestant religion. I am not now praising this new force, or saying that its own ideals are better; all I say is, that they are wholly different. And who will estimate how much the currents of feeling created by Dr. Newman's movements, the keen desire for beauty and sweetness which it nourished, the deep aversion it manifested to the hardness and vulgarity of middle-class liberalism, the strong light it turned on the hideous and grotesque illusions of middle-class Protestantism,—who will estimate how much all these contributed to swell the tide of secret dissatisfaction which has mined the ground under self-confident liberalism of the last thirty years, and has prepared the way for its sudden collapse and supersession? It is in this manner that the sentiment of Oxford for beauty and sweetness conquers, and in this manner long may it continue to conquer!

In this manner it works to the same end as culture,

and there is plenty of work for it yet to do. I have said that the new and more democratic force which is now superseding our old middle-class liberalism cannot yet be rightly judged. It has its main tendencies still to form. We hear promises of its giving us administrative reform, law reform, reform of education, and I know not what; but those promises come rather from its advocates, wishing to make a good plea for it and to justify it for superseding middle-class liberalism, than from clear tendencies which it has itself yet developed. But meanwhile it has plenty of well-intentioned friends against whom culture may with advantage continue to uphold steadily its ideal of human perfection; that this is *an inward spiritual activity, having for its characters increased sweetness, increased light, increased life, increased sympathy.* Mr. Bright, who has a foot in both worlds, the world of middle-class liberalism and the world of democracy, but who brings most of his ideas from the world of middle-class liberalism in which he was bred, always inclines to inculcate that faith in machinery to which, as we have seen, Englishmen are so prone, and which has been the bane of middle-class liberalism. He complains with a sorrowful indignation of people who "appear to have no proper estimate of the value of the franchise"; he leads his disciples to believe,—what the Englishman is always too ready to believe,—that the having a vote, like the having a large family, or a large business, or large muscles, has in itself some edifying and perfecting effect upon human nature. Or else he cries out to the democracy,—"the men," as he calls them, "upon whose shoulders the greatness of England rests,"—he cries out to them: "See what you have done! I look over this country and see the cities you have built, the railroads you have made, the manufactures you have produced, the cargoes which freight the ships of the greatest mercantile navy the world has ever seen! I see that you have converted by your labours what was once a wilderness, these islands, into a fruitful garden; I know that you have created this wealth, and are a nation whose name is a word of power throughout all the world." Why, this is just the very style of laudation with which Mr. Roebuck or Mr. Lowe debauches the minds of the middle classes, and makes such Philistines of them. It is the same fashion of teaching a man to value himself not on what he *is*, not on his progress in sweetness and light, but on the number of the railroads he has constructed, or the bigness of the tabernacle he has built. Only the middle classes are told they have done it all with their energy, self-reliance, and capital, and the democracy are told they have done it all with their hands and sinews. But teaching the democracy to put its trust in achievements of this kind is merely training them to be Philistines to take the place of the Philistines whom they are superseding; and they too, like the middle class, will be encouraged to sit down at the banquet of the future without having on a wedding garment, and nothing excellent can then come from them. Those who know their besetting faults, those who have watched them and listened to them, or those who will read the instructive account recently given of them by one of themselves, the *Journeyman Engineer*, will agree that the idea which culture sets before us of perfection,—an increased spiritual activity, having for its characters increased sweetness, increased light, increased life, increased sympathy,—is an idea which the new democracy needs far more than the idea of the blessedness of the franchise, or the wonderfulness of its own industrial performances.

The pursuit of perfection, then, is the pursuit of sweetness and light. He who works for sweetness and light, works to make reason and the will of God prevail. He who works for machinery, he who works for hatred, works only for confusion. Culture looks beyond machinery, culture hates hatred; culture has one great passion, the passion for sweetness and light. It has one even yet greater!—the passion for making them *prevail*. It is not satisfied till we *all* come to a perfect man; it knows that the sweetness and light of the few must be imperfect until the raw and unkindled masses of humanity are touched with sweetness and light. If I have not shrunk from saying that we must work for sweetness and light, so neither have I shrunk from saying that we must have a broad basis, must have sweetness and light for as many as possible. Again and again I have insisted how those are the happy moments of humanity, how those are the marking epochs of a people's life, how those are the flowering times for literature and art and all the creative power of genius, when there is a *national* glow of life and thought, when the whole of society is in the fullest measure permeated by thought, sensible to beauty, intelligent and alive. Only it must be *real* thought and *real* beauty; *real* sweetness and *real* light. Plenty of people will try to give the masses, as they call them, an intellectual food prepared and adapted in the way they think proper for the actual condition of the masses. The ordinary popular literature is an example of this way of working on the masses. Plenty of people will try to indoctrinate the masses with the set of ideas and judgments constituting the creed of their own profession or party. Our religious and political organisations give an example of this way of working on the masses. I condemn neither way; but culture works differently. It does not try to teach down to the level of inferior classes; it does not try to win them for this or that sect of its own, with ready-made judgments and watchwords. It seeks to do away with classes; to make the best that has been thought and known in the world current everywhere; to make all men live in an atmosphere of sweetness and light, where they may use ideas, as it uses them itself, freely,—nourished, and not bound by them.

This is the *social idea;* and the men of culture are the true apostles of equality. The great men of culture are those who have had a passion for diffusing, for making prevail, for carrying from one end of society to the other, the best knowledge, the best ideas of their time; who have laboured to divest knowledge of all that was harsh, uncouth, difficult, abstract, professional, exclusive; to humanise it, to make it efficient outside the clique of the cultivated and learned, yet still remaining the *best* knowledge and thought of the time, and a true source, therefore, of sweetness and light. Such a man was Abelard in the Middle Ages, in spite of all his imperfections; and thence the boundless emotion and enthusiasm which Abelard excited. Such were Lessing and Herder in Germany, at the end of the last century; and their services to Germany were in this way inestimably precious. Generations will pass, and literary monuments will accumulate, and works far more perfect than the works of Lessing and Herder will be produced in Germany; and yet the names of these two men will fill a German with a reverence and enthusiasm such as the names of the most gifted masters will hardly awaken. And why? Because they humanised *knowledge;* because they broadened the basis of life and intelligence; because they worked powerfully to diffuse sweetness and light, to make reason and the will of God prevail. With Saint Augustine they said: "Let us not leave thee alone to make in the secret of thy knowledge, as thou didst before the creation of the firmament, the division of ligh<sup></sup>

from darkness; let the children of thy spirit, placed in their firmament, make their light shine upon the earth, mark the division of night and day, and announce the revolution of the times; for the old order is passed, and the new arises; the night is spent, the day is come forth; and thou shalt crown the year with thy blessing, when thou shalt send forth labourers into thy harvest sown by other hands than theirs; when thou shalt send forth new labourers to new seed-times, whereof the harvest shall be not yet."

1869

## THOMAS HENRY HUXLEY (1825-1895)

### A LIBERAL EDUCATION

YET it is a very plain and elementary truth that the life, the fortune, and the happiness of every one of us, and, more or less, of those who are connected with us, do depend upon our knowing something of the rules of a game infinitely more difficult and complicated than chess. It is a game which has been played for untold ages, every man and woman of us being one of the two players in a game of his or her own. The chess-board is the world, the pieces are the phenomena of the universe, the rules of the game are what we call the laws of Nature. The player on the other side is hidden from us. We know that his play is always fair, just, and patient. But also we know, to our cost, that he never overlooks a mistake, or makes the smallest allowance for ignorance. To the man who plays well, the highest stakes are paid, with that sort of overflowing generosity with which the strong shows delight in strength. And one who plays ill is checkmated—without haste, but without remorse.

\* \* \* \* \* \*

Well, what I mean by education is learning the rules of this mighty game. In other words, education is the instruction of the intellect in the laws of Nature, under which name I include not merely things and their forces, but men and their ways; and the fashioning of the affections and of the will into an earnest and loving desire to move in harmony with those laws. For me, education means neither more nor less than this. Anything which professes to call itself education must be tried by this standard, and if it fails to stand the test, I will not call it education, whatever may be the force of authority, or of numbers, upon the other side.

It is important to remember that, in strictness, there is no such thing as an uneducated man. Take an extreme case. Suppose that an adult man, in the full vigor of his faculties, could be suddenly placed in the world, as Adam is said to have been, and then left to do as he best might. How long would he be left uneducated? Not five minutes. Nature would begin to teach him, through the eye, the ear, the touch, the properties of objects. Pain and pleasure would be at his elbow telling him to do this and avoid that; and by slow degrees the man would receive an education which, if narrow, would be thorough, real, and adequate to his circumstances, though there would be no extras and very few accomplishments.

And if to this solitary man entered a second Adam, or, better still, an Eve, a new and greater world, that of social and moral phenomena, would be revealed. Joys and woes, compared with which all others might seem but faint shadows, would spring from the new relations. Happiness and sorrow would take the place of the coarser monitors, pleasure and pain; but conduct would still be shaped by the observation of the natural consequences of actions; or, in other words, by the laws of the nature of man.

To every one of us the world was once as fresh and new as to Adam. And then, long before we were susceptible of any other mode of instruction, Nature took us in hand, and every minute of waking life brought its educational influence, shaping our actions into rough accordance with Nature's laws, so that we might not be ended untimely by too gross disobedience. Nor should I speak of this process of education as past for any one, be he as old as he may. For every man the world is as fresh as it was the first day, and as full of untold novelties for him who has the eyes to see them. And Nature is still continuing her patient education of us in that great university, the universe, of which we are all members—Nature having no Test-Acts.

Those who take honors in Nature's university, who learn the laws which govern men and things and obey them, are the really great and successful men in this world. The great mass of mankind are the "Poll," who pick up just enough to get through without much discredit. Those who won't learn at all are plucked; and then you can't come up again. Nature's pluck means extermination.

Thus the question of compulsory education is settled so far as Nature is concerned. Her bill on that question was framed and passed long ago. But, like all compulsory legislation, that of Nature is harsh and wasteful in its operation. Ignorance is visited as sharply as willful disobedience—incapacity meets with the same punishment as crime. Nature's discipline is not even a word and a blow, and the blow first; but the blow without the word. It is left to you to find out why your ears are boxed.

The object of what we commonly call education—that education in which man intervenes and which I shall distinguish as artificial education—is to make good these defects in Nature's methods; to prepare the child to receive Nature's education, neither incapably nor ignorantly, nor with willful disobedience; and to understand the preliminary symptoms of her pleasure, without waiting for the box on the ear. In short, all artificial education ought to be an anticipation of natural education. And a liberal education is an artificial education which has not only prepared a man to escape the great evils of disobedience to natural laws, but has trained him to appreciate and to seize upon the rewards, which Nature scatters with as free a hand as her penalties.

That man, I think, has had a liberal education who has been so trained in youth that his body is the ready servant of his will, and does with ease and pleasure all the work that, as a mechanism, it is capable of; whose intellect is a clear, cold, logic engine, with all its parts of equal strength, and in smooth working order; ready, like a steam engine, to be turned to any kind of work, and spin the gossamers as well as forge the anchors of the mind; whose mind is stored with a knowledge of the great and fundamental truths of Nature and of the laws of her operations; one who, no stunted ascetic, is full of life and fire, but whose passions are trained to come to heel by a vigorous will, the servant of a tender conscience; who has learned to love all beauty, whether of Nature or of art, to hate all vileness, and to respect others as himself.

Such an one and no other, I conceive, has had a liberal education; for he is, as completely as a man can be, in harmony with Nature. He will make the best of her, and she of him. They will get on together rarely: she as his ever beneficent mother; he as her mouthpiece, her conscious self, her minister and interpreter.     1868

## SCIENCE AND CULTURE

For I hold very strongly by two convictions—The first is, that neither the discipline nor the subject-matter of classical education is of such direct value to the student of physical science as to justify the expenditure of valuable time upon either; and the second is, that for the purpose of attaining real culture, an exclusively scientific education is at least as effectual as an exclusively literary education.

I need hardly point out to you that these opinions, especially the latter, are diametrically opposed to those of the great majority of educated Englishmen, influenced as they are by school and university traditions. In their belief, culture is obtainable only by a liberal education; and a liberal education is synonymous, not merely with education and instruction in literature, but in one particular form of literature, namely, that of Greek and Roman antiquity. They hold that the man who has learned Latin and Greek, however little, is educated; while he who is versed in other branches of knowledge, however deeply, is a more or less respectable specialist, not admissible into the cultured caste. The stamp of the educated man, the university degree, is not for him.

I am too well acquainted with the generous catholicity of spirit, the true sympathy with scientific thought, which pervades the writings of our chief apostle of culture to identify him with these opinions; and yet one may cull from one and another of those epistles to the Philistines, which so much delight all who do not answer to that name, sentences which lend them some support.

Mr. Arnold tells us that the meaning of culture is "to know the best that has been thought and said in the world." It is the criticism of life contained in literature

That criticism regards "Europe as being, for intellectual and spiritual purposes, one great confederation, bound to a joint action and working to a common result; and whose members have, for their common outfit, a knowledge of Greek, Roman, and Eastern antiquity, and of one another. Special, local, and temporary advantages being put out of account, that modern nation will in the intellectual and spiritual sphere make most progress, which most thoroughly carries out this program. And what is that but saying that we too, all of us, as individuals, the more thoroughly we carry it out, shall make the more progress?"

We have here to deal with two distinct propositions. The first, that a criticism of life is the essence of culture; the second, that literature contains the materials which suffice for the construction of such criticism.

I think that we must all assent to the first proposition. For culture certainly means something quite different from learning or technical skill. It implies the possession of an ideal, and the habit of critically estimating the value of things by comparison with a theoretic standard. Perfect culture should supply a complete theory of life, based upon a clear knowledge alike of its possibilities and of its limitations.

But we may agree to all this, and yet strongly dissent from the assumption that literature alone is competent to supply this knowledge. After having learned all that Greek, Roman, and Eastern antiquity have thought and said, and all that modern literature have to tell us, it is not self-evident that we have laid a sufficiently broad and deep foundation for that criticism of life which constitutes culture.

Indeed, to any one acquainted with the scope of physical science, it is not at all evident. Considering progress only in the "intellectual and spiritual sphere," I find myself wholly unable to admit that either nations or individuals will really advance, if their common outfit draws nothing from the stores of physical science. I should say that an army, without weapons of precision and with no particular base of operations, might more hopefully enter upon a campaign on the Rhine, than a man, devoid of a knowledge of what physical science has done in the last century, upon a criticism of life.

\* \* \* \* \* \*

The representatives of the Humanists, in the nineteenth century, take their stand upon classical education as the sole avenue to culture, as firmly as if we were still in the age of Renascence. Yet, surely, the present intellectual relations of the modern and the ancient worlds are profoundly different from those which obtained three centuries ago. Leaving aside the existence of a great and characteristically modern literature, of modern painting, and, especially, of modern music, there is one feature of the present state of the civilized world which separates it more widely from the Renascence than the Renascence was separated from the middle ages.

This distinctive character of our own times lies in the vast and constantly increasing part which is played by natural knowledge. Not only is our daily life shaped by it, not only does the prosperity of millions of men depend upon it, but our whole theory of life has long been influenced, consciously or unconsciously, by the general conceptions of the universe which have been forced upon us by physical science.

In fact, the most elementary acquaintance with the results of scientific investigation shows us that they offer a broad and striking contradiction to the opinion so implicitly credited and taught in the middle ages.

The notions of the beginning and the end of the world entertained by our forefathers are no longer credible. It is very certain that the earth is not the chief body in the material universe, and that the world is not subordinated to man's use. It is even more certain that nature is the expression of a definite order with which nothing interferes, and that the chief business of mankind is to learn that order and govern themselves accordingly. Moreover this scientific "criticism of life" presents itself to us with different credentials from any other. It appeals not to authority, nor to what anybody may have thought or said, but to nature. It admits that all our interpretations of natural fact are more or less imperfect and symbolic, and bids the learner seek for truth not among words but among things. It warns us that the assertion which outstrips evidence is not only a blunder but a crime.

The purely classical education advocated by the representatives of the Humanists in our day, gives no inkling of all this. A man may be a better scholar than Erasmus, and know no more of the chief causes of the present intellectual fermentation than Erasmus did. Scholarly and pious persons, worthy of all respect, favor us with allocutions upon the sadness of the antagonism of science to their medieval way of thinking, which betray an ignorance of the first principles of scientific investigation, an incapacity for understanding what a man of science means by veracity, and an unconsciousness of the weight of established scientific truths, which is almost comical.

\* \* \* \* \* \*

The period of the Renascence is commonly called that of the "Revival of Letters," as if the influences then brought to bear upon the mind of Western Europe had been wholly exhausted in the field of literature. I think it is very commonly forgotten that the revival of science, effected by the same agency, although less conspicuous, was not less momentous.

\* \* \* \* \* \*

We cannot know all the best thoughts and sayings of the Greeks unless we know what they thought about natural phenomena. We cannot fully apprehend their criticism of life unless we understand the extent to which that criticism was affected by scientific conceptions. We falsely pretend to be the inheritors of their culture, unless we are penetrated, as the best minds among them were, with an unhesitating faith that the free employment of reason, in accordance with scientific method, is the sole method of reaching truth.

Thus I venture to think that the pretensions of our modern Humanists to the possession of the monopoly of culture and to the exclusive inheritance of the spirit of antiquity must be abated, if not abandoned. But I should be very sorry that anything I have said should be taken to imply a desire on my part to depreciate the value of classical education, as it might be and as it sometimes is. The native capacities of mankind vary no less than their opportunities; and while culture is one, the road by which one man may best reach it is widely different from that which is most advantageous to another. Again, while scientific education is yet inchoate and tentative, classical education is thoroughly well organized upon the practical experience of generations of teachers. So that, given ample time for learning and estimation for ordinary life, or for a literary career, I do not think that a young Englishman in search of culture can do better than follow the course usually marked out for him, supplementing its deficiencies by his own efforts.

\*    \*    \*    \*    \*    \*

Nevertheless, I am the last person to question the importance of genuine literary education, or to suppose that intellectual culture can be complete without it. An exclusively scientific training will bring about a mental twist as surely as an exclusively literary training. The value of the cargo does not compensate for a ship's being out of trim; and I should be very sorry to think that the Scientific College would turn out none but lopsided men.

There is no need, however, that such a catastrophe should happen. Instruction in English, French, and German is provided, and thus the three greatest literatures of the modern world are made accessible to the student.

French and German, and especially the latter language, are absolutely indispensable to those who desire full knowledge in any department of science. But even supposing that the knowledge of these languages acquired is not more than sufficient for purely scientific purposes, every Englishman has, in his native tongue, an almost perfect instrument of literary expression; and, in his own literature, models of every kind of literary excellence. If an Englishman cannot get literary culture out of his Bible, his Shakespeare, his Milton, neither, in my belief, will the profoundest study of Homer and Sophocles, Virgil and Horace, give it to him.

\*    \*    \*    \*    \*    \*

But I am not sure that at this point the "practical" man, scotched but not slain, may ask what all this talk about culture has to do with an institution, the object of which is defined to be "to promote the prosperity of the manufactures and the industry of the country." He may suggest that what is wanted for this end is not culture, nor even a purely scientific discipline, but simply a knowledge of applied science.

I often wish that this phrase, "applied science," had never been invented. For it suggests that there is a sort of scientific knowledge of direct practical use, which can be studied apart from another sort of scientific knowledge, which is of no practical utility, and which is termed "pure science." But there is no more complete fallacy than this. What people call applied science is nothing but the application of pure science to particular classes of problems. It consists of deduction from those general principles, established by reasoning and observation, which constitute pure science. No one can safely make these deductions until he has a firm grasp of the principles; and he can obtain that grasp only by personal experience of the operations of observation and of reasoning on which they are founded.

Almost all the processes employed in the arts and manufactures fall within the range either of physics or of chemistry. In order to improve them, one must thoroughly understand them; and no one has a chance of really understanding them, unless he has obtained that mastery of principles and that habit of dealing with facts, which is given by long-continued and well-directed purely scientific training in the physical and the chemical laboratory. So that there is really no question as to the necessity of purely scientific discipline, even if the work of the college were limited by the narrowest interpretation of its stated aims.

And, as to the desirableness of a wider culture than that yielded by science alone, it is to be recollected that the improvement of manufacturing processes is only one of the conditions which contribute to the prosperity of industry. Industry is a means and not an end; and mankind work only to get something which they want. What that something is depends partly on their innate, and partly on their acquired, desires.

If the wealth resulting from prosperous industry is to be spent upon the gratification of unworthy desires, if the increasing perfection of manufacturing processes is to be accompanied by an increasing debasement of those who carry them on, I do not see the good of industry and prosperity.

Now it is perfectly true that men's views of what is desirable depend upon their characters; and that the innate proclivities to which we give that name are not touched by any amount of instruction. But it does not follow that even mere intellectual education may not, to an indefinite extent, modify the practical manifestation of the characters of men in their actions, by supplying them with motives unknown to the ignorant. A pleasure-loving character will have pleasure of some sort; but, if you give him the choice, he may prefer pleasures which do not degrade him to those which do. And this choice is offered to every man, who possesses in literary or artistic culture a never-failing source of pleasures, which are neither withered by age, nor staled by custom, nor embittered in the recollection by the pangs of self reproach.

If the Institution opened to-day fulfills the intention of its founder, the picked intelligences among all classes of the population of this district will pass through it. No child born in Birmingham, henceforward, if he have the capacity to profit by the opportunities offered to him, first in the primary and other schools, and afterwards in the Scientific College, need fail to obtain, not merely the instruction, but the culture most appropriate to the conditions of his life.

Within these walls, the future employer and the future artisan may sojourn together for a while, and carry, through all their lives, the stamp of the influences then brought to bear upon them. Hence, it is not beside the mark to remind you, that the prosperity of industry depends not merely upon the improvement of manufacturing processes, not merely upon the ennobling of the individual character, but upon a third condition, namely, a clear understanding of the conditions of social life, on the part of both the capitalist and the operative, and their agreement upon common principles of social action. They must learn that social phenomena are as much the expression of natural laws as any others; that no social arrangements can be permanent unless they harmonize with the requirements of social statics and dynamics; and that, in the nature of things, there is an arbiter whose decisions execute themselves.

But this knowledge is only to be obtained by the application of the methods of investigation adopted in physical researches to the investigation of the phenomena of society. Hence, I confess, I should like to see one addition made to the excellent scheme of education propounded for the college, in the shape of provision for the teaching of sociology. For though we are all agreed that party politics are to have no place in the instruction of the college; yet in this country, practically governed as it is now by universal suffrage, every man who does his duty must exercise political functions. And, if the evils which are inseparable from the good of political liberty are to be checked, if the perpetual oscillation of nations between anarchy and despotism is to be replaced by the steady march of self-restraining freedom; it will be because men will gradually bring themselves to deal with political, as they now deal with scientific questions; to be as ashamed of undue haste and partisan prejudice in the one case as in the other; and to believe that the machinery of society is at least as delicate as that of a spinning-jenny, and as little likely to be improved by the meddling of those who have not taken the trouble to master the principles of its action.              1880

## WALTER PATER (1839-1894)

## THE PERCEPTION OF BEAUTY

(From the Preface to *Studies in the History of the Renaissance*)

MANY attempts have been made by writers on art and poetry to define beauty in the abstract, to express it in the most general terms, to find a universal formula for it. The value of such attempts has most often been in the suggestive and penetrating things said by the way. Such discussions help us very little to enjoy what has been well done in art or poetry, to discriminate between what is more and what is less excellent in them, or to use words like beauty, excellence, art, poetry, with more meaning than they would otherwise have. Beauty, like all other qualities presented to human experience, is relative; and the definition of it becomes unmeaning and useless in proportion to its abstractness. To define beauty, not in the most abstract, but in the most concrete terms possible, to find, not a universal formula for it, but the formula which expresses most adequately this or that special manifestation of it, is the aim of the true student of æsthetics.

"To see the object as in itself it really is," has been justly said to be the aim of all true criticism whatever;

and in æsthetic criticism the first step towards seeing one's object as it really is, is to know one's own impression as it really is, to discriminate, to realize it distinctly. The objects with which æsthetic criticism deals, music, poetry, artistic and accomplished forms of human life, are indeed receptacles of so many powers or forces; they possess, like natural elements so many virtues or qualities. What is this song or picture, this engaging personality presented in life or in a book, to *me?* What effect does it really produce on me? Does it give me pleasure? and if so, what sort or degree of pleasure? How is my nature modified by its presence, and under its influence? The answers to these questions are the original facts with which the æsthetic critic has to do; and, as in the study of light, of morals, of number, one must realise such primary data for one's self, or not at all. And he who experiences these impressions strongly, and drives directly at the discrimination and analysis of them, need not trouble himself with the abstract question what beauty is in itself, or what its exact relation to truth or experience—metaphysical questions, as unprofitable as metaphysical questions elsewhere. He may pass them all by as being, answerable or not, of no interest to him.

The æsthetic critic, then, regards all the objects with which he has to do, all works of art, and the fairer forms of nature and human life, as powers or forces producing pleasurable sensations, each of a more or less peculiar and unique kind. This influence he feels, and wishes to explain, analysing it, and reducing it to its elements. To him, the picture, the landscape, the engaging personality in life or in a book, *La Gioconda,* the hills of Carrara, Pico of Mirandola, are valuable for their virtues, as we say in speaking of a herb, a wine, a gem; for the property each has of affecting one with a special unique impression of pleasure. Our education becomes complete in proportion as our susceptibility to these impressions increases in depth and variety. And the function of the æsthetic critic is to distinguish, analyse, and separate from its adjuncts, the virtue by which a picture, a landscape, a fair personality in life or in a book, produces this special impression of beauty or pleasure, to indicate what the source of that impression is, and under what conditions it is experienced. His end is reached when he has disengaged that virtue, and noted it, as a chemist notes some natural element, for himself and others; and the rule for those who would reach this end is stated with great exactness in the words of a recent critic of Sainte-Beuve:—*De se borner à connâitre de près les belles choses, et à s'en nourrir en exquis amateurs, en humanistes accomplis.*

What is important, then, is not that the critic should possess a correct abstract definition of beauty for the intellect, but a certain kind of temperament, the power of being deeply moved by the presence of beautiful objects. He will remember always that beauty exists in many forms. To him all periods, types, schools of taste, are in themselves equal. In all ages there have been some excellent workmen, and some excellent work done. The question he asks is always—In whom did the stir, the genius, the sentiment of the period find itself? who was the receptacle of its refinement, its elevation, its taste? "The ages are all equal," says William Blake, "but genius is always above its age."

Often it will require great nicety to disengage this virtue from the commoner elements with which it may be found in combination. Few artists, not Goethe or Byron even, work quite cleanly, casting off all *débris*, and leaving us only what the heat of their imagination has wholly fused and transformed. Take for instance the writings of Wordsworth. The heat of his genius, entering into the substance of his work, has crystallised a part, but only a part, of it; and in that great mass of verse there is much which might well be forgotten. But scattered up and down it, sometimes fusing and transforming entire compositions, like the Stanzas on *Resolution and Independence* and the *Ode on the Recollections of Childhood,* sometimes, as if at random, turning a fine crystal here and there, in a matter it does not wholly search through and transform, we trace the action of his unique, incommunicable faculty, that strange, mystical sense of life in natural things, and of man's life as a part of nature, drawing strength and colour and character from local influences, from the hills and streams, and from natural sights and sounds. Well! that is the *virtue,* the active principle in Wordsworth's poetry; and then the function of the critic of Wordsworth is to trace that active principle, to disengage it, to mark the degree in which it penetrates his verse.

1873

### CONCLUSION

To REGARD all things and principles of things as inconstant modes or fashions has more and more become the tendency of modern thought. Let us begin with that which is without—our physical life. Fix upon it in one of its more exquisite intervals, the moment, for instance, of delicious recoil from the flood of water in summer heat. What is the whole physical life in that moment but a combination of natural elements to which science gives their names? But these elements, phosphorus and lime and delicate fibres, are present not in the human body alone: we detect them in places most remote from it. Our physical life is a perpetual motion of them—

the passage of the blood, the wasting and repairing of the lenses of the eye, the modification of the tissues of the brain by every ray of light and sound—processes which science reduces to simpler and more elementary forces. Like the elements of which we are composed, the action of these forces extends beyond us; it rusts iron and ripens corn. Far out on every side of us those elements are broadcast, driven by many forces; and birth and gesture and death and the springing of violets from the grave are but a few out of ten thousand resultant combinations. That clear, perpetual outline of face and limb is but an image of ours, under which we group them—a design in a web, the actual threads of which pass out beyond it. This at least of flamelike our life has, that it is but the concurrence, renewed from moment to moment, of forces parting sooner or later on their ways.

Or if we begin with the inward world of thought and feeling, the whirlpool is still more rapid, the flame more eager and devouring. There it is no longer the gradual darkening of the eye and fading of colour from the wall,—the movement of the shoreside, where the water flows down indeed, though in apparent rest,—but the race of the mid-stream, a drift of momentary acts of sight and passion and thought. At first sight experience seems to bury us under a flood of external objects, pressing upon us with a sharp and importunate reality, calling us out of ourselves in a thousand forms of action. But when reflexion begins to act upon those objects they are dissipated under its influence; the cohesive force seems suspended like a trick of magic; each object is loosed into a group of impressions—colour, odour, texture—in the mind of the observer. And if we continue to dwell in thought on this world, not of objects in the solidity with which language invests them, but of impressions unstable, flickering, inconsistent, which burn and are extinguished with our consciousness of them, it contracts still further; the whole scope of observation is dwarfed to the narrow chamber of the individual mind. Experience, already reduced to a swarm of impressions, is ringed round for each one of us by that thick wall of personality through which no real voice has ever pierced on its way to us, or from us to that which we can only conjecture to be without. Every one of those impressions is the impression of the individual in his isolation, each mind keeping as a solitary prisoner its own dream of a world.

Analysis goes a step farther still, and assures us that those impressions of the individual mind to which, for each one of us, experience dwindles down, are in perpetual flight; that each of them is limited by time, and that as time is infinitely divisible, each of them is infinitely divisible also; all that is actual in it being a single moment, gone while we try to apprehend it, of which it may ever be more truly said that it has ceased to be than that it is. To such a tremulous wisp constantly reforming itself on the stream, to a single sharp impression, with a sense in it, a relic more or less fleeting, of such moments gone by, what is real in our life fines itself down. It is with this movement, with the passage and dissolution of impressions, images, sensations, that analysis leaves off—that continual vanishing away, that strange, perpetual weaving and unweaving of ourselves.

*Philosophiren*, says Novalis, *ist dephlegmatisiren vivificiren*. The service of philosophy, of speculative culture, towards the human spirit is to rouse, to startle it into sharp and eager observation. Every moment some form grows perfect in hand or face; some tone on the hills or the sea is choicer than the rest; some mood of passion or insight or intellectual excitement is irresistibly real and attractive for us,—for that moment only. Not the fruit of experience, but experience itself, is the end. A counted number of pulses only is given to us of a variegated, dramatic, life. How may we see in them all that is to be seen in them by the finest senses? How shall we pass most swiftly from point to point, and be present always at the focus where the greatest number of vital forces unite in their purest energy?

To burn always with this hard, gemlike flame, to maintain this ecstasy, is success in life. In a sense it might even be said that our failure is to form habits: for, after all, habit is relative to a stereotyped world, and meantime it is only the roughness of the eye that makes any two persons, things, situations, seem alike. While all melts under our feet, we may well catch at any exquisite passion, or any contribution to knowledge that seems by a lifted horizon to set the spirit free for a moment, or any stirring of the senses, strange dyes, strange colours, and curious odours, or work of the artist's hands, or the face of one's friend. Not to discriminate every moment some passionate attitude in those about us, and in the brilliancy of their gifts some tragic dividing of forces on their ways, is, on this short day of frost and sun, to sleep before evening. With this sense of the splendour of our experience and of its awful brevity, gathering all we are into one desperate effort to see and touch, we shall hardly have time to make theories about the things we see and touch. What we have to do is to be for ever curiously testing new opinions and courting new impressions, never acquiescing in a facile orthodoxy of Comte, or of Hegel, or of our own. Philosophical theories or ideas, as points of view, instruments of criticism, may help us to gather up what might otherwise pass unregarded by us. "Philosophy is the microscope of thought." The theory or idea or system which requires of us the sacrifice of any part of this experience, in consideration of some interest into which we cannot enter, or some abstract theory we have not identified with ourselves, or what is only conventional, has no real claim upon us.

One of the most beautiful passages in the writings of Rousseau is that in the sixth book of the *Confessions,* where he describes the awakening in him of the literary sense. An undefinable taint of death had always clung about him, and now in early manhood he believed himself smitten by mortal disease. He asked himself how he might make as much as possible of the interval that remained; and he was not biassed by anything in his previous life when he decided that it must be by intellectual excitement, which he found just then in the clear, fresh writings of Voltaire. Well! we are all *condamnés,* as Victor Hugo says: we are all under sentence of death but with a sort of indefinite reprieve—*les hommes sont tous condamnés à mort avec des sursis indéfinis:* we have an interval, and then our place knows us no more. Some spend this interval in listlessness, some in high passions, the wisest—at least among "the children of this world"—in art and song. For our one chance lies in expanding that interval, in getting as many pulsations as possible into the given time. Great passions may give us this quickened sense of life, ecstasy and sorrow of love, the various forms of enthusiastic activity, disinterested or otherwise, which come naturally to many of us. Only be sure it is passion—that it does yield you this fruit of a quickened, multiplied consciousness. Of this wisdom, the poetic passion, the desire of beauty, the love of art for art's sake, has most; for art comes to you professing frankly to give nothing but the highest quality to your moments as they pass, and simply for those moments' sake.

1873

## POSTSCRIPT

*(From Appreciations, with an Essay on Style)*

THE words, *classical* and *romantic,* although, like many other critical expressions, sometimes abused by those who have understood them too vaguely or too absolutely, yet define two real tendencies in the history of art and literature. Used in an exaggerated sense, to express a greater opposition between those tendencies than really exists, they have at times tended to divide people of taste into opposite camps. But in that *House Beautiful,* which the creative minds of all generations—the artists and those who have treated life in the spirit of art—are always building together, for the refreshment of the human spirit, these oppositions cease; and the *Interpreter* of the *House Beautiful,* the true æsthetic critic, uses these divisions, only so far as they enable him to enter into the peculiarities of the objects with which he has to do. The term *classical,* fixed, as it is, to a well-defined literature, and a well-defined group in art, is clear, indeed; but then it has often been used in a hard, and merely scholastic sense, by the praisers of what is old and accustomed, at the expense of what is new, by critics who would never have discovered for themselves the charm of any work, whether new or old, who value what is old, in art or literature, for its accessories, and chiefly for the conventional authority that has gathered about it—people who would never really have been made glad by any Venus fresh-risen from the sea, and who praise the Venus of old Greece and Rome, only because they fancy her grown now into something staid and tame.

And as the term, *classical,* has been used in a too absolute, and therefore in a misleading sense, so the term, *romantic,* has been used much too vaguely, in various accidental senses. The sense in which Scott is called a romantic writer is chiefly this; that, in opposition to the literary tradition of the last century, he loved strange adventure, and sought it in the Middle Age. Much later, in a Yorkshire village, the spirit of romanticism bore a more really characteristic fruit in the work of a young girl, Emily Brontë, the romance of *Wuthering Heights;* the figures of Hareton Earnshaw, of Catherine Linton, and of Heathcliffe—tearing open Catherine's grave, removing one side of her coffin, that he may really lie beside her in death—figures so passionate, yet woven on a background of delicately beautiful, moorland scenery, being typical examples of that spirit. In Germany, again, that spirit is shown less in Tieck, its professional representative, than in Meinhold, the author of *Sidonia the Sorceress* and the *Amber-Witch.* In Germany and France, within the last hundred years, the term has been used to describe a particular school of writers; and, consequently, when Heine criticises the *Romantic School* in Germany—that movement which culminated in Goethe's *Goetz von Berlichingen;* or when Théophile Gautier criticises the romantic movement in France, where, indeed, it bore its most characteristic fruits, and its play is hardly yet over, where, by a certain audacity, or *bizarrerie* of motive, united with faultless literary execution, it still shows itself in imaginative literature, they use the word, with an exact sense of special artistic qualities, indeed; but use it, nevertheless, with a limited application to the manifestation of those qualities at a particular period. But the romantic spirit is, in reality, an ever-present, an enduring principle, in the artistic temperament; and the qualities of thought and style which that, and other similar uses of the word *romantic* really indicate, are indeed but symptoms of a very continuous and widely working influence.

Though the words *classical* and *romantic,* then, have acquired an almost technical meaning, in application to certain developments of German and French taste, yet this is but one variation of an old opposition, which may be traced from the very beginning of the formation of European art and literature. From the first formation of anything like a standard of taste in these things, the restless curiosity of their more eager lovers necessarily made itself felt, in the craving for new motives, new subjects of interest, new modifications of style. Hence, the opposition between the classicists and the romanticists—between the adherents, in the culture of beauty, of the principles of liberty, and authority, respectively —of strength and order, or what the Greeks called κοσμιότης.

Sainte-Beuve, in the third volume of the *Causeries du Lundi,* has discussed the question, *What is meant by a classic?* It was a question he was well fitted to answer, having himself lived through many phases of taste, and having been in earlier life an enthusiastic member of the romantic school: he was also a great master of that sort of "philosophy of literature," which delights in tracing traditions in it, and the way in which various phases of thought and sentiment maintain themselves, through successive modifications, from epoch to epoch. His aim, then, is to give the word *classic* a wider, and as he says, a more generous sense than it commonly bears, to make it expressly *grandiose et flottant;* and, in doing this, he develops, in a masterly manner, those qualities of measure, purity, temperance, of which it is the especial function of classical art and literature, whatever meaning, narrower or wider, we attach to the term, to take care.

The charm, therefore, of what is classical, in art or literature, is that of the well-known tale, to which we can, nevertheless, listen over and over again, because it is told so well. To the absolute beauty of its artistic form, is added the accidental, tranquil, charm of familiarity. There are times, indeed, at which these charms fail to work on our spirits at all, because they fail to excite us. *"Romanticism,"* says Stendhal, "is the art of presenting to people the literary works which, in the actual state of their habits and beliefs, are capable of giving them the greatest possible pleasure; *classicism,* on the contrary, of presenting them with that which gave the greatest possible pleasure to their grandfathers." But then, beneath all changes of habits and beliefs, our love of that mere abstract proportion—of music—which what is classical in literature possesses, still maintains itself in the best of us, and what pleased our grandparents may at least tranquillize us. The "classic" comes to us out of the cool and quiet of other times, as the measure of what a long experience has shown will at least never displease us. And in the classical literature of Greece and Rome, as in the classics of the last century, the essentially classical element is that quality of order in beauty, which they possess, indeed, in a preëminent degree, and which impresses some minds to the exclusion of everything else in them.

It is the addition of strangeness to beauty that constitutes the romantic character in art; and the desire of beauty being a fixed element in every artistic organization, it is the addition of curiosity to this desire of beauty, that constitutes the romantic temper. Curiosity and the desire of beauty, have each their place in art, as in all true criticism. When one's curiosity is deficient, when one is not eager enough for new impressions, and new pleasures, one is liable to value mere academical proprieties too highly, to be satisfied with worn-out or conventional types, with the insipid ornament of Racine, or the prettiness of that later Greek sculpture, which passed so long for true Hellenic work; to miss those places where the handiwork of nature, or of the artist, has been most cunning; to find the most stimulating products of art a mere irritation. And when one's curiosity is in excess, when it overbalances the desire of beauty, then one is liable to value in works of art what is inartistic in them; to be satisfied with what is exaggerated in art, with productions like some of those of the romantic school in Germany; not to distinguish, jealously enough, between what is admirably done, and what is done not quite so well, in the writings, for instance, of Jean Paul. And if I had to give instances of these defects, then I should say, that Pope, in common with the age of literature to which he belonged, had too little curiosity, so that there is always a certain insipidity in the effect of his work, exquisite as it is; and, coming down to our own time, that Balzac had an excess of curiosity—curiosity not duly tempered with the desire of beauty.

But, however falsely these two tendencies may be opposed by critics, or exaggerated by artists themselves, they are tendencies really at work at all times in art, moulding it, with the balance sometimes a little on one side, sometimes a little on the other, generating, respectively, as the balance inclines on this side or that, two principles, two traditions, in art, and in literature so far as it partakes of the spirit of art. If there is a great over-balance of curiosity, then, we have the grotesque in art; if the union of strangeness and beauty, under very difficult and complex conditions, be a successful one, if the union be entire, then the resultant beauty is very

exquisite, very attractive. With a passionate care for
beauty, the romantic spirit refused to have it, unless
the condition of strangeness be first fulfilled. Its desire
is for a beauty born of unlikely elements, by a profound
alchemy, by a difficult initiation, by the charm which
wrings it even out of terrible things; and a trace of
distortion, of the grotesque, may perhaps linger, as an
additional element of expression, about its ultimate
grace. Its eager, excited spirit will have strength, the
grotesque, first of all—the trees shrieking as you tear
off the leaves; for Jean Valjean, the long years of con-
vict life; for Redgauntlet, the quicksands of Solway
Moss; then, incorporate with this strangeness, and inten-
sified by restraint, as much sweetness, as much beauty,
as is compatible with that.                          1889

## ROBERT LOUIS STEVENSON (1850-1894)

### A GOSSIP ON ROMANCE

#### (From *Memories and Portraits*)

IN ANYTHING fit to be called by the name of reading,
the process itself should be absorbing and voluptuous;
we should gloat over a book, be rapt clean out of ourselves, and rise from the perusal, our mind filled with
the busiest, kaleidoscopic dance of images, incapable
of sleep or of continuous thought. The words, if the book
be eloquent, should run thenceforward in our ears like
the noise of breakers, and the story, if it be a story, repeat itself in a thousand coloured pictures to the eye.
It was for this last pleasure that we read so closely,
and loved our books so dearly, in the bright, troubled
period of boyhood. Eloquence and thought, character and
conversation, were but obstacles to brush aside as we

dug blithely after a certain sort of incident, like a pig
for truffles. For my part, I liked a story to begin with
an old wayside inn where, "towards the close of the
year 17—," several gentlemen in three-cocked hats were
playing bowls. A friend of mine preferred the Malabar
coast in a storm, with a ship beating to windward, and
a scowling fellow of Herculean proportions striding
along the beach; he, to be sure, was a pirate. This was
further afield than my home-keeping fancy loved to
travel, and designed altogether for a larger canvas than
the tales that I affected. Give me a highwayman and
I was full to the brim; a Jacobite would do, but the
highwayman was my favourite dish. I can still hear
that merry clatter of the hoofs along the moonlit lane;
night and the coming of day are still related in my
mind with the doings of John Rann or Jerry Abershaw;
and the words "postchaise," the "great North road,"
"ostler," and "nag" still sound in my ears like poetry.
One and all, at least, and each with his particular fancy,
we read story-books in childhood, not for eloquence or
character or thought, but for some quality of the brute
incident. That quality was not mere bloodshed or wonder. Although each of these was welcome in its place,
the charm for the sake of which we read depended on
something different from either. My elders used to read
novels aloud; and I can still remember four different
passages which I heard, before I was ten, with the
same keen and lasting pleasure. One I discovered long
afterwards to be the admirable opening of *What will he
Do with It:* it was no wonder I was pleased with that.
The other three still remain unidentified. One is a little
vague; it was about a dark, tall house at night, and
people groping on the stairs by the light that escaped
from the open door of a sickroom. In another, a lover
left a ball, and went walking in a cool, dewy park,

whence he could watch the lighted windows and the figures of the dancers as they moved. This was the most sentimental impression I think I had yet received, for a child is somewhat deaf to the sentimental. In the last, a poet, who had been tragically wrangling with his wife, walked forth on the sea-beach on a tempestuous night and witnessed the horrors of a wreck. Different as they are, all these early favourites have a common note—they have all a touch of the romantic.

Drama is the poetry of conduct, romance the poetry of circumstance. The pleasure that we take in life is of two sorts—the active and the passive. Now we are conscious of a great command over our destiny; anon we are lifted up by circumstance, as by a breaking wave, and dashed we know not how into the future. Now we are pleased by our conduct, anon merely pleased by our surroundings. It would be hard to say which of these modes of satisfaction is the more effective, but the latter is surely the more constant. Conduct is three parts of life, they say; but I think they put it high. There is a vast deal in life and letters both which is not immoral, but simply a-moral; which either does not regard the human will at all, or deals with it in obvious and healthy relations; where the interest turns, not upon what a man shall choose to do, but on how he manages to do it; not on the passionate slips and hesitations of the conscience, but on the problems of the body and of the practical intelligence, in clean, open-air adventure, the shock of arms or the diplomacy of life. With such material as this it is impossible to build a play, for the serious theatre exists solely on moral grounds, and is a standing proof of the dissemination of the human conscience. But it is possible to build, upon this ground, the most joyous of verses, and the most lively, beautiful, and buoyant tales.

One thing in life calls for another; there is a fitness in events and places. The sight of a pleasant arbour puts it in our mind to sit there. One place suggests work, another idleness, a third early rising and long rambles in the dew. The effect of night, of any flowing water, of lighted cities, of the peep of day, of ships, of the open ocean, calls up in the mind an army of anonymous desires and pleasures. Something, we feel, should happen; we know not what, yet we proceed in quest of it. And many of the happiest hours of life fleet by us in this vain attendance on the genius of the place and moment. It is thus that tracts of young fir, and low rocks that reach into deep soundings, particularly torture and delight me. Something must have happened in such places, and perhaps ages back, to members of my race; and when I was a child I tried in vain to invent appropriate games for them, as I still try, just as vainly, to fit them with the proper story. Some places speak distinctly. Certain dank gardens cry aloud for a murder; certain old houses demand to be haunted; certain coasts are set apart for shipwreck. Other spots again seem to abide their destiny, suggestive and impenetrable, "miching mallecho." The inn at Burford Bridge, with its arbours and green garden and silent, eddying river—though it is known already as the place where Keats wrote some of his *Endymion* and Nelson parted from his Emma—still seems to wait the coming of the appropriate legend. Within these ivied walls, behind these old green shutters, some further business smoulders, waiting for its hour. The old Hawes Inn at the Queen's Ferry makes a similar call upon my fancy. There it stands, apart from the town, beside the pier, in a climate of its own, half inland, half marine—in front, the ferry bubbling with the tide and the guardship swinging to her anchor; behind, the old garden with the trees. Americans seek it already for the sake of Lovel and Oldbuck, who dined there at the beginning of the *Antiquary*. But you need not tell me—that is not all; there is some story, unrecorded or not yet complete, which must express the meaning of that inn more fully. So it is with names and faces; so it is with incidents that are idle and inconclusive in themselves, and yet seem like the beginning of some quaint romance, which the all-careless author leaves untold. How many of these romances have we not seen determine at their birth; how many people have met us with a look of meaning in their eye, and sunk at once into trivial acquaintances; to how many places have we not drawn near, with express intimations—"here my destiny awaits me"—and we have but dined there and passed on! I have lived both at the Hawes and Burford in a perpetual flutter, on the heels, as it seemed, of some adventure that should justify the place; but though the feeling had me to bed at night and called me again at morning in one unbroken round of pleasure and suspense, nothing befell me in either worth remark. The man or the hour had not yet come; but some day, I think, a boat shall put off from the Queen's Ferry, fraught with a dear cargo, and some frosty night a horseman, on a tragic errand, rattle with his whip upon the green shutters of the inn at Burford.

Now, this is one of the natural appetites with which any lively literature has to count. The desire for knowledge, I had almost added the desire for meat, is not more deeply seated than this demand for fit and striking incident. The dullest of clowns tells, or tries to tell, himself a story, as the feeblest of children uses invention in his play; and even as the imaginative grown person, joining in the game, at once enriches it with many delightful circumstances, the great creative writer shows as the realisation and the apotheosis of the day-dreams of common men. His stories may be nourished with the realities of life, but their true mark is to satisfy the nameless longings of the reader, and to obey the ideal laws of the day-dream. The right kind of thing should fall out in the right kind of place; the right kind of thing should follow; and not only the characters talk aptly and think naturally, but all the circumstances in a tale answer one to another like notes in music. The threads of a story come from time to time together and make a picture in the web; the characters fall from time to time into some attitude to each other or to nature, which stamps the story home like an illustration. Crusoe recoiling from the footprint, Achilles shouting over against the Trojans, Ulysses bending the great bow, Christian running with his fingers in his ears, these are each culminating moments in the legend, and each has been printed on the mind's eye forever. Other things we may forget; we may forget the words, although they are beautiful; we may forget the author's comment, although perhaps it was ingenious and true; but these epoch-making scenes, which put the last mark of truth upon a story and fill up, at one blow, our capacity for sympathetic pleasure, we so adopt into the very bosom of our mind that neither time nor tide can efface or weaken the impression. This, then, is the plastic part of literature: to embody character, thought, or emotion in some act or attitude that shall be remarkably striking to the mind's eye. This is the highest and hardest thing to do in words; the thing which, once accomplished, equally delights the schoolboy and the sage, and makes, in its own right, the quality of epics. Compared with this, all other purposes in literature, except the purely lyrical or the purely philosophic, are bastard in nature, facile of execution, and feeble in result. It is one thing to write about the inn at Burford, or to describe scenery with the word-painters; it is quite another to seize on the heart of the suggestion and make a country famous with a legend. It is one thing to remark and to dissect, with the most cutting logic, the complications of life, and of the human spirit; it is quite another to give them body and blood in the story of Ajax or of Hamlet. The first is literature, but the second is something besides, for it is likewise art.

English people of the present day are apt, I know not why, to look somewhat down on incident, and reserve their admiration for the clink of teaspoons and the accents of the curate. It is thought clever to write a novel with no story at all, or at least with a very dull one. Reduced even to the lowest terms, a certain interest can be communicated by the art of narrative; a sense of human kinship stirred; and a kind of monotonous fitness, comparable to the words and air of *Sandy's Mull*, preserved among the infinitesimal occurrences recorded. Some people work, in this manner, with even a strong touch. Mr. Trollope's inimitable clergymen naturally arise to the mind in this connection. But even Mr. Trollope does not confine himself to chronicling small beer. Mr. Crawley's collision with the Bishop's wife, Mr. Melnette dallying in the deserted banquet-room, are typical incidents, epically conceived, fitly embodying a crisis. Or again look at Thackeray. If Rawdon Crawley's blow were not delivered, *Vanity Fair* would cease to be a work of art. That scene is the chief ganglion of the tale; and the discharge of energy from Rawdon's fist is the reward and consolation of the reader. The end of *Esmond* is a yet wider excursion from the author's customary fields; the scene at Castlewood is pure Dumas; the great and wily English borrower has here borrowed from the great, unblushing French thief; as usual, he has borrowed admirably well, and the breaking of the sword rounds off the best of all his books with a manly, martial note. But perhaps nothing can more strongly illustrate the necessity for marking incident than to compare the living fame of *Robinson Crusoe* with the discredit of *Clarissa Harlowe*. *Clarissa* is a book of a far more startling import, worked out, on a great canvas, with inimitable courage and unflagging art. It contains wit, character, passion, plot, conversations full of spirit and insight, letters sparkling with unstrained humanity; and if the death of the heroine be somewhat frigid and artificial, the last days of the hero strike the only note of what we now call Byronism, between the Elizabethans and Byron himself. And yet a little story of a shipwrecked sailor, with not a tenth part of the style nor a thousandth part of the wisdom, exploring none of the arcana of humanity and deprived of the perennial interest of love, goes on from edition to edition, ever young, while *Clarissa* lies upon the shelves unread. A friend of mine, a Welsh blacksmith, was twenty-five years old and could neither read nor write, when he heard a chapter of *Robinson* read aloud in a farm kitchen. Up to that moment he had sat content, huddled in his ignorance, but he left that farm another man. There were day-dreams, it appeared, divine day-dreams, written and printed and bound, and to be bought for money and enjoyed at pleasure. Down he sat that day, painfully learned to read Welsh, and returned to borrow the book. It had been lost, nor could he find another copy but one that was in English. Down he sat once more, learned English, and at length, and with entire delight, read *Robinson*. It is like the story of a love-chase. If he had heard a letter from *Clarissa*, would he have been fired with the same chivalrous ardour? I wonder. Yet *Clarissa* has every quality that can be shown in prose, one alone excepted—pictorial or picture-making romance. While

*Robinson* depends, for the most part and with the over-whelming majority of its readers, on the charm of circumstance.

In the highest achievements of the art of words, the dramatic and the pictorial, the moral and romantic interest, rise and fall together by a common and organic law. Situation is animated with passion, passion clothed upon with situation. Neither exists for itself, but each inheres indissolubly with the other. This is high art; and not only the highest art possible in words, but the highest art of all, since it combines the greatest mass and diversity of the elements of truth and pleasure. Such are epics, and the few prose tales that have the epic weight. But as from a school of works, aping the creative, incident and romance are ruthlessly discarded, so may character and drama be omitted or subordinated to romance. There is one book, for example, more generally loved than Shakespeare, that captivates in childhood, and still delights in age—I mean the *Arabian Nights*—where you shall look in vain for moral or for intellectual interest. No human face or voice greets us among that wooden crowd of kings and genies, sorcerers and beggarmen. Adventure, on the most naked terms, furnishes forth the entertainment and is found enough. Dumas approaches perhaps nearest of any modern to these Arabian authors in the purely material charm of some of his romances. The early part of *Monte Cristo,* down to the finding of the treasure, is a piece of perfect story-telling; the man never breathed who shared these moving incidents without a tremor; and yet Faria is a thing of packthread and Dantès little more than a name. The sequel is one long-drawn error, gloomy, bloody, unnatural and dull; but as for these early chapters, I do not believe there is another volume extant where you can breathe the same unmingled atmosphere of romance.

It is very thin and light, to be sure, as on a high mountain; but it is brisk and clear and sunny in proportion. I saw the other day, with envy, an old and a very clever lady setting forth on a second or third voyage into *Monte Cristo*. Here are stories which powerfully affect the reader, which can be reperused at any age, and where the characters are no more than puppets. The bony fist of the showman visibly propels them; their springs are an open secret; their faces are of wood, their bellies filled with bran; and yet we thrillingly partake of their adventures. And the point may be illustrated still further. The last interview between Lucy and Richard Feverel is pure drama; more than that, it is the strongest scene, since Shakespeare, in the English tongue. Their first meeting by the river, on the other hand, is pure romance; it has nothing to do with character; it might happen to any other boy and maiden, and be none the less delightful for the change. And yet I think he would be a bold man who should choose between these passages. Thus, in the same book, we may have two scenes, each capital in its order: in the one, human passion, deep calling unto deep, shall utter its genuine voice; in the second, according to circumstances, like instruments in tune, shall build up a trivial but desirable incident, such as we love to prefigure for ourselves; and in the end, in spite of the critics, we may hesitate to give the preference to either. The one may ask more genius—I do not say it does; but at least the other dwells as clearly in the memory.

\* \* \* \* \* \*

To come at all at the nature of this quality of romance, we must bear in mind the peculiarity of our attitude to any art. No art produces illusion; in the theatre we never forget that we are in the theatre; and while we read a story, we sit wavering between two minds, now merely clapping our hands at the merit of the performance, now condescending to take an active part in fancy with the characters. This last is the triumph of romantic storytelling: when the reader consciously plays at being the hero, the scene is a good scene. Now in character-studies the pleasure that we take is critical; we watch, we approve, we smile at incongruities, we are moved to sudden heats of sympathy with courage, suffering or virtue. But the characters are still themselves, they are not us; the more clearly they are depicted, the more widely do they stand away from us, the more imperiously do they thrust us back into our place as a spectator. I cannot identify myself with Rawdon Crawley or with Eugène de Rastignac, for I have scarce a hope or fear in common with them. It is not character but incident that woos us out of our reserve. Something happens as we desire to have it happen to ourselves; some situation, that we have long dallied with in fancy, is realised in the story with enticing and appropriate details. Then we forget the characters; then we push the hero aside; then we plunge into the tale in our own person and bathe in fresh experience; and then, and then only, do we say we have been reading a romance. It is not only pleasurable things that we imagine in our day-dreams; there are lights in which we are willing to contemplate even the idea of our own death; ways in which it seems as if it would amuse us to be cheated, wounded or calumniated. It is thus possible to construct a story, even of tragic import, in which every incident, detail and trick of circumstance shall be welcome to the reader's thoughts. Fiction is to the grown man what play is to the child; it is there that he changes the atmosphere and tenor of his life; and when the game so chimes with his fancy that he can join in it with all his heart, when it pleases him with every turn, when he loves to recall it and dwells upon its recollection with entire delight, fiction is called romance.                    1887

# NOTES

SPECIAL NOTE ON REFERENCES: A small college dictionary will explain most of the allusions in the text to persons and places and to mythology; the others can be cleared up by consulting an unabridged dictionary; all such references and other necessary information will be found in the new fourteenth edition of the *Encyclopædia Britannica*. The English *Dictionary of National Biography* gives excellent brief accounts of all important Englishmen, including the Victorian authors. Valuable specific references on Victorian literature are Elton's two volumes entitled *A Survey of English Literature, 1830–1880*, Walker's *The Literature of the Victorian Era*, and Volumes XIII and XIV of the *Cambridge History of English Literature*. Origins, relations, and interpretations of individual poems and essays will often be found in editions of individual authors, as, for example, in the Cambridge Edition of Tennyson; but the responsibility for such interpretations should rest primarily on the teacher.

## TENNYSON

Alfred Tennyson was born in 1809, an exact contemporary of Gladstone and Lincoln, of Fitzgerald and Darwin. His birthplace was the village of Somersby near the east coast of England, and the love of rural scenes and of the sea permeates his whole life, as his poetry and his later homes in Surrey and on the Isle of Wight testify. His father, a clergyman, athlete, and man of varied artistic talents, and his mother, the daughter of a clergyman, brought up a family of twelve in very plain living but with high thinking and magnificent romantic playing. Two of his brothers were also poets, and when Alfred was only seventeen the three of them jointly published what they entitled *Poems by Two Brothers* (1827). At Trinity College, Cambridge, he was the close friend of Arthur Henry Hallam. While he was still in college his first volume under his own name, *Poems Chiefly Lyrical* (1830), appeared when he was only twenty-one. In 1832 appeared his second volume, *Poems* (wrongly dated 1833), and though this contained the early forms of *The Lady of Shalott*, *Œnone*, *The Palace of Art*, and *The Lotus-Eaters*, it was severely reviewed. Such severity, the death of Hallam in 1833, and the grinding poverty of his family after the death of his father in the same year discouraged him from further publication for ten years. In these ten years he devoted himself to that serious study of philosophy, science, and literature and to that perfecting of the rhythms and phrasing of his poems which he kept up throughout his long life. In 1842, however, he brought out two volumes entitled *Poems,* and these were hailed with universal applause. A revision of the better of his earlier poems and such favorites as *Morte d' Arthur, Ulysses,* and *Locksley Hall* account for four editions of this collection in four years. After that for nearly fifty years appeared a long list of volumes—*The Princess* in 1847, *In Memoriam* in 1850, *Maud* in 1855, the *Idylls of the King* from 1858 to 1886, up to a total of thirty-six collections of new poems or revised editions after 1842, all ending with *The Death of Œnone, Akbar's Dream,* and *Other Poems* in the year of his death in 1892. Every new edition of his poetry showed that continuous revision, that perfecting of phrase and movement which made him one of the greatest artists in verse of all time.

Though he lived and produced great poetry for forty years afterwards, 1850 was probably his greatest year. In that year he married Emily Sellwood, a marriage postponed for twelve years on account of the poet's poverty; he published *In Memoriam,* by common consent the most representative English poem of the intellectual and moral stress of the Victorian period; and he was made Poet Laureate, an honor he achieved through the Prince Consort's admiration for *In Memoriam.* He was raised to the peerage as Baron Tennyson in 1884, died in 1892, and was buried in Westminster Abbey with a great public funeral. It was a final honor fully deserved by the man everywhere admitted to be the most representative poet of his age.

A rough grouping of the poems in this volume will show the wide range of Tennyson. Two, *The Poet* and *Merlin and the Gleam,* are Tennyson's discussion of his art. A number represent him at his best in the art of pure lyric, in the combination of verbal music and imagery—*Claribel,* and the lyrics from *The Princess* and from *Maud.* Deeper, more personal lyrics are *Move Eastward, Happy Earth, Break, Break, Break,* and *De Profundis.* Patriotic lyrics or semiballads are *You Ask Me Why, Of Old Sat Freedom, The Charge of the Light Brigade,* and *The Revenge.* The poet's interest in the mediæval past is illustrated by *The Lady of Shalott, Morte d' Arthur, Sir Galahad,* and *Merlin and the Gleam;* in the classical past by *Œnone, The Lotus-Eaters, Ulysses,* and *Tithonus.* Poems of doubt and faith, of philosophy, poems illustrative of the great intellectual struggle of the age and of its interest in social questions are *Locksley Hall, In Memoriam, The Higher Pantheism, Flower in the Crannied Wall, De Profundis, By an Evolutionist,* and *Crossing the Bar.*

Page 1. **Claribel.** Claribel's death is told by Spenser. The subtitle—*A Melody*—shows the poet's intention—to write word music—an intention characteristic of the young poet of 1830, a follower of Spenser and Keats.

   2. **The Poet.** Tennyson's interpretation at twenty-one of the mission of the poet. Its Shelley-like vagueness, with the "melting" of "rites and forms," would not be approved by the mature Tennyson.
   **Calpe**—Gibraltar.

**Page 4. Œnone.** The old story of the Judgment of Paris and the desertion of Œnone for Helen. The speech of Pallas is said to indicate Tennyson's own ideals. The scenery is not Grecian but from the Pyrenees. The blank verse is made semilyrical by the repeated "Dear mother Ida, hearken ere I die."

**14.** "I am half sick of shadows" is the theme of the poem. Tennyson says the heroine is taken "out of the region of shadows into that of realities."

**48. Break, Break, Break.** Composed at five o'clock in the morning, while the poet's friend Hallam lay dead at Clevedon far away by the sea.

**51. In Memoriam.** The poet says that the "I" of *In Memoriam* is not always the author speaking of himself, but the voice of the human race speaking through him.
him, line 1—Goethe.

**54. Stanza XCVI, line 1. You.** Probably Tennyson's sister, Emilia, Hallam's fiancée.

**55. One indeed I knew.** Hallam.

**76. The Higher Pantheism.** First read before a philosophical society. Van Dyke says that Tennyson believed all reality is spiritual and the material world exists only as a shadow of the mind of God.

**85.** Originally written on the birth of the poet's eldest son, Hallam, in 1852.

**87. Merlin and the Gleam.** Tennyson says *The Gleam* means the "higher poetic imagination."

**94. Crossing the Bar.** Composed when the poet was eighty-one, and under his direction always put at the end of his poems.

## BROWNING

Browning furnishes a marked contrast to Tennyson in the environment of his life. Robert Browning, the third of the name, was born in a suburb of London, May 7, 1812, in a home of relative wealth. His mother was Scotch and German with an inherited talent for music and art. His father and his grandfather, both Robert Brownings, were officials of the Bank of England, and his great-grandfather was an innkeeper in the south of England. His banker father was a lover of fine books and of art, a linguist and a verse writer, with fine social qualities. The city boy, Robert Browning III, became a city man and remained a city man all of his life. The boy's family inheritance was from middle class business men, not from gentry and clergy, like Tennyson. But in spite of his class and his occupation, the father was no Philistine but a man measuring up in every way to Matthew Arnold's standards of "sweetness and light." Music and art and old books surrounded the boy from his infancy.

His education was largely by absorption from his father, though he did have two years at the modern University of London. He was trained not merely in Latin, Greek, and French but also in riding, boxing, fencing, dancing, music, sculpture, and painting. By the time he was twelve the lad had accumulated enough Byronic verse for a volume, but no publisher, fortunately, would take it. His second poetic passion was for Shelley, and Shelley was a life influence, as we can see by his *Essay on Shelley* in 1852 and his poem *Memorabilia* of 1853.

At the age of twenty-one, in 1833, he published anonymously at his father's expense a Shelleyan poem, *Pauline*, which significantly was a dramatic monologue. It was, of course, unsuccessful. He "read up" exhaustively for his next poem, *Paracelsus*, in the British Museum, and it shows the influence of the new science (see the *Introduction*) and of most of the currents of thought of his time. Appearing in 1835, it at once attracted to him the friendship and sympathy of Forster, Dickens, Leigh Hunt, Landor, Wordsworth, and Macready, the actor. *Pauline* was monologue, and *Paracelsus* conversational drama. Macready urged the young poet to write a poetic drama, and *Strafford*, in 1837, was the result, a first proof that real drama was not Browning's forte. Then by a journey thither began that all-pervasive influence of Italy on his life and work. Italy was Browning's second home. "It was my university," the poet said. The lines of his *De Gustibus* are real:

> "Italy, my Italy!
> Open my heart and you will see
> Graved inside of it 'Italy.'"

*Sordello* of 1840, his first Italian study, alienated a good many of his friends by its obscure style. Later the poet said of *Sordello*: "My own faults of expression were many"; but he recognized his own strength, his own peculiar province in literature, when he said, "my stress lay on the incidents in the development of a soul: little else is worth study." This statement of what was to be his supreme function as a poet links him with the great psychological novelists, George Eliot and Meredith. His next play, *Pippa Passes*, of 1841, was a much more successful result of his interest in Italy, and it appeared as the first of the long series of eight volumes called, Ruskinlike, *Bells and Pomegranates*, what the poet intended to be "the first of a series of dramatical pieces to come out at intervals." From 1842 to 1855 they came out, essentially closet dramas, not so constructed as to be successful on the stage— *King Victor and King Charles, The Return of the Druses, A Blot on the 'Scutcheon, Colombe's Birthday, A Soul's Tragedy, Luria,* and *In a Balcony*. But he had found his true forms earlier in the *Dramatic Lyrics* of 1842—ballad-like marching songs, love lyrics, and dramatic monologues. The world accepts these, along with similar work in the *Dramatic Ro-*

*mances* of 1845, *Men and Women* of 1855, and *Dramatis Personæ* of 1864, as Browning's best work. When *The Ring and the Book* appeared in 1868–69, his most characteristic work was completed. He had been publishing for twenty-five years, and though he continued to publish for twenty more years, the selections in this volume of Victorian Literature, with the exception of the necessary omission of selections from *The Ring and the Book*, illustrate the common opinion that his best work was done by 1864. Only one poem given here appeared after that date, the *Epilogue* to Asolando, published on the day of his death.

Probably the most unusual circumstance in the history of Victorian authors was the union of Robert Browning and Elizabeth Barrett in a perfect marriage. Browning's passionate adoration of his wife affected his life profoundly. For fifteen years they lived in the Italy they both loved, from the wedding in 1846 to Mrs. Browning's death in 1861. The essential healthfulness of Browning's life shows itself in the fact that after his wife's death he made a life of cheerful communion with his friends in London, of devotion to the training of his son, and of continued production of poetry. After long waiting fame and honor came to him these latter years. Though he returned to Italy to die, the English people brought his body back to the Poet's Corner in Westminster Abbey, where he preceded Tennyson by three years.

Page 94. **Porphyria's Lover.** The first (1836) of Browning's dramatic monologues.

96. **Pippa's Song.** Browning's optimism, his philosophy, put into the mouth of the little silk weaver of his drama, *Pippa Passes*.

97. **Marching Along.** Illustrates Browning's magnificent handling of march music.

103. **The Lost Leader.** Browning, like other young liberals, resented the desertion of the liberal cause by Wordsworth. Cf. Whittier's *Ichabod* (Webster).

105. **The Bishop Orders His Tomb.** An epitome of the pagan spirit of the Italian Renaissance.

106. **Epistle side.** The right side of the altar, where the Epistle for the Day is read.

108. **Elucescebat.**—"He was illustrious." Not good Ciceronian Latin.

110. **Memorabilia.** A part of Browning's Shelley worship. Cf. his prose *Essay on Shelley* in the Cambridge edition of his complete works.

110 and 118. **One Word More** and **My Star** are addressed to his wife.

122. **Grammarian.** Renaissance scholar.

125. **Soul-hydroptic.** Soul thirsty.

Page 126. "Hoti" . . . "Oun" . . . "De." Greek particles, mean-
         ing respectively, "that," "therefore," and "towards."
     128. The Ruins. Probably of the Campagna near Rome.
     133. Saint Laurence. The church of San Lorenzo.
     134. The Eight. The magistrates of Florence.
     142. Iste perfecit opus. "This man made the work," referring
         to an inscription on a scroll in the painting, indicating that
         Lippi painted the picture.
     145. The Urbinate. Raphael.
     147. That Francis. Francis I of France, Andrea's first great
         patron.
     150. Rabbi Ben Ezra. Jewish scholar, philosopher, and poet
         of the Middle Ages.
     156. Potter and clay endure. Contrast the attitude here with
         that in the Rubáiyát, stanzas LXXXIX to XCVII. Cf.
         Carlyle, p. 354; for origins, cf. the Bible, Isaiah LXIV, 8
         and Jeremiah XVIII, 1–6.
     159. Bals paré. Fancy dress balls.
     160. Caliban. The beast-man from Shakespeare's Tempest.
         "'Will." For "He will." Caliban habitually thinks of
         himself in the third person. The "He" or "Him" with
         a capital refers to the god Setebos.
     169. Prospice. "Look forward."
     170. Epilogue to Asolando. This poem, with Prospice, gives
         Browning's attitude toward death—an optimism that had
         never faltered. When reading the proof of the Epilogue
         just before his death, he said the third stanza "looks
         like bragging . . . but it's the simple truth; and as it's
         true, it shall stand."

## MRS. BROWNING

Only two women of the Victorian era have any claim to distinction as poets. One of these is Christina Rossetti, and the other is
Mrs. Browning. Elizabeth Barrett Browning was born in 1806, born
to wealth. Her life was wholly uneventful. She had a joyous
childhood in the country; but an accident when she was fifteen in-
jured her spine, and she was an invalid confined to a sofa for practically all her life. She could read Homer in the original Greek
when she was only eight years old, and her father published privately what she called her "great epic," The Battle of Marathon,
when she was only thirteen. The first poets to influence her were
Byron and Pope, and at twenty her father again bore the expense of
publishing a volume, which she entitled, Pope-like, An Essay on Mind
and Other Poems. In the meantime the shut-in recluse read everything, including Plato and all the Greek poets in the original and the
whole Bible in Hebrew. One result of this reading was the publication in 1833 of her translation of Prometheus Bound, of Æschylus,

with some original poems. That year her father brought the family for permanent residence to London. Gradually the invalid built up a circle of pleasant literary friends—Wordsworth, Landor, Miss Mitford, Harriet Martineau, John Kenyon. In 1838 appeared her fourth volume, *The Seraphim and Other Poems*. In 1841–42 she wrote a series of articles on the Greek and the English poets, and these attracted the attention of Browning. In 1843 she published that passionate plea for social justice, *The Cry of the Children*. Then in 1844 appeared a collection of all her work in two volumes, entitled *Poems*.

This led directly to her acquaintance with Browning, and in 1846, owing to the strenuous opposition of her father, the two poets eloped, were married in London, and immediately went to Italy, where they lived for the remaining fifteen years of her life. Marriage, the devotion of Browning, and Italy meant happiness, even much improved health for her, and a full life. Browning was shown only after their marriage the remarkable sonnet sequence inspired by her love for him and written during their courtship, and intensely personal though they were, he insisted that they be published. They appeared in 1847, privately printed as *Sonnets by E. B. B.*, and were reissued publicly under the disguise of *Sonnets from the Portuguese* in 1850. In the meantime her warm-hearted pity for the oppressed induced her to publish in America *The Runaway Slave at Pilgrim Point*. Then in 1849 her son was born. In 1850 she reissued all her poems, with additions, and also published her sonnets. In 1851 her intense sympathy with the cause of Italian liberty found expression in a new volume entitled *Casa Guidi Windows*. In 1853 the public again called for a new edition of her poems. In 1857 she published her long novel *Aurora Leigh* in verse, and it proved so popular a second edition had to be printed in two weeks, a third a few months later, and a fourth in 1859. In 1860 her sympathy for the Italian cause and her hatred for slavery found expression anew in *Poems before Congress*. A volume of *Last Poems* appeared in 1862 after her death. She had died in 1861, and her husband buried her in her beloved Florence.

Page 171. **The Cry of the Children.** Mrs. Browning's passionate revolt against the great social evils of the factory system. Cf. Carlyle, Ruskin, Dickens, Tennyson, Morris, and Swinburne.

176. **Sonnets from the Portuguese.** One of the great sonnet sequences of the language, in its passionate reality wholly unlike the artificial love sonnet sequences of the Elizabethans.

## FITZGERALD

Edward Fitzgerald lived wholly a life of retirement. He was born in 1809, educated at Trinity College, Cambridge, where he became intimate with Thackeray, lived awhile in Paris, and then retired to the country of his birth, Suffolk, to live a life of leisure, making himself busy only with his books, his flowers, his music, his sailing, and his friends. He had a genius for friends and counted among them not only Thackeray but also Tennyson and Carlyle. To both Thackeray and Tennyson he was "Old Fitz," and Tennyson addressed him so in his dedication to "Tiresias":

> "Who live on milk and meal and grass.
> ....................but none can say
> That Lenten fare makes Lenten thought,
> Who reads your golden Eastern boy."

Fitzgerald wrote a Platonic dialog entitled *Euphranor* and a collection of aphorisms called *Patronius*. He was the translator of Calderon, of Æschylus and Sophocles. But his supreme gift for creative translation showed itself in 1859 in the little anonymous booklet entitled *The Rubáiyát of Omar Khayyám*. It was almost stillborn and perhaps might have so remained had not Rossetti and Swinburne discovered it. Two other editions came out, both carefully revised, the second in 1868 (the one used in this volume) and the third in 1872. No one else in the Victorian age wrote such letters as Fitzgerald wrote to his friends, letters searching in literary criticism, human, witty, and altogether delightful. He died in his sleep in 1883.

Page 179 ff. **The Rubáiyát.** The proper names of this poem give the appropriate romantic effects of themselves, without tedious explanations in each case of their exact Persian references.

    **194. The Ball.** In the game of polo, of ancient Persian origin.

## CLOUGH

Arthur Hugh Clough was so closely associated with Matthew Arnold in both life and spirit that the world has insisted on considering them together; yet they were far from being identical either in the circumstances of their lives or in their personalities. Clough was born January 1, 1819, at Liverpool, where his father was a cotton merchant. When Clough was only three years old, his father moved the family to Charleston, South Carolina. When the lad was nine, the family visited England and left the boy in school, one year at Chester and then from 1828 to 1837 with Dr. Thomas Arnold at Rugby. The influence on Clough of Rugby and of Dr. Arnold was profound, and here he began that intimacy with Matthew Arnold that continued until Clough's death. Clough entered Balliol College at Oxford in 1837, where he was joined by Arnold in 1840. Here, besides Arnold, he was closely associated with Jowett, Stanley, Temple, Shairp, and W. G. Ward. He obtained a fellowship and tutorship at Oriel College, where again Arnold became his colleague in a fellowship. Clough's time at Oxford was in the midst of the intellectual, religious, and spiritual conflicts which gathered around the Oxford Movement. Newman and Pusey were then at the height of their influence at Oxford; Ward in Clough's own college was one of the younger leaders of the Tractarians, while Jowett and Stanley and Temple were liberals in religion. Clough felt the necessity as an honest man of freeing himself from a position that implied orthodoxy; accordingly he resigned his fellowship and his tutorship at Oxford. He traveled on the continent during the revolutionary movements of 1848. In 1849 he became principal of University Hall at the University of London but, in spite of a friendship with Carlyle, he was unhappy here among the Unitarians as he had been among the orthodox at Oxford. Through the influence of Emerson in 1852 he went to Cambridge, Massachusetts, to lecture and write; but in 1853 he returned to England to take up work in the Education Office, a work in which Arnold had preceded him by two years. He remained an Education official until his death in Florence in 1861. His best monument is Matthew Arnold's elegy, *Thyrsis*.

Clough is in many ways typical of the sensitive-minded, thinking Englishman of his generation, of a temperament and an environment that made him one of the two chief "poets of doubt." Freed from a bondage by leaving Oxford in 1848, he published that same year the odd-titled "long vacation pastoral," *The Bothie of Tober-na-Vuolich*, a poem full of jests, humor, and bubbling spirits, thus creating an atmosphere never found in Arnold's poetry. The poem is fundamentally serious, however, in its discussion of the social problems of the time and in its love for nature. *Ambarvalia* in 1849 contains shorter poems written before *The Bothie*. *Dipsychus*, an attempted satirical representation of an intellectual and moral world divided against itself, was written at Venice in 1850, but was not published until 1862 after the poet's death.

**Page 202. Qua Cursum Ventus.** "As the wind determines the course."

## ARNOLD

Matthew Arnold was six men in one; or, rather, he was one man who expressed himself in six different directions. He was a poet dissatisfied with life as he found it as a young man. Then he was a government educational official, a political secretary, a schoolmaster, a professor, an essayist, and a publicist, with prose work that took the form of criticism—criticism educational, literary, social, political, and religious. Yet the paralysis of action indicated in his poetry of doubt and disillusionment did not rule his life; on the contrary, he worked for forty years trying to set the world right.

Matthew Arnold had the great advantage of being born the son of the great Dr. Thomas Arnold of Rugby. Three years younger than his friend Clough, he was born in 1822, educated at his father's school with Clough and at the "high thinking" Balliol College at Oxford. Later he was a fellow at Oriel College. In Oxford he was associated with Clough and his intimates. He took prizes for poetry both at Rugby and at Oxford. From 1847 to 1851 he was the political secretary of Lord Lansdowne in Lord John Russell's cabinet. He followed the family bent by becoming an assistant master at Rugby for a time. In 1851 this bent was confirmed as his life work when he received an appointment as inspector of schools, a profession he followed for thirty-five years. Two years before, in 1849, he brought out anonymously his first volume of poetry, *The Strayed Reveler and Other Poems*. It attracted little attention and was later withdrawn from circulation. The same was true of the volume of 1852 entitled *Empedocles on Etna and Other Poems*. Even Clough reviewed these volumes without enthusiasm. In 1853, however, he attached his name to a volume called *Poems*, and he prefixed a noteworthy *Preface* on the nature of poetry which began his career as a literary critic. This volume was received better, and when in 1855 he published a new volume of Poems, it elected him in 1857 to the professorship of poetry at Oxford, a position he held for ten years. Out of the Oxford professorship grew some of his important literary criticisms—*On Translating Homer* in 1861, *Essays in Criticism* (first series) in 1865, *On the Study of Celtic Literature* in 1867. In 1867, also, he brought out his last volume of poetry, entitled *New Poems*. He had already begun to publish educational reports and to make special investigations of schools on the Continent, and this continued throughout his life. In 1869 he began his notable career as a social and political critic in *Culture and Anarchy* and the following year, 1870, he entered the field of religious criticism with *St. Paul and Protestantism*. After this eight different volumes in social, political, religious, and literary criticism appeared before his death in 1888.

Page 209. **He . . . the old man.** Homer.

          **The Wide Prospect.** Translation of the Greek Εὐρώπη—Europe.

          **That halting slave.** Epictetus.

          **Brutal son.** Domitian.

          **Singer of sweet Colonus.** Sophocles.

  214. **Requiescat.** "Let her rest."

  227. **But thou.** Honoring his father, Dr. Thomas Arnold of Rugby.

  418. **Sweetness and Light.** From *Culture and Anarchy;* when Arnold was delivering this material in his lectures as Professor of Poetry at Oxford, his title was *Culture and Its Enemies*. The phrase "Sweetness and Light" came from Swift's *Battle of the Books*—"we . . . chose to fill our lives with honey and wax, thus furnishing mankind with the two noblest of things, which are sweetness and light."

Page 420. **Bishop Wilson.** Thomas Wilson was Bishop of the Isle of Man from 1697 to his death in 1755.

424. **Our modern world, of which the whole civilization is . . . mechanical and external.** This is Carlyle's quarrel with the civilization of the Mid-Victorian age, and it is Ruskin's. For all that follows in Arnold, cf. the contemporary civilization (1932) of both England and America.

425. **Faith in machinery.** Arnold's "machinery" is equivalent to Carlyle's "clothes" (p. 333 ff.)—mere means to ends, old routines, outworn conventions.

**Mr. Roebuck.** A leading Liberal in Parliament.

427. **Philistines.** "Philistine," as Arnold uses it, can be traced back to German student slang of the late eighteenth century. A "Philister" is the tradesman foe of the children of light, *i.e.*, of the students themselves; and therefore— as used by Goethe, Heine, Carlyle, and Arnold—"Philistine" means a "strong, dogged, unenlightened opponent of the chosen people . . . slaves to routine, enemies to light." Cf. *Introduction*, pp. lxiv–lxv.

The Greek words (ἀφυΐα, εὐφυΐα, εὐφυής, ἀφυής) are defined by Epictetus and by Arnold himself.

432. **Independents.** English Congregationalists.

**The Dissidence of Dissent.** From Burke's *Conciliation with America*.

435. **Publicè egestas, privatim opulentia.** From Sallust's *Catiline* —"public want and private wealth."

438. **The great movement.** The Oxford or Tractarian Movement (1833 ff.), led by Newman and Keble, sought to intensify religious faith by a return to the elaborate ceremonials and Catholic traditions of the Middle Ages; the forerunner of the Anglo-Catholic movement in the Established Church in England and in the Episcopal Church in America to-day.

**Quæ regio.** From the *Æneid*—"What region of the earth is not filled with the tale of our woe?"

## ROSSETTI

Dante Gabriel Rossetti was three-fourths Italian. His father was an Italian liberal and poet, who had fled to England for asylum and who became professor of Italian at King's College in London. The poet and painter was born in London in 1828, the oldest of three gifted children, the others being William Michael Rossetti and Christina Rossetti. Rossetti studied art at an early age in the art schools of London and later with Ford Madox Brown. In 1848 at the house of Millais, Rossetti, Holman Hunt, and Millais founded the Pre-Raphaelite Brotherhood. They were joined at once by W. M. Rossetti, Woolner, and Collinson, and later by Morris and Burne-Jones, and still later, in fundamental sympathy at least, by Swinburne and Watts-Dunton. Ruskin became their sponsor, and in spite of the earlier attacks, they became respectable under his patronage. Rossetti exhibited his first picture painted according to the principles of the Brotherhood as early as 1849, when he was barely of age. In 1850 *The Germ*, the organ of the Brotherhood, was founded, and to this Rossetti contributed "The Blessed Damozel" and ten other poems, applying the same principles to poetry he used in his painting. By this time he and the Brotherhood were using as a model a very beautiful milliner's apprentice, Elizabeth Siddal, whom Rossetti painted many times. In 1860 they were married; but his wife died in 1862, and in a frenzy of grief Rossetti buried his manuscript poems in her grave. In the meantime he had become interested with Morris in decorative art, and himself had much to do with the revival of interest in stained glass. He painted and exhibited through the years from 1849 many pictures, the most noted of which are the early *Ecce Ancilla Domini*, and the later *Beata Beatrix* and *Dante's Dream*. In 1869 he was induced to disinter his poems, and they were published in 1870, though many of them had been composed in his youth. He lived the latter part of his life in Cheyne Walk, Chelsea, near Carlyle's home. His *Ballads and Sonnets* appeared in 1881, and he died in 1882, a victim in part of the same use of narcotics that had helped to kill his wife.

Page 235 ff. **Sister Helen.** Note the folk ballad characteristics— story told wholly by dialogue, refrain, incremental repetition, use of the supernatural for chief motive (the waxen image), etc.

245-247. **The House of Life.** Rossetti's beautiful sonnet sequence was written for Elizabeth Siddal, his model for most of his famous pictures (*e.g.*, *Beata Beatrix*), whom he married and in whose grave he buried all his manuscript poems.

# MEREDITH

George Meredith was born at Portsmouth in 1828, an exact contemporary of his friend Rossetti, whom he outlived a quarter of a century. He always insisted on his mixture of Welsh and Irish blood, and undoubtedly that mixture accounts for a good deal in his work. He was educated as a lad in Germany, studied law in London and abandoned it for journalism and literature. While in London he belonged to a group of young radicals, with John Morley and Frederick Harrison as their chief spirits. His first wife was the daughter of Thomas Love Peacock, from whom the son-in-law caught some of his earlier mockery and fantastic humor. He began early to send poetry to the magazines. In 1851 he published a small volume called *Poems*. Tennyson and Kingsley both recognized his value as a poet, his "health and sweetness," as Tennyson said, but the general public was indifferent. In 1855 his first effort at fiction, *The Shaving of Shagpat*, a fantastic Arabian Nights "entertainment," appeared; and this was praised by Rossetti. In 1859 came his first important novel, *The Ordeal of Richard Feverel*, and it represented fully the type of fiction that was to make his fame, the psychological study and interpretation of motive and action. Slowly the long list of novels appeared for some forty years. The novels best known are *Rhoda Fleming* (1865), *Beauchamp's Career* (1875), *The Egoist* (1878), and *Diana of the Crossways* (1885). His second volume of poetry in 1862 he called, clumsily enough, *Modern Love, and Poems of the English Roadside, with Poems and Ballads*. Then followed a series of collections of poetry—*Poems and Lyrics of the Joy of Earth* (1883), *Ballads and Poems of Tragic Life* (1887), *A Reading of Earth* (1888), *Odes in Contribution to the Song of French History* (1888), *A Reading of Life* (1901), and *Last Poems* (1909). It is noteworthy that Meredith got little hearing from the general public for his novels until *Beauchamp's Career*, twenty years after his first publication of fiction. It will be noted also that for twenty years, from 1862 to 1883, he published no poetry, but that in the next quarter of a century he published six different volumes. The explanation of his lack of early popularity and of his comparative lack of it to-day lies partly in his difficult style, a style that makes him one of the triumvirate of difficult styles—Carlyle, Browning, and Meredith. At his death in 1909, however, his fame was high.

Page 248. **Love in the Valley.** Characteristic of Meredith's blending of nature and love. Note that the year of the countryman runs through all its seasons, beginning with "All the girls are out" in early spring and running to "Large and smoky red the sun's cold disk" of winter.

256. **Juggling Jerry.** Illustrates again the blending of nature and love when the old Juggler lies dying in his old wife's arms in the "prime of May," in "God's house on a blowing day."

259. **The chirper.** The ale glass.

260. **Lucifer in Starlight.** A parable. Cf. Browning's "All's right with the world." The embodied Power of Evil, of destruction, cannot stay the stars, "the brain of heaven," which "Around the ancient track marched, rank on rank, The army of unalterable law."

261. **Dirge in Woods.** Death is a prerequisite to life—"And we drop like the fruits of the tree."
**Song in the Songless.** This "dwarf lyric" expresses Meredith's "personal feeling of sympathetic community with inanimate nature."

262. **Youth in Age.** Cf. Wordsworth's "Ode on the Intimations of Immortality."

## MORRIS

William Morris, born in 1834, was the son of a London business man. In his school days he was attracted to architecture and toward the pageantry of the Anglo-Catholic movement. He entered Exeter College, Oxford, in 1853, where, with Burne-Jones and other friends, he read and studied theology, ecclesiastical history, and poetry of the Middle Ages, studied art, and read Tennyson and Ruskin. After college in 1856, he began the study of architecture as a profession, and also studied painting. Rossetti, who now became his friend, urged him to give his whole attention to painting. In 1858 Morris published one of the best of his poems, *The Defence of Guenevere*, fully illustrating that mediæval bent of the Pre-Raphaelites which was to rule most of Morris's poetry. His marriage in 1859 and his building of a new home for himself suggested his permanent life work —home decoration. The artists, Rossetti, Burne-Jones, and Madox Brown, with Morris and others created a company to undertake church decoration, carving, metal work, paper-hangings, and the weaving of chintzes, carpets, and tapestry. Later he began work in artistic book printing, spending some seven years, for example, on the *Kelmscott Chaucer*. Morris was a practical success in doing what Ruskin and Arnold preached, the bringing of beauty into the lives of Englishmen. Early he saw, like his master and inspirer, Ruskin, that the conditions of life must be changed if art was to flourish. Consequently he tried to better things through organization, passed from the Radical section of the Liberal party to the Democratic Federation, and merged this into the Socialist League. Later he was forced out of the socialistic work by the anarchistic wing of the party which got control, and the latter years of his life he gave up to writing and to his art work.

Morris's literary work went on simultaneously with his art work. After *The Defence of Guenevere* appeared *The Life and Death of Jason* in 1867, *The Earthly Paradise* in 1868–70, translations of the *Æneid* and the *Odyssey* in 1867, *Love Is Enough* in 1872, *Sigurd the Volsung* in 1877, and translations of various Norse sagas, *Beowulf*, etc. He published also several volumes of prose fiction and poetry and prose meant to assist the socialist cause. All his work in art and in literature is inspired by the one motive of bringing back into life the beauty of the Middle Ages; but in poetry he recognized that he was a Pre-Raphaelite, an "idle singer of an empty day," even though in his art work he strove as strenuously as Carlyle, Ruskin, and Arnold to make the world better. His poetry was so well received that he was offered the Oxford Professorship in Poetry but refused it. He died in 1896.

Page 263. **The ivory gate.** Greek legends say false dreams come through gates of ivory, true dreams through gates of horn. **"Who strive to build a shadowy isle of bliss."** This is the Pre-Raphaelite motive, the denial of the real world; but cf. *The Day Is Coming*, pp. 282–283.

**Page 269. Sigurd.** From Morris's rendering of the Norse *Volsunga Saga*.

## SWINBURNE

Algernon Charles Swinburne was born in 1837, the year of Queen Victoria's accession to the throne, and he lived almost to the World War, dying in 1908. Like Byron, he was born an aristocrat, and like Byron, he was a rebel against most of the conventions of his class and his time. He was the son of Admiral Charles Henry Swinburne, and his mother was the daughter of an earl. He attended Eton, and in 1857 he entered Balliol College at Oxford, the college of Clough and Arnold. Though a good student, he left without his degree in 1860, and the same year, when only twenty-three, published two dramas inspired by the Elizabethans—*The Queen Mother* and *Rosamond*. He was always strongly responsive to outside influences, to a form of discipleship. In 1862 he took a residence with Rossetti and Meredith as neighbor to Carlyle in Cheyne Row in Chelsea, and much of his later work is essentially Pre-Raphaelite. In 1864 he met Landor in Italy, and Landor's interest in things classical inspired, partly at least, Swinburne's *Atalanta in Calydon*, which he dedicated to Landor. In 1866 his *Poems and Ballads*, written under the influence of the Pre-Raphaelites and of Baudelaire, the French decadent, raised a storm of moral protest, though everybody read them. He became acquainted with Mazzini, the Italian patriot, and with Victor Hugo through correspondence, and the results are *The Song of Italy* in 1867 and *Songs before Sunrise* in 1871. As the first series of *Poems and Ballads* voiced Swinburne's revolt against the Victorian moral and social restraints, so these two later volumes stood for his violent republican and agnostic revolt against kings and priests. He continued to publish steadily volume after volume representing these different influences, and in 1882 added a new interest in his interpretation of the Arthurian material in *Tristram of Lyonesse*. He was influential as a literary critic in his books and articles on Shakespeare and various Elizabethans, on Blake, Charlotte Brontë, Dickens, and Hugo. But his greatest influence was undoubtedly exercised through his marvelous command over lyrical rhythms and tone color. The last thirty years of his life he spent in retirement, deaf and in ill health, in the companionship of his friend Theodore Watts-Dunton.

**Page 284. A Pope.** Pope Pius IX, driven from Rome by the Italian patriot, Garibaldi, was restored by the French army in 1849.

**285. Itylus.** Killed by his mother, Procne, who was changed into a swallow, and by his aunt, Philomela, who was changed into a nightingale.

**290. Proserpine.** Queen of the infernal regions, whose groves formed a realm of shades near the entrance to the underworld.

## HARDY

Thomas Hardy was born in 1840 in that Dorsetshire he has created into a literary world which he has continued to present to his readers for over half a century as "Wessex." It was very literally his homeland—in birth, in the long years of his life, and in the world of his imagination which he has transferred to his novels and to his poems. No great writer of the Victorian era so restricted himself in subject matter to one section of country; with the exception of *The Dynasts*, practically all of Hardy's important work must be referred to the Dorsetshire and the Wiltshire of his "Wessex." Hardy was a trained and successful practicing architect, for ten years a winner of architectural prizes, but he had written poetry and essays before he was of age. Meredith, as reader for the publishers, encouraged him in fiction, and Hardy published his first novel in 1871, beginning his work after the more logical time limit set for the Victorian age. He continued his work as a novelist for a quarter of a century, producing such masterpieces as *Under the Greenwood Tree* (1872), *Far from the Madding Crowd* (1874), which first attained popularity, *The Return of the Native* (1878), and *Tess of the D'Urbervilles* (1891). *Jude the Obscure* (1895) alienated his novel-reading audience, and he turned to poetry.

He had been writing poetry occasionally throughout his life, and at fifty-eight, in 1898, one hundred years after Wordsworth and Coleridge's *Lyrical Ballads*, he published his *Wessex Poems*. This was followed at intervals with other volumes of lyric verse—*Poems of Past and Present* in 1901, *Time's Laughing-Stocks* in 1909, *Satires of Circumstance* in 1914, and four more up to the year of his death in 1928. His greatest work as a poet, some say one of the greatest poems in the language, is *The Dynasts*, published in three volumes in 1904, 1906, 1908 respectively. It is a dramatic poem, primarily epic in intention, presenting England in struggle with Napoleon and written exactly a hundred years after that struggle. Through all his poetry as well as through all his novels runs the pessimistic naturalism that finds no comfort in the indifferent and pitiless control exercised by the blind power of nature and life over human creatures. Hardy lived to the great age of eighty-eight. His ashes are buried in Westminster Abbey, but his heart is interred in his native Wessex parish churchyard.

## MACAULAY

Thomas Babington Macaulay was born with the century, in 1800. His father had been a colonial governor, and in 1800 was an enthusiastic philanthropist working for the abolition of slavery. The precocity of Macaulay is proverbial. At four he told a caller inquiring about an aching tooth, "I thank you, madame, the agony is abated." At eight he was already the author, in manuscript, of a *Compendium of Universal History* and of a metrical romance in three cantos entitled *The Battle of Cheviot*. After attendance at a private school he entered Trinity College, Cambridge, where he wrote prize poems and later became a fellow. He was called to the bar at twenty-six. He had begun speaking in the anti-slavery cause two years earlier. In 1825 his essay on Milton was published in the *Edinburgh Review*, and he became famous over night. The family lost its money, and Macaulay for the next four years had to eke out a living by writing for the reviews. He entered Parliament in 1830 from a "pocket borough" and began work at once to kill all pocket boroughs. His triumphant eloquence was one of the chief factors in passing the first great Reform Bill in 1832. His political success was so great that, young as he was, he was at once given office on the Board of Control for Indian affairs. He helped pass the bill for the abolition of slavery in 1833. In 1834 he took a seat on the Supreme Council for India and spent four years there at ten thousand pounds a year, organizing Indian education, drafting a penal code, and so leading in many directions in the organization of the new Crown government that the effects of his work are seen in India to-day. On his return in 1839 he entered the cabinet, but he quit political life in 1847 when defeated for Parliament in Edinburgh.

Macaulay occasionally from 1825 had been publishing in the periodicals his critical and historical essays. In 1842 he published his declamatory *Lays of Ancient Rome*, and in 1843 published his collected essays. He had been working for years, as politics would permit, on his history. In 1848 appeared the first two volumes of the *History of England* which sold like a best-seller novel of to-day. Volumes III and IV appeared in 1855, and he received in royalties the record-breaking sum of $100,000. The *History* was translated into a dozen modern languages. Its popularity showed that he had accomplished his purpose—to write a history as interesting as a novel. In 1857 he became Baron Macaulay; but his health was failing, and in 1859 he died and was buried in Westminster. He had worked sincerely and most effectively for middle class reform. He had popularized history and literary criticism. If he failed to see the profounder problems of Victorian England, he must be given credit for doing so much.

Page 312. **Beauclerk.** A young intimate of the Johnson circle.
    314. **One of his contemporaries.** Horace Walpole.
        **Another.** Garrick.
        **Hieracles.** Supposed Greek collector of wit and jokes.
    316. **Justice Shallow** in Shakespeare's *2 Henry IV* and *Merry Wives*; **Dr. Caius** in *Merry Wives*; **Fluellen** in *Henry V*; **Alnaschar** in the *Arabian Nights*; **Malvolio** in *Twelfth Night*.
    319. **That celebrated club.** The Literary Club founded by Sir Joshua Reynolds.

## CARLYLE

Thomas Carlyle, the son of a Scotch mason and small farmer, was born, the only writer in this volume, in the eighteenth century, in 1795. In order to live at all the family had to exercise more than Scotch frugality; but the lad's brilliancy in school and his love of books induced the father to try to educate him for the ministry. Young Thomas walked to Edinburgh and entered the University in 1809. He became a schoolmaster in 1814 in his old school at Annan, and then he taught in Kirkcaldy, where Edward Irving became his great friend. He gave up the thought of the ministry because, although profoundly religious, he became wholly unorthodox in his views. His atheistic reaction against Christianity profoundly disquieted him; but in 1822 he went through the crisis he pictures in *Sartor* as the "*Everlasting Yea.*" Goethe now became his chief literary and philosophical hero, and he translated Goethe's *Wilhelm Meister* in 1824. His first literary mission was the introduction of German literature to Englishmen. Meanwhile his acquaintance with brilliant Jane Welsh had ripened into a marriage in 1826, and in 1828 they settled at the out-of-the-way farm of Craigenputtock. Here for nine years he labored at *Sartor Resartus* and at pot-boilers for the publishers.

Carlyle's literary career began properly with the publication of *Sartor Resartus* in *Fraser's Magazine* in 1833–34; but it was so unpopular he could find no publisher for it until Emerson arranged for its publication in America in 1836, and it was not until 1838 it appeared in London. Meanwhile the Carlyles settled in 1834 at No. 24 Cheyne Row in Chelsea, London. Here Carlyle lived for nearly half a century, and the house of the "Sage of Chelsea" is now owned by the public and kept as a memorial museum. Here he finished his *French Revolution*. Its publication in 1837 established his reputation and freed him from money worries, and he was acknowledged as a great historian eleven years before Macaulay attained a like reputation. From 1837 to 1840 he gave courses of lectures in London that proved highly popular, and one of these he published in 1841 as *Heroes and Hero-Worship, and the Heroic in History*. This was only setting forth with many illustrations the doctrine back of his *French Revolution*, and expressed definitely in *Sartor*—that history must always be the study of individual leadership and that it is the business of other men to acknowledge and obey the hero. His interest in social and industrial questions of the strenuous forties is shown in *Chartism* (1839), *Past and Present* (1843), and *Latter-Day Pamphlets* (1850). In his *Cromwell* of 1845 and *History of Frederick II of Prussia* from 1858 to 1865 he illustrates in detail his doctrine of the hero. He prepared his own *Reminiscences* and the *Letters and Memorials* of his wife, but they were not published till 1883. His reputation was so high that he was elected to the rectorship of the University of Edinburgh in 1865; but while in Edinburgh in 1866 to deliver his inaugural, he received a blow from which he never recovered in the sudden death of his wife. He lingered on in seclusion and loneliness at his Chelsea home for fifteen years, visited by such friends as Froude, Ruskin, and Tennyson, and died there in 1881. The nation wished to bury him in Westminster, but following his own desire, his body was taken home to Scotland and buried beside his parents at Ecclefechan.

**Page 325. Landlouper.** Adventurous vagabond.

**Schoolmaster.** Johnson himself.

**327. Gigmanity.** Able to keep a gig; therefore "respectable"! Carlyle humorously explains that all mankind are divided into four classes—"Noblemen, Gentlemen, Gigmen, and Men."

**330. Hero-Worship.** Used here nine years before the publication of *Heroes and Hero-Worship*. Cf. p. 340 ff.

**338. Wisest of our time.** Goethe.

**339. Close thy Byron; open thy Goethe.** Cease imitating the self-centred complainer, and take Goethe's philosophical view of the functions and the rewards of life.

**342. King.** Forced etymology. *King* is from Old English *cyng*, a contraction of *cynning*, from *cynn*, meaning *tribe* or *kin*.

**345. Burns's schoolmaster.** James Murdoch, who guided Burns in his early reading.

**347. Professor Stewart.** Dugald Stewart, Scotch philosopher.

**Lockhart.** John Gibson Lockhart, the biographer of Scott.

**Vauxhall.** A public amusement park in London.

**349. Odin, Burns.** Carlyle began his lectures on heroes with the Norse god, Odin.

# NEWMAN

John Henry Cardinal Newman was born in London in 1801, the son of a banker. He entered Trinity College, Oxford, in 1816. Oxford remained his home for a quarter of a century. After his ordination to the Anglican priesthood, he was appointed vicar at St. Mary's in Oxford, and in 1833 started the High Church movement in the *Tracts for the Times*. In 1842 he left Oxford. In 1845 he was received into the Roman Catholic church. In 1879 he was made a cardinal, a very high honor for a simple priest. He died in 1890, universally respected even in Protestant England.

Newman's work is chiefly in religious controversy; but he also wrote poetry and fiction. It was while still a Protestant that he wrote most of his religious hymns, including "Lead, Kindly Light." In 1854 Newman went to Ireland, to establish a Catholic university, and to this project we owe his *Idea of a University*. When Kingsley attacked Newman's good faith in 1864, the latter began and published in parts his *Apologia pro Vita Sua*. A volume of his poetry appeared in 1868, and his chief volume of apologetics, the *Grammar of Assent*, in 1870.

Page 369. τετράγωνος. Four-square (from Aristotle's *Ethics*).

Nil admirari. To wonder at nothing. Cf. Horace's *Epistles*—"To shun emotion is the sole way, Numicius, to win to happiness and to retain it."

Felix qui potuit. Virgil's *Georgics*—"Happy is he who has power to know the causes of things, and is thus above all fear, master of the dread march of fate, and careless of the wild noise of greedy Acheron."

## THACKERAY

William Makepeace Thackeray was born in 1811 at Calcutta. His father and grandfather were civil servants under the East India Company. Thackeray was a "Bluecoat" boy at the Charterhouse he pictures in *The Newcomes*. He entered Trinity College, Cambridge, but left in 1830 without a degree. His experience was varied. He tried journalism, studied law, studied art. He was an artist, a poet, an editor, an essayist, and a novelist, and good at each. He joined the staff of *Punch* in 1845, and made his first enduring reputation by the *Snob Papers* in 1846. *Vanity Fair* had begun to appear in 1846, but it was not completed till 1848; this immediately placed him among the great English novelists. There followed in order *Pendennis* (1850), *Henry Esmond* (1852), and *The Newcomes* (1854–5). His lecture-essays are *The English Humorists of the Eighteenth Century* in 1853, and *The Four Georges* in 1860. He published the sequel to *Esmond*, called *The Virginians*, in 1859, and in that year became the editor of the *Cornhill Magazine*, where he published his delightfully whimsical *Roundabout Papers*. Thackeray died in 1863, at the relatively early age for the Victorians of fifty-two.

Page 377. 1–10 George IV. The first ten years of George the Fourth's reign—a legal usage.

381. à deux. Two together.

382. Bonne vieille. Dear old lady.

## RUSKIN

John Ruskin's life is quite clearly divided into three parts—his early life to the age of twenty-four, his work as a critic of art and interpreter of nature, and his work as a social reformer. He was born in London in 1819, a contemporary of George Eliot, Kingsley, Clough, and Lowell. No man could have had more fortunate home surroundings or a better æsthetic education. He was trained from early boyhood in the observation of natural objects, in the arts of music, drawing, and reading aloud. His mother forced him to read the Bible through every year. His father read to him from Shakespeare and Scott, and from the great classics of his own and other languages. He began to write both prose and verse as soon as he could read and write. He was educated largely by travel in England, Scotland, and on the Continent. He was sent as a "gentleman-commoner" to Christ Church College in Oxford, but his college career was interrupted by illness, and he did not receive his degree until 1842. This ended his formal preparation for his later work.

In 1843, when Ruskin was only twenty-four, appeared the first volume of *Modern Painters*, a work when completed destined to great influence in the appreciation of nature and art. Other volumes appeared at intervals for nearly twenty years, Volume V, the last, appearing in 1860. In the meantime various volumes appeared on art, including the *Seven Lamps of Architecture* (1849), *Pre-Raphaelitism* (1850), and *The Stones of Venice* (1851–53). In 1869 he became Slade Professor of Art at Oxford, and held the chair almost continuously for nearly a score of years. His lectures were so crowded that only the Sheldonian Theater could accommodate them.

Ruskin, however, had been growing more and more troubled for years before 1860 about the ugliness of modern life. In *The Stones of Venice* he expounded his favorite doctrine that art grows out of life—out of religion, morality, social customs, and racial and national bent. Two series of articles in violent criticism of the orthodox economics of the time were stopped before completion by the editors of the *Cornhill Magazine* and *Fraser's Magazine*, but they appeared later as *Unto This Last* and *Munera Pulveris*. Volume after volume followed in criticism of English social, economic, and political life—all in an effort to better the conditions for true art through noble living. He gave away a fortune in impractical attempts at various practical reforms. But his incessant warfare against evil social conditions, united with the work of the other great Victorians, gradually aroused the social conscience of the English people, and his views on art and social ethics slowly built up for him a group of disciples. A violent disease of the brain attacked him in 1878, and he suffered from this at intervals until his death in 1900. He had written for a half century, and his works fill fifty volumes. In accordance with his wish, the family refused to permit burial in Westminster, and he lies in his parish church at Coniston in the Lake Country.

Page 383. **Præterita.** Things gone by—Ruskin's fanciful name for his autobiography. Cf. such titles of his as *Sesame and Lilies, Crown of Wild Olives*, etc.

410. χρυσέη περόνη. The golden pin or brooch fastening Aglaia's girdle.

## HUXLEY

Thomas Henry Huxley was born in 1825. Though his father was a schoolmaster, the boy received very little formal education. One of the chief influences of his boyhood was Carlyle, and Huxley declared fifty years later that Carlyle's preaching against "cant and shows of all kinds" had "stuck by me all my life." Huxley began the study of medicine in 1842 and in 1845 at graduation published his first scientific paper. He became a naval surgeon and sent home to the Linnean Society paper after paper. At twenty-five he was elected a Fellow of the Royal Society. At thirty he was married and became naturalist to the Geological Survey. His defense of evolution in 1860 was epoch-making. His *Man's Place in Nature* appeared in 1863, *The Classification of Animals* in 1869, and the *Lay-Sermons* in 1870. Public duties and general work in the interests of science and education drew him away from research after 1870. With Matthew Arnold, his friendly foe, he must be given credit for founding a national system of elementary education. The latter part of his life he gave up to philosophical and educational writing. To Huxley more than to any other man we owe the introduction of science into the schools and colleges as an essential part of modern education. He died in 1895.

Page 446. **Test-Acts.** The name of English laws compelling adherence to the Established Church in order to hold office or to receive a university degree.

448. **Science and Culture.** An address delivered October 1, 1880, at the opening in Birmingham of the Science College founded by Sir Josiah Mason.

**Mr. Arnold tells us.** The quotation is from Arnold's *The Function of Criticism at the Present Time* in his *Essays in Criticism*, 1865. Arnold answers Huxley in his lecture entitled *Literature and Science* from *Discourses in America*, 1885.

455. **The Institution.** The Birmingham Science College.

## PATER

Walter Horatio Pater was born in 1839, only two years younger than Swinburne but one year older than Hardy; but, like Hardy and unlike Swinburne, his reputation was made almost wholly after 1870. His father was a doctor, born in New York. Pater was educated at Canterbury and at Queen's College, Oxford. After graduation he settled permanently in Oxford, received a fellowship at Brasenose College, and began slowly his career as a writer of criticism for the reviews. No collection of these early essays was made, however, until they appeared in 1878 as *Studies in the History of the*

*Renaissance.* He became the center of a small circle of followers who accepted his æsthetic gospel, and he was closely associated with the Pre-Raphaelites. He wrote slowly and published even more slowly. His philosophical romance, *Marius the Epicurean,* did not appear till 1885. In 1887 appeared his *Imaginary Portraits;* in 1889, *Appreciations, with an Essay on Style;* in 1893, *Plato and Platonism;* in 1894, *The Child in the House;* and after his death in 1894, *Great Studies, Miscellaneous Studies, Gaston de Latour,* and *Essays from the Guardian.* All his work was permeated by the æsthetic principle, by the love of beauty as the supreme good of life.

Page 457. **To see the object.** From Arnold's *On Translating Homer,* 1861.

458. **The first step.** The foundation of Pater's theory of what constitutes true criticism, *i.e.,* of impressionism. Cf. below—"a special unique impression of pleasure."

459. **De se borner.** "To be at pains to know beautiful things and to feed oneself upon them, as refined amateurs, full-fledged humanists."

462. **Philosophiren.** "To be a philosopher is to rid oneself of inertia, to come to life."

464. **Les hommes sont.** Translated by Pater immediately above.

467. **κοσμιότης.** Translated by Pater as "order," *i.e.,* "decorum."

468. **Order in beauty . . . strangeness to beauty.** The core of Pater's distinction between classic and romantic art.

## STEVENSON

Robert Louis Stevenson was born at Edinburgh in 1850. His health was very poor even as a child. His father was an engineer, and in 1868 the lad began the study of engineering. His health troubling him again, he studied law and was called to the bar in 1875. He never made any attempt to practice law, but gave himself to perfecting a prose style and to writing occasional essays for the periodicals. For the sake of his health he wandered through Scotland, France, and Germany, and these travels resulted in *An Inland Voyage* in 1878 and *Travels with a Donkey* in 1879. He had met Mrs. Osbourne, the future Mrs. Stevenson, while traveling on the Continent. She was an Indiana girl whose home was in California. When Stevenson heard she was seriously ill in 1879, he traveled steerage as an immigrant from Scotland to see her, and they were married the following year. They returned to Scotland, but had to leave on account of Stevenson's health.

In 1881 appeared the first collection of Stevenson's essays, *Virginibus Puerisque.* In 1883 appeared his famous romance *Treasure Island,* which immediately made him popular. In order afterward appeared his chief works: *A Child's Garden of Verses* in 1885, and the romance of *Prince Otto* in the same year; in 1886 came *Dr. Jekyll and Mr. Hyde* and *Kidnapped*; in 1887 his volume of lyrics called *Underwoods*; *Memories and Portraits*; in 1889 *The Master of Ballantrae*; in 1896 *Weir of Hermiston* (unfinished); in 1898 *St. Ives* (completed by Quiller-Couch), and throughout the period a number of lesser works. His health finally drove him to the South Seas in 1888, and he lived the remainder of his life at Vailima on Samoa. He died in 1894, generally acknowledged to be the most attractive personality in literature in a generation that included Hardy and Kipling.

Page 470. **A Gossip on Romance.** Written after Stevenson by his own example in *Treasure Island* had checked the realistic movement fostered by W. D. Howells and Henry James in this country.

471. **Malabar coast.** Part of India.

**Jacobite.** Adherent of the Stewarts after James II was deposed. *Jacobus* is the Latin for *James*.

**John Rann—Jerry Abershaw.** Highwaymen.

**Great North road.** From London to Edinburgh.

**What will He Do with It.** Bulwer-Lytton's novel.

472. **Drama is the poetry of conduct, Romance the poetry of circumstance.** This, the main thesis of Stevenson's essay, necessarily denies the doctrine of Arnold that "conduct is three parts of life." Cf. Arnold's *Literature and Dogma*.

473. **Miching mallecho.** Perhaps "skulking mischief"—from *Hamlet*.

**Nelson—his Emma.** Admiral Nelson and Lady Hamilton.

476. **Trollope's.** Trollope's novels of the English clergy usually merely "chronicle small beer," as unimportant in material as Iago's conclusion to his poem (Othello, II—i).

**Pure Dumas.** Thackeray has stolen Dumas' method with incident, as, for example, in *The Three Musketeers*.

477. **Clarissa Harlowe.** Richardson's psychological character novel (1747–8).

**Byronism.** Romantic melancholy, usually posed and artificial.

479. **Lucy and Richard Feverel.** The chief characters in Meredith's *The Ordeal of Richard Feverel*.

480. **Eugène de Rastignac.** In Balzac's *Père Goriot*.

## INDEX OF AUTHORS

# INDEX OF TITLES

# INDEX OF FIRST LINES OF POEMS